MW00354249

The Money Revolution

The Money Revolution

How to Finance the Next American Century

RICHARD DUNCAN

WILEY

Registered office

John Wiley & Sons Ltd, The Atrium, Southern Gate, Chichester, West Sussex, PO19 8SQ, United Kingdom

For details of our global editorial offices, for customer services and for information about how to apply for permission to reuse the copyright material in this book please see our website at www.wiley.com.

Library of Congress Cataloging-in-Publication Data

Names: Duncan, Richard, 1960- author.
Title: The money revolution : how to finance the next American century / Richard Duncan.
Description: Hoboken, NJ : Wiley, [2022] | Includes bibliographical references and index.
Identifiers: LCCN 2021043246 (print) | LCCN 2021043247 (ebook) | ISBN 9781119856269 (cloth) | ISBN 9781119856276 (adobe pdf) | ISBN 9781119856283 (epub)
Subjects: LCSH: Finance—United States. | Technological innovations—Economic aspects—United States. | Investments—United States. | Monetary policy—United States. | Money—United States. | United States—Economic policy. | United States. Federal Reserve Board.
Classification: LCC HG181 .D85 2022 (print) | LCC HG181 (ebook) | DDC 332.10973—dc23/eng/20211014
LC record available at https://lccn.loc.gov/2021043246
LC ebook record available at https://lccn.loc.gov/2021043247

Cover Design: Wiley
Cover Image: © xtock/Shutterstock

SKY875AEE0C-8CEC-41FA-AFE4-4A4CEFDE0C70_121421

With special thanks to everyone who has subscribed to Macro Watch during the last eight years. Your financial support has made this book possible.

Contents

Introduction

Over the last century, wars, depressions, political ambition, regulatory mistakes, greed, and geopolitical competition have entirely transformed the monetary system of the United States. They have transformed the very nature of money itself. A momentous and irreversible turning point occurred five decades ago when dollars ceased to be backed by gold. Afterwards, a worldwide credit bubble took shape that fundamentally changed the structure of the global economy and the rules that govern how it functions.

That bubble and the global civilization it has created will not survive if left to market forces. Therefore, we have two choices. We can allow the bubble to implode and hope to live through the ensuing cataclysm, which could be far worse than the one that shook the world from 1930 to 1945, following the collapse of an earlier and smaller credit bubble. Alternatively, we can learn how to effectively manage our new economic system to ensure that it prospers rather than disintegrates.

A dangerous pessimism, based on a misunderstanding of how the economy works today, is becoming entrenched in the minds of far too many Americans. Proponents of the Austrian School of Economics preach that due to the United States' egregious transgressions in abandoning sound money and balanced budgets, a harsh day of reckoning inevitably awaits us in the near future, with many arguing, perversely, that since our economic Judgement Day cannot be prevented, the sooner it arrives, the better.

While it is certainly true that the US economy would collapse into a new great depression if the policies advocated by the

Austrian economists were implemented, it is absolutely not true that the doom they foretell is either imminent or inevitable.

This book rejects that pessimistic and debilitating philosophy and argues instead that the new economic environment we find ourselves in today presents us with previously unimaginable opportunities to grow and prosper by investing in the industries of the future on an unprecedented scale. It explains that our economic system has been profoundly altered by the evolution of money and the proliferation of credit over the last century; that, in fact, a Money Revolution has occurred.

Once the nature of our current economic system is properly understood, the correct path forward becomes clear. If we adopt that path our economic future will be bright. This book explains how our economy works now and the opportunities it presents us.

The Money Revolution is divided into three parts. Part One, Money, describes the evolution of money and monetary policy in the United States from the establishment of the Federal Reserve System in 1913 to the eve of the financial crisis of 2008. It also discusses the events that forced the US monetary system to evolve. These seven chapters provide a history of the Federal Reserve System and explain everything necessary to understand how the Fed conducts monetary policy in the twenty-first century. They also demonstrate the colossal power the US central bank has at its disposal.

Part Two, Credit, shows that as the nature of money changed, it brought about a transformation of the economic system as well. It describes the astonishing proliferation of credit in the United States during the five decades since dollars ceased to be backed by gold. It discusses the impact that very rapid credit growth has had on the US economy and shows that economic growth is now dependent on credit growth. It also demonstrates that there are effectively no longer any limits as to how much money the United States government can borrow. Moreover, it shows that if credit fails to expand, the economy will collapse into a depression. Next, it describes the Fed's successful policy response to the financial crisis of 2008 and its current efforts to support the economy through the COVID-19 pandemic. It ends with a survey of the causes of inflation over the last century.

Part Three, The Future, draws on the lessons that can be derived from the history of the Money Revolution detailed in Parts One and Two; and calls for the United States to carry out a multitrillion-dollar investment program over the next 10 years. It begins by explaining why such a large-scale investment program is possible. It then shows that it is also urgently required, since the current level of investment in the United States is dangerously inadequate. It then discusses how this investment program could be structured and the industries it should target. Next, it explains how it could be financed at no cost whatsoever to US taxpayers. Finally, it describes the extraordinary benefits that an investment program of this nature would be sure to deliver.

A Money Revolution has occurred and rewritten all the rules of finance and economics. It presents the United States the opportunity to invest in new industries and technologies on a scale large enough to open up the possibility of curing all the diseases, radically expanding life expectancy, developing limitless clean energy, rehabilitating the environment, and solving many of the other most intractable challenges confronting humanity – not generations from now, but in our own lifetime.

The objective of ***The Money Revolution: How to Finance the Next American Century*** is to persuade the American public and US policymakers that the United States must seize this opportunity. If we do, it is certain that the first American Century will not be the last.

Money

Introduction

Part One of this book presents a history of the Federal Reserve System that details the role the Fed has played in The Money Revolution.

Chapter 1 begins by relating why the Federal Reserve System was created, how it was intended to function, and the constraints originally placed upon it. From there, it explains the Fed's role in distributing the currency and, much more importantly, how the Fed creates money by extending Federal Reserve Credit. The chapter deciphers the arcane jargon that is normally used to discuss monetary policy. It concludes with a simple explanation of the tools and techniques the Fed employs to control credit availability within the United States.

The rest of Part One tells the history of the Federal Reserve System and US monetary policy by analyzing changes in the Fed's balance sheet over six consecutive periods between 1914 and 2007. The changing composition of the Fed's assets and liabilities reveals how the institution evolved from being the relatively passive lender of last resort established by the Federal Reserve Act of 1913 to becoming the US government's most powerful economic policy tool today.

Changes on the liabilities side of the Fed's balance sheet show how the Fed creates *Federal Reserve Credit*, also known as *base money* or *high-powered money*. Changes in the types of assets held by the Fed show how the Fed uses the money it creates. By tracing the changes in the Fed's assets and liabilities over 93 years, Chapters 2–7 disclose how the Fed devised new techniques to conduct monetary policy as circumstances changed, frequently in response to crises.

Part One of *The Money Revolution* describes the indispensable role the Fed played in financing the United States' war effort in World War I and World War II. It examines the Fed's failure to prevent the Great Depression. It traces the gradual reduction and, then, total elimination of the role of gold in the US monetary system. It also considers the political developments that led to the Fed financing an increasing share of the government's budget deficits beginning in the 1960s and then to the breakdown of the Bretton Woods international monetary system in 1971. Finally, it looks at the evolution of monetary policy during the years after dollars ceased to be backed by gold, when the Fed became free to create as much money as it pleased.

Part One conveys a comprehensive understanding of how the Fed operates and the tools at its disposal today. It also sets the stage for Part Two, which describes the profound impact that the transformation of *money* had on *credit* and, consequently, on the way the entire economic system functions.

CHAPTER 1

The Power of the Fed

Attention should be called, first of all, to the fact that the Federal Reserve Act did not establish a central bank.

The 1921 Annual Report of the Federal Reserve Board[1]

The Power to Create Credit

Today, the Fed is one of the world's most powerful institutions. Its power derives from its ability to create limitless amounts of credit. There is no more precise way to demonstrate how the Fed exercises its power than by tracing the evolution of the assets and liabilities on its balance sheet.

Changes on the liabilities side of the Fed's balance sheet show how the Fed creates *Federal Reserve Credit,* also known as *base money* or *high-powered money.* Changes in the types of assets held by the Fed show how it uses the money it creates. This book details the changes in the Fed's assets and liabilities over its 107-year history in order to show how the Fed devised new techniques to conduct monetary policy as circumstances changed, frequently in response to crises; and to show how the Fed's powers became exponentially greater in the process.

This chapter lays out all the basic information the reader will require to understand what the Fed does and how it does it. It explains why the Federal Reserve System was created, how it was intended to function, and the constraints originally placed upon it. It describes the two principal responsibilities assigned to the Fed by the Federal Reserve Act of 1913, distributing the currency and providing short-term loans to commercial banks in times of financial stress. This chapter also explains the five items that have dominated the Fed's balance sheet from its creation up until now and discusses how those items are affected as the Fed carries out its responsibilities. The chapter concludes with a discussion of the tools the Fed deploys to conduct *monetary policy.*

This information is essential for understanding how the Fed wields its power to control the US economy and to create or destroy wealth today.

The rest of Part One narrates how the Fed made use of its powers, sometimes effectively and sometimes not, during the wars and the economic and political upheavals between 1914 and 2007. Subsequent chapters in Part Two describe the extraordinary force the Fed brought to bear to prevent the financial crisis of 2008 and the pandemic that began in 2020 from hurling the United States into a new Great Depression.

In the Beginning

To stop a banking panic, a central bank should lend freely against sound collateral at high interest rates. So Walter Bagehot famously counseled in 1873 in *Lombard Street,*[2] his much-admired book on money markets.

The United States, however, did not have a central bank during most of the nineteenth century. It had not had one since President Andrew Jackson refused to renew the charter of the Second Bank of the United States in 1836.

After the Second Bank of The United States closed, the US suffered through a series of banking panics, many of which inflicted considerable damage on the US economy.

Banking panics generally follow a particular pattern. In the lead up to the crisis, credit growth accelerates and generates an economic boom. Asset prices rise. Investor confidence becomes ebullient. Businesses misjudge future prospects and make poor investment decisions. Production outstrips effective demand. Prices begin to fall. Profits turn to losses. A respected company defaults on its debt obligations. Fears spread that more defaults will follow. Creditors not only cease to make new loans, but also call in their existing lines of credit. Unable to obtain financing for even essential working capital, otherwise sound businesses begin to fail. Panic spreads. Unemployment rises, investment plunges and losses mount. Debt defaults become widespread. A number of banks go under. The downward spiral intensifies, wiping out all those with insufficient capital to withstand the slump.

The Panic of 1907 was especially severe. The damage it wrought was harsh enough to persuade many of the country's most influential bankers, businessmen, and politicians to push for the establishment of a new central bank that could step in to provide credit to sound borrowers during a credit crunch, thereby sparing the economy the unnecessary damage inflicted by excessive credit liquidation during a full-fledged panic.

After much debate, Congress passed the Federal Reserve Act, establishing the Federal Reserve System. The Act was signed into law by President Woodrow Wilson on December 23, 1913.

The Federal Reserve Act of 1913 begins with these words:

An Act To provide for the establishment of Federal reserve banks, to furnish an elastic currency, to afford means of rediscounting commercial paper, to establish a more effective supervision of banking in the United States, and for other purposes.[3]

Notice it is not an act to provide for the establishment of a central bank, but instead "an Act to provide for the establishment of Federal Reserve Banks." Rather than creating one central bank headquartered in Washington or New York, the Federal Reserve Act specified that the Federal Reserve System would be comprised of 12 Federal Reserve Banks that were to be set up in major financial centers all around the country. In part, the sheer size of the United States made this decentralized structure advisable. Business conditions varied from one region to another. Therefore, it was thought desirable to have numerous Reserve Banks located around the country where they could better assess local business conditions and credit requirements at close proximity.

However, the decentralized structure of the Federal Reserve System also reflected the still widespread public opposition to the establishment of a central bank in the United States. Those who believed the United States needed a lender of last resort had to compromise with those who feared the concentration of power that would accrue to one central bank. That compromise took the form of a decentralized Federal Reserve System made up of 12 regional Federal Reserve Banks spread across 12 Federal Reserve Districts plus a seven-member Federal Reserve Board, based in Washington, that would oversee the entire system.

The members of the first Federal Reserve Board took the oath of office on August 10, 1914. The 12 Federal Reserve Banks opened their doors for business on November 16, 1914.

The Fed's Balance Sheet: Two Snapshots

The Federal Reserve System's first consolidated balance sheet was published on November 20, 1914. It is presented in Table 1.1.[4]

Table 1.1 shows that the Federal Reserve System began operations with total assets and total liabilities of $247 million.

To understand the composition of the Fed's first balance sheet some background information is required.

TABLE 1.1 Simplified Balance Sheet of the Federal Reserve System
November 20, 1914

The Fed's First Balance Sheet (Simplified)	
US$ Millions	20-Nov-14
ASSETS	247
Gold	205
Other legal tender	36
Foreign financial assets	0
Bills discounted	6
US government Securities	0
Other or unspecified assets	0
LIABILITIES	247
Foreign liabilities	0
Federal Reserve Notes	1
Member bank deposits, i.e., Bank Reserves	228
Owed to banks, other than banks' reserve deposits	0
Owed to government	0
Net worth	18
Other liabilities	0

Source: Data from *"The Federal Reserve System's Weekly Balance Sheet Since
1914"* and accompanying spreadsheet. Johns Hopkins University, SAE/No.115/
July 2018. See Bibliography.

Long before the Federal Reserve System was established, all
banks had been required by law to hold a certain portion of
their customers' deposits on hand[5] as liquidity reserves in order
to ensure that they would have enough cash readily available to
give their customers their money back whenever their customers decided to withdraw their deposits. The National Bank Act
established reserve requirements at the national level in 1863.[6]

When the Federal Reserve System was established, all
National Banks were required to become members. State banks
and trust companies were given the option to become members.
The banks that joined the Federal Reserve System became
known as *member banks*. By the end of 1917, the Fed estimated
that the membership of the Federal Reserve System represented
about 75% of the total commercial banking assets of the country.[7]

All member banks were required to set up *reserve accounts* at the Federal Reserve Banks in their regions. They were also required to transfer part of their reserves into those new accounts when they became members and the rest by the end of 1917. Finally, they were required, at all times, to hold enough reserves relative to the size of their customers' deposits to meet the mandatory ratio of reserves to deposits, the *required reserve ratio*, set by the Fed.[8,9,10]

The Federal Reserve System's total assets of $247 million on November 20, 2014, were comprised of $205 million of gold, $36 million of other legal tender and $6 million of *bills discounted*. It had obtained most of those assets when the member banks transferred their reserves, amounting to $228 million, into their reserve accounts at the Federal Reserve Banks. It received a further $18 billion from the member banks in the form of paid-in capital when the member banks joined the Federal Reserve System.

Both the reserves and the paid-in capital of the member banks were recorded on the liabilities side of the Fed's balance sheet. As of November 20, 1914, only $1 million of *Federal Reserve Notes* had been issued by the Federal Reserve Banks. They were the Federal Reserve System's only other liability.

During the years since 1914, the Federal Reserve System has grown to a size that its founders could never have imagined. Chart 1.1 shows that its assets have grown from $247 million in 1914 to $8.1 trillion in mid-2021, having expanded by $3.9 trillion or by 94% just since the end of 2019.

This book will show that as the Federal Reserve System grew its assets, it played an important role in shaping the history of the United States and the world.

Table 1.2 updates Table 1.1 by adding a column for June 30, 2021. It provides a snapshot of how the size and composition of the Fed's assets and liabilities have evolved over 107 years.

Throughout its long history, the balance sheet of the Federal Reserve has been dominated by five major components, of which three have been assets and two have been liabilities. The

CHART 1.1 The Fed's Total Assets, 1914 to June 30, 2021

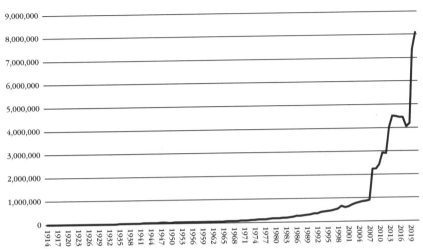

The Fed's Total Assets
US$ Millions, 1914 to June 30, 2021

Source: Data from the Federal Reserve's Annual Reports

significant assets have been gold, loans (originally classified as bills discounted), and US government securities. The significant liabilities have been Federal Reserve Notes and Bank Reserves (originally classified as member banks' deposits).

Between November 1914 and June 2021, on the asset side of the balance sheet, the Federal Reserve System's gold holding increased from $205 million to $11 billion; loans (originally bills discounted) grew from $6 million to $163 billion; and government securities holdings (including GSE securities) soared from $0 to $7.5 trillion.

On the liabilities side, Federal Reserve Notes grew from $1 million to $2.1 trillion, while Bank Reserves (originally member bank deposits) surged from $228 million to $3.5 trillion.

Chapters 2–7 tell the story of the extraordinary transformation of the Federal Reserve System and its balance sheet between 1914 and 2007. The financial crisis of 2008 and the Federal Reserve's policy response to that crisis are taken up in Part

TABLE 1.2 Simplified Balance Sheet of the Federal Reserve Board, November 20, 1914, and June 30, 2021

Simplified Balance Sheet			
US$ Millions	20-Nov-14		June 30, 2021
ASSETS	**247**	**Assets**	**8,078,544**
Gold	205	Gold	11,037
Other legal tender	36	n.a.	-
Foreign financial assets	0	n.a.	-
Bills discounted	6	Loans (including LLCs)	163,004
US government securities	0	US Govt. Securities (incl. GSEs)	7,505,369
Other or unspecified assets	0	Other assets	399,134
LIABILITIES	**247**	**Liabilities**	**8,038,940**
Foreign liabilities	0	Foreign liabilities	5,255
Federal Reserve Notes	1	Federal Reserve Notes	2,134,139
Member bank deposits	228	Bank Reserves	3,511,630
Owed to banks, other than banks' reserve deposits	0	n.a.	-
Owed to government	0	Owed to federal government	851,929
Net worth	18	Net worth	39,604
Other liabilities	0	Other liabilities	1,535,987

The data for 2014 is from "*The Federal Reserve System's Weekly Balance Sheet Since 1914*" and accompanying spreadsheet. Johns Hopkins University, SAE/No.115/July 2018. See Bibliography.
The data for 2021 is from the Fed's "Factors Affecting Reserve Balances" H.4.1 Report

Two, as is the Fed's policy response to counter the economic consequences of the COVID-19 pandemic during 2020 and 2021.

By tracing the evolution of the major items in the Fed's balance sheet from its foundation until the present, these chapters will show exactly how the Federal Reserve has carried out monetary policy throughout its existence. Therefore, no further discussion of the Fed's balance sheet is required here. However, those who seek a more detailed introduction to the Fed's major assets and liabilities will find it in Appendix One of this chapter.

The following sections consider how the Fed carries out the principal responsibilities assigned to it by the Federal Reserve Act of 1913, as well as the constraints that that act placed upon the Fed.

Furnishing an Elastic Currency

Before the Federal Reserve System was established, *United States Notes* were the principal form of *currency in circulation* in the United States. They were issued directly by the Treasury Department.

The Federal Reserve Act authorized the Federal Reserve System to furnish a new form of legal tender, *Federal Reserve Notes*. It also charged the Federal Reserve System with the responsibility of increasing the supply of Federal Reserve Notes when public demand for currency increased and for retiring Federal Reserve Notes when public demand for currency waned. This is what the Federal Reserve Act meant by "to furnish an elastic currency."

This is how the process worked originally and how it still works to this day.

Whenever any individual wishes to hold more cash (Federal Reserve Notes), they withdraw it from their account at a commercial bank. Should that commercial bank find it is running low on cash and it is a member of the Federal Reserve System, it approaches its regional Federal Reserve Bank and requests more. Federal Reserve Notes are paid out by a Federal Reserve Bank to the member bank on request. In exchange for the Federal Reserve Notes, the Federal Reserve Bank debits that member bank's reserve account at the Fed. If the commercial bank is not a member bank, it must obtain the Federal Reserve Notes it requires from a member bank.

The impact of that transaction on the Federal Reserve Bank's balance sheet is as follows. On the liabilities side of its balance sheet, Federal Reserve Notes (or currency in circulation) increase and the reserves of the member bank contract by the same amount, leaving the size of the Federal Reserve Bank's total liabilities unchanged. The asset side of the Federal Reserve Bank's balance sheet is not affected.

Occasionally, the public wishes to hold less currency. When that happens, individuals deposit the unwanted cash back into their accounts at the commercial banks. If those banks find they have more cash than they require, they return it to their regional Federal Reserve Banks (directly if they are member banks and indirectly through member banks if they are not). When the Federal Reserve Banks receive the cash, they credit that sum of money into those member banks' reserve accounts at the Federal Reserve Banks, thus increasing those Federal Reserve Banks' deposit liabilities. However, those Federal Reserve Banks' liabilities for Federal Reserve Notes decrease by an equal amount. The net result is that there is no change in the size of the Federal Reserve Banks' total liabilities or total assets.

And what about the Federal Reserve Banks themselves? How do they obtain Federal Reserve Notes when public demand for currency increases? Whenever any Federal Reserve Bank wishes to obtain additional Federal Reserve Notes it does so from its Federal Reserve agent, a representative of the government. The Treasury Department then has the Federal Reserve Notes printed by its Bureau of Engraving and Printing.

The Federal Reserve Bank obtaining the Federal Reserve Notes must pledge with the Federal Reserve agent an amount of collateral at least equal to the value of the notes issued. Initially, this collateral had to consist of gold, United States Government securities, and eligible short-term paper discounted or purchased by the Federal Reserve Bank. Today, all assets of the Federal Reserve Banks are eligible as collateral for Federal Reserve Notes.[11]

If a Federal Reserve Bank finds it has more Federal Reserve Notes than it requires, it simply returns them to its Federal Reserve agent and reclaims its collateral.

In this way, the amount of currency in circulation (Federal Reserve Notes) expands when the public wishes to hold more cash and contracts when the public wishes to hold less cash. The Federal Reserve Banks do not take the initiative in deciding when to increase or decrease the number of Federal Reserve Notes in circulation. They merely act passively in response to fluctuations in the public's demand to hold cash.

To simplify matters, going forward, no further reference will be made to the 12 Federal Reserve Banks individually. Instead, they will be grouped together and discussed on a consolidated basis. Henceforth, this book will generally refer to them collectively as the Federal Reserve System, the Federal Reserve or, more often, simply as "the Fed," for short. The Fed's balance sheet will always be presented on a consolidated basis.

Providing Credit

Distributing the country's currency is an important job. However, the main reason the Federal Reserve System was created was to prevent banking panics. To do this, it was given the authority to provide credit, Federal Reserve Credit, to individual banks and, thereby, to the banking system as a whole whenever credit conditions began to tighten too abruptly.

The Federal Reserve System can provide credit in one of two ways. First, it can lend money to a member bank in exchange for sound collateral. Alternatively, it can buy a government bond (or other types of debt instruments authorized by Congress) from a bank. The Fed can also buy government bonds and other authorized debt instruments from a non-bank, such as an individual or a corporation, for example. The effect on the banking system is the same as if the Fed bought the bond from a bank because the non-bank entity deposits the cash it receives from the Fed into its commercial bank, thereby increasing the funds available to the banking system. By making a loan to a bank or buying a debt instrument from a bank, the Fed injects additional money into that bank, and, by extension, into the banking system and the economy as a whole.

Discounting Operations

When the Fed lends money to a bank in exchange for collateral, that is referred to as *discounting*, since the recipient of the loan might only receive, for instance, $99 in exchange for collateral worth $100. In this way, the Fed receives its interest payment on the loan up front in advance. The discount is determined by the *discount rate*, the interest rate at which the Fed is willing to lend.

The Federal Reserve Act established the Federal Reserve Banks "to afford means of rediscounting commercial paper." The world *rediscounting* is used because when the Fed lends to commercial banks through a *discounting operation*, it accepts as collateral commercial paper (at a discount) that the commercial banks had already discounted once before when that loan was originally made by the commercial banks. Since the commercial paper is being discounted twice, this process is described as "rediscounting."

When the Fed lends money to a bank in exchange for collateral, the collateral, up through 1971, was recorded as an asset on the Fed's balance sheet under the heading "Bills discounted" as shown in Table 1.1. Since 1972, the collateral has been recorded as an asset under the heading "Loans."[12] In exchange for that collateral, the Fed makes a deposit into that bank's reserve account at the Fed, adding to the bank's reserve balances. That causes an expansion of "Bank Reserves" on the liabilities side of the Fed's balance sheet.

It is important to understand that when the Fed makes such a deposit, it is not transferring funds that were already in existence. Instead, it is creating credit. The act of making the deposit creates the credit. The Federal Reserve Act empowered the Fed to create credit by making deposits into the reserve accounts that commercial banks hold at the Fed. When the Fed makes such a deposit, it is creating and extending Federal Reserve Credit.

When the bank repays its loan from the Fed, the process is reversed. The Fed returns the collateral to the bank, thereby reducing the size of the Fed's assets. At the same time, it debits the commercial bank's reserve account at the Fed by the amount of the loan, thereby reducing the size of the Fed's liabilities and extinguishing the Federal Reserve Credit that came into existence when the loan was first made.

Open Market Operations

The second way the Fed can provide credit to the banking system is to purchase a debt instrument through what is known as an *open market operation*, or, specifically, in this case, an open market purchase. The Federal Reserve Act specified the Fed could acquire US government bonds and certain other types of debt instruments for this purpose.[13]

When the Fed acquires a government bond from a bank, that bond is added to the asset side of the Fed's balance sheet. When the Fed published its first balance sheet, it had not yet purchased any government bonds. But if it had, they would have appeared as "US government securities" in the Simplified Balance Sheet of the Federal Reserve System presented in Table 1.1.

To pay for the government bond it acquires, the Fed makes a deposit into the reserve account of the bank from which it buys the bond. The act of making that deposit creates Federal Reserve Credit exactly as when the Fed makes a deposit into a bank's reserve account through discounting operations.

Later, the Fed may decide to sell a government bond it had acquired earlier. In that case, the Fed would sell the bond to a bank. At the time of the transaction, the Fed would transfer the bond to the bank, reducing the size of the Fed's assets. Simultaneously, the Fed would debit the bank's reserve account at the Fed for the value of the bond, thereby reducing the Fed's bank reserve liabilities (and, consequently, the reserves of the entire banking system) and extinguishing the Federal Reserve Credit that had been created when the Fed originally purchased the bond.

The ability to create Federal Reserve Credit, either through discounting operations or open market operations, is the Fed's "superpower." It can be used to stop a banking panic by supplying credit when no one else will. It can also be used to finance a war, as Chapters 2 and 5 will show. When used properly, it can prevent a great depression, as will be demonstrated in Chapter 12. Finally, under certain circumstances, such as those that prevail today, Federal Reserve Credit can be deployed to radically accelerate economic growth, induce a new technological revolution and alleviate many of humanity's most pressing problems. Part Three of this book will show how Federal Reserve Credit could be used to accomplish those goals.

The chapters ahead provide countless examples of how the Fed uses its power to create Federal Reserve Credit to carry out monetary policy. Those readers seeking a more detailed explanation before reaching those examples will find it in Appendix Two of this chapter.

Federal Reserve Credit and the Monetary Base

The sections above have described how the Fed creates Federal Reserve Credit by making deposits into the reserve accounts that commercial banks hold at the Fed. The funds in those reserve accounts are also known as Bank Reserves. Along with Federal Reserve Notes, Bank Reserves make up the country's *monetary base*. The monetary base, otherwise known as base money, is defined as currency in circulation (i.e., Federal Reserve Notes) plus Bank Reserves. Therefore, when the Fed extends Federal Reserve Credit it is creating base money.

Counterintuitively, when the Fed distributes Federal Reserve Notes, it is not actually creating base money. That is because when the Fed issues the Federal Reserve Notes to a commercial bank, in exchange, it debits that bank's reserve account at the Fed. Therefore, while currency in circulation (i.e., Federal Reserve Notes), one of the components of base money, expands, Bank Reserves, the other component of base money, contracts by the same amount. Therefore, the total amount of base money outstanding remains unchanged. However, with that distinction having been made, it is important to note that the more Federal Reserve Credit the Fed extends by making deposits into the reserve accounts commercial banks hold at the Fed, the more Federal Reserve Notes those banks can obtain by exchanging those reserves for Federal Reserve Notes.

Today, the public often speaks of the Fed "printing" or creating money. It is true that the Fed does create base money when it extends Federal Reserve Credit by making a deposit into the reserve account that a commercial bank holds at the Fed. However, rather than thinking in terms of the Fed creating money, it is less confusing, and, therefore, more useful to think of this process as the Fed creating and extending Federal Reserve Credit. There are numerous definitions of money, as we will see in Part Two. Federal Reserve Credit, on the other hand, has only one meaning. Therefore, when attempting to understand the Fed's powers, it is helpful to think in terms of the Fed creating Federal Reserve Credit, instead of thinking of the Fed creating money.

Constraints

Although times have changed, when the Fed began operations and for many decades thereafter, it was not free to create as much Federal Reserve Credit (i.e., base money) as it pleased.

The Federal Reserve Act spelled out how much gold the Fed had to own relative to the amount of credit it created. The Act specified that:

1. The Fed was required to maintain 40% gold backing for Federal Reserve Notes in circulation; and, to further back the Federal Reserve Notes in circulation, the Fed was also required to hold additional collateral in an amount equivalent to the Federal Reserve Notes received.[14]

2. The Fed was also required to maintain 35% gold backing for the reserves in the commercial banks' reserve accounts at the Fed.

The Fed was required to hold gold against those Bank Reserves because it had the power to create those reserves at will. Therefore, those who drafted the Federal Reserve Act sought to limit the amount of Bank Reserves the Fed could create. Recall that those Reserves are part of the monetary base.

These requirements meant that there were limits to the amount of Federal Reserve Notes the Fed could distribute and the amount of Federal Reserve Credit that the Fed could create.

Over time, as the following chapters will show, the requirement that the Fed hold gold to back Federal Reserve Notes and the Federal Reserve Credit it created was eliminated. However, until it was, the Fed had to ensure that it always held sufficient gold to meet this statutory obligation. The Fed's "gold cover ratio," which measured the Fed's gold assets as a ratio of its currency and deposit liabilities, was published each week along with the Fed's balance sheet information. The Fed began its operations in November 1914 with a gold cover ratio of 105%, meaning the Fed had more than enough gold to back its member bank deposits and Federal Reserve Note liabilities.

Conclusion

The Federal Reserve has become one of the world's most powerful institutions due to is ability to create credit. To understand how the Fed creates credit, it is necessary to understand its balance sheet. Having defined the five major items on the Fed's balance sheet, and how the Fed extends Federal Reserve Credit, we can now untangle the Fed's history by tracing the evolution of its assets and liabilities over time.

The rest of Part One tells the history of the Fed by analyzing changes in the Fed's balance sheet between 1914 and 2007.

(Developments after 2007 are described in Part Two.) This history is broken into six consecutive periods in order to highlight the important stages of the Fed's evolution from being the relatively passive institution established by the Federal Reserve Act of 1913 to becoming the US government's most powerful economic policy tool today.

For each period, we will see the growth in the Fed's total assets and the change in the composition of the Fed's major assets and liabilities. Most importantly, we will see how much credit the Fed created. In the process, it will become clear why the Fed created the credit. The transformative impact that so much credit creation had on the economy will also become apparent.

As we begin, it is important to keep in mind that, for many decades, the quantity of gold held by the Federal Reserve determined how much Federal Reserve Credit the Fed could create, while the size of the commercial banks' reserves, which appear as liabilities on the Fed's balance sheet, determined how much credit the banking system could create.

The rest of Part One will describe how all the constraints that limited the amount of Federal Reserve Credit (i.e., base money) the Federal Reserve System could create were eliminated one after the other. It will also show that once those constraints were removed, the Federal Reserve System created credit on a mind-boggling scale. Part Two will show that a similar process led to an even greater explosion of credit creation through the banking sector and the broader financial system. It will also show that the creation of so much credit fundamentally changed the economic system of the United States by altering the way it functions.

Appendix One

The Fed's Balance Sheet

During the Fed's 107-year history, its balance sheet has been dominated by five major components, of which three have been assets and two have been liabilities. The significant assets have been gold,[15] loans (originally classified as bills discounted), and US government securities. The significant liabilities have been Federal Reserve Notes and Bank Reserves (originally classified as member banks' deposits).

Assets

Gold no longer has any relevance whatsoever as to how the Fed conducts its operations. However, when the Fed was established, gold was the very foundation upon which the entire Federal Reserve System was built. Gold was money. The world was on a gold standard. The amount of gold the Fed held constrained the amount of Federal Reserve Notes the Fed could distribute, and the amount of Federal Reserve Credit the Fed could create.

When gold entered the United States or when it was dug up out of the ground within the United States, it was deposited into commercial banks. As discussed above, commercial banks were legally required to hold a large enough portion of their customers' deposits as reserves (in the form of gold) in their reserve accounts at the Fed in order to meet the required reserve ratio. Therefore, as their customer deposits increased, the commercial banks were required to deposit more gold into their reserve accounts at the Fed. Such deposits caused the Fed's gold holdings to increase on the asset side of its balance sheet and the Bank Reserves (i.e., the deposits of member banks) to increase on the liabilities side of its balance sheet.

Similarly, if gold left the United States, it reduced the level of customer deposits at the commercial banks. As their customer deposits fell, those commercial banks' reserve requirements also fell. That allowed them to reduce the amount of gold they held on deposit at the Fed as reserves. In that case, the Fed's gold holdings would decline in line with the commercial banks' reserves at the Fed.

As explained earlier, the Federal Reserve Act mandated that the Fed was required to maintain 40% gold backing for the Federal Reserve Notes it furnished and 35% gold backing against the reserves that commercial banks held at the Fed. Therefore, the amount of gold held by the Fed determined how many Federal Reserve Notes the Fed could distribute, and the amount of Federal Reserve Credit the Fed could extend by making deposits into the reserve accounts that commercial banks held at the Fed. However, the Fed had no direct control over its own gold holdings. Gold entered and left the United States as the result of trade imbalances or capital flows. These were factors the Fed had only limited power to influence.[16]

The two other assets that have featured most prominently on the Fed's balance sheet are *loans* (originally classified as bills discounted) and *US government securities*. Since 2008, the Fed has also acquired large amounts of bonds issued or guaranteed by government-sponsored enterprises (GSEs). However, these bonds can also be thought of as government securities, since the largest GSEs, Fannie Mae and Freddie Mac, were nationalized by the government during the financial crisis that began that year.

When the Fed obtains these types of assets, it does so by extending Federal Reserve Credit.

Let it be noted that loans and US government securities are all "interest-earning" assets, meaning that the Fed earns income by holding them. This has made the Fed one of the world's most profitable institutions given its enormous portfolio of government securities and loans. In 2020, the Fed earned $86.9 billion, and since 2009 its profits have totaled $963 billion. All of these earnings have been handed over to the US Treasury Department as required by law. Consequently, the government's budget deficits have been substantially reduced by the Fed's income.

Throughout most of its history, the Fed would extend loans through discounting operations. The Fed would lend to commercial banks in exchange for collateral comprised of short-term commercial paper, or, in other words, commercial, industrial, and agricultural loans that commercial banks had made to their customers. The Federal Reserve Act specified that whenever a commercial bank approaches the Fed and asks for a short-term loan, the Fed is obliged to lend money to that bank so long as the bank can offer eligible commercial paper as collateral. The

Fed "discounts" the commercial paper by accepting the commercial paper as collateral at a slight discount to its face value. Originally, this collateral was recorded as "bills discounted" among the Fed's assets. (Since 1972, the collateral is simply recorded as a loan among the Fed's assets.) When the Fed receives the collateral, the Fed deposits money into the reserve account that that commercial bank holds as a deposit at the Fed. Through the act of making that deposit, the Fed creates credit: Federal Reserve Credit.

In more recent years, and particularly since the financial crisis of 2008, the Fed has begun to provide large amounts of loans to commercial banks through *repurchase agreements*, in which the banks can offer government securities as collateral with the understanding that they will repurchase the collateral either the next day or at a specified date in the future.

In discounting operations and with repurchase agreements, the commercial banks take the active role. They approach the Fed and request a loan. The Fed is largely passive. It does not take the initiative in extending Federal Reserve Credit. It simply responds to the commercial banks' requests for loans.

On the other hand, when the Fed acquires US government securities through open market operations, it does so on its own initiative. And it is free to buy or sell these types of assets at its own discretion.

When the Fed wishes to buy a US government security, it does so by making a deposit into the reserve account that the commercial bank from which it acquires the bond holds at the Fed. When the Fed makes the deposit, that creates credit, Federal Reserve Credit. In these transactions, the government security is recorded as an asset and causes the Fed's total assets to expand. The deposit the Fed makes into the reserve account of the commercial bank causes the Fed's reserve liabilities to expand at the same time. The Fed's total liabilities expand by the same amount.

Whenever the Fed wishes to increase the amount of Federal Reserve Credit to stimulate the economy, it does so through open market purchases of US government securities.

Conversely, if the Fed wishes to reduce the amount of Federal Reserve Credit in the financial system in order to slow the economy to reduce inflation, it sells US government securities that it had bought in the past.

In the case where the Fed sells a government security, the Fed's assets contract by the amount of the value of the bond sold. At the same time, the Fed takes payment on the bond it has sold by debiting the reserve account at the Fed belonging to the commercial bank to which it sells the bond. Consequently, on the liabilities side of the Fed's balance sheet, its reserve liabilities contract. Federal Reserve Credit contracts in line with the reduction in the Fed's reserve liabilities.

Up until the early 1930s, the Fed also held a significant amount of "bills bought." Bills bought were typically short-term commercial paper or bankers' acceptances that the Fed obtained through an open market purchase. At that time, the Fed would acquire or sell these types of assets in order to expand or contract Federal Reserve Credit, just as it does with government securities today. After the early 1930s, however, the Fed ceased to buy significant amounts of commercial paper and bankers' acceptances outright. Consequently, "bills bought" all but disappeared from the Fed's balance sheet.

Thus, the Fed expands and contracts Federal Reserve Credit through both discounting operations and open market operations. However, since the Fed is merely the passive agent in discounting operations, it is only through open market operations that the Fed intentionally expands or contracts Federal Reserve Credit in order to loosen or tighten credit conditions throughout the financial system and the economy.

Liabilities

Federal Reserve Notes and *Bank Reserves* have made up the Fed's two principal liabilities throughout its history. As discussed above, the amount of Federal Reserve Notes in circulation is determined by public demand. When individuals wish to hold more cash, they withdraw it from their commercial banks.

When commercial banks run short of cash, they approach the Fed and request more, which the Fed supplies in the form of Federal Reserve Notes. In exchange for the new Federal Reserve Notes, the Fed debits the reserve accounts held at the Fed by the commercial banks obtaining the currency, thereby reducing their reserve balances. In these transactions, the Fed's Federal Reserve Note liabilities expand, while its Bank Reserve liabilities contract by the same amount, leaving the size of the Fed's total liabilities unchanged. The asset side of the Fed's balance sheet is unaffected. No Federal Reserve Credit is created.

When the public wishes to hold less cash, they deposit the unwanted currency into their commercial banks, which, in turn, return it to the Fed. When the Fed receives the currency, it credits the reserve accounts those commercial banks hold at the Fed. Consequently, the Fed's Federal Reserve Notes liabilities contract and its Bank Reserve liabilities expand by the same amount, leaving the size of the Fed's total liabilities unchanged. There is no impact on the asset side of the Fed's balance sheet or upon the amount of Federal Reserve Credit in existence.

Bank Reserves are the last major item to consider. Recall, the original purpose of these reserves was to ensure that the commercial banks had sufficient liquidity reserves readily available to repay their customers' deposits whenever their customers wished to withdraw their funds.

When the Fed began its operations in 1914, Bank Reserves were comprised entirely of the reserves the commercial banks had been required to transfer to the Fed upon becoming members of the Federal Reserve System. Over time, however, the size of the Bank Reserves was also impacted by gold movements, changes in the public's demand for currency and increases and decreases in Federal Reserve Credit outstanding. Gold movements ceased to impact Bank Reserves when the Bretton Woods System collapsed in 1971. Up until then, gold imports had added to Bank Reserves, while gold exports had reduced Bank Reserves.

Today, decreases in currency in circulation and the extension of Federal Reserve Credit cause Bank Reserves to expand, while increases in currency in circulation and contraction of Federal Reserve Credit cause Bank Reserves to contract.[17]

Throughout most of the Fed's history, Bank Reserves determined how much credit the banking system could create. When Bank Reserves expanded, the banking system could create more credit. However, if Bank Reserves contracted to the point where the banking system no longer had sufficient reserves to satisfy the statutory reserve requirement as specified by the required reserve ratio, then the banking sector was required to reduce the amount of credit it had extended.

Since 2008, however, Bank Reserves have ceased to play their traditional role in constraining the amount of credit the banking system can create for two reasons. First, Bank Reserves became superabundant as the result of the Fed's policy response to the financial crisis that year. The Fed created so many Bank Reserves through Quantitative Easing that they no longer served as a constraint on the amount of credit the banking sector could create. Second, and in light of the first reason, in March 2020, the Fed reduced the required reserve ratio to 0%. Consequently, at present, banks are no longer legally required to hold any reserves.

The relation between Bank Reserves and credit creation by the banking system and its evolution over time are explained in Chapter 8, Credit Creation by the Banking Sector.

Appendix Two

Traditional Monetary Policy

The Fed was designed to be a passive institution, distributing currency in line with public demand and supplying short-term loans to commercial banks at their request, so long as the banks could supply sufficient collateral. The Fed did not remain passive for very long, however, as will become clear in Chapter 2.

As time passed, the Fed began attempting to manage the economy through the use of monetary policy. Monetary policy involves controlling the availability of credit within an economy in the effort to prevent that economy from either falling into a depression or from overheating.

Traditionally, the Fed stimulated economic growth by extending credit itself in order to supply additional Bank Reserves to the banking system, thereby enabling the commercial banks to extend bank credit on an even larger scale. It caused the economy – and inflation – to slow by contracting the credit it had already extended in order to reduce Bank Reserves, thereby forcing the banks to slow or even contract bank credit. Since 2008 the Fed has employed much more aggressive tactics: Quantitative Easing to stimulate economic growth and quantitative tightening to guard against inflation.

The Fed has a number of tools that allow it to control the level of credit in the US economy. Here, only the Fed's traditional tools will be described. They are: (1) adjusting the discount rate; (2) conducting open market operations in order to adjust the *federal funds rate*; and (3) adjusting the required reserve ratio. The new tools the Fed adopted in the aftermath of the financial crisis of 2008 will be explained in Chapter 12.

During the Fed's early years, it used the discount rate to influence the amount of credit available in the economy. The discount rate is the interest rate commercial banks pay to borrow Bank Reserves from the Fed through discounting operations. The discount rate is set by the Fed. In the past, if the Fed raised the discount rate, the commercial banks' cost of borrowing Bank Reserves from the Fed increased. When the cost of borrowing from the Fed increased, banks were inclined to reduce their level of Bank Reserves, which, in turn, constrained their ability to make loans. That is because when a bank extends loans, it creates deposits within the banking system. Since the banking sector was required to maintain a specific level of Bank Reserves relative to total customer deposits, if an increase in the discount rate caused Bank Reserves to decline, then the banking system had to reduce its lending, and, thereby, its deposits, in order to meet the level of required reserves it was forced to hold, as specified by the required reserve ratio. This process will be explained in greater detail in Chapter 8.

On the other hand, when the Fed reduced the discount rate, it became less expensive for commercial banks to borrow Bank

Reserves from the Fed. If they borrowed more Bank Reserves, they were able to extend additional bank credit, while still meeting their statutory reserve requirements. Therefore, bank credit tended to expand when the Fed reduced the discount rate.

Over time, borrowing Bank Reserves directly from the Fed came to be seen as a sign of weakness on the part of the borrower. Therefore, it fell out of favor. Instead of borrowing Bank Reserves from the Fed, banks began to borrow Bank Reserves from one another through what became known as the federal funds market. Therefore, the Fed had to develop a process that allowed it to influence the amount of credit in the economy by controlling the level of the federal funds rate, which is the interest rate commercial banks pay to borrow Bank Reserves from one another.

When the Fed increases the federal funds rate, all the other interest rates in the country tend to follow the federal funds rate higher. Therefore, credit becomes less affordable, and businesses and individuals tend to borrow less. Conversely, when the Fed lowers the federal funds rate, credit becomes more affordable, and business and individual tend to borrow more.

Up until 2008, the Fed controlled the federal funds rate by conducting small open market operations to increase or decrease the amount of Bank Reserves in the banking sector. If the Fed wished to push the federal funds rate higher, it would sell government securities (which it had acquired earlier) to the commercial banks. The Fed would take payment on those bonds by debiting the reserve accounts those banks hold at the Fed, thereby reducing the level of Bank Reserves of those individual banks and, by extension, the Bank Reserves of the entire banking system. The Fed would continue this process until Bank Reserves became scarce or, in other words, until some banks no longer held enough Bank Reserves to meet the minimum level of reserves they were required to hold. At that point, if those banks chose not to borrow Bank Reserves from the Fed through discounting operations, they would have to borrow them from other banks. As the demand for Bank Reserves increased, the cost of borrowing Bank Reserves, the federal funds rate, would rise.

On the other hand, if the Fed wanted to push the federal funds rate lower, it would buy government bonds from banks. When the Fed paid for those bonds by making deposits into the reserve accounts those banks hold at the Fed, Bank Reserves would become more plentiful and the cost of borrowing Bank Reserves, the federal funds rate, would fall. After 2008, the Fed was forced to adopt a new technique for controlling the federal funds rates. That technique and the reasons it became necessary will be explained in Chapter 8.

Finally, the Fed has the authority to increase or decrease the required reserve ratio. This is the other tool the Fed has used to influence the amount of credit that the banking sector extends. Throughout most of its history, if the Fed wished to increase the amount of credit in the economy, it could reduce the required reserve ratio, thereby allowing the commercial banks to extend more loans (and create more deposits) relative to their existing level of Bank Reserves. On the other hand, if the Fed wished to reduce the amount of credit in the economy, it could increase the required reserve ratio. Before Bank Reserves became superabundant, a higher required reserve ratio forced the banking sector to contract bank credit in order to shrink deposits enough to enable the banks to meet the new, higher, required reserve ratio, given their existing pool of Bank Reserves. The required reserve ratio is currently set at 0%. However, the Fed does have the power to raise it.

The next six chapters are full of examples of how the Fed has used traditional monetary policy to control the level of credit in the US economy. Those examples will make the concepts laid out in the paragraphs above much easier to understand.

Notes

1. The 1921 Annual Report of the Federal Reserve Board, p. 90.
2. Walter Bagehot, *Lombard Street: A Description of The Money Market* (Henry S. King & Co., 1973).
3. The Federal Reserve Act of 1913. FRASER. Federal Reserve Archival System for Economic Research. Federal Reserve Bank of St. Louis. https://fraser.stlouisfed.org/title/federal-reserve-act-975

4. Note: One balance sheet was published for each of the 12 Federal Reserve Banks and a consolidated balance sheet was published for the Federal Reserve System as a whole. This book will only discuss the consolidated balance sheet of the Federal Reserve System.

5. Reserves could be held as vault cash at each bank or as deposits at other banks in the larger cities that were leading financial centers.

6. Federal Reserve Bulletin, June 1993, p. 572.

7. Fourth Annual Report of the Federal Reserve Board Covering Operations for the Year 1917, Washington Printing Office, 1918, p. 14.

8. The Federal Reserve Act, Section 19: Bank Reserves.

9. The Federal Reserve Act had specified that as much as one-half of all reserves could take the form of rediscounted paper. However, in October 1914, the Board requested member banks to deposit their reserves in the form of gold or gold certificates. Most member banks complied with this request. Source: First Annual Report of the Federal Reserve Board for the Period Ending December 31, 1914, Washington Government Printing Office, 1915, p. 9.

10. The Federal Reserve Act was amended on June 21, 1917. Among other things, it required the member banks to hold all of their reserves in their Deposit Accounts at the Fed. Source: The 1917 Annual Report of the Federal Reserve Board, p. 543.

11. Financial Accounting Manual for Federal Reserve Banks, January 2020, Chapter 5. Federal Reserve Notes. https://www.federalreserve.gov/aboutthefed/chapter-5-federal-reserve-notes.htm

12. See the Fed's Annual Reports for 1971 and 1972. The change occurred in 1972.

13. The Federal Reserve Act, Section 14.

14. The Federal Reserve Act, Sections 13 and 16.

15. Gold certificates after 1934.

16. The influence the Fed wielded over gold flows stemmed from its ability to raise or lower US interest rates. Higher interest rates would attract more gold into the US, but at the price of causing the economy to slow as the cost of borrowing rose. Lower interest rates would support US economic growth, but typically would also cause gold to be shipped abroad in search of a higher return.

17. Changes in the level of funds in the Treasury Department's General Account at the Fed and in reverse repurchase agreements, both Fed liabilities, also came to impact the level of Bank Reserves, but not in a significant way until 2008.

CHAPTER 2

1914 to 1920: World War I

The Federal Reserve system has been of incalculable value during this period of war financing on the most extensive scale ever undertaken by any nation in the history of the world. It would have been impossible to carry through these unprecedented financing operations under our old banking system.
Treasury Secretary William Gibbs McAdoo[1]

World War I erupted in August 1914, three months before the Fed became operational in November 1914. Consequently, the new institution began its existence under conditions radically different from those imagined by its founders. The Federal Reserve Act had structured the Fed to be a relatively passive lender of last resort. It was designed to expand the currency when the public required more cash and to extend short-term loans to member banks when they asked to borrow. The war forced the Fed to take on a much more active role. This chapter describes how the Fed played an invaluable part in financing the debt the United States government had to issue to pay for the war. It also shows how the Fed was transformed in the process.

The Balance Sheet

World War I caused an extraordinary change in the size and composition of the Fed's balance sheet.

The Fed's total assets increased from $250 million at the end of 1914 to $6 billion at the end of 1920, as shown in Chart 2.1.

Chart 2.2 shows how the balance sheet evolved during those six years. Only the largest and most significant items are shown.

Assets are shown as positive numbers. Liabilities are shown as negative numbers. As with all balance sheets, total assets equal total liabilities. A change in the size of one side of the balance sheet is always accompanied by a change on the other side of the balance sheet of exactly the same amount.

CHART 2.1 The Fed's Total Assets, 1914 to 1920

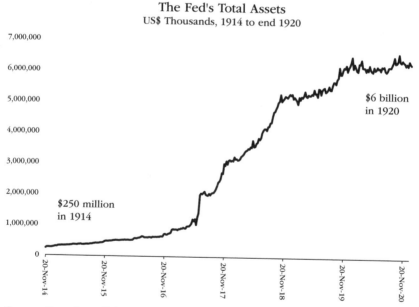

Source: Data from "The Federal Reserve System's Weekly Balance Sheet Since 1914" and accompanying spreadsheet. John Hopkins University, SAE/No.115/ July 2018. See Bibliography.

CHART 2.2 A Breakdown of the Fed's Major Assets and Liabilities, 1914 to 1920

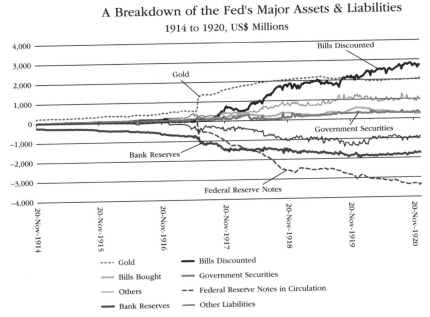

A Breakdown of the Fed's Major Assets & Liabilities
1914 to 1920, US$ Millions

Source: Data from *"The Federal Reserve System's Weekly Balance Sheet Since 1914"* and accompanying spreadsheet. Johns Hopkins University, SAE/No.115/ July 2018. See Bibliography.

Assets

On the asset side, the growth in the Fed's holdings of gold and bills discounted stand out. During the two years and seven months between the beginning of the war in August 1914 and the United States' entry into the war in April 1917, American companies made very large profits selling commodities, supplies, and weapons to England, her allies and to non-belligerent nations. They were paid with gold. (England's naval blockade severely restricted direct US sales to Germany and her allies.) The gold stock of the United States increased by 82% during those 32 months, from $1,566 million to $2,850 million.

When the companies earning those profits deposited their gold into their US bank accounts, their banks had to increase the amount of reserves (i.e., gold or legal tender) they were required to hold on deposit at the Fed to meet their minimum reserve requirements. Consequently, the level of gold held by the Fed increased sharply as a result of World War I. Between November 20, 1914 (the Fed's first balance sheet), and June 15, 1917, the Fed's gold holdings increased from $205 million to $591 million, 188%.

Then, in June 1917, the Fed's gold holdings roughly doubled. Up until then, member banks had been permitted to hold part of their reserves as vault cash or as deposits in commercial banks in the larger financial centers, known as reserve cities and central reserve cities. However, beginning in June 1917, member banks were required to hold all of their reserves with their Federal Reserve banks. The transfer of their reserves to the Fed explains the large increase in the Fed's gold holdings that month.[2]

After the United States entered the war in 1917, the large inflows of gold into the US stopped. Rather than forcing its allies to pay gold for the war materials they bought from the United States, the US government allowed them to finance their purchases with credit. Nevertheless, the amount of gold held by the Fed continued to expand. During the war, bank credit expanded rapidly in the United States. When the commercial banks made loans, that caused the deposits in the banking system to expand as well. Commercial banks therefore were required to continue increasing their reserves against their customers' deposits by adding gold to their reserve accounts at the Fed. The Fed's gold holding increased from $1,295 million on July 29, 1917, to $2,065 million on November 29, 1918, by which time the Fed held 72% of the stock of gold in the United States.

When the United States entered the war, the Fed was compelled to take on a completely different role than that which had originally been envisioned for it. The Fed had been created to serve as a lender of last resort to prevent the recurrence of panics in the banking sector. When the United States entered the war, the Fed's responsibilities changed. Its principal responsibility became to ensure that the US government could borrow as much money as it required to fight and win the war.

To fulfill that duty, the Fed put in place an interest rate structure that guaranteed a profit to member banks when they acquired government bonds. To do that, the Fed announced that it would discount bills that were backed with government securities as collateral at an interest rate that was 1/2% to 1% below the rate of interest offered on government securities. In practice, that meant that a member bank could buy a government Liberty Bond paying 4% interest when it was first sold by the government; and then offer that bond as collateral to the Fed in exchange for a loan that cost the member bank 3.5% interest. The member bank could then take the money that it had received from the Fed as a loan and buy a new government Liberty Bond paying 4% interest, thereby locking in a profit of 1/2 of 1% on every dollar it invested in government bonds.

With both patriotism and profitability in mind, commercial banks were quick to take advantage of this opportunity to earn a guaranteed return. Their holdings of government securities increased from $733 million at the end of 1916 to $5.8 billion at the end of 1919. The jump in the banks' holdings of government securities is shown in Chart 2.3. The banks' holdings of government securities increased by $600 million in 1917, $1.9 billion in 1918 and $2.2 billion in 1919.

The amount of money the banks borrowed from the Fed is reflected on the Fed's balance sheet in the growth in "bills discounted," which increased from just $50 million in June 1917 to a peak of nearly $2.8 billion in November 1920, as shown in Chart 2.2.

The Fed also bought government securities for its own account to help finance the war. At the peak, in October 1918, the Fed owned $350 million of government securities.

When the Fed lent money to member banks, it did so by making deposits into the reserve accounts that those member banks held at the Fed. And when the Fed purchased government securities for its own account, it acquired them from member banks and paid for them by making deposits into the reserve

CHART 2.3 All Banks' Investments in US Government Obligations, Annual $ Change, 1897 to 1920

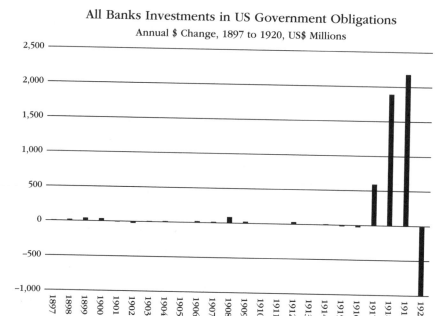

All Banks Investments in US Government Obligations
Annual $ Change, 1897 to 1920, US$ Millions

Source: Data from Historical Statistics of the United States: From Colonial Times to 1957, Chapter 10, Banking and Finance, US Census Bureau

accounts those banks held at the Fed. As discussed in Chapter 1, when the Fed deposits money into a member bank's reserve account at the Fed, it is not depositing money that already exists. Instead, it is paying with credit, Federal Reserve Credit, that is created through the act of making the deposit.

Federal Reserve Credit extended by the Fed increased by just $142 million in 1916. In 1917, it rose by $850 million, in 1918 by $1.4 billion, and in 1919 by $794 million more, as can be seen in Chart 2.4.

Total Federal Reserve Credit outstanding soared from $226 million in April 1917, when the US entered the war, to $3.2 billion in January 1920. Chart 2.5. shows the growth in Federal Reserve Credit between 1914 and 1920, as well as the types of assets the Fed acquired through the process of extending that credit.

CHART 2.4 Federal Reserve Credit, Annual $ Change, 1915 to 1920

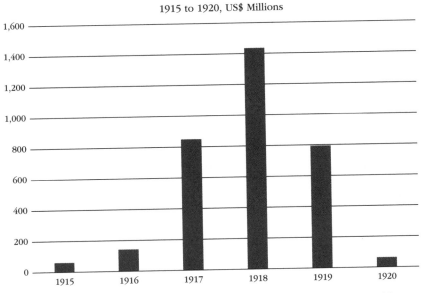

Federal Reserve Credit, Annual $ Change
1915 to 1920, US$ Millions

Source: Data for 1914 to 1917 from "The Federal Reserve System's Weekly Balance Sheet Since 1914" and accompanying spreadsheet. Johns Hopkins University, SAE/No.115/July 2018. See Bibliography.
Data for 1918 to 1920 from The Fed's 2017 Annual Report, page 306

The top (dark gray) line shows the growth in total Federal Reserve Credit from 1914 to 1920. The remining three lines represent the assets the Fed obtained by extending that credit. It can be seen that most of the Federal Reserve Credit that was created was used to make loans to member banks through discounting paper backed by government securities. That is reflected in the black line representing "Bills Discounted." The rest of the Federal Reserve Credit that was created was used to acquire commercial paper (shown as "Bills Bought" in the light gray line) and to acquire government securities (for the Fed's own account), represented by the medium gray line.

As mentioned above, the Fed's assets are comprised primarily of gold and the items acquired through the extension of Federal Reserve Credit. Chart 2.6 shows how the mix between those two types of assets changed between 1914 and 1920.

CHART 2.5 Federal Reserve Credit and Its Components, 1914 to 1920

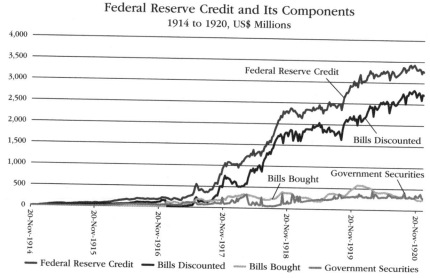

Federal Reserve Credit and Its Components
1914 to 1920, US$ Millions

Source: Data from "The Federal Reserve System's Weekly Balance Sheet Since 1914" and accompanying spreadsheet. John Hopkins University, SAE/No.115/ July 2018. See Bibliography.

The top light gray line represents the Fed's total assets. The dotted line represents the Fed's gold holdings. The dark gray line shows the Fed's assets acquired through the extension of Federal Reserve Credit. Initially, gold made up nearly all of the Fed's assets. However, once the United States entered the war, the assets it acquired through the extension of Federal Reserve Credit began to grow rapidly, until, in September 1918, they accounted for a larger share of the Fed's total assets than gold. In other words, at that point, assets acquired with Federal Reserve Credit overtook gold as the largest item on the asset side of the Fed's balance sheet.

Liabilities

Finally, consider the changes in the Fed's liabilities during these years. These can be seen in Chart 2.2. Gold inflows and the extension of Federal Reserve Credit are accompanied by a corresponding increase in member bank reserves on the liabilities

CHART 2.6 The Fed's Total Assets: Gold vs. Assets Acquired with Federal Reserve Credit, 1914 to 1920

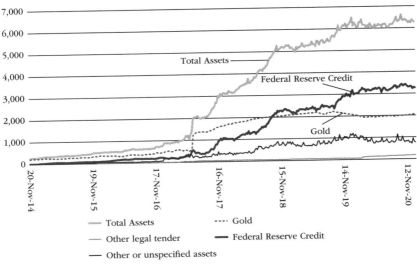

The Fed's Total Assets:
Gold vs. Assets Acquired with Federal Reserve Credit
1914 to 1920, US$ Millions

Source: Data from "*The Federal Reserve System's Weekly Balance Sheet Since 1914*" and accompanying spreadsheet. Johns Hopkins University, SAE/No.115/July 2018. See Bibliography.

side of the Fed's balance sheet. During this period, when gold entered the US, it was deposited into commercial banks. As their deposits grew, those banks were required to deposit more gold at the Fed as reserves against their deposits. Those deposits caused the Fed's gold holdings to expand on the asset side of its balance sheet and its reserve liabilities to increase on the liabilities side of its balance sheet. The extension of Federal Reserve Credit also caused Bank Reserves to expand, since the credit was extended through the act of the Fed making deposits into the member banks' reserve accounts at the Fed.

Chart 2.2 also shows that Bank Reserves (represented by the dark gray line) did grow during these years. However, they did not increase as much as would have been expected given the increase in the Fed's gold holdings combined with the increase in Federal Reserve Credit. That is because the demand for cash increased very sharply during the war. As the public withdrew cash from their commercial banks, those banks obtained more currency in the form of Federal Reserve Notes from the Fed, causing the central bank's Federal Reserve Note liabilities to expand rapidly (as shown in the dashed line). In exchange for giving the commercial banks cash, the Fed debited the reserve accounts the banks held at the Fed. Therefore, growth in Bank Reserves was largely offset by the increase in Federal Reserve Notes in circulation.

Next, consider the impact that the growth in the Fed's assets and liabilities had on its *gold coverage ratio*. Recall that the Fed was required to hold an amount of gold equivalent to at least 40% of the Federal Reserve Notes it issued and also to hold gold equivalent to at least 35% of the reserves that member banks held in their reserve accounts at the Fed. When the Fed opened its doors in November 1914, it held an amount of gold equivalent to 105% of its note and deposit liabilities. However, by May 1920, that ratio had fallen to just 42.6% as the result of the huge expansion of Federal Reserve Notes and Bank Reserves that had occurred during the preceding five and a half years. That was uncomfortably close to the statutory limit. This plunge in the Fed's gold coverage ratio is shown in Chart 2.7.

To summarize then, between 1914 and 1917, the large gold inflows into the United States caused a large expansion of the Fed's assets and liabilities. No new operating procedure was required. As customer deposits at commercial banks expanded, the liquidity reserves that the member banks were required to hold in their reserve accounts at the Fed naturally grew. That was how the Fed was designed to work. Although the Fed's balance sheet grew rapidly during that period, the Fed did not undertake any action to bring about that outcome. It was passive.

When the United States entered the war, however, the Fed adopted new procedures that enabled it to help finance the war at low interest rates. It created as much Federal Reserve Credit as necessary to enable the commercial banks to satisfy the government's funding requirements. If the Fed had not existed in 1917, it would have had to be created to serve that purpose. Wars require extraordinarily large amounts of money; money that

CHART 2.7 Gold Coverage Ratio: Ratio of the Fed's Gold Reserves to Its Note and Deposit Liabilities, 1914 to 1920

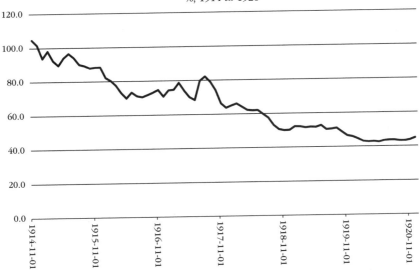

Gold Coverage Ratio

Ratio of the Fed's Gold Reserves to Its Note and Deposit Liabilities %, 1914 to 1920

Source: Data from Ratio of Reserves to Note and Deposit Liabilities, Federal Reserve Banks for United States, St. Louis Fed., 1914 to 1920

governments must obtain through taxes and borrowing. The Fed put in place an interest rate structure that ensured the government could borrow as much credit as it needed to fight the war.

The Fed extended Federal Reserve Credit to the commercial banks, which enabled the banks to purchase government bonds for their own account. That Federal Reserve Credit also allowed the banks to extend additional loans to their customers, enabling them to buy government bonds and also to finance private sector investment in the plant and equipment needed for the war effort. Chart 2.8 shows there was a marked increase in the annual growth of the banks' other loans and investments (excluding their investments in government securities) from 1916 to 1920.

If the Fed had not increased the availability of credit by extending Federal Reserve Credit, government demand for loans

CHART 2.8 All Banks: Loans & Investments Other Than Investments in Government Securities, Annual $ Change, 1897 to 1920

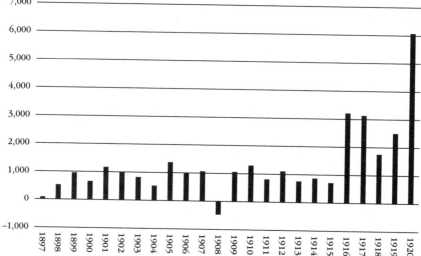

All Banks: Loans & Investments Other Than Investments in Government Securities

Annual $ Change, 1897 to 1920, US$ Millions

Source: Data from Historical Statistics of the United States: From Colonial Times to 1957, Chapter 10, Banking and Finance, US Census Bureau

would have pushed up interest rates to extraordinarily high levels. That, in turn, would have wrecked the economy and made it much more difficult for the United States to successfully conduct the war.

The preceding paragraphs explain why and how the Fed's total assets increased 2,300%, from $250 million to $6 billion, during the first six years of its existence.

Notes

1. Treasury Secretary William Gibbs McAdoo, The Annual Report of the Secretary of the Treasury on the State of the Finances for the Fiscal Year Ending June 30, 1917, p. 22.
2. The Fed's 1916 Annual Report, p. 23, and the Fed's 1917 Annual Report, p. 12.

CHAPTER 3

1920 to 1930: After the War

Taking the year (1923) as a whole and regarding it in the per-spective of the after-war readjustment period, there is abun-dant evidence that, so far as the United States is concerned, economic readjustment has been proceeding at a rapid rate and is now nearing completion.

Tenth Annual Report of the Federal Reserve Board
Covering Operations for the Year 1923.[1]

World War I had set off a torrid economic expansion in the United States. In 1920 that boom came to an end, and in 1921 the country experienced a severe but short-lived depres-sion. When that depression ended in early 1922, the monetary disruptions unleashed by the war finally ceased. This chapter describes the significant impact the Depression of 1921 had on the Fed's balance sheet. It also highlights the relative calm the Fed enjoyed during the rest of the decade.

The Balance Sheet

Assets

Between October 1920 and the end of 1930, the Fed's total assets contracted from $6.6 billion to $5.3 billion, as shown in Chart 3.1. Notice, however, that all of the contraction occurred between October 1920 and January 1922. During that time, the Fed's total assets fell by 27%. Afterwards, they remained more or less stable during the rest of the decade.

The Fed's assets declined during 1921 because the commercial banks sharply curtailed their borrowing from the Fed. This is reflected on the Fed's balance sheet by the plunge in bills discounted from $2.8 billion in October 1920 to only $414 million in January 1922 (see Chart 3.2).

CHART 3.1 The Fed's Total Assets, 1914 to 1930

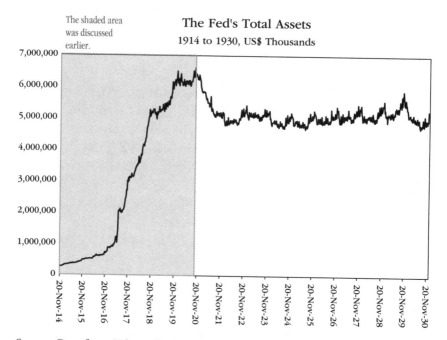

Source: Data from "*The Federal Reserve System's Weekly Balance Sheet Since 1914*" and accompanying spreadsheet. Johns Hopkins University, SAE/No.115/ July 2018. See Bibliography.

Two factors drove the commercial banks' decisions to repay their loans from the Fed. First, a large amount of gold entered the United States during 1921, as the country's allies began to repay some of the money they had borrowed from the United States during the war. That year the country's gold reserves rose by $734 billion, or 28%. When this gold entered the United States, it was deposited into the commercial banks. They used the gold to repay part of their loans from the Fed. The 1921 Annual Report of the Federal Reserve Board attributed 44% of the decline in Fed's "loan account" to these gold inflows.[2] The Fed's gold holdings increased by 50% that year from $2 billion to $3 billion, as shown in Chart 3.2.

CHART 3.2 A Breakdown of the Fed's Major Assets and Liabilities, 1914 to 1930

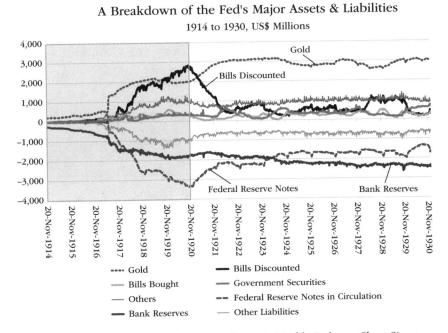

Source: Data from *"The Federal Reserve System's Weekly Balance Sheet Since 1914"* and accompanying spreadsheet. Johns Hopkins University, SAE/No.115/ July 2018. See Bibliography.

The Depression of 1921 is the second reason the commercial banks repaid their loans from the Fed. The postwar economic boom ended with a commodity price crash in 1920, followed by a severe economic slump. During 1921, the total loans and investments of the 800 reporting member banks in leading cities contracted by nearly 11%.[3] The combination of ample gold reserves and weak loan demand meant the commercial banks simply did not need to continue borrowing from the Fed.

The banks repaid the Fed by redeeming the bills they had offered to the Fed as collateral. The bills discounted on the asset side of the Fed's balance sheet fell 85% between October 1920 and January 1922. That explains the 27% contraction in the Fed's total assets during that period despite the large increase in the Fed's gold holdings.

Altogether, Federal Reserve Credit contracted by nearly $1.8 billion during 1921, as shown in Chart 3.3.

CHART 3.3 Federal Reserve Credit, Annual $ Change, 1915 to 1930

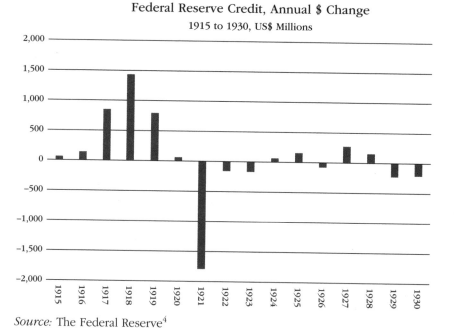

Federal Reserve Credit, Annual $ Change
1915 to 1930, US$ Millions

Source: The Federal Reserve[4]

Chart 3.4 shows that total Federal Reserve Credit, represented in the top line in dark gray, contracted 70%, from a
peak of $3.4 billion in November 1920 to a low of $1 billion in
August 1922.

This collapse was due entirely to the reduction in the Fed's
bills discounted. By comparison, changes in the other two components of Federal Reserve Credit, government securities and
bills bought, were much less significant during those years, as
well as throughout the rest of the decade.

The large inflow of gold and the steep contraction in Federal Reserve Credit resulted in gold once again overtaking assets
acquired with Federal Reserve Credit as the largest component
within the Fed's total assets. Chart 3.5 shows that gold surpassed
the assets acquired with Federal Reserve Credit in mid-1921
and remained the dominant component throughout the rest of
the decade.

CHART 3.4 Federal Reserve Credit and Its Components 1914 to 1930

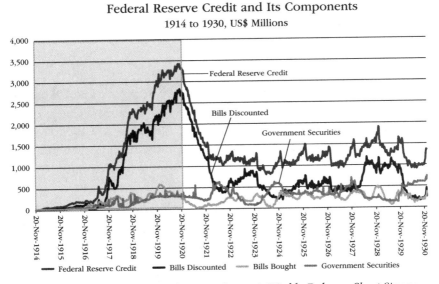

Source: Data from *"The Federal Reserve System's Weekly Balance Sheet Since
1914"* and accompanying spreadsheet. Johns Hopkins University, SAE/No.115/
July 2018. See Bibliography.

CHART 3.5 The Fed's Total Assets: Gold vs. Assets Acquired with Federal Reserve Credit, 1914 to 1930

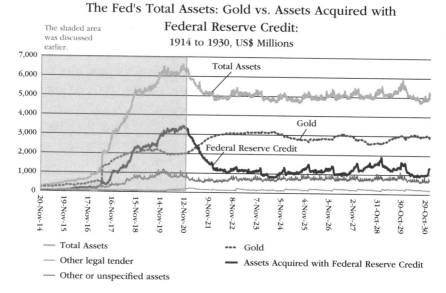

The Fed's Total Assets: Gold vs. Assets Acquired with Federal Reserve Credit: 1914 to 1930, US$ Millions

The shaded area was discussed earlier.

Source: Data from *"The Federal Reserve System's Weekly Balance Sheet Since 1914"* and accompanying spreadsheet. Johns Hopkins University, SAE/No.115/ July 2018. See Bibliography.

Liabilities

On the liabilities side of the Fed's balance sheet, Federal Reserve Notes also contracted sharply between late 1920 and early 1922, by approximately $1.2 billion or 35%. This was another significant development over which the Fed had no control. Once the war ended and the war-induced economic boom came to an end, the public no longer needed or wished to hold as much cash. They deposited it into their accounts at the commercial banks, and the commercial banks returned the unwanted Federal Reserve Notes to the Fed. As the Fed received the cash, in exchange, it credited those banks' reserve accounts at the Fed.

Chart 3.2 shows that the Fed's Federal Reserve Note liabilities shrank as currency was retired. Had no other factors been at play, Bank Reserves would have increased one for one with the decrease in Federal Reserve Notes. However, two other factors were at play. The second factor added to Bank Reserves, while the third factor reduced Bank Reserves.

The second factor, which was discussed above, was the gold inflows into the United States during 1921. When the commercial banks deposited that gold into their reserve accounts at the Fed, it increased the Fed's gold holdings on the asset side of the Fed's balance sheet and it increased the member banks' Reserves on the liabilities side of the Fed's balance sheet.

Therefore, the reduction in Federal Reserve Notes and the gold deposits made by commercial banks both added to Bank Reserves. However, a third factor had the opposite effect. In 1921, when the commercial banks repaid the Fed the credit they had borrowed from the Fed during the war, the Fed took payment by simply debiting the reserve accounts those banks held at the Fed by the amount of the loans repaid, thereby reducing the size of member banks' reserves on the liabilities side of its balance sheet.

The two factors adding to Bank Reserves, the reduction in Federal Reserve Notes and the gold deposits made by commercial banks, were more or less completely offset by the one factor deducting from Bank Reserves: the repayment of the commercial banks' loans from the Fed. As a result, Banks Reserves were little changed between late 1920 and early 1922.

It is also important to note that the reduction in Federal Reserve Notes outstanding, combined with the large additions to the Fed's gold holdings, resulted in an impressive improvement in the Fed's gold coverage ratio. Chart 3.6 shows the ratio of the Fed's gold reserves to notes and reserve liabilities increased from 43.2% in October 1920 to nearly 80% by mid 1922, eliminating, for the time being at least, any concern that the Fed would lack sufficient gold to meet its statutory reserve requirements.

CHART 3.6 Gold Coverage Ratio, 1914 to 1930

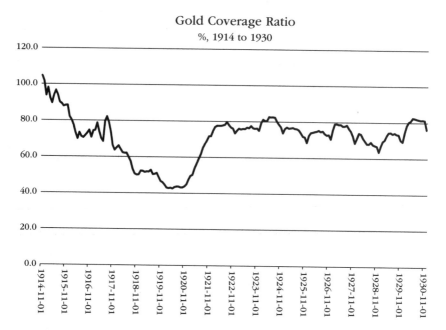

Gold Coverage Ratio
%, 1914 to 1930

Source: Data from Ratio of Reserves to Note and Deposit Liabilities, Federal Reserve Banks for United States, St. Louis Fed., 1914 to 1948

Conclusion

The monetary disruptions that had begun with the outbreak of World War I finally came to an end in February 1922. The Fed had never been intended to be the source of long-term credit. It had been created to supply short-term loans to prevent temporary liquidity shortages from developing into full-blown banking panics. Therefore, the contraction in Federal Reserve Credit during 1921 occurred in full accordance with how the Fed was designed to function. The Fed had supplied Federal Reserve Credit on a large scale as an emergency measure to help finance the war effort. Therefore, the contraction in Federal Reserve Credit during 1921 simply returned the size of the Fed's balance sheet back to a level much closer to where it would have been had World War I never occurred.

During the rest of the 1920s, the Fed functioned as the passive institution that its architects had designed it to be. The Fed periodically responded to commercial bank demand for liquidity through discounting operations. Otherwise, the Fed was largely inactive. There were no significant additional gold inflows from abroad, so the Fed's gold holding remained relatively flat. The amount of Federal Reserve Notes outstanding remained relatively stable and Bank Reserves expanded only gradually. Up through the end of 1930, the Fed's total assets grew little and Federal Reserve Credit grew even less.

The Fed's operating procedures began to evolve during the 1930s. World War II not only radically altered the way the Fed functioned, it radically altered its purpose as well. Afterwards, the Fed never returned to the role set out for it in the Federal Reserve Act of 1913. Chapters 4 and 5 detail how the Great Depression and the World War II transformed the Fed.

Notes

1. Tenth Annual Report of the Federal Reserve Board Covering Operations for the Year 1923, Washington Printing Office, February 15, 1924, p. 1.
2. Eighth Annual Report of the Federal Reserve Board Covering Operations for the Year 1921, Washington Printing Office, 1922, p. 6.
3. Eighth Annual Report of the Federal Reserve Board Covering Operations for the Year 1921, Washington Printing Office, 1922, p. 22.
4. Data for 1914 to 1917 from *"The Federal Reserve System's Weekly Balance Sheet Since 1914"* and accompanying spreadsheet. Johns Hopkins University, SAE/No.115/July 2018. See Bibliography.
   Data for 1918 to 1930 from The Fed's 2017 Annual Report, page 306

CHAPTER 4

1930 to 1941:
The Great Depression

During 1933 changes of a fundamental character occurred in the monetary system of the United States, the most important of which was suspension of gold payments.
Twentieth Annual Report of the Federal Reserve Board
Covering Operations for the Year 1933[1]

Three waves of bank failures during the early 1930s culminated in the worst depression in US history. The Fed had been created to prevent liquidity shortages from developing into full-blown banking panics. Yet, between 1930 and 1933, the Fed failed to supply sufficient funds to keep America's banks solvent; and in early 1933 a third of the banking system collapsed.

The Fed was severely criticized for not preventing the banking crisis of the early 1930s and the Great Depression that resulted from that crisis. In its own defense, the Fed claimed that the Federal Reserve Act placed limitations upon it that had made it impossible for the Fed to take the steps required to contain the crisis. The Glass-Steagall Act of 1932 lessened those limitations and expanded the Fed's powers to create Federal Reserve Credit. However, the huge inflow of gold into the United States

beginning in 1934 made the Fed's enhanced powers superflu-
ous – at least during the rest of that decade.

This chapter analyzes the evolution of the Fed's balance sheet
to explain the most significant monetary developments between
the beginning of the Great Depression and the United States'
entry into World War II.

Total Assets

From the beginning of 1930, when the economic collapse began,
to the end of 1941, when the United States entered World War II,
the Fed's total assets increased from $5.5 billion to $25 billion, as
shown in Chart 4.1.

CHART 4.1 The Fed's Total Assets, 1914 to 1941

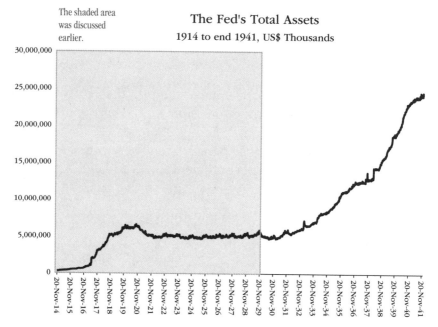

Source: Data from "*The Federal Reserve System's Weekly Balance Sheet Since
1914*" and accompanying spreadsheet. Johns Hopkins University, SAE/No.115/
July 2018. See Bibliography.

The surge in the Fed's total assets occurred for two reasons. First, in 1932 and 1933, the Fed purchased government securities on a large scale through open market operations. Second, a tidal wave of gold entered the United States beginning in 1934. The gold inflows were, by far, the more important factor behind the growth in the Fed's assets during this period. Nevertheless, the Fed's purchases of government securities were also an important development in Federal Reserve policy.

The Great Depression

The US stock market peaked in September 1929. On October 28, the Dow fell 13%. The following day, it fell 12% more. By the time it hit bottom in July 1932, it had lost 89% of its value. The first wave of bank failures began in November 1930. A second followed in mid-1931 and a third in early 1933. By the end of 1933, the total loans and investments of commercial banks had contracted by 38%. Between 1929 and 1933, the size of the US economy shrank by 26% in real terms. In nominal terms, in other words, not adjusting for the change in the price level, the outcome was much worse: the economy contracted by 45%.[2]

As the economic crisis began to unfold, the Fed was slow to respond. The Fed's total assets contracted at the beginning of the Great Depression, from a peak of $5.9 billion in November 1929 to as low as $4.7 billion in February 1931, a 20% drop. Federal Reserve Credit contracted even more, by 47%, from $1.6 billion in November 1929 to $850 million in March 1931, as banks repaid their loans from the Fed and the *bills discounted* on the Fed's balance sheet shrank (see Chart 4.2).

A second wave of bank failures during the second half of 1931 saw the banks turn to the Fed for loans once again. Consequently, Federal Reserve Credit expanded back to $2.2 billion in October, before falling back again to $1.6 billion in March 1932, when that panic subsided.

Eventually, the Fed began buying government securities on a large scale. Between March and June 1932, the Fed's holdings

CHART 4.2 Federal Reserve Credit and Its Components, 1914 to 1941

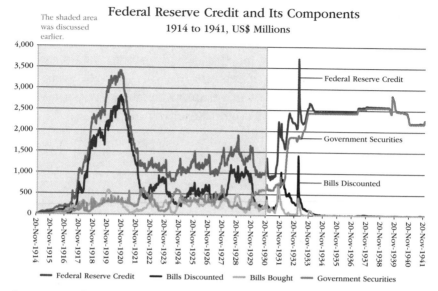

The shaded area
was discussed
earlier.

Federal Reserve Credit and Its Components
1914 to 1941, US$ Millions

Source: Data from "*The Federal Reserve System's Weekly Balance Sheet Since 1914*" and accompanying spreadsheet. Johns Hopkins University, SAE/No.115/ July 2018. See Bibliography.

of government securities increased from $800 million to $1.8 billion, an increase of 125%, as can be seen in Chart 4.2.

This was the first time in the Fed's history that it acquired such a large amount of government debt. It was also the first time the Fed had carried out open market operations on such a large scale.

In early March 1933, at the peak of the third wave of bank failures, bills discounted, reflecting the amount the banks borrowed from the Fed, spiked to $1.4 billion. This drove total Federal Reserve Credit up to $3.7 billion, above the record high of $3.4 billion set in the aftermath of World War I. However, when that bank panic subsided following Franklin Roosevelt's inauguration, bills discounted declined rapidly back to $400 billion by mid-April, bringing total Federal Reserve Credit back below $2.5 billion.

In May, the Fed began purchasing government securities aggressively for a second time, taking its total holdings of government debt up from $1.8 billion in mid-May to $2.4 billion in October.

As the Fed's holdings of government securities increased, its holdings of bills discounted and *bills bought* declined. When the Fed purchased the government securities, it paid for them by making deposits into the reserve accounts at the Fed belonging to the commercial banks from which it had acquired the government bonds. Those banks, seeing no viable investment opportunities in the midst of the Great Depression, simply used the funds they received from the Fed, to pay off the loans they had borrowed from the Fed. Consequently, the bills that they had offered as collateral for those loans were removed from the Fed's assets when those loans were repaid; and the Federal Reserve Credit that had been created when the Fed had discounted those bills was extinguished. The bills bought by the Fed also declined to almost zero after the Fed began to buy government bonds on a large scale, extinguishing still more Federal Reserve Credit.

Therefore, although the Fed did increase its holdings of government securities by $1.6 billion between March 1932 and October 1933, Federal Reserve Credit did not increase by a similar amount. As shown in Chart 4.2, Federal Reserve Credit only increased from $1.6 billion in March 1932 to $2.5 billion in October 1933. From there, it remained relatively flat for the rest of the decade.

Chart 4.3 presents the annual change in Federal Reserve Credit each year. During this period, there was only meaningful growth in 1931, 1932 and 1933.

Friedman and Schwartz argued persuasively in *A Monetary History of The United States* that the Fed could have prevented what was still a recession in 1930 from becoming the Great Depression by 1932 if it had bought government bonds through open market operations earlier and much more aggressively than it eventually did. That would have injected large amounts of Federal Reserve Credit (i.e., newly created base money) into the economy and the financial system. Had it done so, the Fed's

CHART 4.3 Federal Reserve Credit, Annual $ Change, 1915 to 1941

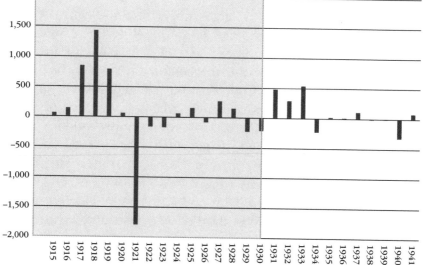

Federal Reserve Credit, Annual $ Change
1915 to 1941, US$ Millions

Source: The Federal Reserve[3]

total assets would have expanded rather than contracting by 20% between November 1929 and February 1931.

The Fed, however, stated in its 1932 Annual Report[4] that it had been unable to undertake a more expansionary monetary policy (i.e., to extend more Federal Reserve Credit) during the early 1930s because its holdings of gold and eligible paper would not have been sufficient to allow it to meet the 100% collateral obligation it was required to hold against Federal Reserve Notes.[5]

Recall from Chapter 1 that the Federal Reserve Act required the Fed to hold gold to back the currency it issued (Federal Reserve Notes) as well as to back the credit it created by making deposits into the reserve accounts that member banks held at the Fed as reserves. The Fed was required to hold 40% gold backing for the Federal Reserve Notes and 35% gold backing for the Bank Reserves. For Federal Reserve Notes, however, in addition to maintaining 40% gold backing, the Fed was also required to hold 60% additional collateral comprised of gold or "eligible paper."[6] Eligible paper was defined as commercial, agricultural, or industrial loans, or loans secured by US government securities rediscounted by member banks; loans to member banks secured by paper eligible for rediscount or by government securities; and bankers' acceptance, i.e., "bills bought" in the terminology of Federal Reserve accounts.[7] However, government securities owned by the Fed were not permitted to be used as eligible paper to serve as collateral for Federal Reserve Notes.

At the beginning of the economic crisis, the Fed had more than enough gold and eligible paper to meet its obligation to back Federal Reserve Notes. In other words, it had excess gold. However, its level of excess gold declined as the depression worsened. A large number of banks failed during 1931. As a result, the public withdrew cash from their banks to protect their savings. Consequently, Federal Reserve Notes in circulation increased as shown in Chart 4.4. The increase in Federal Reserve Notes in circulation is reflected in the Fed's balance sheet as growth in Federal Reserve Note liabilities.

The increase in Federal Reserve Notes in circulation required the Fed to set aside additional gold and collateral backing, which reduced the Fed's excess gold. At the same time, the amount of eligible paper held by the Fed declined. This occurred because member banks borrowed less from the Fed through discounting. After the stock market crash in October 1929, commercial bank lending began to contract. The reduction in bank credit caused the deposits of the commercial banks to contract, as well.

Consequently, the commercial banks had less need to borrow from the Fed. This is reflected in the reduction in the bills discounted held by the Fed during 1930, as shown in Chart 4.2. As a result, the Fed lacked sufficient eligible paper to carry out a more expansionary monetary policy. In other words, the Fed could not conduct large-scale open market purchases because that would have caused an equivalent increase in member bank reserves at the Fed, deposits that required more gold backing than the Fed possessed.

CHART 4.4 A Breakdown of the Fed's Major Assets & Liabilities, 1925 to 1934

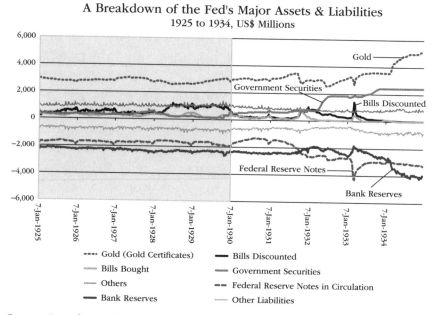

A Breakdown of the Fed's Major Assets & Liabilities
1925 to 1934, US$ Millions

Source: Data from *"The Federal Reserve System's Weekly Balance Sheet Since 1914"* and accompanying spreadsheet. Johns Hopkins University, SAE/No.115/ July 2018. See Bibliography.

The Glass-Steagall Act, enacted on February 27, 1932, removed that problem by making government securities owned by the Fed eligible as collateral to back Federal Reserve Notes. This enabled the Fed to acquire more government securities through open market operations since, thereafter, those government securities could serve as the necessary collateral to back Federal Reserve Notes. It was only after the passage of Glass-Steagall (in fact, immediately after) that the large-scale purchases of government securities discussed above began.

This was the first significant revision to the Federal Reserve Act that expanded the Fed's ability to extend Federal Reserve Credit. It greatly increased the Fed's power to conduct expansionary monetary policy through credit creation.

The authorization for the Fed to use government securities as collateral to back Federal Reserve Notes was initially intended to be only a temporary emergency measure that would expire after one year. However, it was extended every year, until 1945, when it was made permanent by an act of Congress. Had the Fed not been allowed to hold government securities as collateral against Federal Reserve Notes, it would not have been possible for the Fed to supply all the currency that was required during World War II.

In 2008, when the United States was once again on the brink of a new Great Depression, Fed Chairman Ben Bernanke followed Friedman's advice and flooded the financial markets with Federal Reserve Credit through three rounds of *Quantitative Easing*.[8] We'll consider the results of that experiment in Chapter 12.

Turning to the liabilities side of the Fed's balance sheet, the most important development during the early part of the decade was the jump in currency held by the public. When banks began to fail across the country, individuals withdrew their cash from their bank accounts while they still could. At that time, bank deposits were not insured by the government. If a bank failed, its depositors stood to lose all their savings. Federal Reserve Notes in circulation jumped from $1.4 billion in October 1930 to $4.3 billion in March 1933. This can be seen clearly in Chart 4.4, which highlights changes in the Fed's balance sheet during the early years of the Great Depression.

As the public withdrew its cash, the commercial banks were forced to obtain more Federal Reserve Notes from the Fed. Consequently, their reserves at the Fed contracted as the Fed debited their reserve accounts in exchange for the Federal Reserve Notes the Fed provided them. Member bank reserves actually contracted during this time even though the Fed had made deposits into those accounts in payment for the large amount of government securities it had purchased in 1932.

The public run on the banks only ended when President Roosevelt declared a national "bank holiday" during his first days in office and the public became convinced that the new administration would resolve the banking crisis. From January 1, 1934, the government guaranteed all bank deposits up to the amount of $2,500 per depositor. On July 1, 1934, the amount of deposits guaranteed by the government was increased to $5,000 per depositor.[9]

Once the banking crisis ended, the public redeposited the Federal Reserve Notes they had withdrawn from the banking system. The commercial banks returned the unneeded Federal Reserve Notes to the Fed. In exchange, the Fed credited the commercial banks' reserve accounts at the Fed, causing Bank Reserves to expand again, as the Fed's Federal Reserve Note liabilities contracted.

Federal Reserve Notes expanded gradually through most of the rest of the decade. However, the amount of currency in circulation grew significantly again beginning in August 1940 when World War II, already underway in Europe, caused the US economy to heat up and the need for cash to rise. Then, as the commercial banks requested additional cash from the Fed, their reserves began to dip as the Fed debited their reserve accounts in exchange for the Federal Reserve Notes it provided to them. Chart 4.5 best illustrates these changes in the Fed's liabilities after 1933.

Gold

Between the end of January 1934 and April 1941, the Fed's gold holdings increased by more than 450% from $3.6 billion to $20 billion. Chart 4.5 shows that the surge in gold holdings was the outstanding development on the assets side of the Fed's balance sheet during this period.

Greed and fear explain the flood of gold into the US beginning in 1934.

Here some background information is required. During the nadir of the Great Depression, Franklin Roosevelt was elected President in November 1932. He took the oath of office on March 4, 1933.[10] Afterwards, he quickly introduced a series of measures that took the United States off the *gold standard*.

On March 10, an executive order made it illegal to export gold. On April 5, the president issued Executive Order 6102,

CHART 4.5 A Breakdown of the Fed's Major Assets & Liabilities, 1914 to 1941

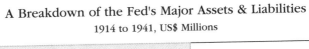

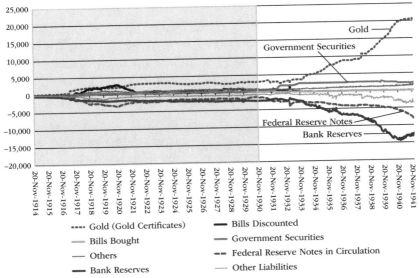

Source: Data from *"The Federal Reserve System's Weekly Balance Sheet Since 1914"* and accompanying spreadsheet. Johns Hopkins University, SAE/No.115/ July 2018. See Bibliography.

which prohibited American citizens from owning gold.[11] Every American was required to hand over their gold to the Federal Reserve by April 28, 1933, or face a fine of up to $10,000 or imprisonment of up to 10 years or both. They were compensated at the prevailing statutory rate of $20.67 per ounce of gold.

In late January 1934, Congress passed the Gold Reserve Act of 1934. It was signed into law by President Roosevelt on January 30. It required the Fed to transfer all of its gold holdings to the US Treasury Department (i.e., the government). In exchange, the Fed was given irredeemable gold certificates. Afterwards, rather than holding gold to back the money it created, as it had been required to do up until then, the Fed was required to "maintain reserves in gold certificates or lawful money of not less than thirty-five per centum against its deposits and reserves in gold certificates of not less than forty per centum against its Federal Reserve Notes in actual circulation."[12]

The Gold Reserve Act of 1934 also gave the president the authority to devalue the dollar against gold. On January 31, the day after the Fed turned over all of its gold to the Treasury Department at the price of US$20.67 per ounce, President Roosevelt devalued the dollar relative to gold by 41%. The dollar price to acquire an ounce of gold increased from $20.67 to $35. This had the effect of also devaluing the dollar against all other currencies that were pegged to gold.[13]

> This devaluation of the dollar meant that the gold held by the Treasury Department became much more valuable when measured in dollars. These extraordinary gains, which amounted to $2.8 billion, according to 1934 Annual Report of the Federal Reserve System (p. 3), were set aside in what came to be known as the Exchange Stabilization Fund. This pool of money was available for the government to use without having to seek permission from Congress. For instance, it was used by the Clinton administration in 1994 to provide loans to Mexico so that country would not default on the debts it owed to US banks and other investors.

The 41% devaluation of the dollar on January 31, 1934, almost immediately resulted in a surge in foreign investment entering the United States. After all, for foreign investors with gold, the dollar devaluation made everything in the United States 41% cheaper.[14]

Capital flight from Europe and Asia also led to much more gold entering the United States as the 1930s progressed. Hitler's rise to power in Germany and Japan's growing aggression in China caused many investors in Europe and Asia to ship their gold to the United States where they believed it would be safe.

These developments explain the sharp rise in the Fed's holdings of gold certificates beginning in 1934, as shown in Chart 4.5.

Before the passage of the Gold Reserve Act, when gold entered the United States, it was deposited into the owner's commercial bank account. The growth in deposits required that bank to add to its gold reserves at the Fed to maintain an appropriate level of required reserves. Therefore, the Fed's gold holdings rose as gold entered the country.

After the passage of the Gold Reserve Act neither private individuals, commercial banks, or the Fed were allowed to own gold. The Treasury Department bought and held all the gold entering the country. The entity selling the gold to the Treasury received Federal Reserve Notes, while the Fed received gold certificates from the Treasury rather than actual gold.[15]

Between the end of 1933 and the end of 1941, the gold stock of the United States increased by 463%, from $4 billion to $18.7 billion, while the gold reserves of the Fed, in the form of gold certificates from February 1934, rose by 450%, from $3.8 billion to $20.8 billion.

Therefore, it was the accumulation of gold certificates rather than the creation of Federal Reserve Credit that drove the surge in the Fed's Total Assets during the 1930s. Chart 4.6 illustrates this point.

Gold Coverage

In mid-1931, the Fed's gold coverage ratio was at 84%, far above the statutory minimum. In August, however, that ratio began to plunge precipitously as the public, fearful that the banking system was not sound, began withdrawing large amounts of Federal Reserve Notes from their banks. Between then and March 1933, when the banking panic subsided, the number of Federal Reserve Notes in circulation increased by roughly $2.5 billion or nearly 150%.

The increase in the Fed's Federal Reserve Note liabilities pulled the Fed's gold coverage ratio down to a low of 51% the month the panic ended, as shown in Chart 4.7.

When the banking crisis ended, the public redeposited much of the cash they had withdrawn from the banks, causing the Fed's gold coverage ratio to rebound to 68% by August 1933. The ratio continued to improve as gold flooded into the US during the rest of the decade. It ended 1941 above 90%.

CHART 4.6 The Fed's Total Assets: Gold vs. Assets Acquired with Federal Reserve Credit, 1914 to 1941

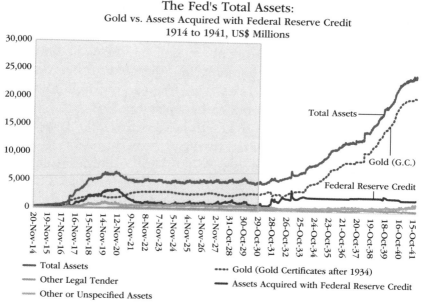

The Fed's Total Assets:
Gold vs. Assets Acquired with Federal Reserve Credit
1914 to 1941, US$ Millions

Source: Data from "*The Federal Reserve System's Weekly Balance Sheet Since 1914*" and accompanying spreadsheet. Johns Hopkins University, SAE/No.115/ July 2018. See Bibliography.

Excess Reserves

One final development during the 1930s deserves attention, particularly as it represents a precedent the Fed would be wise to adopt today.

As discussed above, the devaluation of the dollar in January 1934 was followed by an unprecedented inflow of gold into the United States. That gold was acquired by the Treasury Department. The Treasury paid for that gold by drawing upon its balances in its account at the Fed. This transferred funds from the Treasury account at the Fed to the reserve accounts that member banks held at the Fed. Consequently, the level of bank reserves rose rapidly in line with the surge of gold entering the United States.[16]

CHART 4.7 Gold Coverage Ratio, 1914 to 1941

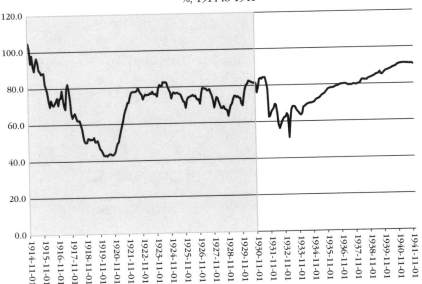

Gold Coverage Ratio
%, 1914 to 1941

Source: Data from Ratio of Reserves to Note and Deposit Liabilities, Federal Reserve Banks for United States, St Louis Fed, 1914 to 1948

Soon, the level of reserves far exceeded the amount commercial banks were required to hold as reserves against their deposits. By late 1935, total reserves had climbed to more than $6 billion, whereas the amount of reserves the banks were required to hold was somewhat less than $3 billion. In other words, the banking system held excess reserves of more than $3 billion.

The Fed became concerned that such a high level of reserves could result in a dangerous expansion of bank credit. The Fed's 1936 Annual Report noted:

On the basis of these excess reserves and the legal reserve ratios then in effect, bank credit could have been expanded to twice the volume in use at the peak of business activity in 1929; and the gold inflow was still in progress.[17]

TABLE 4.1 Member Bank Reserve Requirements

Member Bank Reserve Requirements [Percent of deposits]				
Classes of deposits and banks	June 21, 1917, to Aug. 15, 1936	Aug. 16, 1936, to Feb. 28, 1937	Mar. 1, 1937, to Apr. 30, 1937	Beginning May 1, 1937
On net demand deposits:				
Central reserve city banks	13	19½	22¼	26
Reserve city banks	10	15	17½	20
Country banks	7	10½	12¼	14
On time deposits:				
All member banks................	3	4½	5¼	6

Source: The 1936 Annual Report of the Board of Governors of the Federal Reserve System, p. 11

To preclude that possibility, the Fed doubled the required reserve ratio between July 1936 and May 1937, thereby sharply reducing the level of excess reserves and, by extension, the possibility of excessive credit creation by the banking sector. The increase was implemented in stages. In July 1936, the Fed increased the required reserve ratio by 50% effective August 15, 1936. Then, in January 1937, the Fed raised the required reserve ratio by an equivalent amount again, with one half of the second increase becoming effective on March 1, 1937, and the second half becoming effective on May 1, 1937. These changes are presented in Table 4.1.

In practice, this doubling of the required reserve ratio did not meaningfully influence the amount of credit created by the commercial banks during the rest of the decade. First, demand for loans remained weak and the banks' willingness to lend was also lackluster. Moreover, since gold continued to flood into the United States, soon there was once again a very large level of excess reserves in the banking system even after the required reserve requirement had been doubled.

This episode is nevertheless noteworthy. It shows that the Fed does have the power to reduce excess reserves in the banking system by raising the required reserve ratio. That is important because, today, banks in the United States are once again inundated with excess reserves, this time as the result of the large-scale open market purchases (i.e., Quantitative Easing) the Fed conducted in response to the financial crisis of 2008, and, more recently, the much larger purchases of government securities and mortgage-backed securities in response to the coronavirus crisis. The Fed began paying the banks interest on those reserves in 2008 in order to control the federal funds rate. With that rate now close to 0%, the cost of paying interest on reserves is not very high at present. However, when the Fed eventually does hike the federal funds rate again, the costs to the Fed (and, therefore, US taxpayers) could climb to tens or even hundreds of billions of dollars a year.

The experience of 1936 and 1937 demonstrates that a much less expensive alternative exists. The Fed could simply raise the required reserve ratio high enough to absorb all the excess reserves in the banking system and, thereby, save US taxpayers vast sums of money each year. This subject will be revisited in Part Three.

Next, we turn to the Fed's role in helping to finance World War II.

Notes

1. Twentieth Annual Report on the Federal Reserve Board Covering Operations for the Year 1933, Washington Printing Office, dated May 28, 1934, p. 2.
2. St. Louis Fed.
3. Data for 1914 to 1917 from *"The Federal Reserve System's Weekly Balance Sheet Since 1914"* and accompanying spreadsheet. Johns Hopkins University, SAE/No.115/July 2018. See Bibliography.
   Data for 1918 to 1941 from The Fed's 2017 Annual Report, page 306
4. Nineteenth Annual Report of the Federal Reserve Board covering operations for the year 1932, p. 16

5. "Each Federal Reserve Bank is required by law to pledge collateral at least equal to the amount of currency it has issued into circulation." Source: The Federal Reserve Bank of New York, "How Currency Gets into Circulation." https://www.newyorkfed.org/aboutthefed/fedpoint/fed01.html

6. The Fed must pledge 100% collateral for all the Federal Reserve Notes it obtains from the Treasury Department' Bureau of Engraving and Printing. Source: "How Currency Gets into Circulation," The Federal Reserve Bank of New York. https://www.newyorkfed.org/aboutthefed/fedpoint/fed01.html

7. Friedman and Schwartz (1963), *A Monetary History of the United States, 1867–1960.* First Princeton Paperback Printing Edition, p. 400.

8. A fourth round began in October 2019. It was expanded significantly in response to the coronavirus crisis beginning in March 2020.

9. Friedman and Schwartz (1963), *A Monetary History of the United States, 1867-1960.* First Princeton Paperback Printing Edition, p. 435.

10. The presidential inauguration was moved from March 4 to January 20 beginning in 1937.

11. Americans were allowed to keep gold jewelry, rare gold coins for collections and up to $100 worth of ordinary gold coins. On December 28, the secretary of the treasury issued an order revoking the $100 exemption in connection with the holding of gold coin by the public, and from that date no gold coin (except rare coins) could be legally held. Source: The 1933 Annual Report of the Federal Reserve Board, p. 27.

12. The Gold Reserve Act of 1934, pp. 1 and 2. https://fraser.stlouisfed.org/scribd/?title_id=777&filepath=/files/docs/meltzer/sengol34.pdf

13. "The International Gold Standard and U.S. Monetary Policy from World War I to the New Deal," *The Federal Reserve Bulletin*, June 1989. https://fraser.stlouisfed.org/files/docs/meltzer/craint89.pdf

14. The 1936 Annual Report of the Board of Governors of the Federal Reserve System, p. 5.

15. The 1936 Annual Report of the Board of Governors of the Federal Reserve System, p. 8: "The Treasury pays for gold by drawing upon its balance with the Federal Reserve banks, thus transferring funds from Treasury account to member bank account at the Federal

Reserve banks. The Treasury's balance is reduced by the operation and member bank reserves are correspondingly increased . . . it was the practice of the Treasury to replenish its balance with the Federal Reserve banks by utilizing the newly purchased gold to give the Federal Reserve banks equivalent credits in the gold-certificate account. Replenishment of its balance in this manner had no effect upon member bank reserves, which therefore retained the increase that had occurred when the gold was sold to the Treasury."

16. The 1936 Annual Report of the Board of Governors of the Federal Reserve System, p. 8.

17. The 1936 Annual Report of the Board of Governors of the Federal Reserve System, p. 1.

CHAPTER 5

1941 to 1945: World War II

During the year 1941 the activities of the Federal Reserve System were increasingly geared to facilitating the transition of the nation's economy to a war basis. The Federal Reserve authorities recognized that the primary function of the financial mechanism of the country in wartime is to help meet the requirements of war production.

The 1941 Annual Report of the Board of Governors
of the Federal Reserve System[1]

During World War II, the Fed's primary purpose once again became to ensure the government could borrow all the funds it required to conduct the war at the lowest rate of interest possible – just as it had been during World War I. To carry out this responsibility, the Fed pegged the rate at which it would buy Treasury bills at 3/8 of 1% (37.5 basis points). This arrangement kept the cost of government borrowing low, but it required the Fed to buy government debt and to extend Federal Reserve Credit on a much greater scale than it had ever done before. This chapter describes the indispensable role the Fed played in making credit available to finance the war.

War Financing

Between June 1940 and the end of 1945, the US government raised approximately $380 billion. Of that amount, $152 billion (or 40%) came from taxes. The rest, $228 billion (or 60%) was borrowed. Of the amount borrowed, $133 billion came from selling government securities to non-bank investors. The rest, approximately $95 billion, was raised by selling government securities to the commercial banking system.[2] Currency in circulation increased by nearly $20 billion, or 380%.

During the war, the Fed purchased $22 billion of government securities, thereby injecting reserves into the banking system that made possible both the banks' purchases of government securities and the expansion of currency. The Fed's 1945 Annual Report explained the Fed's purchases of government securities as follows:

> *Federal Reserve purchases of securities provided the basis for the rapid growth of currency in circulation and also supplied the banks with additional reserves needed to support the expansion of bank credit and deposits.*
>
> *Federal Reserve purchases of 22 billion dollars of Government securities, together with 7 billion of reserves in excess of requirements held by member banks in 1940, provided the basis for a wartime currency expansion of 20 billion and a growth of 8 billion in member bank required reserves.[3]*

The following sections describe the evolution of the Fed's assets and liabilities during the war in order to illustrate how the Fed made it possible for the government to borrow all the funds it required to win the war.

Balance Sheet

Assets

During the four years between 1941 and 1945, the Fed's total assets expanded by 80%, from $25 billion to $45 billion, as shown in Chart 5.1.

CHART 5.1 The Fed's Total Assets, 1914 to 1945

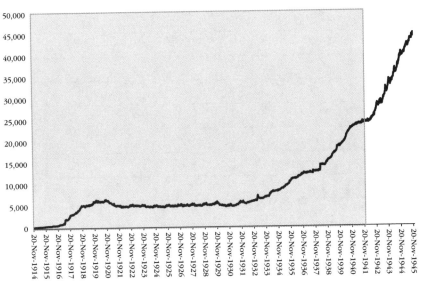

The Fed's Total Assets
1914 to 1945, US$ Millions

Source: Data from "*The Federal Reserve System's Weekly Balance Sheet Since 1914*" and accompanying spreadsheet. Johns Hopkins University, SAE/No.115/ July 2018. See Bibliography.

During the 1930s, a very large increase in the Fed's holdings of gold certificates had been responsible for the surge in the Fed's total assets. That was not the case between 1941 and 1945. During World War II the Fed's total assets jumped because the Fed acquired US government securities by extending Federal Reserve Credit.

The Fed supplied much more Federal Reserve Credit during the Second World War than during the First, as shown in Chart 5.2.

During World War I, the annual increase in Federal Reserve Credit peaked at $1.4 billion in 1918. By contrast, Federal Reserve Credit leapt by $4.2 billion during 1942 and peaked at an annual rate of increase of $7.5 billion during 1944.

Before World War II, Federal Reserve Credit outstanding had peaked at $3.4 billion in 1920. In 1922, it contracted back to $1.0 billion. In December 1941, the month the United States entered the

CHART 5.2 Federal Reserve Credit, Annual $ Change, 1915 to 1945

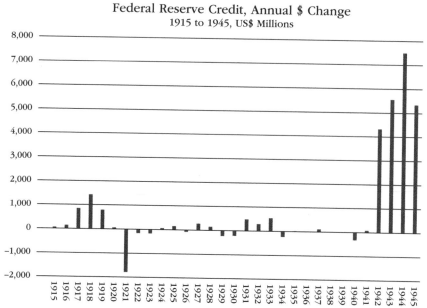

Federal Reserve Credit, Annual $ Change
1915 to 1945, US$ Millions

Source: The Federal Reserve[4]

war, it was still only $2.2 billion. Over the next 12 months, Federal Reserve Credit nearly tripled to $6.0 billion. By the end of 1945, the amount of Federal Reserve Credit outstanding had reached $24.5 billion, more than 10 times its prewar level (see Chart 5.3).

Chart 5.3 shows that practically all of the Federal Reserve Credit took the form of credit to the government through the purchase of US government securities. The Fed did not acquire any other kind of securities, so there were no bills bought. Nor did the Fed extend credit through discounting operations, so its holdings of bills discounted were also at a very low level.

It must be noted that, although the Fed's primary mission was the same in both World War I and World War II, the method the Fed employed to accomplish that purpose was not the same. During World War I, the Fed had used discounting operations to finance government debt indirectly. As described in Chapter 2, the Fed had lent money to commercial banks at an interest rate that guaranteed that the banks would make a profit if they bought government securities. This enabled the government to

CHART 5.3 Federal Reserve Credit and Its Components, 1914 to 1945

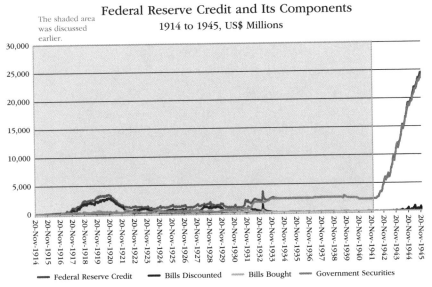

Federal Reserve Credit and Its Components
1914 to 1945, US$ Millions

Source: Data from *"The Federal Reserve System's Weekly Balance Sheet Since 1914"* and accompanying spreadsheet. Johns Hopkins University, SAE/No.115/ July 2018. See Bibliography.

sell as much government debt to the banks (and to the banks' customers) as necessary to finance the war.

During World War II, on the other hand, the Fed bought government securities directly through open market operations. The Fed's holdings of government securities increased from $2 billion in 1941 to $24 billion when the war ended in 1945.

Meanwhile, the Fed's holdings of gold certificates declined during the war, as can be seen in Chart 5.4.

Notice in that chart that the assets acquired with Federal Reserve Credit became a larger component of the Fed's total assets than gold certificates in 1944, prefacing a change that would soon become the norm.

The composition the Fed's assets and liabilities underwent an extraordinary change as the result of the acquisition of so much government debt during the war, as shown in Chart 5.5.

Other than during a brief period in the aftermath of World War I, gold had always been the largest asset on the Fed's

CHART 5.4 The Fed's Total Assets: Gold vs. Assets Acquired with Federal Reserve Credit, 1914 to 1945

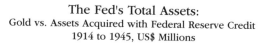

The Fed's Total Assets:
Gold vs. Assets Acquired with Federal Reserve Credit
1914 to 1945, US$ Millions

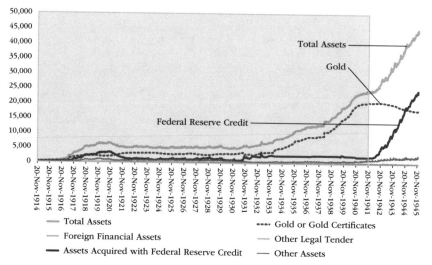

Source: Data from *"The Federal Reserve System's Weekly Balance Sheet Since 1914"* and accompanying spreadsheet. Johns Hopkins University, SAE/No.115/ July 2018. See Bibliography.

balance sheet. By the end of 1945, however, the Fed's holdings of government securities were 36% larger than its holdings of gold certificates. This was an important break from the past. The Federal Reserve Act of 1913, which created the Fed, was crafted to discourage the Fed from owning government securities. At that time, Congress believed that it was undesirable for the central bank to finance government debt.

During World War I, the Fed had provided Federal Reserve Credit by lending money to commercial banks through discounting operations, where, as collateral, the banks offered the Fed loans they had made to their customers which, in turn, were collateralized by government securities. The Fed could then use the bills discounted that it obtained this way as "eligible collateral" to back the Federal Reserve Notes it issued.

CHART 5.5 A Breakdown of the Fed's Major Assets & Liabilities, 1914 to 1945

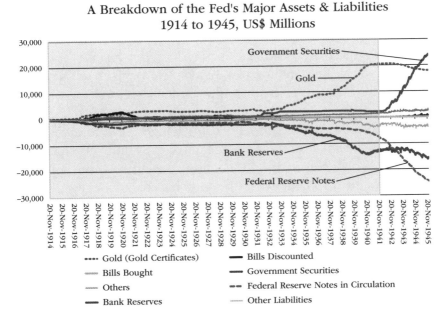

A Breakdown of the Fed's Major Assets & Liabilities
1914 to 1945, US$ Millions

Source: Data from *"The Federal Reserve System's Weekly Balance Sheet Since 1914"* and accompanying spreadsheet. Johns Hopkins University, SAE/No.115/ July 2018. See Bibliography.

During World War II, the Fed bought government bonds outright through open market operations. This change was made possible by the Glass-Steagall Act of 1932 which amended the Federal Reserve Act to allow the Fed to directly use government securities as collateral to back the Federal Reserve Notes it issued. That amendment made it possible for the Fed to purchase government securities on a very large scale during World War II and to use those bonds as "eligible collateral" to back the very large amount of Federal Reserve Notes it issued during the war.

Liabilities

Notice in Chart 5.5, above, that while the growth in the Fed's holdings of government securities dominated the asset side of the Fed's balance sheet, it was the growth in Federal Reserve Notes that dominated the liabilities side.

Between 1941 and 1945, Federal Reserve Notes outstanding surged from $8 billion to $25 billion. This requires some explanation since when the Fed acquired the government securities it paid for them by making deposits into the reserve accounts at the Fed of the commercial banks from which it acquired the bonds. The act of making the deposit created the Federal Reserve Credit.

Had all other factors remained unchanged, the reserves held by member banks at the Fed, the dark gray line in Chart 5.5, would have increased by $22 billion, exactly in line with the amount of government securities purchased by the Fed. Other factors did not remain unchanged, however. The most important change was a surge in demand for currency.

During these years, individuals withdrew cash from their bank accounts for precautionary reasons. The public's desire to hold cash increases during wars and economic crises. Furthermore, businesses needed more cash to carry out production for the war. The government, too, needed more cash to conduct the war. Consequently, Federal Reserve Notes outstanding (the dashed line in Chart 5.5) tripled.

As the demand for currency grew, the Fed provided the Federal Reserve Notes to the commercial banks; and, in exchange for the Federal Reserve Notes, the Fed debited the reserve accounts those commercial banks held at the Fed. So, the increase in Federal Reserve Notes offset the increase in reserves that otherwise would have occurred when the Fed bought the government securities. This explains why Bank Reserves held at the Fed increased only modestly instead of one-for-one with the increase in the Fed's holdings of government securities.

By the time the war ended, the Fed had issued so many Federal Reserve Notes and created so much Federal Reserve Credit that its holdings of gold certificates were on the verge of becoming insufficient to allow the Fed to meet its legal obligation to hold 40% gold certificate backing for Federal Reserve Notes and 35% gold certificate backing for the reserves commercial banks

CHART 5.6 Gold Cover Ratio: Ratio of the Fed's Gold Reserves to Note and Deposit Liabilities, 1914 to 1945

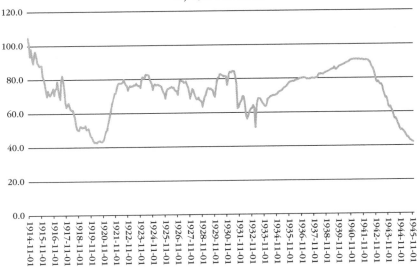

Gold Coverage Ratio
Ratio of the Fed's Gold Reserves to Note and Deposit Liabilities
%, 1914 to 1945

Source: Data from Ratio of Reserves to Note and Deposit Liabilities, Federal Reserve Banks for United States, St. Louis Fed., 1914 to 1948

held in their reserve accounts at the Fed. The Fed's gold cover ratio dipped to just 42% at the end of 1945 (see Chart 5.6)

The drop in the gold cover ratio gave rise to concerns that the Fed's holdings of gold certificates would soon be insufficient to allow the Fed to issue any more currency or Federal Reserve Credit. To eliminate that possibility, Congress, in June 1945, reduced the amount of gold certificates the Fed was required to hold relative to the size of its liabilities. Afterwards, the Fed was required to maintain only 25% gold certificate backing for both Federal Reserve Notes and for the reserves commercial banks held in their reserve accounts at the Fed. This important revision to the Federal Reserve Act significantly increased the amount of credit the Fed could create relative to the amount of gold certificates it owned.

Here is how the Fed later described this unprecedented change:

> . . . *the decline in the Reserve Banks' ratio of reserves to combined note and deposit liabilities during World War II threatened the Federal Reserve's freedom of policy action. In this situation the Congress in 1945 deemed it wise to reduce the reserve requirements of the Reserve Banks from 40 per cent for Federal Reserve notes and 35 per cent for deposits to 25 per cent for each kind of liability.*[5]

Federal Reserve Credit and Commercial Bank Credit

During the 1930s, the huge inflow of gold into the United States supplied the commercial banks with far more reserves than they needed to satisfy the statutory reserve requirements set out by the required reserve ratio. Even though the Fed doubled the required reserve ratio during 1936 and 1937, as described in Chapter 4, the banking system's excess reserves continued to grow as gold kept pouring into the country. Excess reserves peaked at $7 billion in October 1940.[6] The following year, the demand for currency increased, causing Bank Reserves to fall, since when the Fed provides the banks with Federal Reserve Notes it debits their reserve accounts at the Fed, in exchange. Nevertheless, at the end of 1941, excess reserves still amounted to $3.1 billion.

Although that was an exceptionally high level of excess reserves compared with past norms, they quickly proved to be insufficient given the growth in demand for cash during the war. As noted above, the amount of Federal Reserve Notes in circulation expanded by $17 billion during the war, from $8 billion in 1941 to $25 billion in 1945. In 1941, total Bank Reserves amounted to only $12.5 billion, including the $3.1 billion of excess reserves.[7]

An increase in Federal Reserve Notes reduces Bank Reserves one-for-one. Therefore, the increase in currency in circulation would have quickly eliminated all Bank Reserves had the Fed not supplied the banking system with more reserves by acquiring $22 billion of government securities. Recall that when the Fed acquires a government bond, it pays for it by making a deposit into the reserve account at the Fed of the bank from which it acquires the bond. That transaction adds to that bank's level of reserves and, by extension, to the level of reserves of the entire banking system. In other words, by acquiring government securities, the Fed supplied the banking system with sufficient reserves to meet their legal reserve requirements, despite the extraordinary drain of reserves brought about by the large increase in Federal Reserve Notes in circulation.

It is also important to note that the banking systems' reserve requirements expanded during the war because of the very sharp rise in the amount of deposits held by the banking system.

Deposit Creation by Commercial Banks

Commercial banks create deposits by extending credit. This process will be explained in detail in Chapter 8. However, the extent to which this occurred during the war is so striking that it is useful to highlight it here.

It is counterintuitive that banks create deposits by extending credit. It seems as though banks should only be able to lend out deposits they already possess. That is not the case, however. Banks create deposits when they lend.

During the four years between 1941 and 1945, deposits at commercial banks more than doubled from $82 billion to $166 billion, as shown in Chart 5.7.

The deposits held by commercial banks grew because the banks bought government bonds. The government's budget deficit exploded when the war began. In 1941, the deficit was $5 billion, the largest since 1919 in the immediate aftermath of World War I. In 1942, the deficit jumped to more than $20 billion. The cumulative deficit during the four years of war came to $170 billion (see Chart 5.8).

CHART 5.7 Commercial Banks: Total Deposits, 1914 to 1945

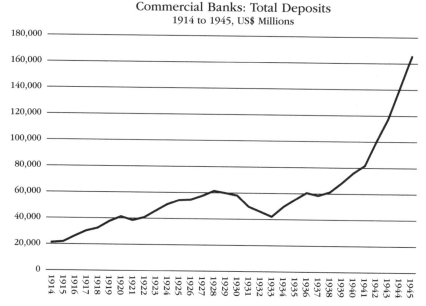

Commercial Banks: Total Deposits
1914 to 1945, US$ Millions

Source: Data from Board of Governors of the Federal Reserve System (U.S.), 1935-. Banking and Monetary Statistics, 1914–1941; Board of Governors of the Federal Reserve System (U.S.), 1935-. Banking and Monetary Statistics, 1941–1970.

The commercial banks bought $69 billion of government securities during those four years, as depicted in Chart 5.9.

That took their portfolio of government securities up from $22 billion to $91 billion; and increased their total loans and investments from $51 billion to $124 billion (see Chart 5.10).

By the end of the war, the commercial banks holdings of government securities made up 73% of all their loans and investments combined (see Chart 5.11).

Each time a commercial bank bought a government bond from the government, the commercial bank financed its acquisition of that bond by creating bank credit, not by transferring funds that already existed. When the government spent the money it obtained from selling that government bond, whoever received the money the government spent deposited that money

CHART 5.8 US Government Budget Surplus or Deficit (–),
1900 to 1945

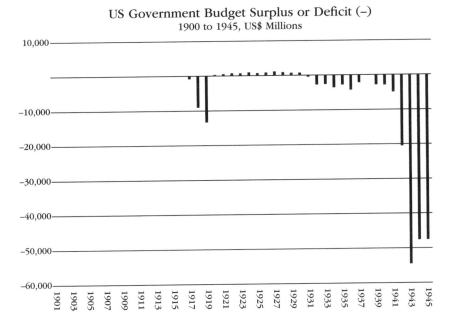

US Government Budget Surplus or Deficit (–)
1900 to 1945, US$ Millions

Source: Data from the Office of Management and Budget, Historical Tables,
the White House.

into their bank account, which added to the deposit base of
the entire banking system. In 1941, the entire deposit base of the
commercial banks was only $82 billion. By the end of the war,
it had grown to $166 billion. Those deposits were created when
the banks extended credit as they acquired government securities. Until then, they did not exist.

The process through which banks create deposits by extending credit will be explained in detail in Chapter 8.

Bretton Woods

Finally, it is necessary to mention the establishment of the Bretton Woods international monetary system and the constraints it
placed on the Fed's "freedom of policy action."

CHART 5.9 Commercial Banks' Holdings of Government Securities, Annual Dollar Change, 1915 to 1945

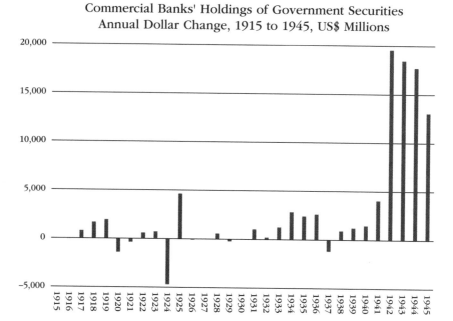

Commercial Banks' Holdings of Government Securities
Annual Dollar Change, 1915 to 1945, US$ Millions

Source: Data from Board of Governors of the Federal Reserve System (U.S.), 1935-. Banking and Monetary Statistics, 1914–1941; Board of Governors of the Federal Reserve System (U.S.), 1935-. Banking and Monetary Statistics, 1941–1970.

As the end of the war approached, efforts to rebuild the global financial architecture got underway. The Bretton Woods system was created at the United Nations Monetary and Financial Conference held at Bretton Woods, New Hampshire, in July 1944. Its purpose was to establish a rule-based system to regulate international trade and monetary relations so as to promote balanced growth in international trade. The conference was a tremendous success. Never before had an "international monetary system" been created by an agreement between nations. The gold standard had simply emerged over the course of centuries because gold had proven to be the most reliable medium of exchange.

CHART 5.10 Commercial Banks: Total Loans & Investments vs.
Holdings of Government Securities, 1914 to 1945

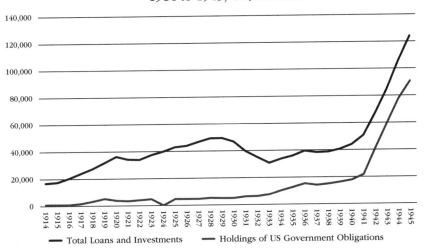

Commercial Banks:
Total Loans & Investments vs. Holdings of Government
Securities
1914 to 1945, US$ Millions

Source: Data from Board of Governors of the Federal Reserve System (U.S.),
1935-. Banking and Monetary Statistics, 1914–1941; Board of Governors of
the Federal Reserve System (U.S.), 1935-. Banking and Monetary Statistics,
1941–1970.

The Bretton Woods system was designed to replicate the
best aspects of the gold standard. It was structured to prevent
member countries from pursuing unfair trade practices that had
contributed to the Depression. In particular, it sought to prevent
unilateral currency devaluations and trade tariffs.

Simply returning to the gold standard was not an option. By
the end of the war, the victors held most of the world's gold.
Gold was not distributed widely enough around the world to
allow international trade to recommence. The United States
had by far the largest gold holdings, followed by France. Moreover, the United States had become the largest creditor nation
in history.

CHART 5.11 Commercial Banks' Holdings of Government Securities as a Percentage of Total Loans & Investments, 1914 to 1945

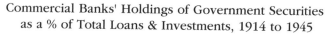

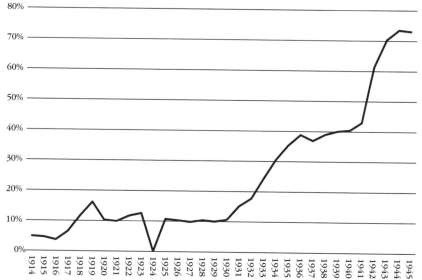

Source: Data from Board of Governors of the Federal Reserve System (U.S.), 1935-. Banking and Monetary Statistics, 1914–1941; Board of Governors of the Federal Reserve System (U.S.), 1935-. Banking and Monetary Statistics, 1941–1970.

To overcome this unequal distribution of gold, the Bretton Woods Agreement established a system of fixed exchange rates in which the US dollar served as the anchor currency. The United States pegged the dollar to gold at the fixed rate of $35 per ounce; and agreed to buy or sell gold to or from the monetary authorities of other countries in order to prevent any fluctuation in the dollar's value relative to gold. Other member countries undertook to maintain the value of their currency near an agreed par value, allowing fluctuation within only a narrow margin. In practice, most countries pegged their currency to the dollar and intervened by buying or selling dollars in order to prevent any significant change in their currency's value relative to the dollar. They also had the right to exchange the dollars held by their monetary authorities for gold held as reserves by the United States via the "gold window" at the Treasury Department.

The monetary authorities at the conference believed that no international trading system could survive for long if trade between nations did not balance. Trade had to be paid for. Imbalances could be financed on credit only over the short run, at best. To ensure trade did balance, the Bretton Woods system was designed to have the same automatic adjustment mechanism as the gold standard. Trade deficits would cause monetary contraction and trade surpluses would cause monetary expansion, in both cases setting off macroeconomic forces that would restore balance. During the conference, the architects of the system created the International Monetary Fund (IMF) to help ease the adjustment process.

The international monetary system created at Bretton Woods worked well for a quarter of a century. So long as the world's leading industrialized nations abided by its rules, it provided a structure in which international trade could (and did) flourish.

However, the Bretton Woods systems imposed constraints on the Fed. If the Fed undertook expansionary monetary policy (i.e., created too much Federal Reserve Credit), it could result in gold leaving the United States. For example, if the Fed created too much Federal Reserve Credit, the US economy would strengthen, employment would rise, consumption would increase, US demand for foreign products would grow, ultimately leading to an increase in imports entering the United States and a deterioration in the country's trade balance. A trade deficit would have to be settled by sending dollars abroad. The recipients of those dollars had the right to exchange them for US gold. If the US lost too much gold, there would not be enough gold left in the country to allow the Fed to meet its obligation to hold gold backing for Federal Reserve Notes and for the Bank Reserves held at the Fed. Furthermore, if the trade deficit persisted for long enough, the United States would lose all its gold, at which point it would become impossible for the United States to allow other countries to convert any more dollars into gold. The same outcome would occur if the Fed reduced interest rates to a level substantially below the interest rates of other large countries. Dollars would have left the United States to profit from the higher interest rates offered abroad.

Therefore, the Bretton Woods system forced the Fed to think carefully before providing monetary stimulus to support economic growth. Dollar convertibility was the cornerstone of the Bretton Woods system. The system would not survive if the United States was unable to meet its obligations to allow dollars to be converted into gold. Eventually, the Bretton Woods system did collapse for exactly that reason. However, the breakdown did not occur until 1971. Until then, the Fed had to consider how its actions would impact the United States' balance of payments and its gold stock.

Conclusion

The Fed provided invaluable service to the country during the war. Its 10-fold expansion of Federal Reserve Credit allowed the government to borrow as much money as it required to win the war, while simultaneously underwriting a 200% increase in Federal Reserve Notes in circulation. In 1945, Congress significantly increased the Fed's power to create credit by reducing the amount of gold certificates the central bank was required to hold relative to its notes and reserve liabilities.

When the war ended, it was generally assumed that the Fed would gradually return to functioning as the relatively passive institution its founders had created in 1913, just as it had done following World War I. Chapter 6 explains why that did not happen. World War II marked a turning point for the Fed. There would be no going back.

Notes

1. The 1941 Annual Report of the Board of Governors of the Federal Reserve System, p. 1.
2. The 1945 Annual Report of the Board of Governors of the Federal Reserve System, p. 1.
3. The 1945 Annual Report of the Board of Governors of the Federal Reserve System, pp. 9–10.
4. Data for 1914 to 1917 from *"The Federal Reserve System's Weekly Balance Sheet Since 1914"* and accompanying spreadsheet. Johns Hopkins University, SAE/No.115/July 2018. See Bibliography.
   Data for 1918 to 1945 from The Fed's 2017 Annual Report, page 306
5. Purposes and Functions, The Federal Reserve System, pp. 174–175. https://fraser.stlouisfed.org/files/docs/historical/federal%20reserve%20history/bog_publications/bog_frs_purposes_1963.pdf
6. The 1940 Annual Report of the Board of Governors of the Federal Reserve System p. 52.
7. The 1941 Annual Report of the Board of Governors of the Federal Reserve System p. 48.

CHAPTER 6

1945 to 1971:
The Bretton Woods Era

If the position of foreign countries is further strengthened by adoption of the proposals agreed on at the International Monetary and Financial Conference held at Bretton Woods, there will be every reason to expect more stability, order, and freedom in international exchange relationships in the postwar world.

Thirty-First Annual Report of the Board of
Governors of the Federal Reserve
System Covering Operations
for the Year 1944.[1]

The Bretton Woods era can be divided in two halves. The first half was characterized by fiscal and monetary restraint. The second half was not.

During the first half, from 1945 to 1960, the Fed once again operated as it was originally designed to. Federal Reserve Credit expanded in some years and contracted in others. The outstanding stock of Federal Reserve Credit was $25 billion in 1945. It fell to as low as $17 billion in 1949 and then rose back to $28 billion in 1960, only 12% higher than at the end of the war. During the second half of this period, Federal Reserve Credit surged by 160%, from $28 billion in 1960 to $73 billion in 1971.

A significant change in the government's fiscal policy explains the sharp contrast in monetary policy before and after 1960. During the first half, the government's budget was roughly balanced. After 1960, however, the government ran large budget deficits and the Fed was called upon to help finance those deficits at low interest rates, which it did by acquiring government bonds with Federal Reserve Credit.

The government's large budget deficits and the Fed's willingness to help accommodate them had far reaching consequences. Most importantly, they resulted in a large outflow of gold from the United States that reduced the country's gold reserves – and the Fed's holdings of gold certificates – by half during the 1960s. The loss of gold forced Congress, in 1965, to eliminate the requirement that the Fed hold gold certificates to back the reserves banks held in their reserve accounts at the Fed. Three years later, Congress removed the final constraint on the Fed's ability to create credit by rescinding the requirement that the Fed hold gold certificates to back the Federal Reserve Notes it issued. Finally, in August 1971, the Bretton Woods system collapsed altogether because the United States no longer had enough gold to abide by its commitment to allow the governments of other countries to convert the dollars they accumulated into US gold. That commitment had been the cornerstone of the Bretton Woods system.

The breakdown of the Bretton Woods system completely and permanently severed the link between dollars and gold, unleashing a new era of purely fiat money that transformed the world. This chapter describes how these events were reflected in the evolution of the Fed's balance sheet.

Assets

From 1945 to 1960, the Fed's total assets remained roughly flat. But between 1960 to 1971, they increased by 80% (see Chart 6.1).

CHART 6.1 The Fed's Total Assets, 1914 to 1971

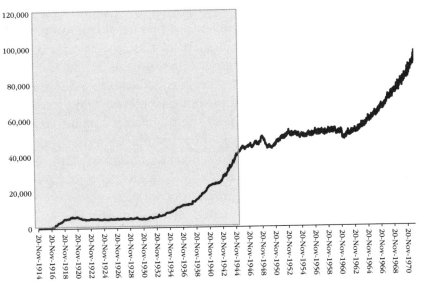

The Fed's Total Assets
1914 to 1971, US$ Millions

Source: Data from *"The Federal Reserve System's Weekly Balance Sheet Since 1914"* and accompanying spreadsheet. Johns Hopkins University, SAE/No.115/ July 2018. See Bibliography.

What was responsible for this disquieting increase in the Fed's assets after 1960? To answer that question, it is necessary to explain how the Fed conducted monetary policy after World War II ended.

The Fed continued to hold the yield on government securities fixed up until 1951. However, that year, the Fed reached an "Accord" with the Treasury Department that freed it from that World War II commitment.

Afterwards, the Fed's primary objective shifted from financing the government's debt at low interest rates to producing monetary conditions that would foster economic growth without creating inflation. The Fed used open market operations as its principal monetary policy tool to accomplish that objective. When the Fed wished to loosen monetary conditions to support more rapid economic growth it conducted open market purchases of government securities, thereby adding reserves to the banking system and, consequently, lowering interest rates. Additional reserves enabled the banking system to lend more, while lower interest rates encouraged more private sector borrowing. When the Fed wished to tighten monetary conditions to slow the economy and deter inflationary pressures, it conducted open market sales of government securities, which drained reserves from the banking system and pushed up interest rates, which, in combination, deterred lending by the commercial banks.

This process required the Fed to first make an assessment of what the appropriate level of monetary accommodation should be and then to conduct open market operations to achieve the level of accommodation it deemed appropriate.

Between 1951, when it reached its Accord with the Treasury Department, and 1960, the Fed was required to make only relatively small adjustments to its holdings of government securities to maintain the level of monetary accommodation that it desired. After 1960, however, much larger open market purchases were necessary. A fundamental change in fiscal policy was responsible for that change in monetary policy.

Between 1946 and 1958, the government's budget was more or less in balance. The cumulative deficit during those 13 years was just $4 billion. In 1959, however, the government ran a large budget deficit of $13 billion. Afterwards, deficits were the norm rather than the exception. The cumulative deficit during the 13 years between 1959 and 1971 was $95 billion. Chart 6.2 shows the government's budget deficits each year from 1946 to 1971.

Presidents Truman and Eisenhower believed in balanced budgets. Between 1946 and 1952, the Truman administration ran a small budget surplus, despite very large military expenditures related to the Korean War. The Eisenhower administration was also quite fiscally conservative, at least up through 1957. The recession of 1958, however, resulted in a large budget deficit the following year. The Kennedy and Johnson administrations ran budget deficits every year between 1961 and 1968, with a

CHART 6.2 US Government's Budget Surplus or Deficit, 1946 to 1971

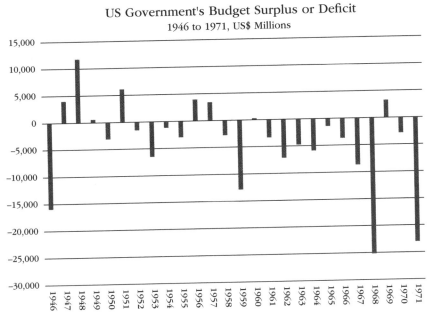

US Government's Budget Surplus or Deficit
1946 to 1971, US$ Millions

Source: Data from the Office of Management and Budget Historical Tables, the White House

particularly large deficit in the final year. President Nixon also produced a very large budget deficit in 1971.

The surge in government borrowing necessitated by large budget deficits exerted upward pressure on interest rates. This required the Fed to purchase larger amounts of government securities in order to hold interest rates at the level it believed appropriate to support economic growth. Moreover, as the government's budget deficits grew during the 1960s, the Fed came under increasing political pressure to help finance them at low interest rates.

The Great Depression and World War II had brought about a radical change in public opinion regarding the government's responsibility for managing the economy. Beginning in 1933, the Roosevelt administration had introduced a wide series of experimental policies in the attempt to end the Depression. When World War II began, the government took over direct management of nearly every aspect of the economy, including production, distribution, money, prices, and labor. By the time the war ended, the public expected the government to continue managing the economy.

The public had come to believe it was the government's responsibility to manage the economy so that people could find jobs. Congress passed legislation that made it the government's legal obligation to do so. In February 1946, President Truman signed into law the Employment Act of 1946, which, according to the first sentence of that law, was "An Act to declare a national policy on employment, production, and purchasing power, and for other purposes."

Section 2 of the Act states:

> *The Congress hereby declares that it is the continuing policy and responsibility of the Federal Government to use all practicable means consistent with its needs and obligations and other essential considerations of national policy, with the assistance and cooperation of industry, agriculture, labor, and State and local governments, to coordinate and utilize all its plans, functions, and resources for the purpose of creating and maintaining, in a manner calculated to foster and promote free competitive enterprise and the general welfare, conditions under which there will be afforded useful employment opportunities, including self-employment, for those able, willing, and seeking to work, and to promote maximum— employment, production, and purchasing power.[2]*

William Martin, Fed chairman from 1951 to 1970, held the view that it was the duty of the Congress and the president to decide how large the government's budget deficit would be and that it was the duty of the Fed to help finance those deficits at reasonable interest rates.[3] Arthur Burns, who succeeded Martin as Fed chairman in February 1971, is generally believed to have succumbed to

CHART 6.3 A Breakdown of the Fed's Major Assets and Liabilities, 1914 to 1971

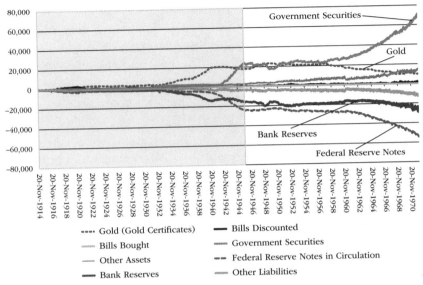

A Breakdown of the Fed's Major Assets & Liabilities
1914 to 1971, US$ Millions

Source: Data from "*The Federal Reserve System's Weekly Balance Sheet Since 1914*" and accompanying spreadsheet. Johns Hopkins University, SAE/No.115/ July 2018. See Bibliography.

pressure from President Nixon to keep monetary policy accommodative ahead of Nixon's campaign for reelection in 1972.[4]

With this political environment in mind, let's look more closely at the evolution of the Fed's balance sheet.

Balance Sheet

During the first half of the Bretton Woods era, when the government was fiscally conservative, all the Fed's major assets and liabilities remained roughly unchanged, as Chart 6.3 shows.

On the asset side, the Fed's holdings of government securities increased only from $24 billion in 1945 to $27 billion in 1960, while the Fed's holdings of gold certificates also increased modestly from $18 billion to $19 billion over the same period. On the liabilities side of the balance sheet, the reserves commercial banks held at the Fed rose from $16 billion in 1945 to $17 billion in 1960, while Federal Reserve notes in circulation increased from $25 billion to $30 billion.

The change in the Fed's balance sheet tells a very different story after 1960, however, once the government began running persistently large budget deficits. The most notable development on the asset side was an extraordinary surge in the Fed's holdings of government securities, which more than doubled from $27 billion in 1960 to $70 billion in 1971.

The Fed's holdings of US government securities not only increased sharply in absolute dollar amounts, but they also increased sharply relative to the total amount of government debt outstanding. In 1961, the Fed owned 10% of all such securities. By 1971, it owned 17% of the total. In other words, by 1971, the Fed had monetized 17% of the government's debt. This fact is all the more startling given the very large increase in US government debt outstanding during those years (see Chart 6.4).

A second development to take note of on the asset side of the Fed's balance sheet is that the Fed's holdings of gold certificates fell sharply starting in 1958, as shown in Chart 6.3.

Huge amounts of dollars left the United States during the 1960s. The US government gave its allies large military grants, particularly for use in the war in Vietnam. US corporations and banks also made large investments in Europe that resulted in dollars going abroad. The capital outflows were greater than the United States trade and current account surpluses. Consequently, the United States balance of payments was in deficit. Dollars went abroad to pay for that deficit. Some of those dollars were converted into US gold. As a result, the United States lost more than half of its gold reserves during the 1960s. Consequently, the Fed's holdings of gold certificates declined from $23 billion in 1957 to $10 billion in 1971.

Between 1945 and 1957, the Fed held roughly an equal amount of Treasury securities and gold certificates. By 1971, the Fed held nearly seven times as many Treasury securities as gold certificates, as can be seen in Chart 6.3.

CHART 6.4 The Fed's Ownership of US Treasury Securities as a
Percentage of Gross Federal Debt, 1945 to 1971

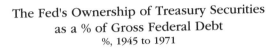

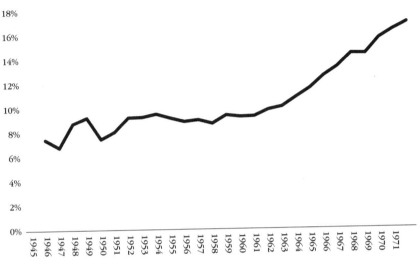

The Fed's Ownership of Treasury Securities
as a % of Gross Federal Debt
%, 1945 to 1971

Source: Data from Board of Governors of the Federal Reserve System, The
Fed's Annual Reports 1945 to 1971

Chart 6.5 shows the contribution of both Treasury securities
and gold certificates to the Fed's total assets during these years.

On the liabilities side of the Fed's balance sheet, it is the
growth in Federal Reserve Notes that stands out. Before World
War II, the public increased its holdings of cash during wars
and economic crises, but then redeposited the currency once
the emergency had passed. That did not happen at the end of
World War II. Currency outside banks (Federal Reserve Notes)
remained larger than Bank Reserves even after the war ended.
In fact, more than six decades would pass before the Fed's
reserve liabilities once again exceeded it liabilities for Federal
Reserve Notes.

This is all the more surprising since, when the Fed began
buying more government securities from the early 1960s, it paid
for those securities by making deposits into the reserve accounts

CHART 6.5 The Fed's Total Assets: Gold vs. Assets Acquired with Federal Reserve Credit, 1914 to 1971

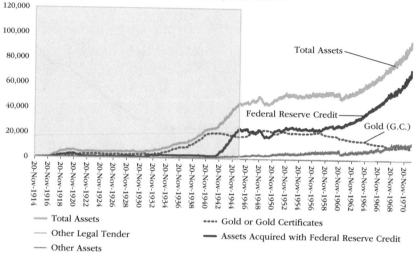

The Fed's Total Assets:
Gold vs. Assets Acquired with Federal Reserve Credit
1914 to 1971, US$ Millions

Source: Data from "*The Federal Reserve System's Weekly Balance Sheet Since 1914*" and accompanying spreadsheet. Johns Hopkins University, SAE/No.115/ July 2018. See Bibliography.

of the commercial banks from which it bought the bonds. Therefore, growth in commercial bank reserves should have dominated the liabilities side of the Fed's balance sheet during the 1960s. But that was not the case. Instead, currency outside banks increased much more than Bank Reserves. Federal Reserve notes in circulation increased from $30 billion in 1960 to $54 billion in 1971.

In the early 1960s, the outstanding amount of Federal Reserve Notes in circulation began to increase rapidly. As demand for cash grew, the public withdrew Federal Reserve Notes from their bank accounts; and when the banks ran short of cash they obtained more from the Fed. When the Fed provided the banks with additional Federal Reserve Notes, the Fed debited their reserve balances at the Fed. Consequently, the growing demand for Federal Reserve Notes resulted in a large and persistent drain of Bank Reserves.

In part, the increase in demand for cash was the result of a regulatory change. Beginning in 1959, the Fed permitted vault cash, i.e., the cash banks hold at their place of business, to be counted as reserves. Up until then the commercial banks could only satisfy their liquidity reserve requirements by holding funds on deposit in their reserve accounts at the Fed. This change lowered the level of reserves that banks had to hold idle in an account at the Fed and increased the banks' demand for Federal Reserve Notes. A higher rate of inflation during the second half of the decade also explains part of the increase in the demand for cash, since higher prices required a greater volume of currency.

Although Federal Reserve Notes grew more, the deposits banks held in their reserve accounts at the Fed also expanded. That is the final development to take note of on the liabilities side of the Fed's balance sheet. As the 1960s progressed, bank deposits grew. Consequently, the level of reserves that the banks were required to hold relative to their deposit base also grew. Between 1963 and 1971, the Fed's reserve liabilities increased from $17 billion to $28 billion, despite the drain caused by the increase in the number of Federal Reserve Notes in circulation (see Chart 6.3).

Federal Reserve Credit

During the 1960s, Federal Reserve Credit grew every year, with the rate of growth accelerating throughout the decade. Such a rapid and prolonged increase in Federal Reserve Credit was unprecedented. The significance of this development must not be overlooked. Astonishingly, Federal Reserve Credit grew more in 1971 than it did in 1944, at the peak of World War II. This is shown in Chart 6.6.

Federal Reserve Credit consisted almost exclusively of credit extended to the government through the Fed's acquisition of US government securities, as shown in Chart 6.7. Notice that there were practically no bills discounted among the Fed's assets. Before the Great Depression, the Fed carried out monetary

CHART 6.6 Federal Reserve Credit, Annual $ Change, 1915 to 1971

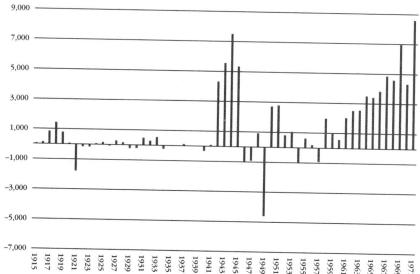

Federal Reserve Credit, Annual $ Change
1915 to 1971, US$ Millions

Source: Data for 1915 to 1917 from "*The Federal Reserve System's Weekly Balance Sheet Since 1914*" and accompanying spreadsheet. Johns Hopkins University, SAE/No.115/July 2018. See Bibliography. Data for 1918 to 1971 from The Fed's 2017 Annual Report, p. 306

policy primarily by extending Federal Reserve Credit through its discounting operations, during which it accumulated bills discounted as collateral. From 1932, however, the Fed provided Federal Reserve Credit primarily through open market operations instead. Afterwards, bills discounted nearly ceased to register on the Fed's balance sheet. The same is true for bills bought, since, after 1934, when the Fed conducted open market purchases it acquired government securities rather than commercial paper.

The End of Gold-Backed Money

By the mid-1960s, it was becoming clear that within a very short period of time, the United States simply would not have enough

CHART 6.7   Federal Reserve Credit and Its Components, 1914 to 1971

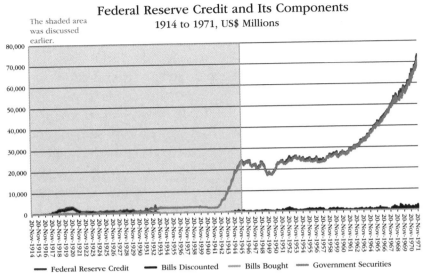

Source: Data from *"The Federal Reserve System's Weekly Balance Sheet Since 1914"* and accompanying spreadsheet. Johns Hopkins University, SAE/No.115/ July 2018. See Bibliography.

gold left to enable it to meet its obligation to allow the governments of other countries to convert the dollars they accumulated into US gold – as it was required to do under the rules of the Bretton Woods system – unless it radically altered both its fiscal and monetary policy.

The Fed could have stopped or even reversed the gold outflows by pushing up interest rates to a much higher level. Higher US interest rates would have encouraged US banks and corporations to stop investing in Europe and to bring their capital back home by making the returns on US bonds more attractive. Higher US interest rates would have also caused the US current account surplus to grow larger, since higher interest rates would have caused a recession in the US that deterred consumption and imports. A larger current account surplus would have brought more gold into the United States.

However, the Fed was committed to the government's goal of maintaining full employment. Higher interest rates would have thrown Americans out of work and undermined the government's efforts to create more jobs.

The Employment Act of 1946 required the Fed to take actions that would help achieve full employment. The Bretton Woods Agreement required the Fed to conduct monetary policy in a manner that would prevent the United States from losing gold through a balance of payments deficit. Clearly, those two requirements were incompatible. Loose monetary policy designed to support full employment would result in a balance of payments deficit and the loss of gold. Tight monetary policy designed to prevent the loss of gold would lead to higher unemployment.

The Fed could not pursue both policies at once. It chose to support employment. The Fed believed that government policies – budget deficits and capital outflows stemming from military grants – were responsible for the drain of US gold reserves. It was unwilling – and politically unable – to tighten monetary policy enough to stop the United States' loss of gold.

The combination of the loss of US gold and the increase in Federal Reserve Notes in circulation brought about a rapid deterioration in the Fed's gold coverage ratio, which fell from 46.6% in 1958 to 27.7% in 1965, as shown in Chart 6.8.

To enable the Fed to continue accumulating government securities without falling below its statutory gold coverage obligations, Congress, in 1965, changed the law so that the Fed was no longer required to maintain any gold certificate backing for the reserves commercial banks held at the Fed. That caused the Fed's gold coverage ratio to move back up to 41.2%. However, with the Fed continuing to buy government securities on a large scale and currency in circulation expanding rapidly, that relief did not last long.

In 1968, Congress changed the law again so that the Fed was not required to hold gold certificates to back Federal Reserve Notes either.

Once President Johnson signed Public Law 90-269 into effect on March 19, 1968, the Fed was freed of its obligation to hold gold certificates to back the money it created. In fact, the Fed no longer faced any domestic constraints on how many Federal

CHART 6.8 Gold Coverage Ratio, 1914 to 1968

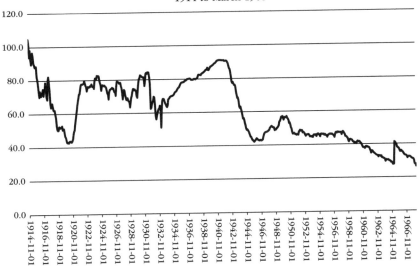

Gold Coverage Ratio:
Ratio of the Fed's Gold Reserves to Note and Deposit Liabilities
1914 to March 1968

Source: Data for 1914 to 1948, Ratio of Reserves to Note and Deposit
Liabilities, Federal Reserve Banks for United States, St. Louis Fed. Data for 1949
to 1968, Factors Affecting Reserve Balances of Depository Institutions and
Condition Statement of Federal Reserve Banks, St. Louis Fed.

Reserve Notes it could issue or how much Federal Reserve
Credit it could create. The United States moved from a gold-
backed monetary system to a pure fiat monetary system. The
men who passed the Federal Reserve Act that had created the
Fed in 1913 would have been appalled. Afterwards, only the fear
that inflation would result from an overly expansive monetary
policy kept the Fed in check.

When US gold reserves began to dwindle during the 1960s,
the governments of other countries became concerned that the
United States soon would not have enough gold left to allow
them to convert the dollars they had accumulated into US gold.
The more these concerns grew, the faster those countries converted their dollars into gold.

President Johnson had asked Congress in 1968 to end the
Fed's obligation to back dollars with gold certificates in the hope

that such a change would calm those fears and restore international confidence in the dollar.

Confidence in the dollar was not restored, however. The rest of the world was not convinced that the United States would tighten fiscal and monetary policy enough to swing the US balance of payments from deficit back into surplus. The run on the dollar continued and US gold reserves continued to shrink.

On August 15, 1971, President Nixon unilaterally declared the United States would no longer abide by its commitment to allow other governments to convert dollars into gold. By that time, the US simply did not have enough gold left to allow dollar convertibility to continue.

Nixon's announcement was the death knell of the Bretton Woods system. The regime in which all currencies were directly or indirectly pegged at a fixed exchange rate to gold disintegrated. Fixed exchange rates gave way to a new system of floating exchange rates. Soon thereafter international trade ceased to balance and cross-border capital flows ballooned. Credit growth exploded. This Money Revolution fundamentally changed the nature of the global economic system that had emerged under the gold standard. A new era, financed merely with fiat money, got underway. This new monetary regime quickly transformed the global economy.

Notes

1. Thirty-First Annual Report of the Board of Governors of the Federal Reserve System Covering Operations for the Year 1944, dated April 28, 1945, p. 24.

2. Employment Act of 1946, St. Louis Fed. https://fraser.stlouisfed.org/files/docs/historical/trumanlibrary/srf_014_002_0002.pdf

3. Source for William Martin's view: Allan H. Meltzer, *A History of the Federal Reserve*, Volume 2, Book 1, 1951–1969. p. 85

4. Source for statement regarding Arthur Burns: "Nixon tapes reveal political pressures on the Fed." Burton A. Abrams, professor of economics and acting chairperson of the Department of Economics in UD's Lerner College of Business and Economics. http://www1.udel.edu/PR/UDaily/2007/nov/fed111706.html]

CHAPTER 7

1971 to 2007: After Gold

We must protect the position of the American dollar as a pillar of monetary stability around the world.

President Richard Nixon[1]

The last link between money and gold was severed in 1971. The consequences were revolutionary. The parameters within which monetary – and fiscal – policy had traditionally operated expanded well beyond what earlier generations had imagined possible.

Once the Fed was no longer required to hold gold to back Federal Reserve Notes and the reserves that commercial banks held at the central bank, it was free to create as much credit as it wished, simply by making deposits into the commercial banks' reserve accounts at the Fed. That meant the Fed could engineer an extraordinary expansion of commercial bank credit as well as central bank credit, since when the Fed added to the reserves of the banking sector that enabled the banks to extend additional bank credit, while still meeting the statutory required reserve ratio.

Suddenly there seemed to be no limit as to how much credit the United States financial system could create. Soon, credit growth began to accelerate, not only when measured in dollars but also relative to the size of the economy. Before long, credit growth became the principal driver of economic growth. That theme will be developed in later chapters. First, this chapter will describe the transformation of the Fed's balance sheet once its golden fetters had been removed.[2]

Assets

Between 1971 and 2007, the Fed's total assets increased 10-fold from $95 billion to $950 billion, as shown in Chart 7.1.

The Fed's balance sheet shows which items were responsible for that growth.

The composition of the Fed's balance sheet became much simpler between 1971 and 2007, as shown in Chart 7.2. Government securities became the Fed's only major asset and Federal Reserve Notes became its only major liability. All the other items were relatively insignificant.

CHART 7.1 The Fed's Total Assets, 1914 to 2007

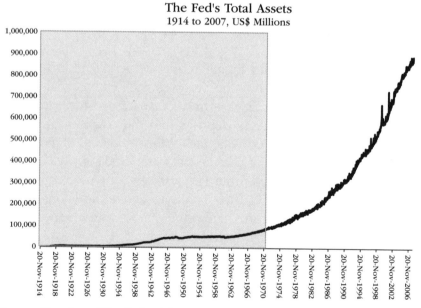

Source: Data from "*The Federal Reserve System's Weekly Balance Sheet Since 1914*" and accompanying spreadsheet. Johns Hopkins University, SAE/No.115/ July 2018. See Bibliography.

On the asset side, the Fed's holdings of government securities soared by $670 billion, from $70 billion in 1971 to $740 bil-
lion in 2007. On the liabilities side of the balance sheet, Federal
Reserve Notes in circulation increased even more, skyrocketing
by $720 billion from $54 billion in 1971 to $774 billion in 2007.
First, let's consider the reason behind the growth in the Fed's
holdings of government securities. As mentioned in the previous chapter, after its 1951 Accord with the Treasury Department,
the Fed's stated objective in carrying out monetary policy was
to facilitate sustainable economic growth at low rates of inflation. To accomplish that objective the Fed would first determine what the appropriate amount of monetary accommodation
should be. It then would add or, less frequently, remove reserves

CHART 7.2 A Breakdown of the Fed's Major Asset and Liabilities,
1940 to 2007

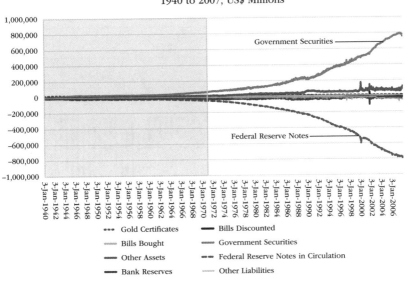

Source: Data from *"The Federal Reserve System's Weekly Balance Sheet Since
1914"* and accompanying spreadsheet. Johns Hopkins University, SAE/No.115/
July 2018. See Bibliography.

from the banking system using open market operations. Open market purchases of government securities would add to reserves, which would stimulate economic growth by making credit more available. Open market sales of government securities would remove reserves and tighten credit availability, which would slow the economy and dampen inflationary pressures.

During the 1950s, when the government's budget was generally in balance, the Fed had little difficulty achieving its policy objectives. Its task became much more difficult once the government began running large and persistent budget deficits, however. Budget deficits became a problem during the 1960s. They then became much worse. By 1976, the budget deficit was larger than it had been at the peak of World War II. In 1983, the deficit had grown to four times the World War II peak; and by 2004, it was nearly eight times larger (see Chart 7.3).

CHART 7.3 US Budget Balance: Surplus or Deficit, 1940 to 2007

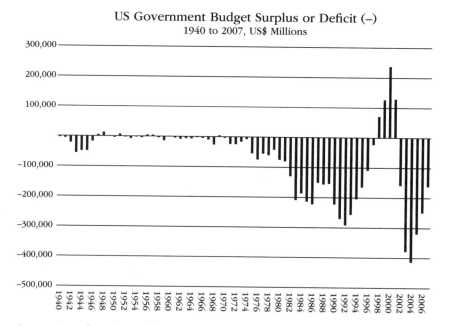

Source: Data from the Office of Management and Budget, Historical Tables, the White House

Increased government borrowing put upward pressure on interest rates, which the Fed countered by purchasing increasing amounts of government securities in order to support economic growth and employment. The Fed paid for the government securities it acquired by making deposits into the reserve accounts that commercial banks held at the Fed. In other words, the Fed created Federal Reserve Credit to finance its purchases of government debt.

The larger the budget deficits became, the more government securities the Fed bought. This can be seen by comparing Chart 7.4, which shows the annual change in Federal Reserve Credit outstanding, with Chart 7.3, which shows the growth in the government's annual budget deficits.

It was noted in the previous chapter that Federal Reserve Credit expanded more in 1971 than it did at the peak of World War II. After 1971, it did so nearly every year. Altogether, between 1971 and 2007, the Fed created $825 billion of Federal Reserve Credit

CHART 7.4 Federal Reserve Credit, Annual $ Change, 1940 to 2007

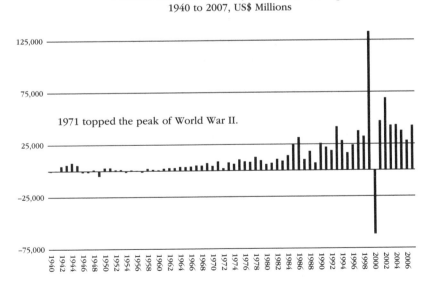

Federal Reserve Credit, Annual $ Change
1940 to 2007, US$ Millions

Source: Data from Board of Governors of the Federal Reserve System, The Fed's 2017 Annual Report Tables 6A and 6B

and acquired $672 billion of government securities.[3] That amounted to 8% of the increase in government debt during that period.

Had the Fed not bought so much government debt, either other investors would have had to buy those bonds, or the government would have had to run smaller budget deficits. If other investors had bought the bonds, then they would have had less money to invest in other bonds or in equities, meaning that bond prices would have been lower and that interest rates would have been higher, while stock prices would have risen less or fallen. If the government had run smaller deficits, there would have been less economic growth. Either way, the public would have been far worse off.

Despite monetizing an additional $672 billion of government debt during this period, the share of government debt owned by the Fed still declined. At the peak, in 1971, the Fed owned 17% of all government debt. In 2007, its ownership share had fallen to 8% (see Chart 7.5). However, as Chapter 10 will show, by

CHART 7.5 The Fed's Holdings of Treasury Securities, as a Percentage of Gross Federal Debt, 1945 to 2007

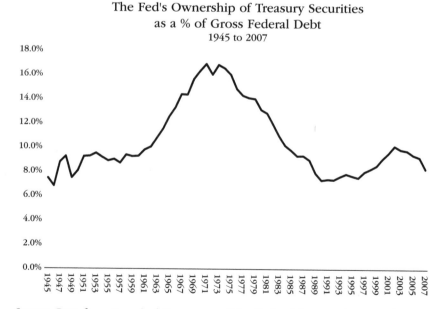

The Fed's Ownership of Treasury Securities
as a % of Gross Federal Debt
1945 to 2007

Source: Data from Board of Governors of the Federal Reserve System, The Fed's Annual Reports 1945 to 2007

then, other central banks had monetized even more US govern-ment debt than the Fed. When central banks outside the United States began financing US government debt, the Fed was no longer compelled to finance as much.

By 2007, Federal Reserve Credit accounted for nearly all of the Fed's total assets; and Federal Reserve Credit was com-prised almost entirely of credit extended to the government by the Fed's acquisition of US government securities, as shown in Chart 7.6 and Chart 7.7.

Liabilities

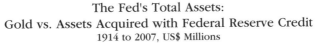

As mentioned above, when the Fed bought government secu-rities, it paid for them by making deposits into the reserve accounts that commercial banks hold at the Fed. Those deposits

CHART 7.6 The Fed's Total Assets: Gold vs. Assets Acquired with Federal Reserve Credit, 1914 to 2007

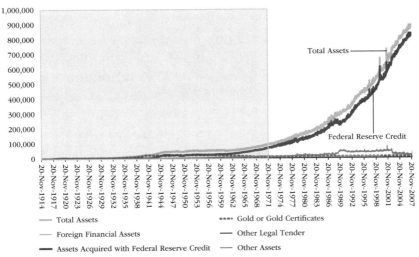

Source: Data from *"The Federal Reserve System's Weekly Balance Sheet Since 1914"* and accompanying spreadsheet. Johns Hopkins University, SAE/No.115/ July 2018. See Bibliography

CHART 7.7 Federal Reserve Credit and Its Components, 1940 to 2007

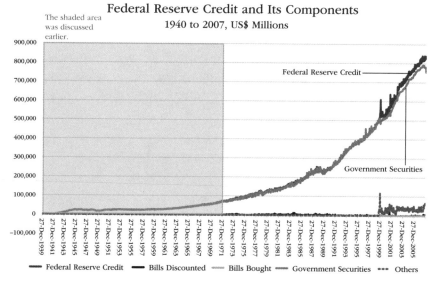

Source: Data from "The Federal Reserve System's Weekly Balance Sheet Since 1914" and accompanying spreadsheet. Johns Hopkins University, SAE/No.115/ July 2018. See Bibliography.

did not remain in the commercial banks' reserve accounts, however. Chart 7.2 shows that despite the surge in the Fed's holdings of government securities during this period, its reserve account liabilities hardly increased. The number of Federal Reserve Notes in circulation expanded instead – by $720 billion, from $54 billion in 1971 to $774 billion in 2007.

Before going any further, it is important to emphasize that the explosion of Federal Reserve Notes in circulation after 1971 would have been entirely impossible if the Fed had still been required to hold 25% gold backing for the Federal Reserve Notes it issued, as had been the case up until 1968. In 2007, the Fed would have had to have held $193 billion worth of gold certificates to back $774 billion of Federal Reserve Notes. It held only $11 billion worth. Its holdings of gold certificates had not changed since 1971.

Increased demand for cash drains Bank Reserves. That is because the Fed debits the reserve accounts of the commercial bank in exchange for the Federal Reserve Notes it provides

CHART 7.8 Federal Reserve Notes per Capita, 1945 to 2019

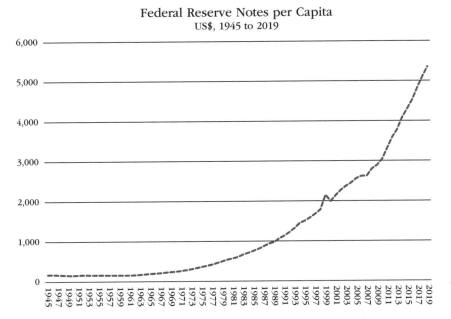

Federal Reserve Notes per Capita
US$, 1945 to 2019

Source: Data from Board of Governors of the Federal Reserve System (U.S.), The Fed's Annual Reports 1945 to 2019

them. Chart 7.2 shows that increased public demand for cash was so great that it completely offset all of the reserves the Fed injected into the commercial banking system to pay for the $620 billion of government securities it bought during those years.

The unprecedented growth in the number of Federal Reserve Notes that began in the early 1960s was mentioned in the previous chapter, as was the mystery surrounding the reasons behind it. Yet the public's desire to hold cash became even more voracious during the decades following the collapse of the Bretton Woods system, for reasons that are difficult to identify.

The number of Federal Reserve Notes per capita surged from $160 in 1960 to $260 in 1971 and then to $2,600 in 2007 – and to $5,350 in 2019. That is $5,350 of cash for every man, woman, and child in the United States (see Chart 7.8).

The demand for cash soared even though credit card use became widespread during the 1970s and should have lowered the demand for cash. Why?

Some of the increase can be attributed to inflation. A higher price level requires more currency to conduct transactions. However, inflationary pressures abated after 1980, when Federal Reserve Notes per capita amounted to just $550. Therefore, inflation can account for only part of the increase in the demand for physical dollars.

A more important factor is that a growing number of Federal Reserve Notes began to be accumulated outside the United States due to the widespread international acceptance of dollars as a store of value and a medium of exchange. For instance, Panama, Ecuador, and El Salvador have adopted the dollar as their currency; and many other countries are partially "dollarized." Drug lords are known to stockpile $100 bills. And it is very likely that dollar bills are used for a variety of other criminal transactions around the world, as well.

No one knows how many dollars are held abroad, but estimates range from between 40% and 70% of the total. In 2007, there were $800 billion Federal Reserve Notes in circulation. In 2019, there were $1.8 trillion. If 40% of those $1.8 trillion of Federal Reserve Notes were held overseas, the per capita amount remaining in the United States would be $3,300. If 70% were held abroad, US per capita holdings would be $1,650. Either of those figures would still represent a very large and difficult to explain surge in cash holding per capita within the United States relative to the level of 1980, which was $550.

The author is unable to find a satisfactory explanation for why, at the time of writing, more than 2 trillion non-interest bearing physical Federal Reserve notes are currently in circulation.

Conclusion

In 2007, the Fed had little in common with the institution created by the Federal Reserve Act of 1913. No one doubted that it was a central bank. Gold had become irrelevant to its operations. It had gained the power to create an infinite amount of credit. It could control interest rates at any level it chose. It was free to monetize some or all of the government's debt. And, it could even create wealth by extending Federal Reserve Credit and pushing up the price of property and stocks.

The following chapters will show that during the years after dollars ceased to be backed by gold, the Fed oversaw a phenomenal expansion of credit in the United States that supercharged the global economy and pulled hundreds of millions of people out of poverty. Unfortunately, the credit structure that existed in 2007 was built on weak foundations. In 2008, it began to collapse. If it had, it would have decimated the entire US financial sector and destroyed most of the country's savings and wealth.

That did not happen because in 2008 the Fed created and extended more Federal Reserve Credit in one year than it had during its near-century of existence prior to 2008, as shown in Chart 7.9.

And that was only the beginning. Fed policy ensured there would be no replay of the Great Depression.

CHART 7.9 Federal Reserve Credit, 1940 to 2008

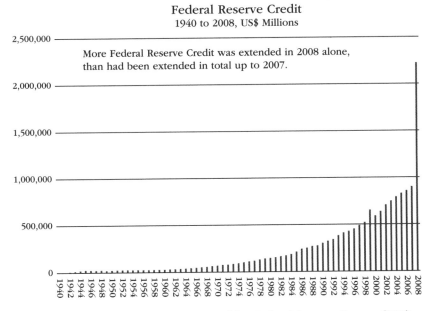

Federal Reserve Credit
1940 to 2008, US$ Millions

More Federal Reserve Credit was extended in 2008 alone, than had been extended in total up to 2007.

Source: Data from Board of Governors of the Federal Reserve System (U.S.), The Fed's 2018 Annual Report

Notes

1. Office of the Federal Register (Ed.), Richard Nixon, containing the
   public messages, speeches and statements of the president - 1971,
   Washington: US Government Printing Office, 1972, 1362 p. (Public Papers of the Presidents of the United States), pp. 886–890.
   https://www.cvce.eu/content/publication/1999/1/1/168eed17-f28b-
   487b-9cd2-6d668e42e63a/publishable_en.pdf
2. This is a reference to Barry Eichengreen's influential book, *Golden
   Fetters: The Gold Standard and the Great Depression* (Oxford University Press, 1992).
3. The 2017 Annual Report of the Board of Governors of the Federal
   Reserve System, Tables 6A and 6B.

PART II

Credit

Introduction

After dollars ceased to be backed by gold five decades ago, a radical acceleration of credit growth occurred that fundamentally altered the way economic growth is generated. Part Two describes the proliferation of credit in the United States since 1971. It details the impact that very rapid credit growth has had on the US economy. It explains how the economy became dependent on credit growth, and it discusses what these developments mean for the US economy during the years ahead. In this way, this part of the book completes the description of the Money Revolution that Part One began.

Total credit in the United States exceeded $1 trillion for the first time in 1964. By 2007, it had expanded 50-fold to $50 trillion. That phenomenal growth in credit set off a worldwide economic boom that pulled hundreds of millions of people around the world out of poverty.

However, at the same time, economic growth became dependent on credit growth. When the heavily indebted US private sector began to default on its debt in 2008, credit began to contract and the US – and the global – economy began to spiral into depression.

Fortunately, US policymakers had learned from the policy errors of the early 1930s. Between 1930 and 1933, credit had been allowed to contract, and the economy collapsed. That mistake would not be repeated. Between 2007 and 2014, the government nearly doubled its debt, from $9.2 trillion to $18.1 trillion, while the Fed concurrently created $3.5 trillion to help finance that expansion of government debt at low interest rates. Consequently, credit growth resumed, and the economy recovered.

Most surprisingly, this extraordinarily aggressive combination of fiscal and monetary stimulus did not cause inflation. Milton Friedman taught that "Inflation is always and everywhere a monetary phenomenon." Events following the financial crisis of 2008 have demonstrated that Friedman was mistaken.

There are three lessons to be learned from the decades-long surge in credit that led to the crisis of 2008 and from the policy response that successfully resolved that crisis. First, following the Money Revolution described in the first two parts of this book, our economic system requires credit growth to generate economic growth. Without credit growth there will be a depression. Second, there are limits as to how much the private sector can borrow. Third, it is possible for the US government to borrow many trillions of dollars and for the Fed to create trillions of dollars to help finance that debt over a short space of time, without causing high rates of inflation.

The inescapable conclusion that must be drawn from these lessons – lessons that were strongly reinforced by the results of the government's aggressive economic policy response to the COVID-19 pandemic - is that the US government will have to continue to borrow heavily during the years ahead to keep the economy from collapsing into a new depression. This begs the question: How should the government spend the money it will be forced to borrow?

The first three chapters of Part Two describe the sharp surge in credit creation by the US banking sector, by the broader US financial system, and by foreign central banks, particularly during the years after dollars ceased to be backed by gold.

Chapter 11 then shows how credit growth became the principal driver of economic growth. Chapter 12 discusses the financial crisis of 2008 and the forceful policy response that successfully resolved it. Chapter 13 examines how, and to what ends, the Fed conducted monetary policy between the crisis of 2008 and 2019, while Chapter 14 describes the extraordinary measures the Fed implemented to help carry the economy through the COVID-19 pandemic during 2020 and the first half of 2021. Chapter 15 surveys the differing causes of inflation each decade from the 1920s to the present.

Part Three will show that rather than threatening US prosperity, the circumstances brought about by the Money Revolution have opened up extraordinary opportunities that the United States must grasp and fully realize.

CHAPTER 8

Credit Creation by the Banking System

Only commercial banks and trust companies can lend money that they manufacture by lending it.

Irving Fisher[1]

The Fed's power over the economy stems from its ability to create or destroy credit. When the Board of Governors of the Federal Reserve System decides economic growth should accelerate, the Fed takes actions that cause credit to expand more rapidly. When it feels the economy is at risk of overheating, it adopts policies that cause credit growth to slow, or, if necessary, to contract. Monetary policy involves nothing more than implementing actions that determine the rate of credit expansion.

Part One demonstrated how the Fed creates credit directly, Federal Reserve Credit, when it makes deposits into the reserve accounts that commercial banks hold at the Fed.

This chapter will show that the Fed also controls the amount of credit that the banking system can create. This power is of crucial importance to the conduct of monetary policy and to the economy because, under normal circumstances, the banking system creates a great deal more credit than the Fed does. For that reason, the Fed generally achieves its policy objectives by influencing the volume of bank credit.

This chapter begins by explaining how the banking system creates credit. Next it describes the tools and methods the Fed employs to control the amount of credit the banking system creates. Finally, it shows that over time the Fed steadily revised its regulations to enable the banking system to create ever larger amounts of credit in order to stimulate economic growth. Eventually, these changes facilitated the creation of so much credit that credit growth became the most important driver of economic growth, fundamentally transforming the nature of our economic system.

Subsequent chapters will show that economic growth became dependent on credit growth, which explains why the Fed is so desperate to ensure that credit continues to expand. The Fed understands that credit growth drives the economy and that if credit contracts there will be a depression.

Commercial Banks Create Money, Too

Part One described how the Fed creates money. But, the Fed is not alone in its ability to create money. The commercial banking system also creates money by extending loans and creating deposits. The deposits that individuals, businesses, and other entities hold in commercial banks are considered to be a second kind of money because deposits can be withdrawn as cash and spent, or they can be spent simply by writing a check on a deposit in a checking account.

The money that a central bank creates is called base money or the monetary base. As explained in Part One, the US monetary base is comprised of the reserves that commercial banks hold in their reserve accounts at the Fed, and currency.

"M1" and "M2" are broader measures of money that include money that the banking system creates.

M1 is defined as the sum of currency held by the public and transaction deposits at depository institutions (i.e., checking account deposits).

M2 is defined as M1 plus savings deposits, small-denomination time deposits and retail money market mutual fund shares.

Chart 8.1 shows the monetary base, M1 and M2 for the United States from 1959 to 2007.

M2 is far larger than the monetary base, meaning that commercial banks in the US create far more money than the Fed does.

This chapter will show how the commercial banking system creates money (i.e., bank deposits) when it extends loans. It will also show that the money created in this way allows the banking

CHART 8.1 The Monetary Base, M1 & M2, 1959 to 2007

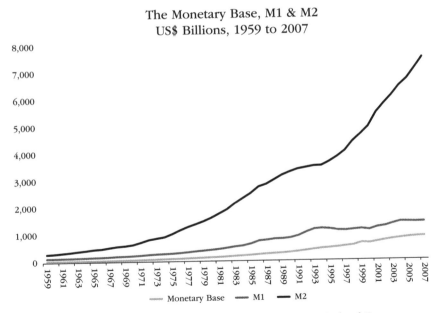

Source: Data from FRED Graph Observations, 1959–2007, Federal Reserve Economic Data

system to extend still more credit and to create still more money in a circular process that ultimately results in the creation of an amount of credit and money that is a multiple of the initial loan.

The maximum amount of money and credit that can be created through this process is determined by regulations governing the banks. We will see that the amount of money and credit created by the US banking system became extraordinarily large as bank regulations governing this process were relaxed.

How the Process Works

When a bank accepts a deposit, it is legally required to set aside part of that deposit as "reserves" to ensure that it will have enough liquid assets to meet its customers' requests to withdraw their deposits at any time.[2] Every bank must hold its reserves either in its account at the Fed or else as vault cash, which is physical cash at the bank's place of business.

Since the depositors are generally content to leave their money in their bank accounts for long periods of time and generally don't all withdraw their money at the same time, banks are only required to hold a fraction of their total deposits as reserves. The Fed decides the amount of reserves that banks must hold as a percentage of their deposits. This ratio is called the required reserve ratio. For example, if the required reserve ratio is 20%, banks must hold $20 of reserves at the central bank (or as vault cash) for every $100 of deposits the banks accept from their customers.

Table 8.1 demonstrates how the process works, assuming an initial deposit of $100 and a required reserve ratio of 20%.

When the initial deposit of $100 is made, the bank that receives that deposit sets aside a reserve of $20 and then lends out the remaining $80 in order to earn interest income. Regardless of how the recipient of that loan uses the money, before long it will be deposited somewhere back in the banking system. It makes no difference if the $80 is deposited into one bank or several banks. Either way, $16 (20% of $80) will be set aside

TABLE 8.1 Money Creation Through Fractional Reserve Banking

Money Creation through Fractional Reserve Banking			
Assuming:		The "Money Multiplier" is:	
1: As initial deposit of $100 by the Fed		$1 \div$ the Required Reserve Ratio	
2: A Required Reserve Ratio of 20%		$1 \div 20\% = 5$ times $\$100 \times 5 = \$500$	
	Deposit	Reserves	Loan
Round 1	100	20	80
Round 2	80	16	64
Round 3	64	13	51
Round 4	51	10	41
Round 5	41	8	33
Round 6	33	7	26
Round 7	26	5	21
Round 8	21	4	17
Round 9	17	3	13
Round 10	13	3	11
Round 11	11	2	9
Round 12	9	2	7
Round 30	0.2	0.0	0.1
Round 31	0.1	0.0	0.1
Total	500	100	400

by the banking system as reserves and the remaining $64 will be lent out again. The process will be repeated again and again until ultimately, the banking system will have set aside $100 of reserves and extended $400 of loans. In the process, the amount of deposits in the banking system grows to $500.

Since bank deposits are considered to be a kind of money, by extending credit, the banking system can create an amount of money that is a multiple of the initial deposit. The multiple, known as the *money multiplier*, can be calculated as follows:

The money multiplier = 1 ÷ the required reserve ratio

Therefore, if the required reserve ratio is 20%, as in the example above, the money multiplier is 5 times (1 ÷ 20%) and the banking system can create an amount of money that is five times the initial deposit: $100 X 5 = $500.

If the required reserve ratio is 10%, the money multiplier is 10 times (1 ÷ 10%) and the banking system can create an amount of money 10 times the size of the initial deposit.

The lower the required reserve ratio, the more credit the banking system can create.

Two Factors Determine How Much Credit Banks Can Create

Two main factors determine the amount of credit that the banking system can create. Both are controlled by the Fed. The first is the required reserve ratio. The second is the level of Bank Reserves, also known as Reserve Balances. Over time, the Fed adjusted the regulations affecting these factors in a way that allowed an explosion of credit creation by the banking system. The Fed made these changes with the express purpose of allowing credit to expand in order to fuel additional economic growth.

The next section of this chapter shows how the Fed can control credit creation by the commercial banks by adjusting either the required reserve ratio or the level of Reserve Balances in the banking system. Subsequent sections then discuss the growth of the commercial banks' reserves, customer deposits and total loans and investments over three time periods (1914 to 1945, 1945 to 1970 and 1970 to 2007) in order to show the evolution of credit creation by the banking system over time and to highlight the extraordinary extent to which credit expanded relative to reserves after dollars ceased to be backed by gold five decades ago. Finally, the chapter concludes by discussing the regulatory changes that permitted credit creation by the banking system to expand so radically.

The Required Reserve Ratio

The Fed can tighten monetary conditions by raising the required reserve ratio. Typically, the banking system maintains only just enough reserves to meet the required reserve ratio. Therefore, when the Fed increases the required reserve ratio, the banking system is forced to contract its deposit base. To do that, it is forced to reduce its outstanding loans. As a result, credit then becomes less available, interest rates tend to rise and the economy tends to slow.

Conversely, the Fed can loosen monetary conditions by lowering the required reserve ratio, thereby allowing the banking system to extend more credit and, as a byproduct, create more deposits without breaching the new, lower required reserve ratio. As liquidity becomes more plentiful, interest rates tend to fall and economic growth tends to accelerate.

Expressed differently, increasing the required reserve ratio lowers the money multiplier, while lowering the required reserve ratio increases the money multiplier.

Bank Reserves

Next, consider how the Fed traditionally influenced the amount of credit the banking system could create by adding or deducting Bank Reserves through open market operations.

Before 2008, when reserves in the banking system were still scarce,[3] if the Fed wanted the banking system to extend more bank loans, it would acquire a government bond and pay for that acquisition by making a deposit into the reserve account of the bank from which it bought the bond. For example, if the Fed acquired $1 billion worth of government bonds from a bank, it would deposit $1 billion into that bank's reserve account at the Fed. That deposit would directly increase the level of Reserve Balances of that bank, and, therefore, of the entire banking system, by $1 billion.

A higher level of Reserve Balances would allow the banking system to make additional loans while still satisfying the required reserve ratio. The additional credit creation by the banking system would stimulate the economy and generate more growth and employment.

On the other hand, if the Fed were concerned that the economy was overheating and threatened by rising inflation, it could force the banking system to contract the amount of money it had lent by draining reserves from the banking system.

For example, the Fed could sell some of the government bonds that it had acquired in the past. If the Fed sold $1 billion worth of bonds to a bank, it would hand the bonds over to the bank and, at the same time, debit that bank's reserve account at the Fed by $1 billion, thereby reducing the level of Reserve Balances in the banking system by $1 billion.

Assuming that there were no excess reserves in the banking system at the time of this transaction (and, typically, before 2008 there were not), the banking system would no longer have sufficient reserves to meet the statutory required reserve ratio. Therefore, it would be forced to reduce the size of its deposit base by calling in loans and contracting credit.

The contraction of bank credit would cause the economy to slow, putting an end to the inflationary pressures that had concerned the Fed.

In sum, then, by adjusting the level of Bank Reserves or the required reserve ratio, the Fed controlled the amount of credit the banking system could create, which, in turn, gave the Fed the power to speed up or slow down the growth rate of the US economy.

Credit Creation by Commercial Banks: 1914 to 2007

Credit creation by commercial banks has played a leading role in shaping the economic history of the United States and it will continue to do so in the future. This section briefly describes the developments that determined the amount of credit that commercial banks created between the establishment of the Federal Reserve System in 1914 and the economic crisis of 2008.

This history is divided into three parts in order to more clearly explain the most important events that affected the banks' ability to create credit. The first period, 1914 to 1945, covers World War I, the Great Depression, and World War II. The second period considers the period between the end of World War II and 1970, the year roughly corresponding to the time when dollars ceased to be backed by gold. The third period covers the years from 1970 to 2007, when credit "slipped its leash," as the regulatory constraints that had earlier held credit creation in check were removed one after the other.

1914 to 1945

Today, gold movements into and out of the United States have no impact on the level of Bank Reserves or on the ability of the banking sector to extend credit. But the role of gold was very different up until the late 1960s. For instance, between 1914 and 1945, two large waves of gold inflows into the United States resulted in a surge in Bank Reserves, which, in turn, permitted a surge in credit creation.

US gold holdings nearly doubled between 1914, when World War I began, and 1917, when the United States entered the war. As that gold entered the US it was deposited in US banks and, as a result of increased deposits, those banks were required to set aside a higher level of reserves at the Fed. The next wave of gold inflows entered the US between 1933 and 1940. US gold holdings increased by 440% during those seven years.

Chart 8.2 shows those gold inflows into the United States. It also shows that Bank Reserves expanded as gold entered the country.

The growth in Bank Reserves permitted the commercial banks to extend more credit and, thereby, to create more deposits while remaining within the limits set by the required reserve ratio. Chart 8.3 compares the level of Bank Reserves to bank deposits and to the total loans and investments made by the banks between 1914 and 1945.

CHART 8.2 US Gold & Bank Reserves, 1914 to 1945

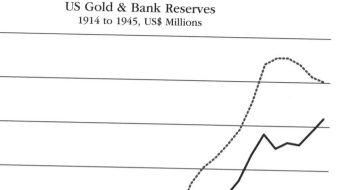

US Gold & Bank Reserves
1914 to 1945, US$ Millions

---- The Gold Stock of the United States   — Bank Reserves at the Fed

Source: Data from Banking And Monetary Statistics 1914 to 1941 and 1941 to 1970, and the Federal Reserve's Annual Report for 2017

The surge in Bank Reserves between 1914 and 1920 (more easily seen in Chart 8.2) permitted a rapid expansion of bank credit (both loans and investments) and deposits. Reserves peaked in 1919 and then contracted by 7% by 1921. Credit and deposits also both contracted in 1921, causing a severe, but short-lived, economic depression that year.

Bank Reserves expanded by 48% between 1921 and 1928, while bank credit and bank deposits increased by 45% and 60%, respectively. The credit expansion during those seven years is the principal reason the Roaring Twenties roared.

When the boom of the 1920s turned to bust, creditors defaulted, banks failed and individuals withdrew their savings from banks. The sharp contraction of credit between 1929 and 1933 produced the Great Depression.

CHART 8.3 Commercial Banks: Reserves, Deposits, and Loans and Investments, 1914 to 1945

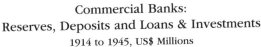

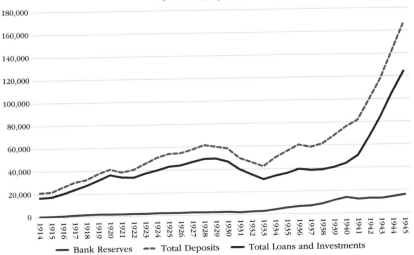

Source: Data from Friedman and Schwartz, "A Monetary History Of The United States," Table A-2, p. 737; and the Federal Reserve's Annual Report for 2017

When World War II began, credit surged as banks acquired government bonds to help finance the war. It is interesting to note that by the end of the war, government securities made up nearly 73% of the commercial banks' total loans and investments, up from 11% in 1930 and 40% in 1940. In other words, by 1945, nearly three-quarters of all bank credit outstanding was extended to the government (see Chart 8.4).

The surge in bank credit between 1940 and 1945 enabled the government to spend vast sums fighting the war. Credit-financed government spending during the war ended the Great Depression. It also produced a very large increase in deposits as a byproduct. Recall that when banks extend credit, they also create deposits through the money multiplier effect inherent to the system of fractional reserve banking.

CHART 8.4 Commercial Banks: Government Securities Held as a Percentage of Total Loans and Investments 1914 to 1945

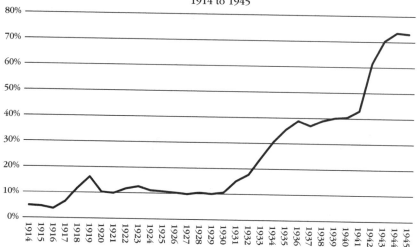

Commercial Banks:
Government Securities Held
as a Percent of Total Loans & Investments
1914 to 1945

Source: Data from Board of Governors of the Federal Reserve System (U.S.), 1935-. Banking and Monetary Statistics, 1914–1941; Board of Governors of the Federal Reserve System (U.S.), 1935-. Banking and Monetary Statistics, 1941–1970.

Chart 8.5 shows the ratio of Bank Reserves to bank deposits between 1917 and 1945. This chart does not represent the required reserve ratio set by the Fed. It depicts the actual ratio of reserves to deposits, reflecting numerous factors including the willingness of savers to hold their savings in banks as deposits, the willingness of banks to lend and the inflow of gold into the United States. It fluctuated in a narrow range between 4% and 5% from 1917 to 1931 because reserves increased nearly as much as deposits at commercial banks during those years. After 1931, however, the ratio began to move up very rapidly, first as bank deposits contracted during the Depression and then as Bank Reserves soared with the surge of gold inflows into the

CHART 8.5 The Ratio of Bank Reserves to Bank Deposits,
1917 to 1945

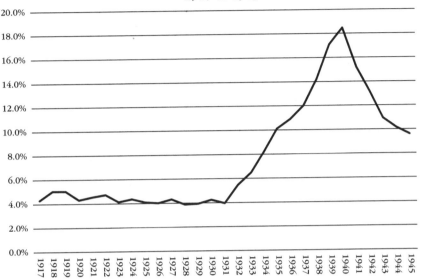

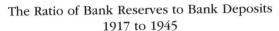

Source: Data from Friedman and Schwartz, "A Monetary History Of The United States," Table A-2, p. 737; and the Federal Reserve's Annual Report for 2017

US beginning in 1934. The ratio peaked at 18.5% in 1940. These ample reserves made it possible for the commercial banks to extend vast amounts of credit by acquiring government bonds during World War II while still satisfying the statutory required reserve ratio. By the end of the war the ratio of reserves to deposits had fallen to 9.6%.

The ratio of deposits to Bank Reserves is the exact inverse of the ratio of reserves to deposits; and it is a good measure of leverage within the banking system. Chart 8.6 shows that the ratio of bank deposits to Bank Reserves fell from 25 times in 1931 to only 5 times in 1940, but then expanded again to 10 times in 1945.

CHART 8.6 The Ratio of Bank Deposits to Bank Reserves,
1917 to 1945

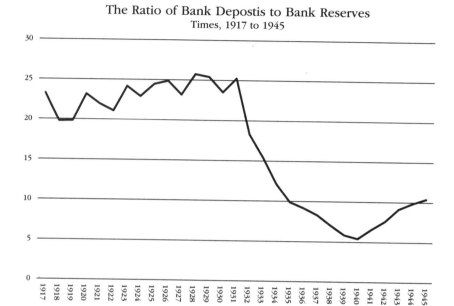

The Ratio of Bank Depostis to Bank Reserves
Times, 1917 to 1945

Source: Data from Friedman and Schwartz, "A Monetary History Of The United States," Table A-2, p. 737; and the Federal Reserve's Annual Report for 2017

Between 1914 and 1945, bank credit (total loans and investments) contracted three times: in 1920 and 1921, between 1930 and 1933 and in 1937, as shown in Chart 8.7. The first two contractions caused economic depressions. The third caused a recession within a depression.

On the other hand, during periods of rapid credit growth, as during World War I, most of the 1920s and, especially, during World War II, the economy boomed.

This pattern was recognized not only by economists, but by policymakers as well. During the years that have followed, the Fed has worked diligently in the effort to prevent credit from ever contracting again.

CHART 8.7 Total Loans and Investments: Annual Dollar Change,
1915 to 1945

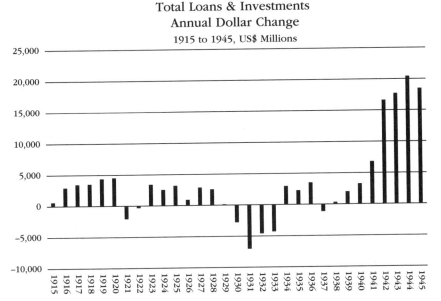

Total Loans & Investments
Annual Dollar Change
1915 to 1945, US$ Millions

Source: Data from Board of Governors of the Federal Reserve System (U.S.),
1935-. "Part I" in Banking and Monetary Statistics, 1914–1941; Board of
Governors of the Federal Reserve System (U.S.), 1935-. Banking and Monetary
Statistics, 1941–1970.

1945 to 1970

Bank credit did not contract during any year between 1945 and
1970. In fact, it grew very rapidly. Bank credit expanded more in
1958 than at the peak of World War II. And after 1961, it did so
nearly every year, as shown in Chart 8.8.

The growth in Bank Reserves was pedestrian in comparison.
Gold inflows, which had inflated Bank Reserves before World
War II, peaked in 1949 and then turned into outflows, particularly after 1957. Consequently, the growth in Bank Reserves was
unimpressive during this period; and the growth in reserves that
did occur after 1963 was the result of open market operations by
the Fed (see Chart 8.9).

CHART 8.8 Total Loans and Investments: Annual Dollar Change,
1915 to 1970

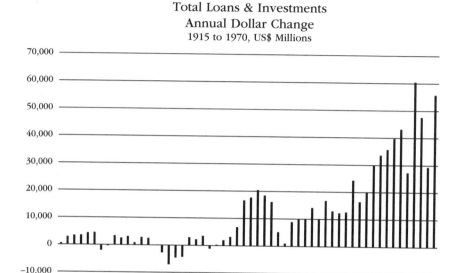

Total Loans & Investments
Annual Dollar Change
1915 to 1970, US$ Millions

Source: Data from Board of Governors of the Federal Reserve System (U.S.),
1935-. "Part I" in Banking and Monetary Statistics, 1914–1941; Board of
Governors of the Federal Reserve System (U.S.), 1935-. Banking and Monetary
Statistics, 1941–1970.

The large extension of bank credit produced a similar rise
in bank deposits, in another example of money creation by the
banking sector. Chart 8.10 shows the growth in the reserves,
deposits, and loans and investments of the commercial banks
between 1914 and 1970.

Notice that during the postwar years, the commercial banks' loans and investments became larger than their
deposit base. This occurred because the banks began to borrow some of their funds from the credit markets, rather than
relying solely on deposits as they traditionally had done. This
important development will be discussed in greater detail in
Chapter 9.

Next, bank deposits grew much more rapidly than Bank
Reserves. Chart 8.11 shows very clearly that that was the case.

CHART 8.9 US Gold & Bank Reserves, 1914 to 1970

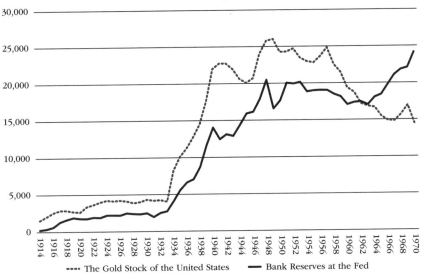

US Gold & Bank Reserves
1914 to 1970, US$ Millions

--- The Gold Stock of the United States **—** Bank Reserves at the Fed

Source: Data from Friedman and Schwartz, "A Monetary History Of The United States," Table A-2, p. 737; and the Federal Reserve's Annual Report for 2017

By 1970, the ratio of Bank Reserves to bank deposits had fallen from 18.5% in 1945 to just 3.7%, roughly on par with, and slightly below, where it had stood throughout the 1920s.

Inverting that ratio shows that in 1970 the commercial banks' deposits were 27 times as large as their reserves at the Fed, up from 10 times in 1945 and 5 times in 1940 (see Chart 8.12).

Consequently, by 1970, the leverage of the commercial banks (as measured by the ratio of deposits to reserves) exceeded the point reached at the peak of the Roaring Twenties. What would come next, however, would make that level of leverage appear highly conservative.

1970 to 2007

US gold reserves peaked in 1949, held fairly steady though 1957, and then began to fall rapidly afterwards as the US balance of

CHART 8.10 Commercial Banks: Reserves, Deposits, and Loans and Investments, 1914 to 1970

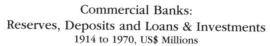

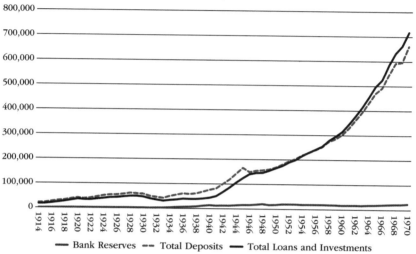

Commercial Banks:
Reserves, Deposits and Loans & Investments
1914 to 1970, US$ Millions

— Bank Reserves -- Total Deposits — Total Loans and Investments

Source: Data from Friedman and Schwartz, "A Monetary History Of The United States," Table A-2, p. 737; and the Federal Reserve's Annual Report for 2017

payments deteriorated. In 1965, Congress eliminated the requirement that the Fed hold gold to back the reserves that commercial banks held at the Fed. Three years later, Congress freed the Fed from the obligation of holding gold to back the currency it issued. And, in 1971, with the breakdown of the Bretton Woods system, gold ceased to have any relevance whatsoever for the conduct of US monetary policy.

Chart 8.13 shows that Bank Reserves continued to expand until 1986 even as the stock of US gold contracted. Reserves expanded due to open market operations (purchases) by the Fed.

However, what is most striking about this chart is how little Bank Reserves grew. In fact, they peaked in 1986 at just $46 billion and then fell sharply to a postwar low of only $8 billion in

CHART 8.11 The Ratio of Bank Reserves to Bank Deposits, 1917 to 1970

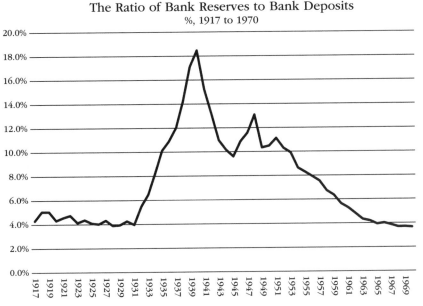

The Ratio of Bank Reserves to Bank Deposits
%, 1917 to 1970

Source: Data from Friedman and Schwartz, "A Monetary History Of The United States," Table A-2, p. 737; and the Federal Reserve's Annual Report for 2017

2001. In 2007, Bank Reserves were $14 billion, which was $2 billion less than in 1945.

Given that bank deposits and bank credit are limited by the level of Bank Reserves and by the required reserve ratio, they, too, would have contracted in line with Bank Reserves after 1986 had the ratio of reserves the banks were required to hold relative to deposits remained unchanged.

Chart 8.14 dramatically illustrates that bank deposits and bank credit were not constrained by the depressed level of Bank Reserves, however. Both leapt phenomenally.

Bank deposits surged from $660 billion in 1945 to $8.5 trillion in 2007, while the credit extended by the banks as loans and investments rose even more from $720 billion to $11.4 trillion.

CHART 8.12 The Ratio of Bank Deposits to Bank Reserves, 1917 to 1970

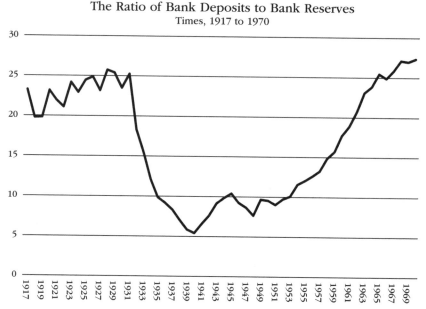

The Ratio of Bank Deposits to Bank Reserves
Times, 1917 to 1970

Source: Data from Board of Governors of the Federal Reserve System (U.S.),
1935-. "Part I" in Banking and Monetary Statistics, 1914–1941; Board of
Governors of the Federal Reserve System (U.S.), 1935-. Banking and Monetary
Statistics, 1941–1970.

After 1970, credit growth by the commercial banks became
so large each year that by comparison, the credit extended
to finance World War II appears as only a very small blip in
Chart 8.15, which shows the growth in credit extended by the
commercial banks each year between 1915 and 2007.

Note that bank credit did contract once between 1970 and
2007, during 1990 and 1991. The United States experienced a
recession as a result.

The ratio of Bank Reserves to bank deposits, sank from 10%
in 1945 to only 0.16% in 2007.

The ratio of bank deposits to Bank Reserves shot up from 10
times in 1945 to 607 times in 2007 (having peaked at 681 times
in 2005), reflecting a mind-boggling expansion of leverage in the
banking system.

These ratios are shown in charts Chart 8.16 and Chart 8.17.

CHART 8.13 US Gold and Bank Reserves, 1914 to 2007

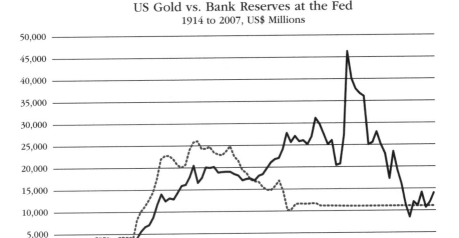

US Gold vs. Bank Reserves at the Fed
1914 to 2007, US$ Millions

···· The Gold Stock of the United States   ▬ Bank Reserves at the Fed

Source: Data from Friedman and Schwartz, "A Monetary History Of The United States," Table A-2, p. 737; and the Federal Reserve's Annual Report for 2017

Why Bank Credit Grew Much Faster than Bank Reserves

So, how was it possible that bank deposits and bank credit grew so much relative to Bank Reserves?

The level of Reserve Balances ceased to increase in line with the level of deposits in the banking system for five main reasons. First, in 1959 the Fed began to permit member banks to use their vault cash, i.e., the physical cash the banks held in their offices, as part of their reserves.

Up until then, only the deposits that member banks held in their reserve accounts at the Fed could be counted as Bank Reserves. After this change, both deposits at the Fed and vault cash were counted as reserves. Allowing banks to use vault cash as reserves reduced the level of deposits, i.e., Reserve Balances, that banks were required to hold at the Fed.

CHART 8.14 Commercial Banks: Reserves, Deposits, and Loans and Investments, 1914 to 2007

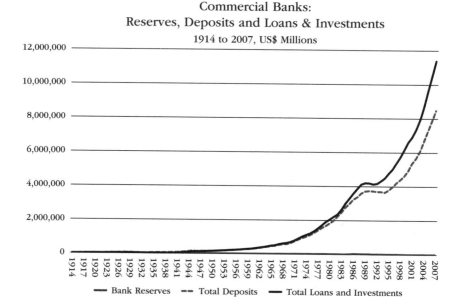

Source: Data from Friedman and Schwartz, "A Monetary History Of The United States," Table A-2, p. 737; and the Federal Reserve's Annual Report for 2017

This change only explains a small part of the surge in the leverage of the banking system, however. Even after vault cash was added to Bank Reserves held at the Fed, the ratio of total reserves to bank deposits still fell very sharply. By 2007, it had fallen to only 0.9%, as shown in Chart 8.18. With the effective reserve ratio at 0.9%, the money multiplier was 111 times just before the economic crisis struck in 2008.

The second factor that reduced Reserve Balances was that banks began to raise a growing portion of their funds by borrowing money through the credit markets rather than obtaining their funding solely from customers' deposits. This maneuver began in the late 1950s and accelerated thereafter. Banks were not required to hold any reserves against borrowed funds, so this too reduced the level of Reserve Balances held by the banking system.[4]

CHART 8.15 Total Loans and Investments, Annual Dollar Change, 1915 to 2007

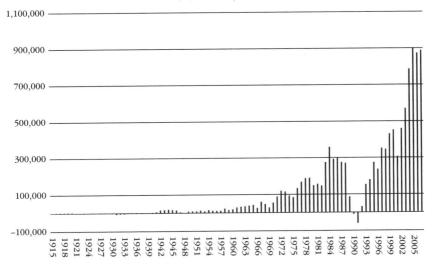

Total Loans & Investments
Annual Dollar Change
1915 to 2007, US$ Millions

Source: Data from Board of Governors of the Federal Reserve System (U.S.), 1935-, "Part I" in Banking and Monetary Statistics, 1914–1945; Board of Governors of the Federal Reserve System (U.S.), 1935-. Banking and Monetary Statistics, 1941–1970.

Third, the banks developed and put in place techniques that reduced the level of reserve they were required to hold. The Fed had always set the required reserve ratio much higher on demand deposits than on time deposits. Since the banks' customers can withdraw their money from demand deposits (such as checking deposits) without suffering any penalty, demand deposits are more likely to be withdrawn suddenly than are time deposits. Consequently, banks were traditionally required to set aside a higher level of reserves for such deposits. Over time, banks found ways to persuade their customers to shift their deposits out of normal demand deposit accounts into new kinds of deposit accounts that required lower levels of reserves.

CHART 8.16 The Ratio of Bank Reserves to Bank Deposits, 1917 to 2007

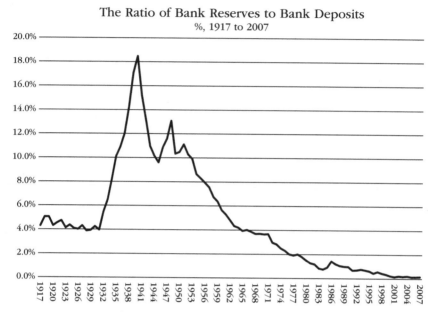

The Ratio of Bank Reserves to Bank Deposits
%, 1917 to 2007

Source: Data from Friedman and Schwartz, "A Monetary History Of The United States," Table A-2, p. 737; and the Federal Reserve's Annual Report for 2017

The establishment of sweep account programs beginning in the mid-1990s was particularly effective in lowering Bank Reserves. The programs involved the banks implementing automated computer programs that analyzed their customers' use of demand deposits and "sweeping" unused demand deposits into savings deposit accounts with lower reserve requirements.[5]

Fourth, Congress enacted laws that reduced the level of reserves banks were required to hold. For instance, the Monetary Control Act of 1980 established a "low reserve tranche" whereby the amount of net transaction accounts subject to a reserve requirement ratio of 3% was established, while net transaction accounts in excess of the low reserve tranche were reservable at 10%. Similarly, the Garn-St. Germain Act of 1982 exempted the first $2 million of reservable liabilities from reserve requirements.

CHART 8.17 The Ratio of Bank Deposits to Bank Reserves, 1917 to 2007

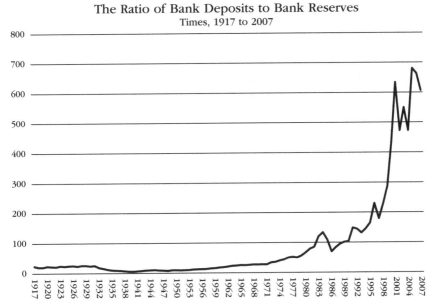

The Ratio of Bank Deposits to Bank Reserves
Times, 1917 to 2007

Source: Data from Friedman and Schwartz, "A Monetary History Of The United States," Table A-2, p. 737; and the Federal Reserve's Annual Report for 2017

These laws also specified that the low reserve tranche amount and the exemption amount would be adjusted each year. By 2007, the former had been increased to $43.9 million and the latter to $9.3 million. By 2019, they had moved up to $124 million and $16 million, respectively.

Finally, the Fed itself steadily reduced the required reserve ratio. In 1948, the required reserve ratio peaked at 26% on net demand deposits and 7.5% on time deposits. It was reduced time and again thereafter. For instance, in 1990, the required reserve ratio on non-transactions accounts was cut from 3% to zero, while in 1992, the requirement on transaction deposits was reduced from 12% to 10%. Finally, in March 2020, the Fed reduced the required reserve ratio to 0%, thereby entirely eliminating the requirement for banks to hold any reserves against their deposits.

CHART 8.18 The Ratio of Bank Reserves at the Fed plus Vault Cash as a Percentage of Bank Deposits, 1945 to 2007

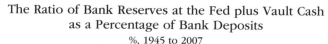

Source: Data from Fed, Flow of Funds, US-Chartered Depository Institutions 1945–2007

Table 8.2 shows every adjustment to the required reserve ratio between 1913 and 2020.

By the 1990s, the Fed had come to view reserves as largely pointless. It explained that forcing banks to hold reserves at the Fed was like a tax on the banking system – a tax that was no longer necessary. The banks concurred wholeheartedly, and lobbied vigorously for the "reserve tax" to be reduced or eliminated altogether.

The Fed pointed out that the government guaranteed bank deposits up to $100,000 per account through the Federal Deposit Insurance Corporation (FDIC); and it argued that these guarantees made old-fashioned bank runs, where frightened depositors all demanded the return of their deposits at once, very unlikely. Moreover, the Fed also emphasized that, in the unlikely event

TABLE 8.2 Changes in the Required Reserve Ratio from 1913 to the Present

A.1. Reserve requirements based on geographic distinction among member banks, 1913–66

	Percent of deposits			
Effective date	Net demand deposits			Time deposits (all classes of banks)
	Central reserve city banks	Reserve city banks	Country banks	
1913–December 23	18	15	12	5
1917–June 21	13	10	7	3
1936–August 16	19.5	15	10.5	4.5
1937–March 1	22.75	17.5	12.25	5.25
May 1	26	20	14	6
1938–April 16	22.75	17.5	12	5
1941–November 1	26	20	14	6
1942–August 20	24	↑	↑	↑
September 14	22			
October 3	20			
1948–February 27	22			
June 11	24	↓	↓	↓
September 24, 16	26	22	16	7.5
1949–May 5, 1	24	21	15	7
June 30, July 1	↑	20	14	6
August 1	↓	20	13	6
August 11, 16	23.5	19.5	12	5
August 18	23	19	↑	↑
August 25	22.5	18.5		
September 1	22	18	↓	↓
1951–January 11, 16	23	29	13	6
January 25, February 1	24	20	14	↑
1953–July 9, 1	22	19	13	↓
1954–June 24, 16	21	19	13	5

(Continued)

TABLE 8.2 *(Continued)*

A.1. Reserve requirements based on geographic distinction among member banks, 1913–66

July 29, August 1	20	18	12	↑
1958–February 27, March 1	19.5	17.5	11.5	
March 20, April 1	19	17	11	
April 17	18.5	17	↑	
April 24	18	16.5		
1960–September 1	17.5	↑	↓	
November 24	17.5		12	
December 1	16.5		↑	
1962–July 28	↑			
October 25, November 1	↓	↓	↓	4

A.2. Reserve requirements based on geographic distinction among member banks and on the level of deposits, 1966–72

	Percent of deposits						
Effective date	Net demand deposits				Time deposits (all classes of banks)		
	Reserve city banks (deposit intervals in millions of dollars)		Country banks (deposit intervals in millions of dollars)		Savings	Other time (deposit intervals in millions of dollars)	
	0–5	More than 5	0–5	More than 5		0–5	More than 5
1966–July 14, 21	16.5	16.5	12	12	4	4	5
September 8, 11	↑	↑	↑	↑	4	4	6
1967–March 2					3.5	3.5	↑
March 16		↓		↓	3	3	
1968–January 11, 18	↓	17	↓	12.5	↑	↑	
1969–April 17	17	17.5	12.5	13			↓
1970–October 1	17	17.5	12.5	13	↓	↓	5

A.3. A graduated reserve requirement schedule for member banks, 1972–80

Percent of deposits

Effective date	Net demand deposits (deposit intervals in millions of dollars)					Time and savings deposits						
							Time (deposit intervals in millions of dollars)					
							0–5, by maturity			More than 5, by maturity		
	0–2	2–10	10–100	100–400	More than 400	Savings	30–179 days	180 days to 4 years	4 years or more	30–179 days	180 days to 4 years	4 years or more
1972–November 9	8	←→	12	16.5	17.5	3	3	3	3	5	5	5
November 16	10	10	12	13	17.5	↕	↕	↕	↕	↕	↕	↕
1973–July 19	10.5	10.5	12.5	13.5	18					6	3	3
1974–December 12	10.5	10.5	12.5	13.5	17.5					↕	↕	↕
1975–February 13	7.5	←→	←→	←→	16.5							
October 30	←→	←→	←→	←→					1			1
1976–January 8	←→	←→	←→	←→	2.5			2.5			2.5	
December 30	7	9.5	11.75	12.75	16.25			2.5			2.5	

(Continued)

TABLE 8.2 *(Continued)*

A.4. Reserve requirements since passage of the Monetary Control Act of 1980

Effective date	Percent	
	Net transaction accounts	Non-transaction accounts
1980–November 13	12	3
1990–December 26	12	0
1992–April 2	10	0
2020–March 26	0	0

Source: "Reserve Requirements: History, Current Practice, and Potential Reform" pp. 587-589. Board of Governors of the Federal Reserve System 1935- and Federal Reserve Board, 1914-1935, "June 1993," Federal Reserve Bulletin (June 1993), Public Domain

that a liquidity crisis did arise, the Fed itself could provide as much liquidity as necessary to resolve the crisis through discounting operations and/or open market operations. Consequently, the Fed posited, there was no longer any justification for imposing a "reserve tax" on the banking system.

These developments, taken together, allowed the commercial banking sector to create credit and to grow its deposit base vastly more than the reserves it set aside as Reserve Balances at the Fed.

Consequently, the effective required reserve ratio declined to such a low level that for all intents and purposes it ceased to limit how much money the banking system could create. Therefore, long before the crisis of 2008 struck, neither the Fed nor the banking sector was constrained in the amount of money it could create.

When the crisis began, Bank Reserves, including vault cash, amounted to only $74 billion, compared with $8.5 trillion of deposits and $11.4 trillion of loans and investments. They may as well have been nonexistent.

Of course, had the banking sector acted prudently, it would have been careful to only create as much credit through extending loans as their customers could realistically afford to repay. The bankers did not act prudently, however. Up through 2007, the banking system created credit on an extraordinary scale with little to no concern for the ability of their customers to repay even the interest on the credit that the banks provided to them so freely.

Notes

1. Irving Fisher, 100% Money, chapter 3. http://fisher-100money.blogspot.com

2. The Fed eliminated the requirement that commercial banks hold reserves against their deposits, effective March 26, 2020. Source: Reserve Requirements, The Fed. https://www.federalreserve.gov/monetarypolicy/reservereq.htm

3. After 2008, when Quantitative Easing had caused Bank Reserves to become superabundant, the Fed changed its operating procedure, as will be described in Chapter 20.

4. Banks began issuing large Certificates of Deposit (CDs) in 1961 to raise funds. These CDs were subject to Reserve Requirements until 1991. Source: "US Monetary Policy and Financial Markets" p. 38, Ann-Marie Meulendyke. Federal Reserve Bank of New York, 1998

5. "Federal Reserve Board Data on OCD Sweep Account Programs," St. Louis Fed. https://research.stlouisfed.org/aggreg/swdata.html; Sweep Accounts, "The wholesale adoption of Sweep programs in 1995," The Fed's Annual Report for 2001, p. 101.

Credit Creation by the Financial Sector

When the music stops, in terms of liquidity, things will be complicated. But as long as the music is playing, you've got to get up and dance. We're still dancing.

Charles Prince, Citigroup CEO, July 9, 2007[1]

The previous chapter described the surge in credit creation by the commercial banks, the corresponding sharp increase in leverage of the banking sector and the regulatory and technical changes that allowed those developments to occur.

This chapter describes the much larger surge in credit extension by the broader financial sector, of which the commercial banks comprise only one part. It documents the rapid rise of the non-bank creditors in the financial sector from the early 1970s and discusses the profound impact their lending had on the US economy as it drove the leverage of the entire economy much higher.

The chapter also addresses the important question concerning the source of the funds that allowed those non-bank lenders to extend so much credit. We will see that the entire financial sector finances the credit it extends in essentially the same way the commercial banks do; that is, when non-bank creditors extend credit, they too create the funds that finance additional credit creation. Just as banks create money (deposits) in a system of fractional reserve banking when they make loans, non-bank creditors in the financial sector create bank deposits and other types of financial sector liabilities that serve to provide the funding for the next round of credit extension.

Creditopia

Between 1970 and 2007, the stock of outstanding credit extended by the financial sector surged by more than 50 times, from $714 billion in 1970 to $38 trillion in 2007. Of the $38 trillion total in 2007, the *private depository institutions* (comprised primarily of US commercial banks, but also of foreign banking offices in the United States, banks in US-affiliated areas and credit unions) accounted for only $11 trillion, or 29%. The remaining $27 trillion was extended by non-bank creditors (see Chart 9.1).

CHART 9.1 Credit Provided by the Entire Financial Sector vs. Credit Provided by Private Depository Institutions, 1945 to 2007

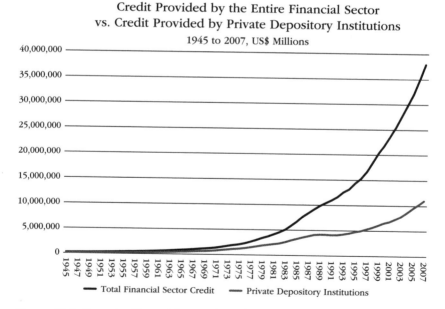

Credit Provided by the Entire Financial Sector
vs. Credit Provided by Private Depository Institutions
1945 to 2007, US$ Millions

— Total Financial Sector Credit   — Private Depository Institutions

Source: Data from the Financial Accounts of the United States 1945–2007, The Fed

Not only did the credit extended by the financial sector grow extraordinarily rapidly, it also expanded relative to the size of the US economy. Total credit provided by the financial sector was 102% of GDP in 1945. It rose to 117% in 1970 and to 130% in 1980. From that point, there was a marked acceleration. By 1990, financial sector credit to GDP hit 175%. In 2000, the ratio was 213% and by 2007, it had jumped to 263% of GDP (see Chart 9.2).

This sharp surge in financial sector credit fueled economic growth in the United States. Therefore, this rise in the ratio of financial sector credit to GDP is even more striking than it appears at first glance. That is because the credit growth made the economy grow faster than it otherwise would have. In other words, the denominator in this ratio (GDP) was made larger by the increase in the numerator (financial sector credit).

CHART 9.2 Total Financial Sector Credit as a Percentage of GDP, 1945 to 2007

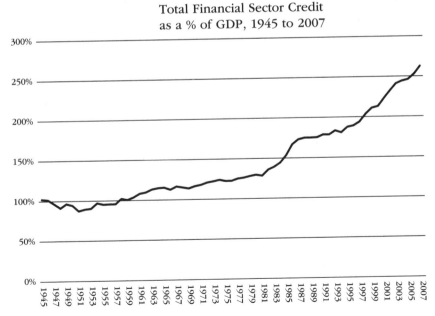

Source: Data from the Financial Accounts of the United States, 1945–2007, The Fed

Had financial sector credit growth not made the economy expand, the increase in this ratio would have been far larger.

The growth in the annual amount of credit extended by the financial sector each year has been truly astonishing. Total credit provided by the financial sector increased by $92 billion in 1970. By 1986, the annual increase had climbed to nearly $1 trillion. It topped $2 trillion in 2003. And, in 2007, it hit $3 trillion. That surge in financial sector credit played a leading role in blowing the US economy into the economic bubble that popped in 2008. See Chart 9.3.

As great as the increase in private depository institutions lending was (as described in the previous chapter), it was lending by non-bank creditors within the financial sector, rather than lending by the private depository institutions, that was primarily responsible for the explosion of total financial sector credit.

CHART 9.3 Total Financial Sector Credit, Annual $ Change, 1946 to 2007

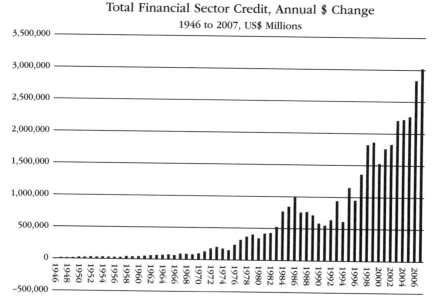

Source: Data from the Financial Accounts of the United States, 1945–2007, The Fed

Chart 9.4 shows that the ratio of credit provided by the private depository institutions to GDP changed relatively little between 1945 to 2007, ranging between 51% and 79%. The credit provided by the rest of the financial sector, on the other hand, rose steadily from 39% of GDP in 1945 to 54% of GDP in 1975, from which point it then accelerated dramatically, reaching 186% of GDP in 2007.

In 1970, private depository institutions provided $55 billion of new credit out of the $92 billion of new credit the financial sector provided in total that year, whereas in 2007, they provided just $809 billion of new credit out of a total of $3 trillion. This can be seen in Chart 9.5, which shows the annual increase in credit provided by the private depository institutions compared with the annual increase in credit provided by the entire financial sector. That chart clearly illustrates the diminishing role played by the private depository institutions in providing

CHART 9.4 **Credit Provided by Private Depository Institutions vs. the Rest of the Financial Sector as a Percentage of GDP, 1945 to 2007**

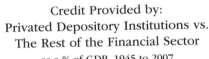

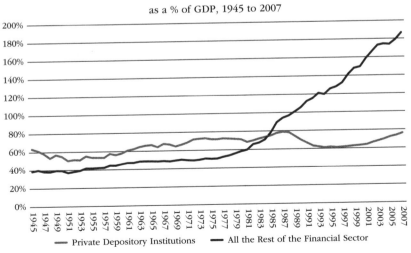

Source: Data from the Financial Accounts of the United States, 1945–2007, The Fed

CHART 9.5 The Annual Dollar Change in Total Financial Sector Credit vs. Private Depository Institution Credit, 1970 to 2007

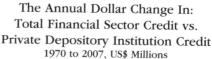

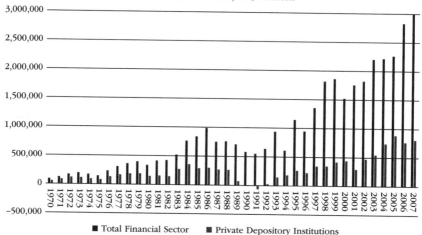

Source: Data from the Financial Accounts of the United States, 1970–2007, The Fed

credit in comparison with the non-bank lenders. Succeeding paragraphs will show that the extraordinary growth of non-bank lenders transformed the nature of the US financial system.

The private depository institutions' market share of total financial credit had ranged between 56% and 62% from the end of World War II to 1970. However, after 1972, it began to decline steadily, falling to just 29% by 2007. The market share of the rest of the financial sector, the non-bank creditors, surged from 40% in 1972 to 71% in 2007, as shown in Chart 9.6.

The Non-Bank Financial Sector Creditors

So, what are the non-bank institutions that make up the financial sector along with the private depository institutions?

CHART 9.6 Market Share of Credit Extended by the Financial Sector: Private Depository Institutions vs. the Rest of the Financial Sector, Percentage of Total, 1945 to 2007

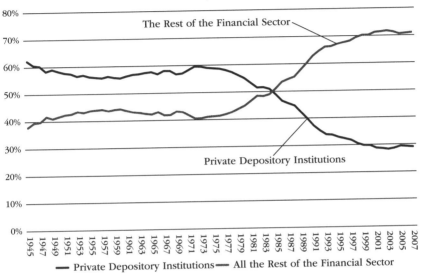

Market Share of Credit Extended by the Financial Sector: Private Depository Institutions vs. The Rest of the Financial Sector % of Total, 1945 to 2007

Source: Data from the Financial Accounts of the United States, 1945–2007, The Fed

The financial sector is comprised of 18 types of lenders. They are shown in Table 9.1, listed according to the amount of credit provided by each in 2007.

Private depository institutions are the largest type of lender in the financial sector. They accounted for $11 trillion of the $38 trillion of credit that had been extended by the financial sector in 2007.

The *government-sponsored enterprises* and *GSE-backed mortgage pools* came next with $7.3 trillion of credit extended, followed by *asset-backed securities issuers* with $4.4 trillion and *life insurance companies* with $2.9 trillion.

The growth in these four largest financial sector creditors from 1945 to 2007 is shown in Chart 9.7 and Chart 9.8. Those charts

TABLE 9.1 The Financial Sector: 2007

Credit Provided by the Financial Sector: 2007	
	US$ Millions
Private Depository Institutions	11,012,462
GSEs & GSE-Backed Mortgage Pools	7,293,959
ABS Issuers	4,394,258
Life insurance companies	2,864,421
Mutual funds	2,100,121
Money market funds	1,992,717
Finance companies	1,822,058
Security brokers and dealers	1,128,635
Federal government retirement funds	1,058,184
Property–casualty insurance companies	903,235
State & local Govt. employee defined benefit retirement funds	869,657
Private pension funds	767,985
The Fed	740,611
Funding corporations	495,690
REITS	246,474
Closed-end funds	167,173
Holding companies	59,894
Exchange-traded funds	34,692
Total	37,952,226

Source: Data from the Financial Accounts of the United States, The Fed

also include two other lines: the first shows the increase in the amount of credit extended by the Fed; the second the increase in the amount of credit extended by all the rest of the financial sector (i.e., the 13 other types of financial sector creditors, combined).

The Culprits

The US economy was profoundly impacted by the credit extended by the government-sponsored enterprises (GSEs) from the early 1970s and by the credit extended by the issuers of asset-backed securities from the mid-1980s.

CHART 9.7 A Breakdown of the Market Share of Financial Sector Creditors

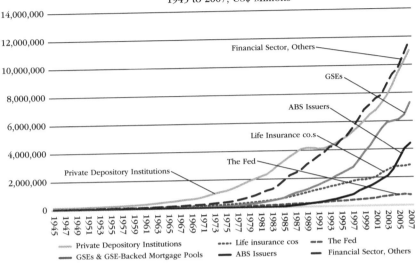

A Breakdown of the Market Share of
Financial Sector Creditors
1945 to 2007, US$ Millions

Source: Data from the Financial Accounts of the United States, 1945–2007, The Fed

The credit provided by the GSEs, primarily Fannie Mae and Freddie Mac, rose from only 3% of total financial sector credit in 1969 to 22% in 2002. At its peak, in 2007, GSE credit expanded by $862 billion in that one year alone. By the end of 2007, total GSE-related credit outstanding reached $7.3 trillion. See Charts 9.7 and 9.8, which show the breakdown of the market share of the financial sector creditors in dollars and percent terms.

The credit that Fannie and Freddie pumped into the economy by acquiring or guaranteeing mortgages drove up property prices and was instrumental in creating the US property bubble that blew apart in 2008.

The issuers of asset-backed securities were equally culpable. Asset-backed securities are made up of a pool of assets such as mortgages, credit cards, auto loans, equipment leases, corporate loans, and trade receivables. This segment of the financial sector

CHART 9.8 A Breakdown of the Market Share of Financial Sector
Creditors: Percentage of Financial Sector Credit, 1945 to 2007

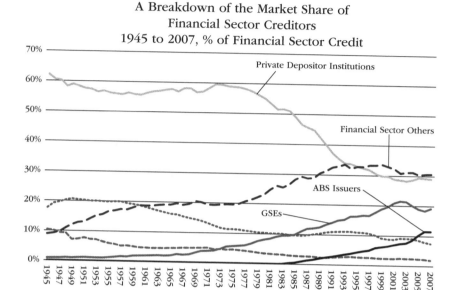

Source: Data from the Financial Accounts of the United States, 1945–2007,
The Fed

only began extending credit on a meaningful scale in 1983.
By 2007, they had provided $4.4 trillion of credit or 12% of all
the credit extended by the financial sector. Their annual credit
growth peaked at roughly $750 billion in both 2005 and 2006.
The money they lent played a leading role in inflating the credit
bubble that developed in the United States in the years leading
up to 2008.

Chart 9.9 compares the annual credit growth of the private
depository institutions, the GSEs and the issuers of asset-backed
securities (ABS) each year between 1970 to 2007. It clearly illustrates the rapid rise of the GSEs and the ABS issuers as credit
providers, particularly after the mid-1980s.

Most strikingly, the growth in credit extended by the GSEs
exceeded that of the private depository institutions during 12 out

CHART 9.9 The Annual Dollar Change in Credit Extended by Private Depository Institutions, GSEs & ABS Issuers, 1970 to 2007

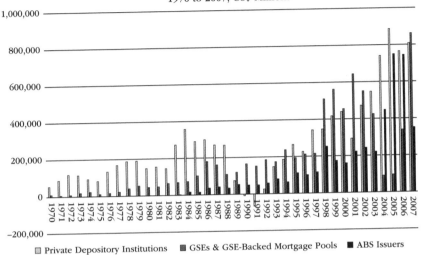

The Annual Dollar Change in Credit Extended by
Private Depository Institutions, GSEs & ABS Issuers
1970 to 2007, US$ Millions

☐ Private Depository Institutions ■ GSEs & GSE-Backed Mortgage Pools ■ ABS Issuers

Source: Data from the Financial Accounts of the United States, 1970–2007, The Fed

of the 19 years between 1989 and 2007. By 2007, the GSEs and the issuers of asset-backed securities, combined, had extended $11.7 trillion of credit in total, compared with only $11.0 trillion for the commercial banks.

Finally, the rest of the financial sector combined (the financial sector excluding the private depository institutions, the GSEs, ABS-issuers, life insurance companies, and the Fed) had $11.6 trillion in total credit outstanding in 2007. That amounted to 31% of all financial sector credit, up from only 9% in 1945.

The three largest among these in 2007 were mutual funds, money market funds and finance companies with $2.1 trillion, $2.0 trillion, and $1.8 of credit extended, respectively. See Chart 9.10.

CHART 9.10 The Largest of the Remaining Financial Sector Creditors (those with more than $750 billion credit extended in 2007), 1945 to 2007

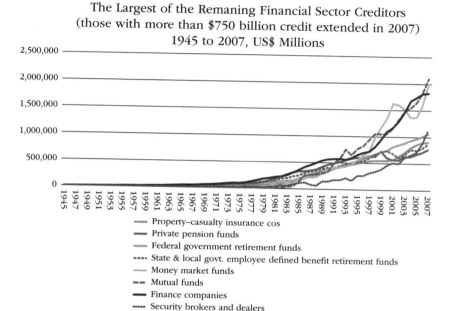

The Largest of the Remaning Financial Sector Creditors
(those with more than $750 billion credit extended in 2007)
1945 to 2007, US$ Millions

- Property–casualty insurance cos
- Private pension funds
- Federal government retirement funds
- State & local govt. employee defined benefit retirement funds
- Money market funds
- Mutual funds
- Finance companies
- Security brokers and dealers

These non-bank credit providers injected credit into the financial markets helping to further inflate the asset price bubbles there.

Funding Through Credit Creation

The extension of $27 trillion of credit by non-bank financial sector lenders fueled US economic growth and ultimately blew the economy into a bubble. This process will be described in greater detail in Chapter 11.

The sum of $27 trillion is an extraordinarily large amount of money. It is not possible to fully understand the growth and evolution of the US economy during recent decades without understanding where the money came from that financed the extension of so much credit.

The appendix to this chapter explains in detail (perhaps too much detail for the general reader) how the non-bank financial sector creditors financed the credit they extended. In short, it shows that the non-bank creditors in the financial sector create credit when they extend loans, just as the banks do.

Credit Without Reserves

As the non-bank creditors came to dominate the financial sector, debt rather than deposits began to supply the majority of funding that financed financial sector lending. Chart 9.11 shows that debt surpassed deposits as the largest source of financial sector funding in 1994. By 2007, financial sector debt was twice as large as the level of deposits it held.

The commercial banks, which relied on deposits, were required to hold liquidity reserves at the Fed. Institutions that financed themselves by issuing debt instruments were not.

CHART 9.11 The Financial Sector Funding: Deposits vs. Debt, 1945 to 2007

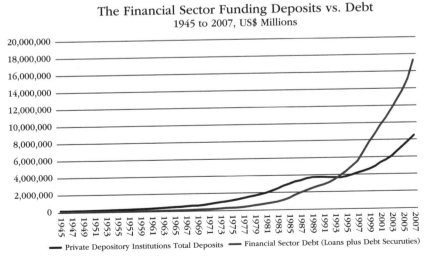

Source: Data from the Financial Accounts of the United States, 1945–2007, The Fed

Therefore, as the financial sector grew less and less dependent on deposits, the overall level of liquidity reserves it held relative to the amount of credit it extended shrank. Chart 9.12 shows that whereas the ratio of reserves held at the Fed as a percentage of total financial sector credit was above 8% in the late 1940s; by 2007 it had declined to just 0.04%.

As the crisis of 2008 approached, just as there was no gold to back the money the Fed created, there were effectively no liquidity reserves to back the credit that the financial sector had created.

Given that liquidity reserve requirements had for all intents and purposes been abolished, the only constraint on how much credit the financial sector could create was the ability of the debtors to pay interest on the money they had borrowed; and

CHART 9.12 **Bank Reserves at the Fed as a Percentage of Total Financial Sector Credit, 1945 to 2007**

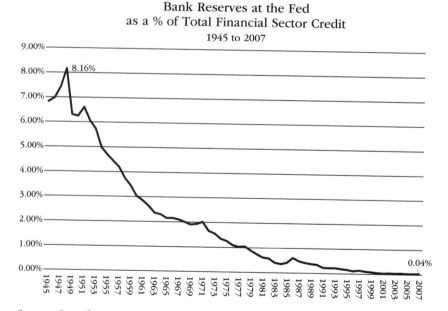

Bank Reserves at the Fed
as a % of Total Financial Sector Credit
1945 to 2007

Source: Data from the Financial Accounts of the United States 1945–2007, The Fed; and the Federal Reserve's Annual Report for 2017

that was a constraint that the chief executives of America's financial institutions chose to ignore.

Appendix

Where Does the Money Come From?

Only the private depository institutions can accept deposits. The non-bank financial sector creditors cannot. The credit extended by the financial sector far exceeds the amount of deposits held by the private depository institutions, however. Chart 9.13 shows that by 2007 the financial sector had extended $38 trillion of credit, but that the private depository institutions held only $8.5 trillion of deposits.

CHART 9.13 Total Credit Provided by the Financial Sector vs. Total Deposits of Private Depository Institutions, 1945 to 2007

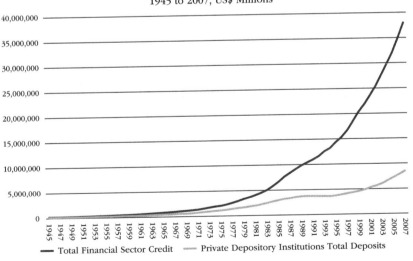

Source: Data from the Financial Accounts of the United States, 1945–2007, The Fed

Where, then, does the financial sector obtain the rest of the money it extends as credit? The answer is that it creates that money through the process of extending credit, just as the commercial banks create money (i.e., deposits) and credit when they make loans. The process is very similar to money creation by banks in a system of fractional reserve banking, but it is more complex due to the greater number of financial intermediaries involved.

The next few pages show how bank deposits were transformed into other types of financial sector liabilities as the US financial system grew and evolved from World War II to 2007. They also illustrate how those new liabilities funded the creation of still more credit.

Just Like the Banks

As explained in the previous chapter, when commercial banks extend credit, either by making a loan or by acquiring a debt security, they create deposits. Loans and investments appear as assets on the banks' balance sheets, while deposits are recorded as liabilities.

Those deposits are considered to be one type of money and they are counted as part of the *money supply*. Bank deposits make up by far the largest part of the *monetary aggregate*, M2.

When non-bank creditors within the financial sector extend credit by making a loan or an investment that also sets off a process that results, not only in credit creation, but also in the creation of liabilities that finance additional credit creation. The extension of credit creates new assets and new liabilities within the broader financial sector. If the credit is extended as a loan, that loan is recorded as an asset on the balance sheet of the entity that extended the loan. Similarly, if the credit is extended through the acquisition of a bond, then the bond is recorded as an asset on that institution's balance sheet.

What the recipient of the loan or the seller of the bond ultimately does with the money they receive determines the kind of liability that is created within the financial sector. If they deposit the money into a commercial bank and leave it there, it becomes a deposit liability of a commercial bank and, consequently, part of the money supply. On the other hand, if they use the money to buy a new bond issued by Fannie Mae[2], for instance, that money makes it possible for Fannie to obtain additional financing; and that financing is recorded as a debt liability on the balance sheet of Fannie Mae. It adds to the total liabilities of the financial sector, but it does not increase the money supply, since, unlike commercial bank deposits, the liabilities of the GSEs are not considered to be "money" and are not included as part of the monetary aggregates. Nevertheless, the liability that has been created on Fannie Mae's balance sheet enables Fannie Mae to extend more credit.

Therefore, the key to understanding how the broader financial sector creates credit, just as commercial banks do, is to look at the liabilities of the non-bank creditors in the same way that we look at bank deposits. Both allow the creation of more credit. The only difference is that bank deposits are considered to be *money* and part of the money supply, whereas the liabilities of non-bank entities within the broader financial sector are not considered to be money or part of the money supply.

The Deposits Escaped from the Banks

Until the early 1970s, most individuals and businesses held the greatest part of their savings as deposits in banks or credit unions. There were few other alternatives. After 1970, however, the financial sector began offering individuals and businesses alternative investment vehicles, such as mutual funds and money market funds. From that point, money began leaking out of commercial bank deposit accounts and moving into other kinds of products, often in search of higher returns.

Afterwards, what had been a relatively straightforward process in which the private depository institutions created money and credit through the system of fractional reserve banking became more complicated.

Bank deposits gradually ceased to be the most important source of funding for the financial sector because depositors took their money out of banks and invested it in the other investment products that non-bank financial institutions began to offer them.

The Creation of Non-deposit Liabilities by Commercial Banks

The way the financial sector created money and credit evolved during the second half of the twentieth century. To understand this evolution, let's first look at the commercial banks and the other private depository institutions to see how their pattern of extending credit changed. We will find that over this period the financial sector began lending relatively less to non-financial sector end users of the funds, such as the federal government and state and local governments, and relatively more to other entities within the financial sector, thereby providing them with funds they could use to extend credit themselves.

At the end of World War II, investments in US government bonds accounted for a full 72% of all the credit extended by the private depository institutions. Loans made up only 22% of their total portfolio of loans and investments. The composition of these institutions' portfolios changed very rapidly after the war, however. By the early 1960s, the relative proportion of government bonds and loans in the private depository institutions' portfolios had been reversed, with the former falling to below 20% of the total and the latter rising above 70%.

Between the mid-1960s and 2007, loans continued to account for 70% to 80% of these institutions' total assets. Their holdings of government securities continued to decline, however. Meanwhile, their investments in municipal securities, GSE debt and corporate bonds grew. These changes are shown in Chart 9.14.

The changes in the composition of the private depository institutions' investment portfolio can be seen much more clearly in Chart 9.15, which presents the breakdown of the debt securities they owned between 1945 and 2007.

CHART 9.14 A Breakdown of the Private Depository Institutions' Total Loans and Investments, Percentage of Total, 1945 to 2007

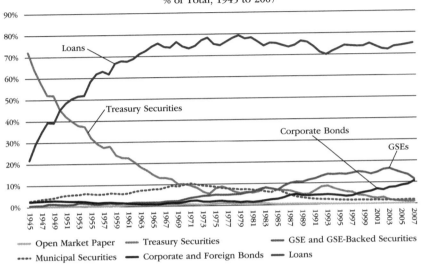

A Breakdown of the Private Depository Institutions' Total Loans and Investments
% of Total, 1945 to 2007

Source: Data from the Financial Accounts of the United States, 1945–2007, The Fed

There it can be seen that Treasury securities, which accounted for 92% of all the debt securities owned by these institutions in 1945, had fallen to just 4% of the total by 2007. From the end of the war to the mid-1970s, the private depository institutions' holdings of municipal securities (bonds sold by state and local governments) rose rapidly and partially offset the decline in the holdings of Treasury securities. During the first half of the 1970s, these institutions held more municipal securities than any of the other types of debt securities.

After the mid-1970s, however, investments in municipal securities declined significantly relative to the size of the entire portfolio of debt securities. The private depository institutions' investments in GSE debt accelerated from the late 1960s and became the largest type of debt security held by private depository institutions from the mid-1980s. Next, the private depository

CHART 9.15 A Breakdown of the Debt Securities Owned by the Private Depository Institutions, Percentage of Total, 1945 to 2007

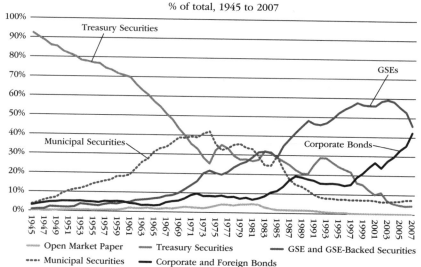

Source: Data from the Financial Accounts of the United States, 1945–2007, The Fed

institutions' investments in corporate bonds grew rapidly beginning in the early 1980s.

By 2007, GSE securities plus corporate bonds accounted for 88% of all the debt securities held by the private depository institutions, whereas federal government and municipal securities, combined, made up only 11% of the total.

That year the private depository institutions held $1.3 trillion of GSE-related debt and $1.2 trillion of corporate bonds, versus just $200 billion of municipal securities and $120 billion of Treasury securities, as shown in Chart 9.16.

This shift in the composition of the private depository institutions' investment portfolio away from federal and state and local government debt and into debt issued by the GSEs and by corporations is significant because it brought about a fundamental change in the way the financial sector financed the credit it created.

CHART 9.16 A Breakdown of the Debt Securities Owned by the Private Depository Institutions, 1945 to 2007

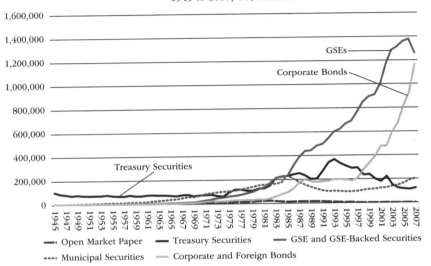

A Breakdown of the Debt Securities Owned by
the Private Depository Instituions
1945 to 2007, US$ Millions

Source: Data from the Financial Accounts of the United States, 1945–2007, The Fed

When the federal government or state and local governments borrowed from the private depository institutions by issuing bonds, that borrowing served only to finance government expenditure. On the other hand, when the GSEs issued bonds, their borrowing served to finance new lending by the GSEs themselves, which allowed credit creation to occur outside the commercial banks and within the broader financial sector.

The same is also true for much of the private depository institutions' holdings of corporate bonds, because a large portion of those corporate bonds were bonds that had been issued by borrowers from within the financial sector, including bonds issued by the issuers of asset-backed securities. At the end of 2007, the total amount of domestic corporate bonds outstanding amounted to $9.4 trillion. Of that amount, $5.9 trillion (or 63%) had been issued by financial sector entities, including

$3.6 trillion of corporate bonds that had been issued by the issuers of asset-backed securities.

When the private depository institutions invested in corporate bonds issued by other financial sector institutions, that provided funds that allowed those institutions themselves to extend credit, permitting credit creation to occur outside the private depository institutions and within the broader financial sector.

Stepping back, then, and reconsidering the process of money and credit creation by the commercial banks and other private depository institutions through the system of fractional reserve banking, we can see that the commercial banks invested some of the money (deposits) they created into debt instruments issued by the GSEs, the issuers of asset-backed securities and other non-bank financial sector institutions. That investment provided funding that allowed those entities to extend additional credit. In other words, from the late 1960s, a significant amount of the deposits that were being created by the commercial banks began to be invested by the commercial banks into debt securities issued by non-bank financial sector institutions rather than being extended as traditional bank loans.

The commercial banks were not required to hold liquidity reserves against the debt securities they bought, whereas they were required to hold reserves against their customers' deposits. Moreover, the GSEs, the ABS issuers, and the other non-bank financial sector institutions were not required to hold any liquidity reserves against the liabilities on their balance sheets. The net result was more credit creation and fewer liquidity reserves throughout the entire financial sector and throughout the economy more broadly.

The Creation of Financial Sector Liabilities (and Credit) by the Non-bank Financial Sector Creditors

The section above focused on the evolution of the composition of the private depository institutions' investment portfolio and the impact that change had on the way the financial sector creates credit. It explained that as the private depository institutions increased their holdings of bonds issued by the GSEs, the issuers of asset-backed securities and other non-bank financial sector institutions, they supplied funds that allowed those entities to extend additional credit. However, the private depository institutions provided only a portion of the funding the broader financial sector required.

In 2007, private depository institutions provided less than 20% of the GSEs' total funding and less than 30% of the funding of the ABS issuers. The rest of the financing came from other sources. Some of that funding came from abroad, as will be explained in the next chapter. The majority, however, was derived from credit that the broader financial sector actually created itself.

Up through the late 1960s, most Americans kept the greatest part of their savings in bank deposits. The financial sector was tightly regulated, and few other investment vehicles were widely accessible to the general public.

From the early 1970s, however, new investment channels such as mutual funds and money market funds emerged that offered different ways for the public to save and invest. Money that would have traditionally stayed in commercial banks as deposits began to flow out of the banks and onto the balance sheets of other credit providers within the financial sector.

Expressed differently, deposits that had been created by commercial banks did not all remain as deposits within the banks or even as other kinds of non-deposit liabilities at the banks. Instead, those deposits began to be withdrawn from the banks and placed with other financial sector institutions where they were recorded on the balance sheet not as deposits, but as debt securities or mutual fund shares. Although the deposits of the financial sector continued to grow, the non-deposit liabilities grew much more.

First consider the role of mutual funds. When banks extended loans, those loans still created deposits when the recipients of the loans deposited the money they had borrowed into their bank accounts. That money did not necessarily stay in the banking system as deposits for long, however. For instance, some of the deposits were withdrawn from the banks and invested in mutual funds instead.

At that point, the mutual funds had the money that the banking system had created by extending credit; and the mutual funds were free to invest that money in the stock market, in government bonds, in corporate bonds, in bonds issued by Fannie Mae and Freddie Mac[3] or elsewhere. In other words, when deposits left the banks to be invested in mutual funds, the money the commercial banks had created ceased to be bank deposits. Instead, it was transformed into other kinds of liabilities, both equities and debt securities.

Next, look at the role played by the GSEs. The GSEs became important creditors from the early 1970s, and, in the process, they began to create credit. In most instances, the GSEs did not originate mortgage loans themselves. Instead, commercial banks or mortgage companies, like Countrywide, would extend a mortgage loan to a home buyer. The mortgage originator would keep an origination fee and then either sell the mortgage to Fannie Mae or Freddie Mac, or, more often, obtain a guarantee for that loan from Fannie or Freddie (which the GSEs provided for a fee) and then sell the GSE-guaranteed mortgage to some other investor.

The credit instrument created by the bank, i.e., the mortgage, would move from the bank's balance sheet to the balance sheet of the investor that had acquired the mortgage, thereby reducing the size of the bank's assets and, consequently, the amount of capital the bank was required to hold against its assets. This permitted an expansion of leverage throughout the financial system since the GSEs and the other non-bank investors were not required to hold any liquidity reserves against the bonds they issued to finance their mortgage purchases, and also because the GSEs had much lower capital adequacy requirements than the banks.

Meanwhile, when the individual who took out the mortgage deposited the money he received from the mortgage into his bank account (and later transferred it to the bank account of the person from whom he would acquire his new home) that deposit enabled the banking system to extend still more loans or to invest in additional debt securities. The process of money and credit creation through the banking system not only continued, but it was also facilitated and accelerated by the intermediation of Fannie Mae, which could raise funds by selling bonds (carrying an implicit government guarantee) without having to maintain any liquidity reserves against those bonds.

Some of the deposits that were created in this process were withdrawn from the banks and used to buy the bonds that Fannie and Freddie sold to finance their rapidly growing investment portfolio which was made up of mortgages and of the mortgage pools that they had guaranteed.

As Fannie and Freddie grew by selling ever larger amounts of bonds, they acquired or guaranteed an ever-larger portfolio of mortgages. The effect was to push up property prices and to increase the overall leverage of the financial sector and the economy in general.

Later, the issuers of asset-backed securities followed a similar strategy as the GSEs, producing a similar effect. Many, and probably the majority, of the issuers of asset-backed securities, were in reality *special purpose vehicles* (SPVs) created by the largest commercial banks and the large investment banks, such as Citigroup and Lehman Brothers. The banks and investment banks originated mortgages and consumer credit and then repackaged that debt into securities with various degrees of risk, which they sold to their own SPVs and other investors, after keeping an origination fee. Even though in most cases the banks and investment banks remained the true owners of the SPVs, they were not required to hold liquidity reserves against those SPVs' liabilities.

Moreover, in many cases, the banks took their customers' deposits and invested them in the SPVs they controlled, reducing the overall level of deposits in the banking system, and minimizing the level of liquidity reserves the banks were required to hold against such deposits. The SPVs then used the funds received in this way to extend still more credit.

Again, the original extension of credit by the banks set off the process of money and credit creation, with the ABS issuers acting as intermediaries to make it appear that the risky assets were not on the books of the banks. The more credit that was extended in this way, the more deposits (money) flooded back into the banks, financing still more lending. In this way, leverage increased throughout the economy and drove asset prices higher.

Notes

1. David Wighton, "What we have learned 10 years after Chuck Prince told Wall St to keep dancing," Financial News. https://www.fnlondon.com/articles/chuck-princes-dancing-quote-what-we-have-learned-10-years-on-20170714
2. The Federal National Mortgage Association, a US government-sponsored enterprise, is commonly known as Fannie Mae.
3. The Federal Home Loan Mortgage Corporation is a US government-sponsored enterprise commonly known as Freddie Mac.

CHAPTER 10

Credit Creation by Foreign Central Banks

I don't know whether, to what extent you can attribute anything to anything. . . .

Alan Greenspan, in a conversation with the author on
January 18, 2017

One of the most extraordinary failures of the economics profession in the twenty-first century has been its inability to understand that foreign central banks have played a leading role in destabilizing the US economy by injecting trillions of dollars of central bank credit into the United States during recent decades. By 2007, foreign central banks had financed approximately 8% of all US debt and had injected nearly six times more credit into the United States than the Fed had.

The surge in foreign central bank money into the United States after 1997 was a major contributing factor in the creation of the NASDAQ bubble in 1999. The even larger inflows between 2004 and 2007 caused the Fed to lose control over US interest rates and made it impossible for the US central bank to prevent the property bubble that wreaked havoc around the world when it imploded in 2008. This chapter describes credit creation by foreign central banks and the extraordinary impact that that credit has had on the United States.

The Financial Sector Is Not Alone

The financial sector is not alone in providing credit to American borrowers. The non-financial sector and the "rest of the world" are also credit providers. Chart 10.1 shows that while by 2007 the financial sector had extended $38 trillion of credit, the rest of the world had extended an additional $7.3 trillion (up from just $3 billion in 1945) and the non-financial sector had extended $7.1 trillion (up from only $127 billion in 1945).

Chart 10.2 shows the credit extended by each of these sectors as a percentage of GDP. The surge in the financial sector's credit, which was discussed in the previous chapter, is the most striking. It leapt from 102% of GDP in 1945 to 263% in 2007. The non-financial sector is the least interesting. Relative to GDP, the credit provided by that sector changed little, moving only

CHART 10.1 Credit Extended by Financial Sector, Rest of the World, & Non-financial Sector, 1945 to 2007

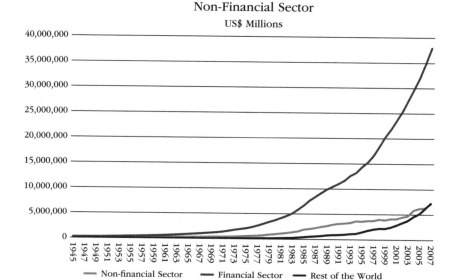

Source: Data from the Financial Accounts of the United States, 1945–2007, The Fed

CHART 10.2 Credit Extended by Financial Sector, the Rest of the World, & Non-financial Sector as a Percentage of GDP, 1945 to 2007

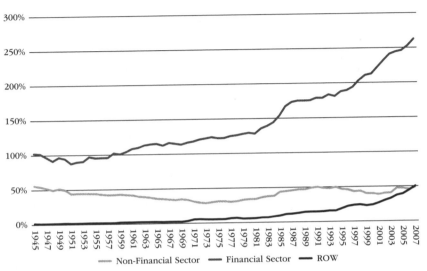

Credit Extended by Financial Sector, The Rest of The World & Non-Financial Sector as a % of GDP

Source: Data from the Financial Accounts of the United States, 1945–2007, The Fed

from 56% of GDP in 1945 to 49% in 2007. The change in the amount of credit provided by the rest of the world is noteworthy, however. It increased from 1% of GDP in 1945 to 50% of GDP by 2007, and accounted for 14% of all credit in the United States that year. The following paragraphs will show that of the $7.3 trillion of credit extended to the United States by the rest of the world, approximately $4.3 trillion or 60% of that credit was extended by foreign central banks.

The substantial increase in credit injected into the US economy from abroad had a powerful influence on the US economy and financial markets. That is the subject of this chapter. First, however, let's look quickly at the details of lending by the non-financial sector.

The creditors from the domestic non-financial sector are households, state and local governments, the federal government,

CHART 10.3 The Non-financial Sector Creditors as a Percentage of GDP, 1945 to 2007

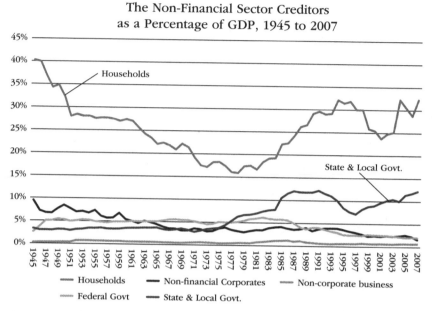

Source: Data from the Financial Accounts of the United States, 1945–2007, The Fed

non-financial corporations and non-corporate businesses. Chart 10.3 shows the amount of credit they extended relative to GDP between 1945 and 2007. As developments here were not particularly interesting, no more will be written about the credit provided by the non-financial sector.

The Rest of the World

The emergence of "the rest of the world" as a major source of credit to American borrowers, on the other hand, powerfully influenced the evolution of the US economy during the years following the breakdown of the Bretton Woods system. In fact, foreign credit played a leading part in inflating the NASDAQ bubble in the late 1990s and ultimately caused the Fed to lose control over US interest rates and, therefore, over the US economy during the years leading up to the crisis of 2008.

The rest of this chapter will show that the majority of the credit entering the United States from abroad between 1970 and 2007 was created by foreign central banks. It will show that foreign central banks created the equivalent of trillions of dollars, used that new money to acquire US dollars in order to hold down the value of their own currencies and then invested those dollars into dollar-denominated assets. It is impossible to understand the history of the US economy or the global economy during recent decades without understanding the impact produced by the credit created by central banks outside the United States. This story, like so many others in this book, becomes most interesting when money ceased to be backed by gold.

Trade Deficits and Capital Flows

When the Bretton Woods system collapsed in 1971, all currencies ceased to be backed by gold, not only the US dollar. Thereafter, every central bank was free to create as much of its own currency as it pleased, just as the Fed was free to create as many dollars as it pleased. Not surprisingly, inflation rose sharply in the United States and globally during the 1970s. What did come as a surprise, however, is that trade between nations ceased to balance. Most strikingly, the United States, by far the world's largest economy, began running large and persistent trade deficits from the early 1980s. Even more astonishingly, the central banks of the trade surplus countries began creating money and lending it to the United States so that the US could continue buying goods from their countries. The following paragraphs explain how that process worked.

Chart 10.4 shows that the US Current Account was more or less in balance between 1950 up until the breakdown of Bretton Woods system in the early 1970s. Then this began to change. The truly radical break from the past only began during the early 1980s, however, when the US began running very large

CHART 10.4 US Current Account Balance, 1950 to 2007

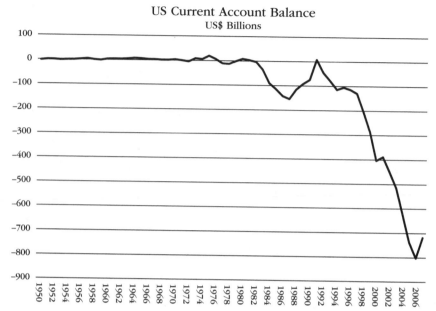

Source: Data from US Current Account Balance 1950–2007, St Louis Fed

trade deficits for the first time. By 1987, the US Current Account deficit had reached 3.3% of US GDP. By 2006, it had grown to 6% of US GDP or to more than $800 billion. These were trade deficits on a scale the world had never before encountered.

The Balance of Payments

Every country's balance of payments must balance, just as every family's accounts must balance. If a family spends more than it earns, it must make up the difference either by borrowing or by selling things to cover the shortfall. Similarly, when a country runs a current account deficit, it must borrow from abroad or sell its assets to foreign investors. Such transactions appear as a surplus on the country's Financial and Capital Accounts.

Chart 10.5 shows that the surplus on the US Financial and Capital Accounts is the mirror image of the US Current Account deficit.

CHART 10.5 Mirror Image: The US Current Account = The Financial Account and the Capital Account, 1960 to 2007

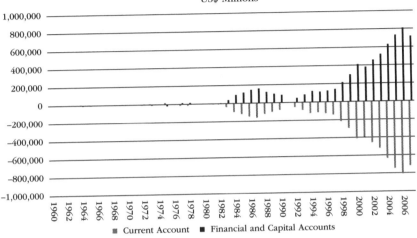

Mirror Image
The Current Account = The Financial and Capital Accounts
US$ Millions

■ Current Account ■ Financial and Capital Accounts

Source: Data from U.S. International Trade in Goods and Service, U.S. Bureau of Economic Analysis

In other words, the capital inflows into the United States reflected on the Financial and Capital Accounts finance the country's Current Account deficit.

The cumulative Current Account deficit for the United States from 1970 to 2007 amounted to $6.5 trillion, as shown in Chart 10.6. The cumulative surplus on its Financial and Capital Accounts combined also amounted to $6.5 trillion.

Had the Bretton Woods system lasted, it would not have been possible for other countries to provide $6.5 trillion in capital to finance the US Current Account deficit during those years. The rest of the world did not have $6.5 trillion worth of gold, far from it. After only a few years of lending money to the United States, the countries in the rest of the world would have run out of gold. That would have made it impossible for the US Current Account deficit to persist.

CHART 10.6 The Cumulative US Current Account Deficit, 1950 to 2007

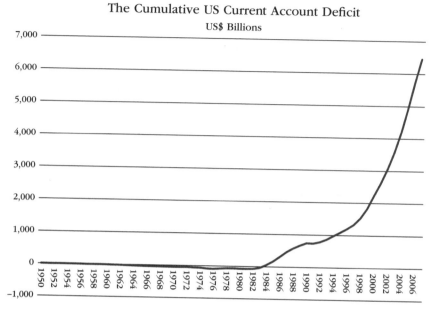

The Cumulative US Current Account Deficit

US$ Billions

Source: Data from Cumulative US Current Account Deficit from 1950 to 2007, U.S.Bureau Of Economic Analysis

But the Bretton Woods system had fallen apart in 1971. Countries and central banks were no longer constrained by the amount of gold they owned. The rules of the game had changed completely. Other countries were able to lend the United States $6.5 trillion between 1970 and 2007 because their central banks were free to create as much money as they desired; and they chose to create enough new money to finance the United States' enormous trade deficit.

This can be seen by the growth in the total foreign exchange reserves of the world, which reflects how much money central banks created for the purpose of acquiring the currencies of other countries. Chart 10.7 shows the total amount of foreign exchange reserves held by all the world's central banks from 1950 to 2007.

When a central bank acquires the currency of another country, it is classified as foreign exchange reserves on the asset side

CHART 10.7 Total Foreign Exchange Reserves, 1950 to 2007

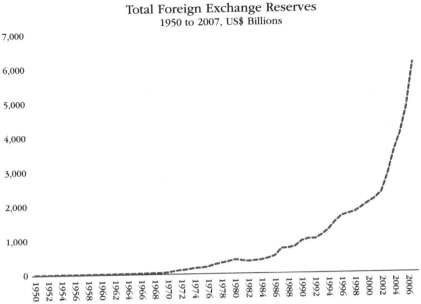

Total Foreign Exchange Reserves
1950 to 2007, US$ Billions

Source: Data from the International Monetary Fund, Total Foreign Exchange Reserves: 1950 to 2007

of that central bank's balance sheet. Central banks acquire the currencies of other countries by creating money, just as the Fed acquires US government securities by creating money. Therefore, the total level of foreign exchange reserves in the world reveals how much money has been created for the purpose of acquiring the currencies of other countries. As shown in Chart 10.7, by 2007 central banks had created the equivalent of $6.1 trillion for this purpose, whereas in 1970, the year before the Bretton Woods system broke down, total foreign exchange reserves amounted to only $56 billion. Of course, only the Fed can create dollars. The other central banks can only create their own currencies. But once other central banks have created their own currencies, they can use that currency to buy the currencies of other countries; and the currency they acquire in most cases is the US dollar.[1]

The US Current Account deficit sends dollars to the countries that have a current account surplus with the United States. That is because the foreign companies that sell their goods in the United States are paid in dollars. Those companies take the dollars they earn back home and convert them into their own currency. This process would push up the value of the currencies of all the trade surplus countries if left to market forces. To prevent that, the central banks of many of the trade surplus countries buy most of the dollars entering their countries. The amounts are very large, in total, roughly the same size as the entire US Current Account deficit. Nevertheless, the central banks of the trade surplus countries can afford to buy all the dollars entering their countries because they can create all the money they need to do so.

Chart 10.8 shows that total foreign exchange reserves have risen more or less in line with the cumulative US Current Account deficit. That is because the central banks of the trade surplus countries financed the US Current Account deficit by creating money,

CHART 10.8 The Cumulative US Current Account Deficit vs. Total Foreign Exchange Reserves, 1950 to 2007

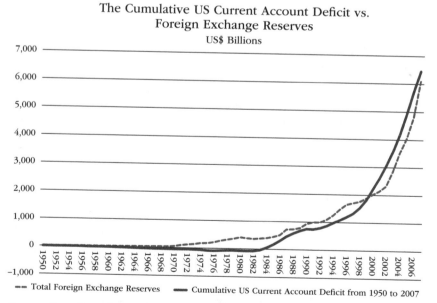

Source: Data from the International Monetary Fund, Total Foreign Exchange Reserves: 1950 to 2007

buying US dollars and then investing those dollars into US dollar-denominated assets, preferably US government securities. Had they not financed the US Current Account deficit in this way, that deficit could not have persisted. In that case, the United States would have had to buy less from the rest of the world and the economy of the rest of the world would have grown much more slowly.

Not all foreign exchange reserves are made up of US dollars. Central banks also acquire euros, pounds, yen, and other currencies. The exact currency breakdown of total foreign exchange reserves is unknown because China, the largest holder of foreign exchange reserves, keeps the composition of its foreign exchange reserves a secret. For all the other countries that do report the composition of their reserves, dollars make up 61% of the total.[2]

China has run an extraordinarily large trade surplus with the United States for three decades. China's cumulative trade surplus with the US between 1990 and 2007 was $1.7 trillion (with that figure increasing to $5.7 trillion by 2019). Given that Chinese companies are paid in dollars when they sell their products to the United States, it is very likely that the great majority of China's foreign exchange reserves are comprised of dollars. That strongly suggests that the dollar accounts for a larger portion of total foreign exchange reserves in the world than the 61% indicated by the countries that do report the composition of their foreign currency reserves. Therefore, here it will be assumed that dollars make up 70% of all foreign exchange reserves.

At the end of 2007, total foreign exchange reserves amounted to $6.1 trillion. Assuming 70% of those reserves were comprised of dollars, then foreign central banks held 4.3 trillion dollars at that time. Those dollars would have been invested in US dollar-denominated assets. Total US debt outstanding (i.e., the combined debt of all sectors of the US economy) amounted to $52.6 trillion at the end of 2007. Therefore, it is reasonable to conclude that foreign central banks had financed more than 8% of all US debt at that point.

This arrangement, whereby the United States would run very large trade deficits and the central banks of the trade surplus countries would finance those deficits by creating money and buying dollar-denominated assets, was extraordinarily advantageous for both the government of the United States and for the trade surplus countries. The US government was able to run larger budget deficits and have other countries finance them. This allowed the US government to spend more on both the military and on domestic welfare programs than it otherwise could have done. If other countries had been unwilling to finance the government's budget deficits, then either the US government would have had to run smaller budget deficits (by spending less or taxing more) or else the Fed would have had to create even more money to finance the large deficits. If the Fed had created more money than it was already creating, it would have risked causing much higher rates of inflation in the United States. When other central banks created the money that financed the US budget deficits, that avoided the inflationary pressures that would have arisen in the United States if the Fed had had to create more dollars to finance the budget deficits. Chapter 15 will explain this in greater detail.

The trade surplus countries benefited from this arrangement because it allowed them to pursue export-led economic growth strategies that produced very rapid economic growth in their countries. To make this work, the central banks of the trade surplus countries created their own currency and used it to buy dollars in order to depress the value of their currency. Weak currencies allowed those countries to continue running large trade surpluses with the United States by making their manufactured goods more competitive than goods manufactured in the United States. Rapid export growth meant rapid job creation and accelerated economic growth in the countries with a trade surplus.

Not surprisingly, then, numerous central banks around the world created their own currencies and bought dollars. Once they had acquired dollars, it made sense to invest them in order to generate additional income. Dollars must be invested in dollar-denominated assets. US government securities were (and still are) the dollar-denominated asset of choice for risk-adverse central bankers. Buying US government securities with newly created money was seen as a small price to pay in exchange for rapid economic growth and rapid job creation. In fact, the price paid was zero, since the money that was used to buy the US government debt had cost nothing to create.

The world economy was transformed as a direct result of these developments. Much of Asia, in particular, underwent an industrial revolution in the course of only a few decades. Hundreds of millions of people around the world were pulled out of poverty because of the United States trade deficits and the money that the central banks of the trade surplus countries created to finance them.

In practice, this meant that not only was the Fed creating money (Federal Reserve Credit) and using it to finance the US government's budget deficit by acquiring US government securities, but that the central banks of other countries were also creating money and using it to acquire US government securities. By 1977, the "rest of the world" owned more US government securities than the Fed did, as shown in Chart 10.9.

CHART 10.9 US Government Debt Owned by the Fed and the Rest of the World, 1945 to 2007

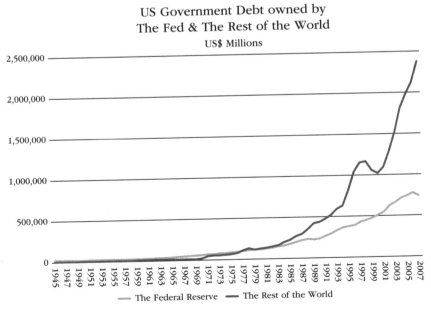

US Government Debt owned by
The Fed & The Rest of the World
US$ Millions

— The Federal Reserve　— The Rest of the World

Source: Data from the Financial Accounts of the United States, 1945–2007, The Fed

CHART 10.10 The Share of US Government Debt Owned by the Fed and the Rest of the World, 1945 to 2007

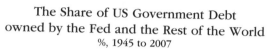

The Share of US Government Debt
owned by the Fed and the Rest of the World
%, 1945 to 2007

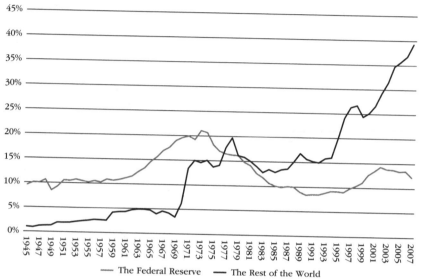

— The Federal Reserve   — The Rest of the World

Source: Data from the Financial Accounts of the United States, 1945–2007, The Fed

By the end of 2007, the Fed owned 12.2% of all US government debt, while the rest of the world owned 39.3%. This can be seen in Chart 10.10.

So, while the Fed's holdings of US government securities increased very sharply between 1970 and 2007, other central banks' holdings of US government securities increased a great deal more. This development had important consequences. Since other central banks were creating money and buying US government securities (i.e., monetizing US government debt), that enabled the Fed to create less money and to acquire fewer US government securities than it otherwise would have had to do.

Put differently, the central banks of the trade surplus countries were creating central bank credit (in the same way that the Fed creates Federal Reserve Credit, as explained in Chapter 1)

and extending it to the United States by first buying dollars and then investing those dollars in US government securities, bonds issued by Fannie Mae and Freddie Mac, and other US dollar-denominated debt instruments.

The Liquidity Gauge

This arrangement worked out very well for almost everyone concerned – up until the time that the US Current Account deficit grew so huge that the matching capital inflows became too large to be absorbed in the US economy without blowing it into an economic bubble. Remember, the capital inflows (recorded in the Financial and Capital Accounts) are the mirror image of the US Current Account deficit. So, as the Current Account deficit expanded so did the capital inflows into the United States that financed that deficit.

Everything worked smoothly so long as the US government budget deficit was larger than the capital inflow, or, to say the same thing in a different way, so long as the US budget deficits were larger than the US Current Account deficits. The government would sell government securities to finance its budget deficit and the central banks of the trade surplus countries could simply invest the dollars they had acquired into those new government securities.

The trouble began, however, when the annual capital inflows grew larger than the US government's annual budget deficits, starting in 1997, as shown in Chart 10.11.

For 11 years in a row, from 1997 to 2007, the capital inflows (i.e., the surplus on the Financial and Capital Account) were larger than net government borrowing (which is quite similar to, but not exactly the same size as, the US government's budget deficit). That meant that the US government was not selling enough new bonds to absorb all the dollars that the central banks of the trade surplus countries had acquired and needed to invest during those years. Therefore, those central banks had to find some other dollar-denominated assets in which to invest

CHART 10.11 The Surplus on the US Financial Account and Capital Account vs. Net Government Borrowing, 1990 to 2008

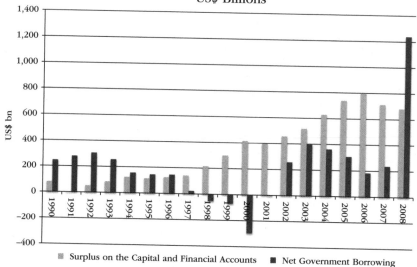

The Surplus on the US Financial & Capital Accounts vs. Net Government Borrowing (similar to the Budget Deficit) US$ Billions

■ Surplus on the Capital and Financial Accounts   ■ Net Government Borrowing

Source: Data from the Financial Accounts of the United States, The Fed; U.S.Bureau of Economic Analysis

those dollars. Their options were relatively limited. They could buy US corporate bonds, the bonds issued by Fannie Mae and Freddie Mac, US equities, US property or other real assets in the United States, or they could buy existing US government securities that the government had sold in earlier years. They did some of all these things. The result was that US asset prices rose and US interest rates fell. When there is heavy demand for bonds, bond prices rise and that causes bond yields (i.e., interest rates) to fall.

To better illustrate this point, I have created what I call the Liquidity Gauge, which is simply the difference between the surplus on the Financial and Capital Accounts (which is the mirror image of the Current Account deficit) and net government borrowing. When the Liquidity Gauge shows a positive number

CHART 10.12 Liquidity Gauge, 1990 to 2008

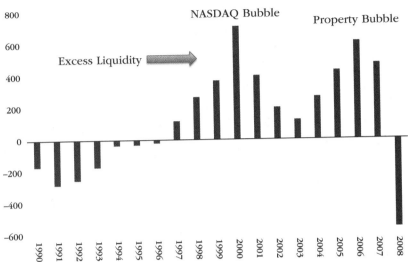

Liquidity Gauge, 1990 to 2008, US$ Billions
The Gap between the Financial & Capital Account Surplus
& Net Govt. Borrowing

Source: Data from the Financial Accounts of the United States, The Fed;
U.S.Bureau Of Economic Analysis

there is excess liquidity and asset prices tend to rise. When the Liquidity Gauge indicates a negative number, there is a liquidity shortage and asset prices tend to fall. Chart 10.12 shows the Liquidity Gauge from 1990 to 2008.

The huge amounts of money that the central banks of the trade surplus countries created and invested in the United States played a significant role in blowing the US economy into a bubble. Notice in Chart 10.12 the years 1998 to 2001. During those years, the Clinton administration ran rare government budget surpluses. That meant the government sold no new government securities. Instead, it repaid some of the government securities that had financed the budget deficits in earlier years, thereby retiring government securities and compounding the problem the foreign central banks faced in finding suitable investments for the money they had created. The NASDAQ bubble was the result.

This was similar to the 1920s, when the US government paid down its debt, forcing money out of government bonds and into stocks. That reduction in government debt outstanding contributed to the stock market bubble of the late 1920s and the crash in 1929.

Money is fungible. That means regardless of where the foreign central banks invested their money in the United States, it affected the price of every asset class. For instance, if they bought government bonds that had been issued in earlier years, whomever they bought those bonds from had cash that they had to invest somewhere else – somewhere else like NASDAQ.

Next, consider the period beginning 2004. That year, the Fed, concerned that the property market was running out of control, began hiking the federal funds rate. Between June 2004 and July 2006, the Fed hiked the federal funds rate 17 times, pushing up short-term interest rates. Long-term interest rates, which matter much more for the economy than short-term rates, barely budged, however. The Fed pushed up the federal funds rate by 425 basis points, but the yield on 10-year government bonds was only 36 basis points higher in July 2006 than it was when the Fed began hiking nearly two years earlier. Chart 10.13 shows the movement in the federal funds rate and the 10-year bond yield during this period.

Normally when the Fed pushes up short-term interest rates, long-term interest rates move up as well. That did not happen in the mid-2000s because the central banks of the trade surplus countries were creating so much money and buying so many long-term US government securities, thereby supporting the price of those bonds, that the yield on those securities would not rise. Bond yields rise when bond prices fall. In short, the central banks of the trade surplus countries were monetizing so much US government debt that the Fed lost control over US interest rates and, therefore, lost control over the US economy. Unable to make long-term interest rates rise, the Fed was powerless to stop the property bubble from inflating. In 2008, that bubble popped and nearly dragged the world into a new Great Depression.

I asked Alan Greenspan about this in January 2017.

CHART 10.13 The Federal Funds Rate vs. the 10-Year Government Bond Yield, 1980 to 2007

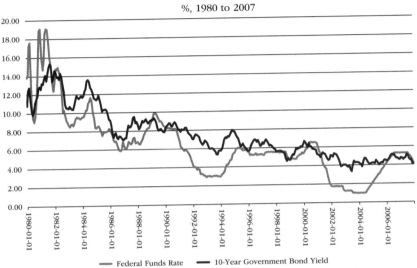

The Federal Funds Rate vs.
The 10-Year Government Bond Yield
%, 1980 to 2007

Source: Data from the Federal Reserve Bank of St. Louis

Thanks to Bill Bonner, founder of Agora Inc. and The Daily Reckoning, I had the opportunity to meet former Fed Chairman Alan Greenspan on January 18, 2017, at the Agora Economics Roundtable 2017 in Baltimore. Below is the transcript of the questions I asked him and his replies. Please keep in mind that this was a discussion. We only had one hour with Dr. Greenspan. Roughly 15 to 20 questions were put to him by a dozen participants. Time was short. I had only a very limited time to ask my question and to get a meaningful response. I believe the question I asked is of historic importance. I was determined to get an answer. I did.

Please note that I have added a few comments in **bold type** to help clarify points that may not be obvious to those who have not followed this subject closely.

A Transcript of My Q&A with Alan Greenspan

Richard Duncan: Dr. Greenspan, we know almost everything about the crisis of 2008 by this point, but there is one very important thing that we don't know, in my opinion, and that is what was your thinking about the fiat money creation that was being carried out by the central banks of the trade surplus countries? They created trillions of dollars between 2000 and 2007 and they invested 70% of those into US dollar-denominated assets, mostly treasury bonds.

For instance, during the "conundrum years", mid-2004 to mid-2006, foreign exchange reserves went up by one and a quarter trillion dollars; and $900 billion of those reserves were held in US dollars. Those dollars were invested in US dollar-denominated assets, mostly treasury bonds. That was enough to finance the entire US government budget deficit for those two years, with $200 billion left over. Doesn't that explain "the conundrum"? And how did you think of that at the time?

The Conundrum: Between mid-2004 and mid-2006, the Fed increased the federal funds rate by 425 basis points, but longer-term interest rates (such as the yield on 10-year US government bonds) did not go up as they normally do when the Fed hikes short-term interest rates. In reference to this development, Chairman Greenspan said in Congressional testimony, "For the moment, the broadly unanticipated behavior of world bond markets remains a conundrum."[3]

Alan Greenspan: I don't think it does. If you look at double-entry bookkeeping in the national accounts, the type of transactions you're talking about don't directly affect that. That is, if you get a central bank, let's say the case in which is the most general way, in 2008 the federal reserve, because everyone wanted to hold dollars, which I found very fascinating as it was as late as . . . Remember, we were a fiat currency, we were a weak fiat currency, but stronger than everybody else so through that crisis reserves were US dollars and the federal reserve made a large number of swaps, which were temporary exchange of dollars for lira, for euros, any foreign currencies of other central banks.

They were unwound shortly thereafter so it's not . . . The basic problems are, you get bubbles because human nature is what it is. People get euphoric. We know by experience that fear is a far more formidable force in human activity than euphoria and as a result, for example, recessions go down far more sharply than recoveries and the stock market behaves exactly the same way so that you've got these very odd patterns. Without getting into too much detail, most economic models that work try to integrate human nature into the asymmetries that we're seeing. What I've seen at the moment is that you would not have gotten a crisis in 2008 if we took, say, eliminated Dodd–Frank completely and merely substituted a significant increase in equity capital requirements in the commercial banking industry for everything else.

The reason I say that is we have data going back in the United States to 1869 since the beginning of the control of the currency and that shows that income, net income of commercial banks to equity assets has been a remarkably stable five . . .

Richard Duncan: I'm sorry, could I interrupt? This wasn't a swap, this was a central bank, the PBOC, printing money, buying dollars and buying treasury bonds, pushing up their price and pushing down their yield.

Alan Greenspan: Everybody does that but you can't push the yield down if the market's running against you.

Richard Duncan: You were trying to push them up by hiking the federal funds rate by 425 basis points . . .

Alan Greenspan: I wasn't there.

Richard Duncan: This was when you were hiking rates in 2004, 2005 and 2006, but the 10-year bond yield didn't go up . . .

Chairman Greenspan retired from the Fed in January 2006.

Alan Greenspan: No, what happened then is what I call "the conundrum."

Richard Duncan: Yes.

Alan Greenspan: We thought, what we thought was that we had to tighten the markets and as we did the only tool that we had was the federal funds rate and historically we did not trade in the long end of the market.

Richard Duncan: My question is, the long end didn't go up because the PBOC was printing RMB, buying dollars, and buying treasury bonds.

Alan Greenspan: No, that's not the reason. The reason was that the cold war came to an end and the Berlin wall came down and you have a huge increase in the number, it was something like a billion people came out from behind the iron curtain and tried to integrate with the remainder of the world's economy and obviously the economic ruin behind the iron curtain that was exposed when that wall came down was a great shock to everybody. You had all of these semi-skilled people moving into the west and there was enough of a downward pressure on wages because big new supply occurred that you've got interest rates going down.

For example, I remember extraordinarily well that Mexico was able to issue a 20-year peso-backed bond at a reasonable interest rate, not terribly much above the United States. This is within a relatively few years. Remember in 19 . . . I'm trying to think, it was when Mexico was about to go bankrupt, which was 1984 and it had tesobonos, which were basically not backed by anything and we bailed them out, the United States bailed out Mexico at that particular point. They were able to come back very few years later with a 20-year issue in pesos and they couldn't . . . For decades, I don't think they ever were able to issue a 20-year peso-denominated anything.

Richard Duncan: The creation of the equivalent of 10 trillion dollars by the foreign central banks between 2000 and 2014 had no impact on the global savings glut?

The event organizers were signaling (and had already signaled a few times) that my time was up. . . .

Global Savings Glut: Both Ben Bernanke and Alan Greenspan explained that the Fed was unable to prevent the property bubble in the United States (and, consequently, the global economic crisis) because there was a "global savings glut". By that they meant that people in the developing economies had a very high savings rate and they chose to invest their savings in US dollar-denominated assets, instead of investing at home. Their investments caused US bond prices to rise and US bond yields (i.e., interest rates) to fall. And, consequently, there was nothing the Fed could do about it, at least, according to Bernanke and Greenspan.

Alan Greenspan: We don't know because you can't tell. There were so many forces at play at that time it was difficult to separate them. We were confronted with the fact that with this huge increase in savings, because remember, the income of the previously behind the iron curtain countries was not spent, they saved a good part of it because there were no institutions for savings. That drove down the long-term rates in the market of both the US dollar and all other rates. In that type of condition, you've got a very difficult problem on the part of the federal reserve who was trying to raise rates but the flood, the savings glut, was coming from the movement of funds from behind the iron curtain, basically.

These were people who were literally blocked off until you got a huge increase and the rates kept going down for a number of years.

I don't know whether, to what extent you can attribute anything to anything, but that was critically the major factor in retrospect.

I find his final remark especially fascinating: "I don't know whether, to what extent you can attribute anything to anything. . . ."

Also, I am not sure how much money the people behind the iron curtain had saved up, but I am sure it was nowhere near $10 trillion dollars. I would be surprised if as much as $100 billion of savings moved from Eastern Europe to the United States. The iron curtain fell in 1989. The conundrum occurred between mid-2004 and mid-2006.

If Chairman Greenspan did not know why longer-term interest rates were not moving higher, he should have. Government bond yield did not move higher because a number of central banks from other countries were buying hundreds of billions of dollars' worth of US government bonds, pushing up their price and holding down their yields.

I find it difficult to believe that Chairman Greenspan did not understand that. The data was publicly available. Central bankers communicate with each other daily, as do monetary officials in the world's treasury departments. The main function of central banks is to create money and credit. It is inconceivable that the thousands of economists employed by the Federal Reserve System would have simply overlooked the fact that central banks outside the United States were creating the equivalent of trillions of dollars, using that money to buy dollars and then investing those dollars into US dollar-denominated assets – and that those economists would have failed to understand the impact those investments were having on US interest rates, asset prices, and the entire economy. If they did fail to understand what was happening, they were grossly incompetent.

On the other hand, if Chairman Greenspan and his colleagues at the Fed did, in fact, understand what was happening, it is fascinating to consider why he denied knowing that he did. Is this a topic that central bankers are simply not permitted to discuss? Are they not allowed to acknowledge that US government officials had entered into an arrangement with foreign governments whereby the United States agreed to run large trade deficits so long as foreign central banks would finance them? Is it too sensitive because this arrangement benefits the profits of US corporations and banks and financed US government spending at low interest rates, but at the cost of the loss of millions of jobs in the US manufacturing sector and downward pressure on US wages in general? I believe that may be the reason.

Chairman Greenspan may be right in saying, "I don't know whether, to what extent you can attribute anything to anything. . . ." However, I would prefer to attribute the deindustrialization of the United States and the economic crisis that followed in 2008 as the largely unintended outcome of the arrangement described above than to the possibility that the Central Bank and Treasury Department of the United States were too dim-witted to understand what was happening right in front of them.

In any case, there can be no doubt that the injection of $4.3 trillion of foreign central bank credit into the United States by 2007 – an amount that financed 8% of all the outstanding debt in the United States that year – had a profound impact on the US economy. That money drove up asset prices and helped inflate the economic bubble that imploded in 2008.[4]

Notes

1. Japan is an exception. Japan's foreign exchange reserves are held by the Ministry of Finance rather than by the Japanese Central Bank, the Bank of Japan.
2. IMF Currency Composition of Official Foreign Exchange Reserves, COFER. https://data.imf.org/?sk=E6A5F467-C14B-4AA8-9F6D-5A09 EC4E62A4
3. Testimony of Chairman Alan Greenspan, Federal Reserve Board's semiannual Monetary Policy Report to the Congress, Before the Committee on Banking, Housing, and Urban Affairs, U.S. Senate, February 16, 2005. https://www.federalreserve.gov/boarddocs/hh/ 2005/february/testimony.htm
4. $4.3 trillion assumes that 70% of all foreign exchange reserves were dollars in 2007.

CHAPTER 11

Creditism

Once a nation parts with the control of its credit, it matters not who makes the laws.

William Lyon Mackenzie King,
Canadian Prime Minister, 1935[1]

After money ceased to be backed by gold, credit growth accelerated so dramatically that it became the principal driver of economic growth. More than that, the unprecedented proliferation of credit fundamentally changed the nature of our entire economic system. Saving and investment had fueled economic growth in earlier decades. Businessmen would invest. Some of them would make a profit. They would accumulate that profit as capital and then invest again. That was the dynamic that generated economic growth in the age of Capitalism.

Our economic system no longer works that way. Today, credit creation and consumption have replaced saving and investment as the dynamic that makes the economy grow. *Creditism* is a more appropriate name than Capitalism for the economic system that prevails in the world today. Credit creation, not capital accumulation, is the force that powers the global economy in the twenty-first century.

This chapter explains how Creditism works. It begins by documenting the tremendous surge in total credit that has occurred since World War II and, particularly, from the early 1970s. Next, it discusses the debtors, those who borrow and spend the credit; and the impact that their borrowing and spending has on the economy. The chapter then describes how credit creation pushes up asset prices, creating a wealth effect that finances even more consumption. It concludes by revealing Creditism's Achilles' heel. It explains that Creditism requires perpetual credit growth to survive.

A Credit Bonanza

Total credit in the United States is comprised of all the credit extended in the country. That includes the credit extended by commercial banks and the broader financial sector, by households, corporations, non-corporate businesses, the federal government, by state and local governments, and by the rest of the world.

Total credit first hit $1 trillion in 1964. By 2007, it had increased to $53 trillion, a 53-fold increase in just 43 years. Chart 11.1 shows this extraordinary surge in credit.

There is far more credit than there is money. Chart 11.2 compares the *credit supply* to the *money supply*. Clearly, by 2007, total credit outstanding dwarfed the money created by the Fed (*base money*), as well as the money created by the banking system (M2).

The gap between total credit and *total money* has not always been so large. It grew wider over many decades, however, as total credit increased much more rapidly than the money supply, even though the money supply was growing very rapidly at the same time. The ratio of total credit to the *monetary base* rose from 19 times in 1959 to 61 times in 2007, as shown in

CHART 11.1 Total Credit 1952 to 2007

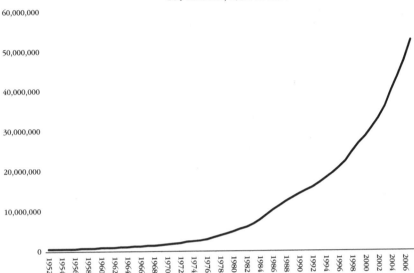

Total Credit
US$ Millions, 1952 to 2007

Source: Data from the Financial Accounts of the United States, The Fed

CHART 11.2 The Monetary Base, M2, and Total Credit, 1959 to 2007

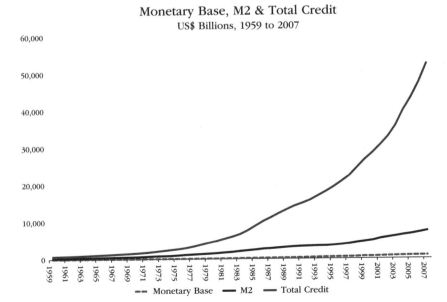

Monetary Base, M2 & Total Credit
US$ Billions, 1959 to 2007

-- Monetary Base ── M2 ── Total Credit

Source: Data from the Financial Accounts of the United States, The Fed; and the Federal Reserve Bank of St. Louis

CHART 11.3 The Ratio of Total Credit to the Monetary Base 1959 to 2007

Times

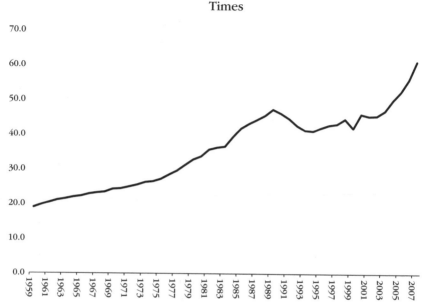

Source: Data from the Financial Accounts of the United States, The Fed; and the Federal Reserve Bank of St. Louis

Chart 11.3. The widening gap between total credit and total money is further evidence of the increase in leverage in the United States during those decades.

Total credit was equivalent to 159% of GDP in 1945. That ratio declined to a postwar low of 133% in 1951. From there it began to rise gradually, but did not exceed the level reached at the end of the war until 1977. Beginning in the early 1980s, however, the ratio of total credit to GDP accelerated sharply, rising from 170% of GDP in 1980 to 239% in 1990, 279% in 2000, and 364% in 2007. The marked change that occurred around 1980 stands out in Chart 11.4, which presents the ratio of total credit to GDP from 1945 to 2007.

The rest of this chapter describes how this extraordinary surge in credit changed the way the economy worked as credit became the fuel that made the economy grow.

CHART 11.4 The Ratio of Total Credit to GDP, 1945 to 2007

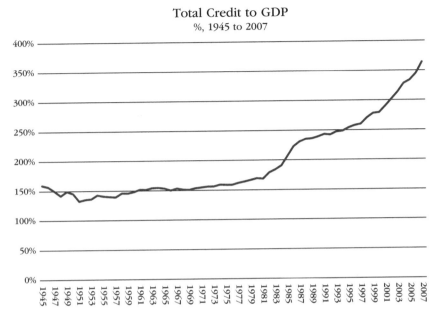

Total Credit to GDP
%, 1945 to 2007

Source: Data from the Financial Accounts of the United States, 1945–2007, The Fed

The Debtors

Total credit is equal to *total debt*. The first three chapters of Part Two focused on the credit providers. But, of course, for every dollar of credit extended there is a dollar borrowed. This section looks at who borrowed the money, as well as how the expenditure of the borrowed money transformed the economy and the economic system itself.

The Fed classifies debtors into three major sectors: the non-financial sector, the financial sector, and the rest of the world. Chart 11.5 illustrates the change in these three sectors' debt relative to GDP from 1945 to 2007. Each of these sectors will be discussed in turn.

CHART 11.5 The Ratio of Debt to GDP by Major Sector, 1945 to 2007

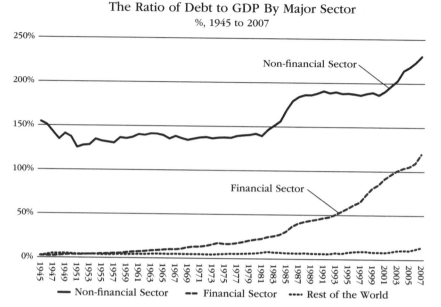

The Ratio of Debt to GDP By Major Sector
%, 1945 to 2007

Source: Data from the Financial Accounts of the United States, 1945–2007, The Fed

The Non-financial Sector Debtors

The largest of the three is the *non-financial sector*. It is comprised of five sub-sectors: the federal government, households and non-profit organizations, corporate businesses, non-corporate businesses, and state and local governments.

Detailed data for most of these sub-sectors is only available from 1945. However, the data for government debt goes back further. Chart 11.6 shows the growth in federal government debt between 1900 and 1945.

There was so little federal government debt before World War I that it cannot be distinguished in this chart. During World War I, however, the government's debt jumped from $3 billion in 1917 to $25 billion in 1919. During World War II, it jumped again, from $49 billion to $259 billion. The investments financed by the surge in US government debt during World War II not only ended the Great

CHART 11.6 The Public Debt of the Federal Government, 1900 to 1945

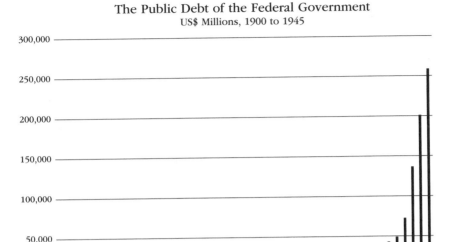

The Public Debt of the Federal Government
US$ Millions, 1900 to 1945

Source: Data from Historical Statistics of the United States: Colonial Times to 1970, US Census Bureau

Depression, it set off an economic boom in the United States that lasted for more than 30 years.

The ratio of federal government debt to GDP rose from 16% in 1930 (GDP data only began to be calculated in 1930) to 44% in 1934. That increase was largely due to the collapse in the government's tax revenues during the Great Depression. Government debt to GDP remained relatively flat from 1934 until 1941, but then spiked again from 42% that year to 114% in 1945 when World War II ended. See Chart 11.7. The 1945 peak in government debt to GDP was not exceeded until 2020.

Starting from 1945, the data for all the other sub-sectors of the economy become available. Chart 11.8 shows the change in the ratio of debt to GDP for all five sub-sectors of the non-financial sector from 1945 and 2007.

The most remarkable change during the first three decades following World War II was the plunge in the ratio of federal

CHART 11.7 Government Debt to GDP, 1930 to 1945

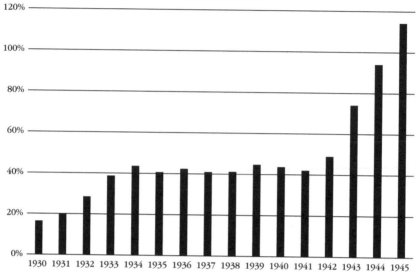

Government Debt to GDP
%, 1930 to 1945

Source: Data from Historical Statistics of the United States: Colonial Times to 1970, US Census Bureau

government debt to GDP from 114% in 1945 to just 26% in 1974. This decline in government debt relative to the size of the economy was partially offset by a rise in household sector debt, which increased from 13% of GDP in 1945 to 47% of GDP in 1965. The ratio of debt to GDP of the other three categories also rose, although at a more gradual pace than household sector debt.

Consequently, rather than the non-financial sector's debt contracting relative to GDP as the ratio of federal government debt to GDP declined, the overall ratio of debt to GDP for the non-financial sector remained relatively unchanged between 1945 and 1980, due to an offsetting rise in the debt of the other four sub-sectors of the non-financial sector. This can be seen in Chart 11.5.

Ronald Reagan completely changed the debt trajectory of the United States, however. His policies resulted in huge budget deficits that caused government debt to skyrocket. In 1980, the

CHART 11.8 The Non-financial Sector Debt to GDP by Category, 1945 to 2007

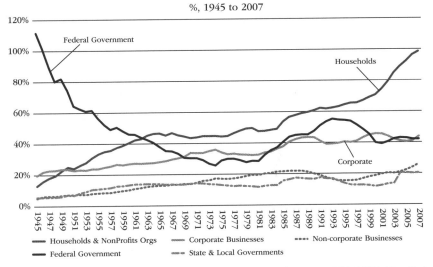

The Non-Financial Sector
Debt to GDP by Category
%, 1945 to 2007

Source: Data from the Financial Accounts of the United States, 1945–2007, The Fed

year Reagan was elected, the US budget deficit was already at a record high of $74 billion. Within three years it had nearly tripled. The highest budget deficit during the Reagan years was $221 billion in 1986.

President Reagan was followed as president by George H. W. Bush. In 1992, the final year of the Bush administration, the budget deficit reached $290 billion. See Chart 11.9.

During the eight years of the Reagan presidency, federal government debt nearly tripled from $812 billion in 1980 to $2.4 trillion in 1988. It then increased by an additional $778 billion to $3.5 trillion during George H. W. Bush's four years as president. Altogether, during those 12 years, US federal government debt rose by 330% and the ratio of government debt to GDP nearly doubled from 28% to 54% of GDP.

The Reagan years are often cited as a period of great economic rejuvenation and prosperity, while the role played by the surge in government debt in creating the Reagan boom is

CHART 11.9 US Government Budget Surplus or Deficit (–), 1960 to 1992

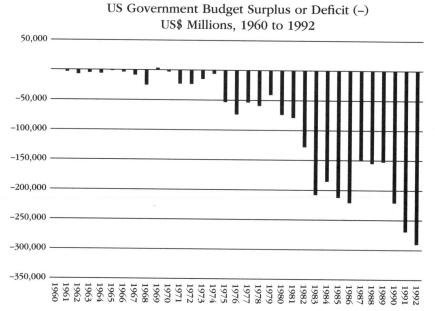

US Government Budget Surplus or Deficit (–)
US$ Millions, 1960 to 1992

Source: Data from Office of Management and Budget, Historical Tables, The White House

ignored. That is a mistake. The surge in government debt was the principal reason for the economic rejuvenation and prosperity during the Reagan era. The record-setting budget deficits of that period were the result of large tax cuts that sharply boosted personal consumption expenditure, combined with greatly increased government investment in the US military, which generated large profits for the defense industry as well as inducing a new surge in business investment across the country. Here is another example of a sharp expansion of government debt producing a surge in US prosperity.

Household sector debt and corporate debt also expanded notably during the 1980s, the former increased from 50% of GDP in 1980 to 61% in 1990 and the latter from 32% in 1980 to 47% in 1990. Increased household debt financed additional personal consumption expenditure, while the growth in business debt paid for additional investment, with both consumption and investment boosting economic growth. Beginning in 1990, however, corporate and non-corporate business debt dipped, tipping the United States into a mild recession. The ratios of corporate and non-corporate debt to GDP each fell roughly five percentage points over the next few years.

In 1993, the ratio of government debt to GDP stabilized. Then, in 1997, it began to decline. From 1998 to 2000, the US government ran uncharacteristic budget surpluses and paid down some of the outstanding government debt.

During the 1990s, the reduction in corporate, non-corporate, and government debt relative to the size of the economy offset the continued increase in the ratio of household sector debt to GDP. That held the overall ratio of non-financial sector debt to GDP flat at just under 190% during the 1990s. See Chart 11.5 and Chart 11.8.

From 2000, however, household sector debt accelerated sharply, growing by more than $1 trillion every year between 2003 and 2006, as shown in Chart 11.10.

CHART 11.10 The Annual Change in Household Sector Debt, 1946 to 2007

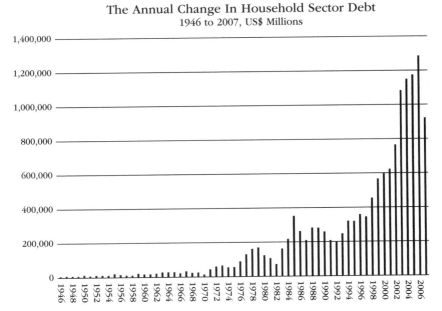

The Annual Change In Household Sector Debt
1946 to 2007, US$ Millions

Source: Data from the Financial Accounts of the United States, 1945–2007, The Fed

That took the ratio of household sector debt to GDP up from 71% in 2000 to 99% in 2007. It was also the main factor driving the ratio of non-financial sector debt to GDP up from 186% in 2000 to 231% in 2007.

That surge in household sector borrowing was unprecedented, as was its impact on the economy. The jump in household borrowing for mortgages pushed up home prices and fueled a construction boom. It also created a *wealth effect* that financed additional consumption. The large increase in household borrowing of consumer credit for car loans and credit card purchases threw even more fuel on the blazing US economy. The resulting economic boom in the United States spilled over into the rest of the world as the US Current Account deficit blew out to an unpreceded $800 billion in 2006, a number equivalent to 6% of US GDP that year. During these years, the US credit bubble set off a worldwide economic boom.

The Financial Sector Debtors

Next consider the surge in borrowing by the financial sector. At the end of World War II, the financial sector borrowed very little. Financial sector debt accounted for only 2% of all outstanding debt that year. By 2007, however, financial sector debt accounted for one-third of all the debt in the United States.

The extraordinary increase in borrowing by the financial sector enabled that sector to lend much more and to invest much more in debt securities and equities than it otherwise would have been able to do. The additional lending to consumers and businesses boosted consumption and business investment, while the increase in the financial sector's investments drove up property prices and the stock market. Consequently, the US economy grew much more rapidly than it otherwise would have; and, as Americans consumed more and imported more from abroad, the economy of the rest of the world also grew much more than it could have otherwise done.

As explained in Chapter 9, up until the mid-1970s, the financial sector was dominated by commercial banks, which used their customers' deposits as the source of funds for the credit they extended. Their deposit base was more than sufficient to finance their lending activities. They did not need to borrow additional funds through the debt market.

Similarly, life insurance companies, the second largest financial sector lender, used the premiums they received from their policy holders to finance the loans and investments they made. They did not use external borrowing either.

The structure of the financial sector began to change during the 1970s, however, as shown in Chart 11.11. Three developments stand out. First, there was a particularly rapid increase in the debt of the government-sponsored enterprises (GSEs), beginning at that time. Next, from the early 1980s, the debt of many of the smaller institutions in the financial sector also accelerated sharply. Finally, the issuers of asset-backed securities (ABS) became heavy borrowers starting around 1990.

The GSEs, primarily Fannie Mae and Freddie Mac, issued debt directly. They also guaranteed the debt issued by GSE-backed

CHART 11.11 Breakdown of the Financial Sector Debtors, 1945 to 2007

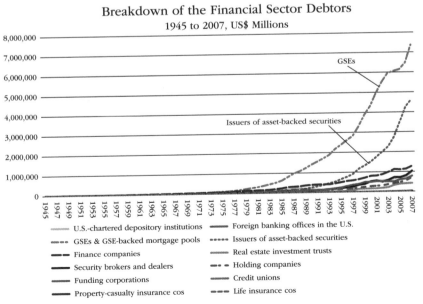

Source: Data from the Financial Accounts of the United States, 1945–2007, The Fed

mortgage pools. Taken together, their combined debt jumped from $43 billion in 1970 to $7.4 trillion in 2007, an increase of more than 170 times over 37 years. Similarly, the debt borrowed by the issuers of asset-backed securities surged from $269 billion in 1990 to $4.6 trillion in 2007, a 16-fold increase over 17 years.

The GSEs and the issuers of asset-backed securities were, simultaneously, large debtors and large creditors. They borrowed trillions of dollars, which they then invested in debt instruments tied to home mortgages and, in the case of the ABS issuers, in debt instruments tied to consumer credit as well.

The combined debt of the 10 other types of institutions that comprise the rest of the financial sector ramped up from $98 billion in 1970 to $5.3 trillion in 2007, a 53-fold increase over 37 years. This is shown in Chart 11.12.

CHART 11.12 Financial Sector Debt Excluding the GSEs and Issuers of Asset-Backed Securities, 1945 to 2007

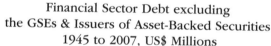

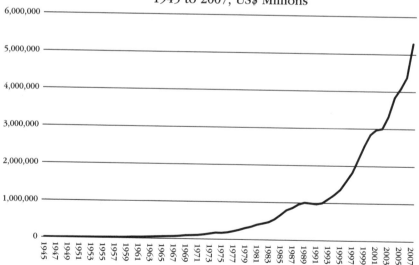

Source: Data from the Financial Accounts of the United States, 1945–2007, The Fed

Chart 11.13 shows the growth in debt of each of these 10 smaller sub-sectors of the entire financial sector between 1945 and 2007. Finance companies owed $1.3 trillion in 2007; followed by security brokers and dealers, $1 trillion; US-chartered depository institutions, $1 trillion; funding corporations, $786 billion; and holding companies, $710 billion. It is quite certain that much of the funds borrowed by these institutions were used for speculative purposes that drove up asset prices.

Chart 11.14 shows the incredible increase in the annual borrowing of the financial sector from the mid-1970s. Focusing on the milestones, financial sector debt grew by $17 billion in 1970, by $103 billion in 1981, by $575 billion in 1996, by $1.1 trillion two years later, and by $2.2 trillion in 2007.

Chart 11.15 shows how dominate a role the financial sector came to play in the debt market by comparing the amount it

CHART 11.13 Breakdown of the Financial Sector Debt Excluding GSEs and ABS Issuers, 1945 to 2007

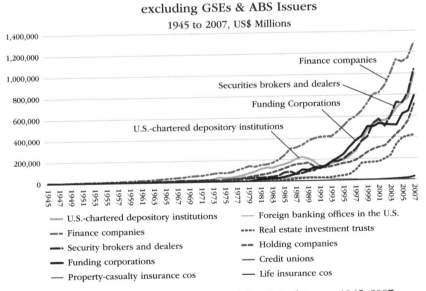

Breakdown of the Financial Sector Debt
excluding GSEs & ABS Issuers
1945 to 2007, US$ Millions

Source: Data from the Financial Accounts of the United States, 1945–2007, The Fed

CHART 11.14 The Annual Change in Financial Sector Debt, 1946 to 2007

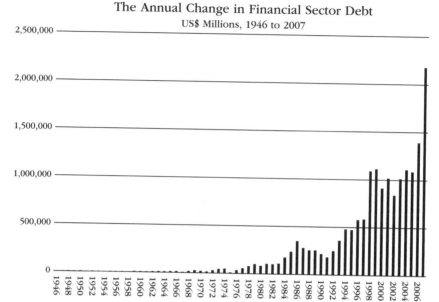

The Annual Change in Financial Sector Debt
US$ Millions, 1946 to 2007

Source: Data from the Financial Accounts of the United States, 1945–2007, The Fed

CHART 11.15 The Annual Dollar Change in the Debt of the Household Sector, the Government Sector, and the Financial Sector 1946 to 2007

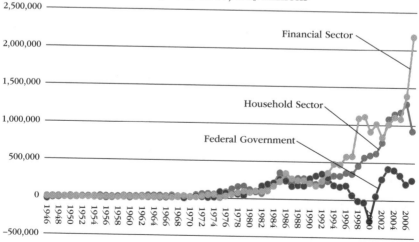

The Annual Dollar Change In the Debt of
the Household Sector, the Government & the Financial Sector
1946 to 2007, US$ Millions

Source: Data from the Financial Accounts of the United States, 1945–2007, The Fed

borrowed annually with the sums borrowed by the government and the household sector. In 2007, the financial sector added $2.2 trillion to its debt load. That was more than twice as much as the $923 billion increase in the debt of the household sector and eight times as much as the $270 billion increase in government debt that year.

Credit and Wealth

When credit growth began to accelerate in both absolute amounts and relative to GDP from the early 1980s, it began to push up the price of stocks, property, and many other asset classes. Rising asset prices made Americans richer and created a wealth effect that boosted consumption and economic growth.

Chart 11.16 shows that when the ratio of total credit to GDP began to accelerate in the early 1980s, the Dow Jones exited the long bear market of the 1970s and began to soar. As the ratio of

CHART 11.16 Debt and the Dow: The Ratio of Total Debt to GDP vs. the Dow Jones Industrial Average, 1953 to 2007

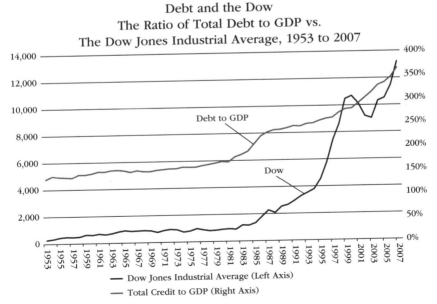

Debt and the Dow
The Ratio of Total Debt to GDP vs.
The Dow Jones Industrial Average, 1953 to 2007

Source: Data from the Financial Accounts of the United States 1953–2007, The Fed; and the Bureaus of Economic Analysis; CEIC

credit to GDP rose from 170% in 1980 to 364% in 2007, the Dow Jones Industrial index skyrocketed from 895 to 13,200, a 15-fold increase over 27 years.

The property market boomed as well. The value of real estate owned by the household sector jumped nearly eightfold between 1980 and 2007, the largest increases occurring during the 1990s when the issuers of asset-backed securities joined the GSEs in extending trillions of dollars' worth of mortgage loans to American households (see Chart 11.17).

As credit expanded, it created wealth. In fact, the wealth of the United States is floating on an ocean of debt. Chart 11.18 clearly shows that as credit grew, the wealth of the household sector grew along with it.

Just as the ratio of credit to GDP rose well above its traditional range by 2007, so did the ratio of *household net worth* to GDP. The average for that ratio between 1945 and 2007 was

CHART 11.17 **Real Estate Owned by the Household Sector: Owner-Occupied Real Estate (at market value), 1945 to 2007**

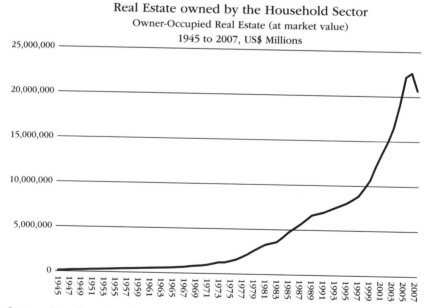

Real Estate owned by the Household Sector
Owner-Occupied Real Estate (at market value)
1945 to 2007, US$ Millions

Source: Data from the Financial Accounts of the United States, 1945–2007, The Fed

CHART 11.18 Wealth and Credit: Household Sector Net Worth vs. Total Credit (Total Debt), 1946 to 2007

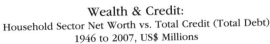

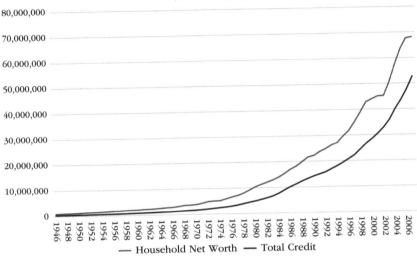

Wealth & Credit:
Household Sector Net Worth vs. Total Credit (Total Debt)
1946 to 2007, US$ Millions

— Household Net Worth — Total Credit

Source: Data from the Financial Accounts of the United States, 1945–2007, The Fed

384%. It hit 445% at the peak of the NASDAQ bubble in 1999 and then rose to a new record high of 490% in 2006 during the credit-induced property bubble (see Chart 11.19).

From the early 1980s onward, the increase in the wealth of the household sector each year became another important driver of economic growth. Household net worth is calculated by deducting all the debt of the US households from all their assets. The annual increase in household sector net worth exceeded $1 trillion for the first time in 1979. It broke above $2 trillion in 1995, hit $3 trillion in 1999 and reached a pre-crisis peak of nearly $7 trillion in 2004, as can be seen in Chart 11.20.

The evidence is clear, after money ceased to be backed by gold, credit broke free of the bindings that had constrained its expansion until the 1970s. Afterwards, credit grew so markedly that it became the most important driver of economic growth by directly financing more consumption and investment, while at the same time pushing

CHART 11.19 The Ratio of Household Net Worth to GDP, 1945 to 2007

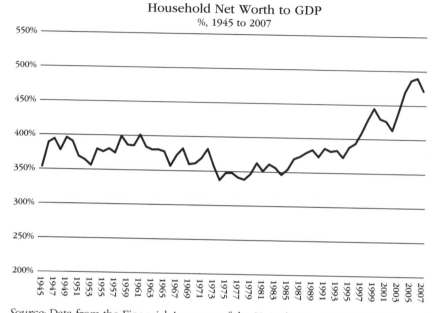

Household Net Worth to GDP
%, 1945 to 2007

Source: Data from the Financial Accounts of the United States, 1945–2007, The Fed

CHART 11.20 Household Net Worth, Annual Dollar Change, 1946 to 2007

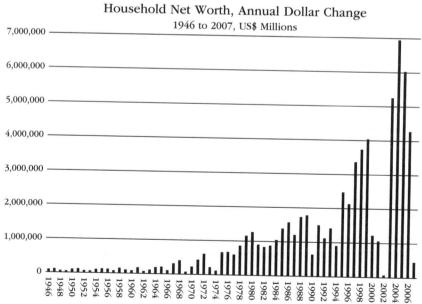

Household Net Worth, Annual Dollar Change
1946 to 2007, US$ Millions

Source: Data from the Financial Accounts of the United States, 1945–2007, The Fed

up asset prices and creating unprecedented amounts of wealth that allowed the American public to spend freely.

Credit creation and consumption replaced saving and investment as the principal dynamic generating economic growth. In the process, our economic system evolved from Capitalism into Creditism.

Credit Creation, Not Savings

It is important to understand that credit creation, not savings, financed the surge in lending and borrowing that has driven economic growth since the early 1970s. If the economy had had to rely only on savings, then there would have been far less growth and the economy would be a great deal smaller today than it is.

Chart 11.21 compares *net private savings*[2] each year with the annual increase in credit. Chart 11.22 presents the ratio of credit

CHART 11.21 Net Private Savings vs. the Increase in Total Credit, 1947 to 2007

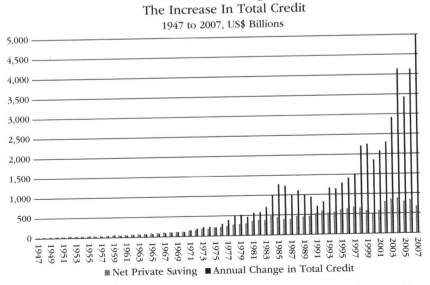

Net Private Savings vs.
The Increase In Total Credit
1947 to 2007, US$ Billions

■ Net Private Saving ■ Annual Change in Total Credit

Source: Data from the Financial Accounts of the United States, 1945–2007, The Fed; U.S. Bureau of Economic Analysis, Net Private Saving, 1947–2007

CHART 11.22 The Ratio of Annual Credit Growth to Annual Net Private Savings, 1947 to 2007

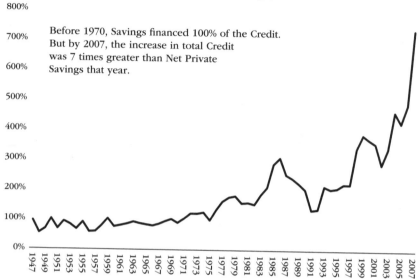

The Ratio of Annual Credit Growth
to Annual Net Private Savings, 1947 to 2007

Before 1970, Savings financed 100% of the Credit.
But by 2007, the increase in total Credit
was 7 times greater than Net Private
Savings that year.

Source: Data from the Financial Accounts of the United States, The Fed; U.S. Bureau of Economic Analysis, Net Private Saving

growth to net private savings. As both charts make clear, savings did finance 100% of all the credit extended each year between 1947 and 1970. After 1970, however, credit began to expand much more rapidly than private sector savings. By 1986, credit growth was three times greater than net private savings. By 2007, it was seven times larger. That year, credit expanded by $5 trillion, while net private savings amounted to only $680 billion.

By 2007, total credit outstanding had reached $53 trillion, whereas the cumulative savings of the private sector was still less than $20 trillion, as shown in Chart 11.23.

Many of the charts in this chapter have shown the sharp increase in credit relative to GDP. But credit growth played an even more important role in driving economic growth than those charts reflect. That is because rapid credit growth caused the economy to grow more rapidly than it would have if credit had

CHART 11.23 Total Credit vs. Cumulative Net Private Savings, 1945 to 2007

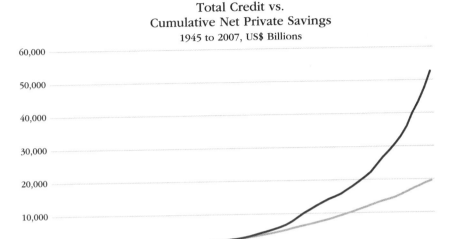

Total Credit vs.
Cumulative Net Private Savings
1945 to 2007, US$ Billions

Source: Data from the Financial Accounts of the United States, The Fed; U.S. Bureau of Economic Analysis

only expanded in line with savings. As government and private sector debt expanded rapidly, the government and the private sector spent more than they would have been able to had they not borrowed so much. Consequently, the economy, business profits and disposable personal income all grew more than they would have. Higher business profits and higher disposable personal income allowed business and households to save more than they otherwise could have done. Consequently, credit creation is the origin of a significant portion of the savings that did occur.

Creditism's Achilles' Heel

This chapter has demonstrated that credit growth has driven economic growth in the United States for decades, transforming Capitalism into Creditism in the process.

Creditism has one very serious flaw, however. It requires credit to expand. When it doesn't, the economy doesn't grow. If fact, Creditism requires credit to expand by roughly 2% a year, adjusted for inflation. Otherwise, the economy falls into recession and does not recover until credit growth rebounds. This can be seen in Chart 11.24, which compares credit growth with GDP growth (both adjusted for inflation) from 1952 to 2009.

Credit, adjusted for inflation, grew by less than 2% nine times during those 57 years. Every time, the United States fell into recession. That tells us that Creditism requires credit growth to generate economic growth.

Worst still, if credit contracts significantly, Creditism is engulfed in crisis. That is what occurred in 2008. That year, a large portion of the household sector in the United States was unable to service even the interest expense on the credit they had borrowed. When those households defaulted, most of

CHART 11.24 Credit Growth vs. GDP Growth, Adjusted for Inflation, 1952 to 2009

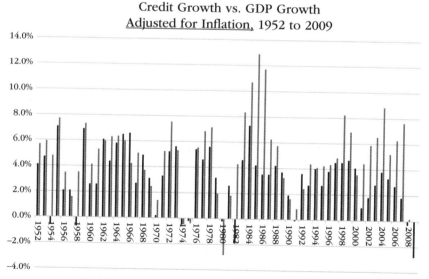

Source: Data from the U.S. Bureau of Economic Analysis; The Financial Accounts of the United States 1952–2009, The Fed

the financial sector became incapable of servicing the interest expense on the credit it had borrowed. Credit began to contract, and the United States economy began to spiral into crisis, pulling the global economy down with it.

The Great Depression occurred because credit contracted sharply between 1930 and 1933. Chart 11.25 shows the sharp contraction in the total loans and investment of the US commercial banks during those years. By the end of 1933, the US economy was 45% smaller than it had been in 1929 in nominal terms and 26% smaller in real terms. It contracted less in real terms than in nominal terms because of the severe deflation at that time.

When credit began to contract in 2008, the US economy came very close to collapsing into a new great depression. Chapter 12 describes the policy response that prevented that calamity from happening.

CHART 11.25 Commercial Banks: Total Loans and Investments, Annual Dollar Change, 1915 to 1940

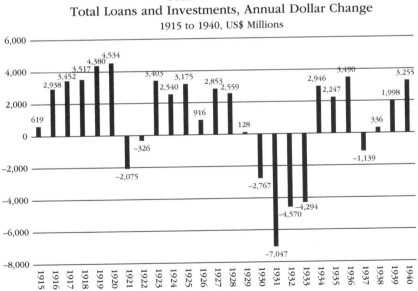

Source: Data from Board of Governors of the Federal Reserve System in Banking and Monetary Statistics, 1914–1945

Notes

1. IMDb Mini Biography By: Garchomp's Alliance, IMDb: https://www
   .imdb.com/name/nm0455383/bio
2. Net private saving is the amount by which disposable income
   exceeds private spending. Source: heteconomist http://heteconomist
   .com/government-deficits-and-net-private-saving/

CHAPTER 12

2007 to 2016: Crisis and Response

As a scholar of the Great Depression, I honestly believe that September and October of 2008 was the worst financial crisis in global history, including the Great Depression.

Ben Bernanke[1]

Introduction

This chapter begins by describing the 2008 financial sector meltdown that brought the world to the brink of a new Great Depression. It then describes the extraordinarily aggressive policy measures the Federal Reserve implemented to prevent that worst-case outcome. It details how the Fed used *discounting operations* to prevent the collapse of the global financial system and then *open market operations* to fuel economic recovery. The success of these policies prevented an economic catastrophe that our civilization may not have survived.

Meltdown

More than 13 years have gone by since the crisis of 2008. As time passes, memories fade. Therefore, this chapter will begin with a quick review of the events that nearly destroyed the global financial system.

Beginning in the Spring of 2007, the United States greatest financial institutions began falling like dominos.

In April 2007, New Century Financial Corporation, the second largest subprime mortgage lender in the United States, filed for bankruptcy. Its 2005 annual report, the last it published, showed total assets of $26 billion.

Countrywide Financial, with $212 billion of assets in 2007, also began encountering funding difficulties at that time. Countrywide was not only the largest subprime mortgage lender, it was the largest mortgage lender. It had originated nearly half a trillion dollars of loans during 2006 alone. In August 2007, Bank of America (BOA) came to Countrywide's rescue with a $2 billion investment. In January 2008, Bank of America bought the rest of Countrywide for $4 billion. This was an acquisition that Bank of America came to regret.

In March 2008, Bear Stearns was the United States' 17th largest financial institution. It had reported total assets of $395 billion in 2007. It was also on the brink of collapse. It was saved by Morgan Stanley and the Fed. The New York Fed agreed to lend Morgan Stanley $30 billion to facilitate its takeover of Bear Stearns. The Fed also agreed to take all the losses that might arise on Bear's assets after the first $1 billion of loses was borne by Morgan Stanley.

IndyMac, which was seized and shut down by the Office of Thrift Supervision and the FDIC in July, 2008, reported $33 billion of total assets in its 2007 annual report.

By early September, Fannie Mae and Freddie Mac were on the verge of bankruptcy. At that point, they were funding roughly 75% of all new mortgages in the country. They owned or guaranteed $5 trillion of mortgage debt. To put that into perspective, the total gross debt of the US government was $9 trillion in 2008.[2]

Their leverage ratio (i.e., the ratio of debt to equity) was 75 times. On September 8, they were placed in "conservatorship" by the government to prevent their collapse. According to the New York Fed, "Under these agreements, U.S. taxpayers ultimately injected $187.5 billion into Fannie Mae and Freddie Mac."[3] Fannie Mae had reported $883 billion in total assets in 2007, while Freddie Mac had reported $794 billion.

Merrill Lynch was also experiencing a funding crisis that month. They were acquired by Bank of America on September 14. This acquisition also cost BOA heavily during the quarters ahead. Merrill Lynch's 2007 annual report showed total assets of $1,020 billion.

The next day, Lehman Brothers filed for bankruptcy. It was by far the largest bankruptcy in US history. Lehman Brothers had $691 billion in total assets at the end of 2007.[4]

The day after that, the Fed lent AIG $85 billion to keep it afloat. Taxpayers received a 79.9% equity stake in AIG in return. AIG was one of the largest financial service companies in the world, with operations in more than 80 countries, tens of thousands of employees and a trillion-dollar balance sheet. The Fed's $85 billion capital infusion was not enough. The Fed and the Treasury ultimately committed more than $180 billion to its rescue.[5]

On September 21, Goldman Sachs and Morgan Stanley, the last two surviving investment banks, were hastily converted into bank holding companies in the attempt to reassure the financial markets that they would be able to tap emergency funding from the Fed.

Washington Mutual was shut down by the FDIC on September 25. With $300 billion in assets, it was the largest FDIC-insured bank ever to fail.

It looked as though Wachovia would be next in line. It was twice as large as Washington Mutual. It was saved in the nick of time on September 29, when Citigroup offered to acquire most of the company for $1 per share, in a deal in which the government offered to absorb any losses that exceeded $42 billion. In October, Wells Fargo made a better offer and acquired Wachovia.

On October 14, the government announced it would inject $125 billion of capital into the nine largest banks. JPMorgan, Wells Fargo, and Citi received $25 billion each. Bank of America got $15 billion. Morgan Stanley, Goldman Sachs, and Merrill Lynch were given $10 billion each. Bank of New York got $3 billion and State Street received $2 billion.

That was not enough to save Citi or Bank of America. On November 23, the government injected a further $20 billion of capital into Citigroup. On January 16, 2009, the government announced an additional $20 billion rescue package for Bank of America. Citigroup required still further government assistance in February 2009, by which point the government owned 36% of the bank.

The financing arms of the US automobile industry were also in crisis. Beginning in November 2008, the government provided $79.7 billion to General Motors, Chrysler, Ally Financial, Chrysler Financial, and automotive suppliers through the federal Auto Industry Financing Program.

If any one of the 10 largest US financial institutions had failed, in all probability that would have set off a chain of events that would have bankrupted practically every large financial institution in the world, wiping out most of the world's savings and dragging the global economy down into a new Great Depression in the process.

This calamity came about for four related reasons. First, the financial sector made risky loans, many of which eventually went bad. Second, the leverage ratio of the financial sector was far too high. In other words, the financial institutions lent much more than they should have, relative to the size of their capital. Third, the financial sector relied far too heavily on short-term sources of funding. And finally, the liquidity reserves of the banks were grossly inadequate – verging on nonexistent.

When the risky loans began to default, the capital of many institutions was too small to absorb the losses. As the severity of the problem came to be understood, a growing number of financial institutions found they could no longer borrow in the overnight money markets. Unable to borrow, many were soon unable to pay their creditors on time. Distress spread rapidly, and soon panic set in. Those with funds to lend, not knowing which institution would be next to fail, preferred not to lend at all. This situation grew steadily worse and in September 2008 the capital markets ceased to function altogether.

Saving the Financial System Through Discounting Operations

The Fed had been established with the principal purpose of stopping bank runs. It was given the power to create money (i.e., to extend Federal Reserve Credit) so that it could inject new money into the financial system when other sources of liquidity dried up. It had failed to prevent the collapse of the banking system during the early 1930s. It was determined not to fail again.

Therefore, as the crisis intensified, the Fed developed a series of programs to inject money into every corner of the financial system.[6]

1. The Term Auction Facility (TAF): TAF was introduced in December 2007 to alleviate pressures in short-term funding markets. It allowed depository institutions to borrow from the Fed against a wide variety of collateral, initially for a period of 28 days, later expanded to 84 days. Traditionally, the Fed had only lent to banks overnight.

2. The Term Securities Lending Facility (TSLF): Introduced in March 2008, TSLF was a program through which the Fed lent Treasury securities to primary dealers for a term of 28 days in exchange for other investment-grade debt securities. Its purpose was to strengthen the financing position of primary dealers.

3. The Primary Dealer Credit Facility (PDCF): Also introduced in March 2008, PDCF was intended to improve the ability of primary dealers to provide financing to participants in securitization markets in order to bolster market

liquidity and promote orderly market functioning. Collateral pledged to secure loans under this facility was initially limited to investment-grade debt securities, but subsequently was expanded to include all collateral eligible for pledge in triparty funding arrangements through the major clearing banks.

4. The Asset-Backed Commercial Paper Money Market Mutual Fund Liquidity Facility (AMLF): Under this program, which was initiated in September 2008, the Fed extended nonrecourse loans to US depository institutions and bank holding companies to finance their purchases of high-quality asset-backed commercial paper from money market mutual funds. This initiative was intended to assist money funds that hold such paper in meeting demands for redemptions by investors and to foster liquidity in the asset-backed commercial paper markets and broader money markets.

5. The Commercial Paper Funding Facility (CPFF): In October 2008, the Fed authorized the CPFF to provide a liquidity backstop to US issuers of commercial paper. The CPFF was intended to improve liquidity in short-term funding markets and thereby increase the availability of credit for businesses and households. Under the CPFF, Federal Reserve Credit was provided to a special purpose vehicle that, in turn, purchased commercial paper of eligible issuers.

6. The Money Market Investor Funding Facility (MMIFF): Also in October 2008, the Fed announced the creation of MMIFF to facilitate the purchase of US dollar-denominated certificates of deposit and commercial paper issued by highly rated financial institutions. By backstopping the sale of money market instruments in the secondary market, the MMIFF was designed to improve the liquidity of money market investors, thus increasing their ability to meet redemption requests and their willingness to invest in money market instruments.

7. The Term Asset-Backed Securities Loan Facility (TALF): In November 2008, the Fed announce TALF in order to help market participants meet the credit needs of households and small businesses by supporting the issuance of

asset-backed securities collateralized by student loans, auto loans, credit card loans, and loans guaranteed by the Small Business Administration.

Thus, the Fed put in place an array of lending facilities that flooded the capital markets with new money until practically any financial institution could borrow from the Fed using nearly any kind of debt instrument as collateral. The banks were able to borrow all they wanted from the Fed through TALF. The condition of the primary dealers was helped out by TSLF and PDCF. AMLF and TALF re-liquefied the asset-backed securities market. CPFF injected money into the commercial paper market. MMIFF and AMLF restored calm to the money markets.

During its near century of existence up to mid-2008, the Fed had created less than $1 trillion altogether. In the second half of 2008 alone, it created $1.3 trillion more. Chart 12.1 reflects this radical development.

CHART 12.1 The Fed's Total Assets, 1914 to 2008

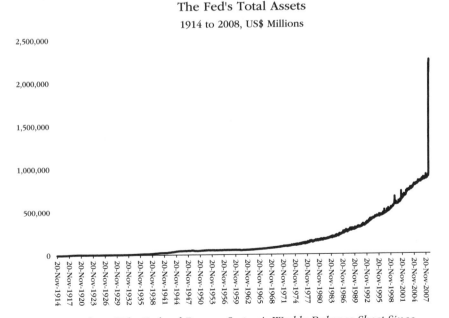

The Fed's Total Assets
1914 to 2008, US$ Millions

Source: Data from "*The Federal Reserve System's Weekly Balance Sheet Since 1914*" and accompanying spreadsheet. Johns Hopkins University, SAE/No.115/ July 2018. See Bibliography.

CHART 12.2 Federal Reserve Credit Extended Through Discounting Operations, 2006 to 2010

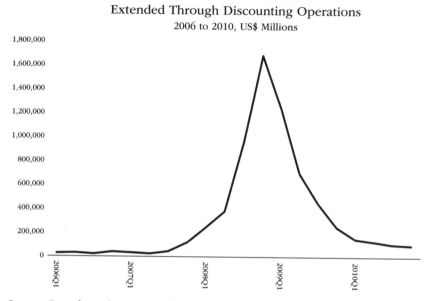

Federal Reserve Credit
Extended Through Discounting Operations
2006 to 2010, US$ Millions

Source: Data from the Financial Accounts of the United States, Table L. 109, Monetary Authority. The Federal Reserve[7]

The Fed injected this new money into the financial system by extending Federal Reserve Credit through discounting operations. Between mid-2007 and the end of 2008, the Fed's lending blew out from $25 billion to $1.7 trillion, as shown in Chart 12.2. That amount, $1.7 trillion, was nearly twice as large as the Fed's total assets had been in mid-2008.

Chart 12.3 shows how these loans were classified on the asset side of the Fed's balance sheet.

Ranked according to peak size, they were:

1. Nonofficial foreign currencies (swap lines), which peaked at $554 billion in the fourth quarter of 2008. These were currency swaps the Fed entered into with foreign central banks to provide the rest of the world with badly needed dollar liquidity.

CHART 12.3 A Breakdown of the Fed's Discounting Operations, 2006 to 2010

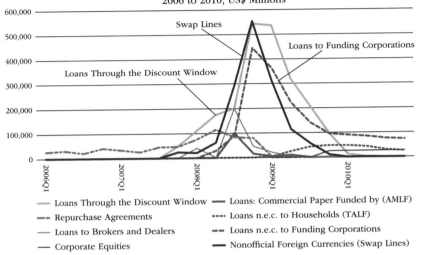

A Breakdown of the Fed's Assets
Acquired Through Discounting Operations
2006 to 2010, US$ Millions

Source: Data from the Financial Accounts of the United States, Table L. 109, Monetary Authority. The Federal Reserve[8]

2. Loans through the discount window, which peaked at $544 billion in the fourth quarter of 2008. These were the most traditional form of Fed lending, in which the Fed lends money to domestic banks in exchange for sound collateral (as envisioned in the Federal Reserve Act of 1913).

3. Loans (not elsewhere classified, n.e.c.) to funding corporations, which peaked at $445 billion in the fourth quarter of 2008.

4. Loans to brokers and dealers, which peaked at $200 billion in the third quarter of 2008.

5. Repurchase agreements (repos), which peaked at $115 billion in the second quarter of 2008.

6. Loans: commercial paper funded by (AMLF), which peaked at $100 billion in the third quarter of 2008.

7. Loans not elsewhere classified (n.e.c.) to households (TALF), which peaked at $47 billion in the fourth quarter of 2009.

Discounting is a common practice the Fed has employed from the time it was created. What makes the discounting operations during the crisis uncommon is the type of institutions the Fed lent to and the collateral the Fed was willing to accept in exchange for loans. To make these kinds of loans, the Fed revived "an obscure provision found in Section 13(3) of the Federal Reserve Act to extend credit to nonbank financial firms for the first time since the 1930s."[9] Section 13(3) allows the Fed to make such loans "in unusual and exigent circumstances."

The Fed's greatest mistake in 2008 was to allow Lehman Brothers to fail. Lehman's failure set off shock waves and induced panic throughout the global financial system.

After Lehman Brothers' bankruptcy, however, the Fed's policy response to the crisis was very effective. Using various types of discounting operations, it found the means to extend Federal Reserve Credit to practically every type of financial institution that requested it.

The Fed injected so much liquidity into the financial system so quickly that the financial system did not collapse. This successful outcome demonstrates that a central bank can, by creating money on a large enough scale, stop a liquidity crisis even in a financial system suffering under trillions of dollars of seriously impaired assets.

Reflating the Economy Through Open Market Operations

The Fed's discounting operations ended the liquidity crisis that had paralyzed the capital markets during the last few months of 2008. However, the lack of short-term liquidity was only the beginning of the problems confronting the US financial system and the US economy more generally.

Exposure to bad loans, inadequate capital and plunging collateral values meant that a great number of financial institutions were still threatened with insolvency, even if their immediate liquidity problems were overcome.

Furthermore, the financial/credit crisis was simultaneously an economic crisis. For decades, the US economy had been driven by credit growth. When credit growth slowed sharply during 2008, the US economy began to collapse. GDP contracted by 8.2% in the fourth quarter of 2008 (at an annualized rate).[10] Fed lending through discounting operations, even on an extraordinary scale, could not restore failing financial institutions to solvency. Nor could it generate sufficient aggregate demand to stop the economy's descent into depression. Very large-scale open market operations were required to overcome those crises.

On November 25, 2008, the Fed launched an audacious new phase of its policy response to the crisis by announcing that it would acquire up to $600 billion of debt instruments issued or guaranteed by the government-sponsored enterprises (GSEs): Fannie Mae, Freddie Mac, and Ginnie Mae. The Fed had often purchased debt securities through open market operations in the past, but never on a scale anything like this. This program became known as *Quantitative Easing* or QE for short. It proved to be so effective in reflating the economy that the Fed enlarged and extended the initial phase of QE; and later launched a second round in 2010 and a third round in 2012. Financial commentators referred to these successive rounds of Quantitative Easing as QE1, QE2, and QE3.[11]

Here are the details:

QE1

On November 25, 2008, the Fed announced "it would initiate a program to purchase up to $100 billion in direct obligations of housing-related government-sponsored enterprises and up to $500 billion in mortgage-backed securities (MBS) backed by Fannie Mae, Freddie Mac, and Ginnie Mae."[12]

Then, at its March 2009 FOMC meeting, the Fed announced it would expand its asset purchases. "The Committee announced that, to provide greater support to mortgage lending and housing markets, it would increase the size of the Federal Reserve's balance sheet further by purchasing up to an additional $750 billion of agency MBS, bringing its total purchases of these securities up to $1.25 trillion in 2009, and that it would increase its purchases of agency debt this year by up to $100 billion to a total of up to

$200 billion. Moreover, to help improve conditions in private credit markets, the Committee decided to purchase up to $300 billion of longer-term Treasury securities over the next six months."[13]

Altogether, between late 2008 and early 2010, the Fed acquired $1.425 trillion of debt securities issued or guaranteed by the GSEs; and a further $300 billion of Treasury securities. That put the total size of QE1 at $1.725 trillion.[14]

QE2

At its August 2010 FOMC meeting, the Fed announced it would purchase an additional $600 billion of Treasury securities by the end of the second quarter of 2011. That took the Fed's holdings of Treasury securities up to $1.6 trillion by mid-2011.[15]

QE3

In September 2012, the Fed announced additional purchases of MBS at the pace of $40 billion per month. Shortly thereafter, in December 2012, the Fed announced that it would also purchase additional Treasury securities at the pace of $45 billion per month.[16]

Between December 2012 and December 2013, the Fed acquired $85 billion of debt securities each month. This was by far the Fed's most aggressive asset purchase program to date. The Fed then began to gradually "taper" the pace of its purchases and ended them altogether in October 2014. During the third round of Quantitative Easing, the Fed purchased $786 billion of Treasury securities and $736 billion of mortgage-backed securities.

Thus, altogether, during these three rounds of Quantitative Easing, the Fed acquired approximately $1.7 trillion of Treasury securities and $1.7 trillion of debt issued or guaranteed by the GSEs.

By the time QE3 was brought to a halt at the end of the third quarter of 2014, in total, the Fed owned $2.5 trillion of Treasury securities (up from $790 billion in mid-2007) and $1.7 trillion of

CHART 12.4 The Fed's Holdings of Treasury Securities and GSE-Backed Mortgage Debt, 2000 to 2016

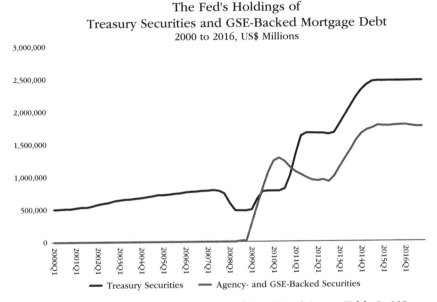

Source: Data from the Financial Accounts of the United States, Table L. 109, Monetary Authority. The Federal Reserve[17]

debt issued or guaranteed by the GSEs (up from $0 as recently as mid-2008), as shown in Chart 12.4.

Notice in Chart 12.4 that when the crisis began in 2008, the Fed's holdings of Treasury securities declined from $790 billion in mid-2007 to $480 billion in mid-2008. That occurred because the Fed sold down some of its holdings of Treasury securities in order to be able to fund its initial discounting operations.

Notice next that the Fed's large-scale purchases of mortgage-backed securities got underway at the very end of 2008, as already noted. A few months later, after the Fed expanded its asset purchases to include government bonds, its holdings of Treasury securities began to grow again.

Interestingly, the Fed ran down part of its holdings of mortgage-backed securities between mid-2010 and the third quarter of 2012, before reversing course and expanding its

CHART 12.5 A Breakdown of the Fed's Assets, 2000 to 2016

A Breakdown of the Fed's Assets
2000 to 2016, US$ Millions

Legend:
- – – U.S. Official Reserve
- ●●●● Federal Reserve Float
- ━━●● Repurchase Agreements
- – – – Loans n.e.c. to Households (TALF)
- – – Corporate Equities
- ━━━ SDRs
- – – Loans Through the Discount Window
- ━━━ Treasury Securities
- ━━━ Loans to Brokers and Dealers
- – – – Nonofficial Foreign Currencies (Swap Lines)
- ━━ ━ Treasury Currency
- ━━ ━ Loans: Commercial Paper Funded by (AMLF)
- ━━━ Agency- and GSE-Backed Securities
- ━━━━ Loans n.e.c. to Funding Corporations
- ━━━ Unidentified Miscellaneous

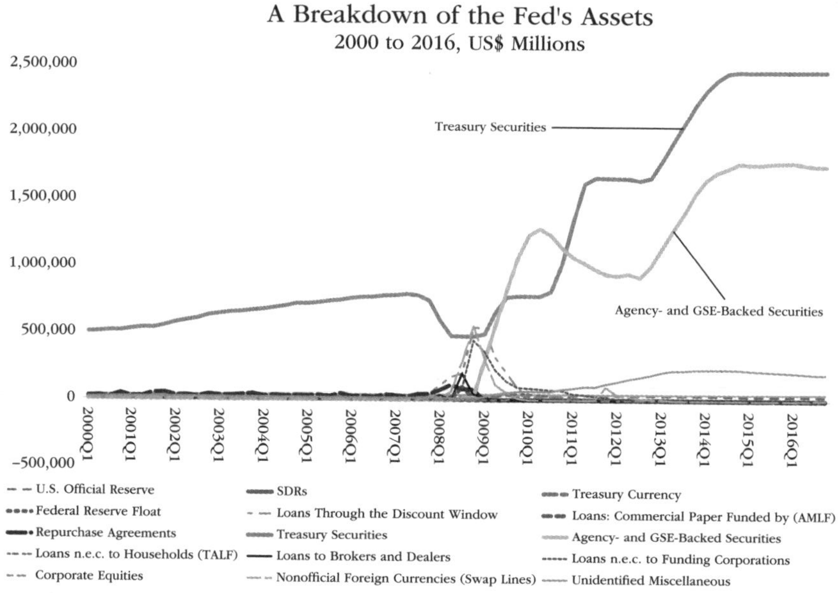

Source: Data from the Financial Accounts of the United States, Table L. 109, Monetary Authority. The Federal Reserve[18]

holdings of these assets to significantly higher levels by the end of 2014.

To put the enormity of the Fed's open market purchases of Treasury securities and mortgage-backed securities into perspective, it is useful to present them along with the assets the Fed had accumulated as collateral through its discounting operations (described above) in one chart, showing a breakdown of the Fed's total assets. This is done in Chart 12.5.

The mortgage-backed securities and the Treasury securities that the Fed acquired through open market operations quickly dwarfed the assets it had accumulated as collateral in its discounting operations.

It is also important to understand that as the Fed flooded the financial markets with liquidity during the first round of Quantitative Easing, that liquidity enabled its recipients in the financial sector to repay the loans they had all received from the

CHART 12.6 Assets Obtained Through Discounting Operations vs. Assets Purchased Through Open Market Operations, 2000 to 2016

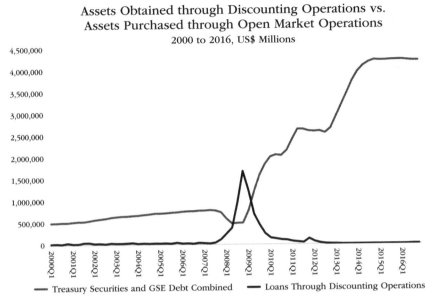

Assets Obtained through Discounting Operations vs. Assets Purchased through Open Market Operations
2000 to 2016, US$ Millions

━━ Treasury Securities and GSE Debt Combined   ━━ Loans Through Discounting Operations

Source: Data from the Financial Accounts of the United States, Table L. 109, Monetary Authority. The Federal Reserve[19]

Fed through the Fed's emergency discounting operations. Consequently, as the central bank's holdings of mortgage-backed securities and Treasury bonds expanded, the collateral assets the Fed had obtained in exchange for the loans it had extended through discounting operations contracted, eventually returning to more normal levels by 2011. This can be seen more easily in Chart 12.6, which compares the assets the Fed obtained through its discounting operations with those it bought through its open market purchases.

Altogether, the Fed's total assets, which it acquired by extending Federal Reserve Credit, skyrocketed from $950 billion at the end of 2007 to $4.5 trillion at the end of 2014. That was nearly a fivefold increase over seven years (see Chart 12.7). During World War II, the Fed's total assets had increased by only 80%.

CHART 12.7 The Fed's Total Assets, 2000 to 2016

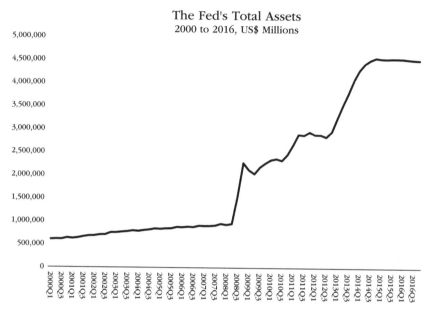

The Fed's Total Assets
2000 to 2016, US$ Millions

Source: Data from the Financial Accounts of the United States, Table L. 109, Monetary Authority. The Federal Reserve[20]

When the Fed extends a loan to a bank through a discounting operation it does so by making a deposit into that bank's reserve account at the Fed. Similarly, when the Fed buys a bond through an open market operation, it pays for that bond by making a deposit into the seller's reserve account at the Fed. The act of making the deposit creates the money that is deposited. This process was explained at length in Part One.

The evolution of Bank Reserves is shown, along with that of all the Fed's other liabilities, in Chart 12.8, which presents a breakdown of the Fed's total liabilities between 2000 and 2016.

The Fed had all but done away with the requirement that banks hold reserves against their deposits long before the crisis of 2008 struck. At the end of 2007, Bank Reserves amounted to only $21 billion. By the time QE3 ended in October 2014, reserves had grown to more than $2.5 trillion as the result of the massive extension of Federal Reserve Credit during those years.

CHART 12.8 A Breakdown of the Fed's Liabilities, 2000 to 2016

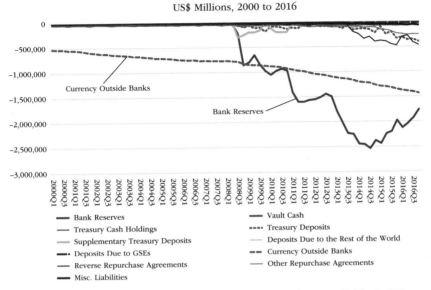

A Breakdown of the Fed's Liabilities
US$ Millions, 2000 to 2016

▬ Bank Reserves	▬ Vault Cash
— Treasury Cash Holdings	•••• Treasury Deposits
⋙ Supplementary Treasury Deposits	— Deposits Due to the Rest of the World
▬• Deposits Due to GSEs	▬▬ Currency Outside Banks
— Reverse Repurchase Agreements	— Other Repurchase Agreements
▬ Misc. Liabilities	

Source: Data from the Financial Accounts of the United States, Table L. 109, Monetary Authority. The Federal Reserve[21]

Reserves expanded less than the $3.5 trillion increase in the Fed's total assets because some of the reserves the Fed created were absorbed during those seven years by the increase in currency, $450 billion; the increase in Treasury deposits at the Fed, $140 billion; an expansion of reverse repo agreements entered into by the Fed, $300 billion; and by the less sizable expansion of various other Fed liabilities.

Nonetheless, the monetary base of the United States expanded by roughly 380% during that period.

Why QE Worked

Quantitative Easing played a leading and indispensable role in reigniting economic growth in the United States after 2008. It helped drive the economic recovery in three overlapping ways.

First, it financed much of the US government's massive budget deficits, permitting government spending to stimulate the economy and generate growth. Second, it pushed up asset prices, which, initially, helped restore many financial institutions and individuals to solvency and, subsequently, created a wealth effect that fueled consumption and economic growth. Finally, QE pushed interest rates lower, making mortgages and other kinds of consumer credit more affordable for individuals and making investment more profitable for businesses.

Financing the Budget Deficit

The crisis of 2008 caused a severe deterioration in the government's finances. Tax receipts plunged from $2,568 billion in 2007 to $2,105 billion in 2009. At the same time, government expenditure jumped from $2,729 billion in 2007 to $3,518 billion in 2009. Chart 12.9 shows these changes.

CHART 12.9 US Government Receipts and Outlays, 2000 to 2014

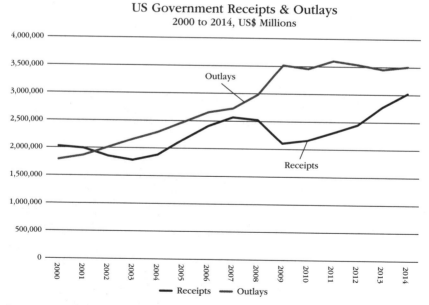

Source: Data from Office of Management and Budget, Historical Tables, The White House

CHART 12.10 US Government Surplus or Deficit, 2000 to 2014

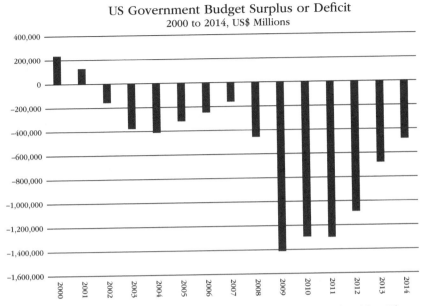

US Government Budget Surplus or Deficit
2000 to 2014, US$ Millions

Source: Data from Office of Management and Budget, Historical Tables, The White House

The 18% drop in revenues combined with a 29% increase in expenditures produced the largest peacetime government budget deficits in the country's history. The budget deficit hit $1.4 trillion in 2009. It exceeded $1 trillion a year for the next three years, as well (see Chart 12.10).

The cumulative budget deficit between 2009 and 2014 amounted to nearly $6.3 trillion. Government borrowing on that scale would normally have pushed interest rates higher. Property prices had begun falling sharply from the second quarter of 2007. Higher interest rates would have driven them even lower, as well as damaging the economy in innumerable other ways. The Fed intervened to prevent interest rates from rising.

Just as in World War I and World War II, the Fed extended Federal Reserve Credit in order to finance the government's large budget deficits at low interest rates at a time of national emergency. From the start of the crisis to the time the third round of Quantitative Easing ended in October 2014, the Fed purchased

CHART 12.11 US Government Debt Owned by the Fed, 1945 to 2016

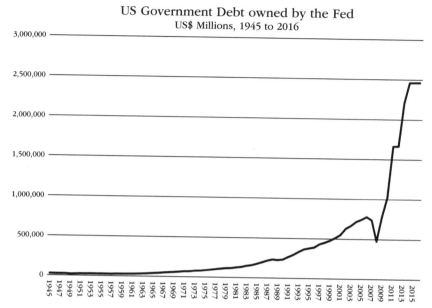

US Government Debt owned by the Fed
US$ Millions, 1945 to 2016

Source: Data from the Financial Accounts of the United States, Table L. 109, Monetary Authority. The Federal Reserve[22]

an additional $1.7 trillion of Treasury securities, an amount equivalent to 27% of the cumulative budget deficits between 2009 and 2014 (see Chart 12.11). If the Fed had not bought those bonds, the private sector would have had to. The issuance of so much new government debt to the private sector would have driven interest rates significantly higher.

In addition, the Fed also purchased $1.7 trillion of debt issued or guaranteed by the GSEs. That also helped finance the government's large deficits. When the Fed acquired the GSE-related debt, whomever it acquired that debt from had money to invest elsewhere. Much of that money moved straight into Treasury securities. Money is fungible. That means when the central bank creates money and injects it into the financial system, it increases the supply of money in the system and affects the prices of all asset classes. By acquiring GSE-related debt, the Fed made another $1.7 trillion available to purchase Treasury securities and other assets. That was another important Fed policy measure that helped to hold interest rates down despite the government's heavy borrowing.

In other words, by creating $3.4 trillion during three rounds of QE, the Fed, in effect, financed 54% of the government's budget deficits between 2009 and 2014.

During the crisis, the government increased its spending sharply even though its tax receipts plunged. That government spending directly boosted economic growth at a time when the private sector, both households and businesses, spent much less. Had the government not increased its spending, the economic crisis would have been much deeper and more protracted. Far worse still, had the government attempted to balance its budget by cutting its spending as its tax receipts shrank, the United States economy would, without question, have collapsed into a new Great Depression.

Without the assistance of the Fed, government borrowing of $6.3 trillion over only six years would have pushed interest rates up. The damage caused by the higher interest rates would have offset, to some extent, and perhaps even outweighed, the benefits of the increased government spending. Quantitative Easing, however, held interest rates down and allowed the full benefits of the government stimulus to work its way all through the economy. This combination of very aggressive fiscal policy and very aggressive monetary policy was extraordinarily effective in pulling the economy out of its nosedive and restoring economic growth.

Pushing Up Asset Prices

Next, Quantitative Easing pushed up asset prices, creating a wealth effect that boosted consumption and fueled economic recovery. That process worked in two ways. First, QE pushed down the interest rates available on bonds and bank accounts. Investors, discouraged by low interest rates on debt instruments, moved their money out of bonds and bank accounts and invested it, instead, in the stock market and the property market. That pushed stock prices and property prices higher.

Second, QE also pushed asset prices higher through a process the Fed calls the "portfolio effect." As the Fed acquired

CHART 12.12 QE & the S&P

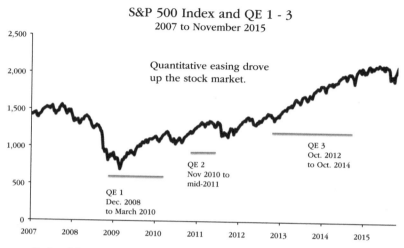

S&P 500 Index and QE 1 - 3
2007 to November 2015

Source: Federal Reserve Bank of St Louis

$3.4 trillion of Treasury securities and GSE-related debt, the previous owners of those debt instruments were forced to invest their money somewhere else. Many chose to invest it in stocks and property, which inflated values in those markets.

Chart 12.12 shows how the S&P 500 Index responded to Quantitative Easing.

Stock prices went higher with every round of Quantitative Easing. Before the first round of QE began, stock prices were in freefall. They rebounded soon after QE began. When QE1 ended, so did the stock market rally. The rally resumed when QE2 was launched, and it ended again in mid-2010 when QE2 was terminated. The third round of Quantitative Easing, which was large and initially open-ended, had the same effect. It drove the stock market higher. During QE1, the S&P 500 Index rose 29%; during QE2, it rose 26%; and during QE3, it rose 40% more.

Property prices also benefited from low interest rates and QE's portfolio effect. Chart 12.13 shows that home prices plunged dramatically from the second quarter of 2007 until mid-2009. They then bounced, but fell again, setting a post-crisis low

CHART 12.13 S&P/Case Shiller 20 City Composite Home Price Index, 2000 to 2014

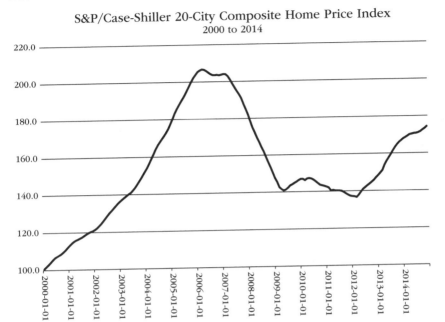

S&P/Case-Shiller 20-City Composite Home Price Index
2000 to 2014

Source: Data from the S&P Case-Shiller 20-City Composit Home Price Index

in March 2012. From there they began to rebound quickly. By the end of 2014, they had recovered more than half their losses.

Rising stock prices and property prices made anyone with a home, a stock portfolio, or a pension richer. Chart 12.14 shows US household net worth, which is calculated by deducting all the liabilities from all the assets of the household sector. Thanks to Quantitative Easing and low interest rates, by the end of 2014, household net worth was $30 trillion or 54% higher than at the depth of the crisis in 2009. In fact, and rather astonishingly, it was $16 trillion or 24% higher than its pre-crisis peak in 2007, when the stock market and the property market were both bubbles.

Rising asset prices created wealth and allowed many millions of Americans to spend more, thereby boosting consumption and economic growth. At the same time, higher asset prices returned

CHART 12.14 Household Net Worth, 1952 to 2014

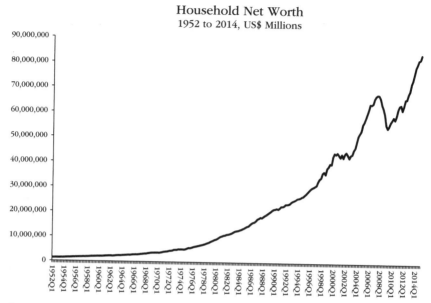

Household Net Worth
1952 to 2014, US$ Millions

Source: Data from the Financial Accounts of the United States. Table B.101.
The Federal Reserve

many banks, businesses, and individuals to solvency by pushing
the value of their assets back above the level of their debt. In
this way, QE helped bring the crisis in the financial sector to an
end, while at the same time strengthening the economy's funda-
mentals by boosting purchasing power.

Pushing Down Interest Rates

Finally, Quantitative Easing helped revitalize the economy by
making borrowing more affordable. QE pushed interest rates
down and held them down. The yield on 10-year Treasury securities fell from 4.0% at the end of 2007 to 2.2% at the end of 2014.
Over the same period, interest rates on 30-year fixed mortgages
and on new auto loans fell from 6.2% to 3.9% and from 7.6%
to 4.1%, respectively. Low mortgage rates and cheap auto financing boosted home sales and car sales. Similarly, corporate
financing costs, which move in line with, although at a spread

above, 10-year Treasury yields, fell and encouraged new business investment by making those investments more profitable.

The Fed, therefore, deserves great praise for the way it responded to the crisis. During the second half of 2008, through its discounting operations, the Fed flooded the capital markets with liquidity until calm was restored and financing once again became plentiful. Then, beginning in December 2008, the Fed, using open market operations, started to reflate the economy by acquiring trillions of dollars of debt instruments by extending Federal Reserve Credit. The Fed's discounting operations ended the financial crisis. Its open market operations played a vital role in ending the economic crisis.

Bank Reserves Are Just a Byproduct of QE

Many people mistakenly believe that Quantitative Easing has no effect on the economy. They point to the buildup in Bank Reserves that occurs when the Fed carries out Quantitative Easing and they argue that QE is ineffective because all the money the Fed creates simply gets stuck in the banks as reserves and, therefore, does not provide any stimulus to the economy. This idea is mistaken, however. It grows out of a misunderstanding of what Bank Reserves actually are. Here a short explanation of what reserves are will help dispel this misunderstanding.

When the Fed buys government bonds, it enables the government to spend that amount of money providing direct support to the economy, as described in the paragraphs above.

The Fed does not buy the bonds directly from the government, however. It buys them from banks. The banks are simply the middlemen. Once the banks have sold the bonds to the Fed, they typically use the proceeds they receive from the Fed to buy more government bonds.

When the Fed buys government bonds from the banks, it pays for those bonds by making deposits into the reserve accounts that those banks hold at the Fed.

In this process, the Fed is not depositing money that already exists. The act of making the deposit creates the money, as explained in Chapter 1.

Of course, the Fed does not really deposit anything physical into the banks' reserve accounts. It just digitally credits those accounts. To help clarify what Bank Reserves really are, imagine that instead of paying for those bonds by digitally crediting the banks' reserve accounts, picture that the Fed pays for the bonds with pennies. Yes, imagine that when the Fed carries out QE that it hands the banks trillions of dollars' worth of pennies – a mountain of pennies – in exchange for those bonds.

The banks are free to spend those pennies on anything they like. For example, they can lend them or invest them. But lending or investing the pennies would not make the mountain of pennies any smaller. Some other bank would end up with the pennies. The pennies will never go away no matter how much the banks lend or invest.

The pennies would go away, however, if the Fed were to sell the bonds it bought from the banks, back to the banks. In this case, when the Fed sells the bonds to the banks, the banks would pay for those bonds by giving the Fed back its pennies. Then there would be fewer pennies in the banking system. When the Fed gets its pennies back, it destroys them. But it is free to create them again any time it wants.

It is the same with Bank Reserves. When the Fed buys bonds from the banks, it pays by making deposits into the reserve accounts that the banks hold at the Fed, thereby creating Bank Reserves. Those reserves are money and the banks can do anything they want with them. They can lend them or invest them, but, when they do, some other bank ends up with the reserves. Lending reserves doesn't reduce the number of reserves, it just sends the reserves to some other bank. That is because when a bank makes a loan, whoever receives the loan then deposits that money into their bank, so the reserves move to their bank. An increase in the level of Bank Reserves simply reflects the increase of liquidity in the financial system. When liquidity increases, financial conditions loosen, interest rates tend to fall, and asset prices tend to rise.

If the Fed were to sells the bonds it bought from the banks back to the banks, then the reserves would disappear. This is what occurs when the Fed conducts open market sales. When the Fed sells bonds back to the banks, in exchange, it debits the reserve accounts that those banks hold at the Fed.

When it debits those reserve accounts, that makes the reserves disappear.

The Fed does not have its own bank account in which it keeps trillions of dollars of reserves. Why would it? The Fed can create reserves any time it wants.

So, the buildup of Bank Reserves in the accounts that the banks hold at the Fed, is simply just a by-product that occurs when the Fed buys government bonds, just as the mountain of pennies would be, if the Fed paid for the bonds it bought with pennies.

Hopefully, this explanation clears up the misunderstanding about Bank Reserves once and for all, because Quantitative Easing is the country's most powerful economic policy tool. It is important to understand that QE works. It is not possible to understand the government's policy response to economic crises in the twenty-first century without understanding that QE does effectively stimulate economic growth.

The Fed Was Helped by Other Central Banks

The Fed was not the only central bank acting to reflate the US economy, however. Other central banks also pumped liquidity into the US economy by creating money and buying US dollar-denominated debt. Chart 12.15 shows total foreign exchange reserves from 1970 to 2014.

A central bank obtains foreign exchange reserves by creating its own currency and using it to buy the currencies of other countries. Total foreign exchange reserves increased by $5.7 trillion between 2007 and 2014, from $6.1 trillion to $11.6 trillion.

If it is assumed that 70% of all foreign exchange reserves are made up of US dollars,[23] that means that the dollar holdings of central banks outside the United States increased by $4 trillion ($5.7 trillion multiplied by 70%) between 2007 and 2014. As those dollars were acquired, they were invested in US

CHART 12.15 Total Foreign Exchange Reserves, 1970 to 2014

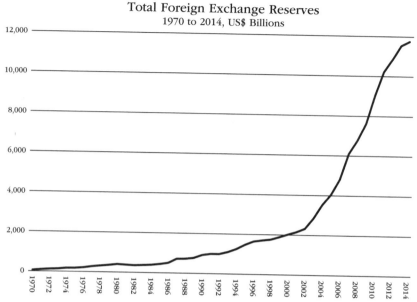

Source: The International Monetary Fund

dollar-denominated assets. Central banks are risk adverse and invest most of their foreign exchange holdings in government bonds. Chart 12.16 shows that between 2007 and 2014, the rest of the world's holdings of US Treasury securities increased by $3.8 trillion to $6.2 trillion. It is very likely that central banks were the buyers of a great majority of those Treasury securities.

Even if those foreign central banks used their newly acquired dollars to invest in US dollar-denominated assets other than Treasury securities, their investments would still have pushed money into Treasury securities. For example, if the People's Bank of China bought $50 billion of GSE-related debt or of US corporate bonds, whomever it bought those bonds from would have had $50 billion of cash to invest and, sooner or later, much, if not all, of that money would have ended up in US Treasury securities. This is in part because there is only a limited amount of investable securities of all types at any one time and also, in part, because the investment in GSE-related debt would have

CHART 12.16 US Government Debt Owned by the Rest of the World, 1970 to 2014

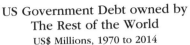

US Government Debt owned by
The Rest of the World
US$ Millions, 1970 to 2014

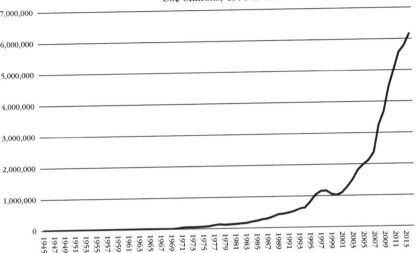

Source: Data from the Financial Accounts of the United States. Table L.133. The Federal Reserve

pushed down the yield on all GSE-related debt, making the yield on US Treasury securities relatively more attractive on a risk-adjusted basis.

In short, then, the Fed was not alone in monetizing US government debt. In fact, central banks outside the United States monetized more US government debt than the Fed did between 2007 and 2014. The rest of the world's holdings of US Treasury securities increased by $3.8 trillion during those years, whereas the Fed's holdings of US Treasury securities increased by "only" $1.7 trillion. By the end of 2014, as shown in Chart 12.17, out of the $19 trillion of US government debt outstanding at the end of 2014, the rest of the world owned $6.2 trillion, whereas the Fed owned just $2.4 trillion.

The monetization of US government debt by foreign central banks has not been recognized by the economics profession; and, if it has been understood by those behind the

CHART 12.17 US Government Debt Owned by the Fed and the Rest of the World, 1970 to 2014

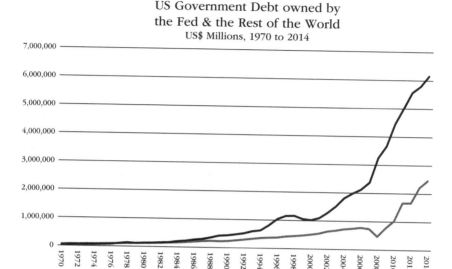

US Government Debt owned by
the Fed & the Rest of the World
US$ Millions, 1970 to 2014

— The Federal Reserve — The Rest of the World

Source: Data from the Financial Accounts of the United States. Tables L.109 and L.113. The Federal Reserve

"smart money" in the financial markets, they have kept that information to themselves. The sooner this fact is commonly understood, the better. Total foreign exchange reserves peaked at more than $12 trillion during 2014, rising from less than $2 trillion at the turn of the century. That means that the central banks of the trade surplus countries created the equivalent of $10 trillion in just 14 years. It is likely that approximately 70% of that amount, or $7 trillion, ended up being invested in US dollar-denominated assets, primarily Treasury bonds. That dwarfs the $3.6 trillion the Fed created during the first three rounds of Quantitative Easing. That new central bank money profoundly impacted US interest rates and, consequently, the rate of economic growth in the United States and all around the world. Its extraordinary impact further exemplifies the significance of the Money Revolution that occurred once money ceased to be backed by gold five decades ago.

Four Charts

Part One traced the evolution of the Fed's balance sheet over six consecutive periods, covering 1914 to 2007. For each period, four charts were used to illustrate changes in the Fed's balance sheet in order to explain Fed policy:

1. The Fed's Total Assets
2. A Breakdown of the Fed's Major Assets and Liabilities
3. The Annual Change in Federal Reserve Credit
4. Federal Reserve Credit and Its Components

Those charts will now be presented and discussed here for the period 2007 to 2016.

The Fed's total assets increased from $950 billion at the end of 2007 to $4,555 billion at the end of 2014, an increase of 379% over seven years. The third round of Quantitative Easing, which, at its peak, reached $85 billion per month, ended in October 2014. Between 2014 and 2016, the Fed's total assets remained relatively unchanged, ending the period at $4,510 billion. This crisis-driven surge in the Fed's total assets is shown in Chart 12.18.

The evolution of the Fed's major assets and liabilities between 1945 to 2016 is presented in Chart 12.19. Since the preceding paragraphs have discussed the major developments on both the assets side and the liabilities side of the Fed's balance sheet in considerable detail, no further comments will be added here.

The Fed is one of the world's most powerful (and profitable) institutions due to its ability to create credit: Federal Reserve Credit. The Federal Reserve Act of 1913 had envisioned that the Fed would only extend relatively limited amounts of short-term credit to prevent banking crises; and that such credit as the Fed did create would be retired once the panics had passed. As we have seen, that is not how things worked out.

CHART 12.18 The Fed's Total Assets, 1945 to 2016

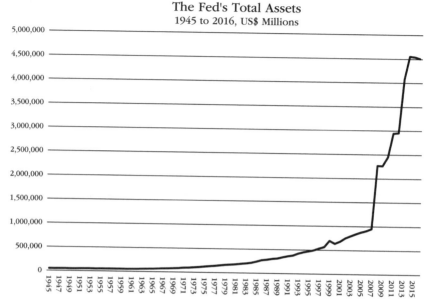

The Fed's Total Assets
1945 to 2016, US$ Millions

Source: Data from the Financial Accounts of the United States, Table L. 109, Monetary Authority. The Federal Reserve[24]

The Fed created $1.4 billion of Federal Reserve Credit in 1918 at the peak of the United States involvement in World War I. Not until World War II did the Fed create so much credit in one year again. The largest annual increase of Federal Reserve Credit during World War II was $7.5 billion in 1944. That peak in credit creation by the Fed was not exceeded until 1971, when the Fed extended $8.6 billion of Federal Reserve Credit.

New record highs were set frequently after 1971, but milestones included 1986, when Federal Reserve Credit expanded by $31 billion, and 1993, when it expanded by $41 billion. The largest amount of Federal Reserve Credit extended in any one year before the crisis of 2008 occurred in 1999, when the Fed flooded the financial markets with liquidity over concerns related to Y2K. It grew by $133 billion that year, but $61 billion of that credit was extinguished the following year. Other than the Y2K-affected year of 1999, the pre-crisis, all-time record expansion of Federal Reserve Credit was $69 billion in 2002.

CHART 12.19 A Breakdown of the Fed's Major Assets and Liabilities, 1945 to 2016

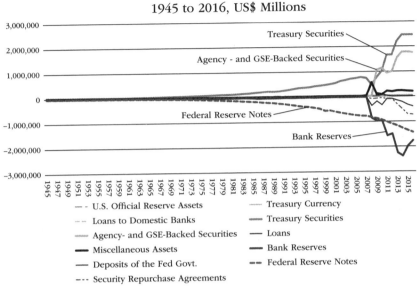

A Breakdown of the Fed's Major Assets & Liabilities
1945 to 2016, US$ Millions

Legend:
- − ‒ U.S. Official Reserve Assets
- − − Loans to Domestic Banks
- ═══ Agency- and GSE-Backed Securities
- ▬ Miscellaneous Assets
- ▬ Deposits of the Fed Govt.
- - - - Security Repurchase Agreements
- ▬ Treasury Currency
- ▬ Treasury Securities
- ▬ Loans
- ▬ Bank Reserves
- ▬▬ Federal Reserve Notes

Source: Data from the Financial Accounts of the United States, Table L. 109, Monetary Authority. The Federal Reserve[25]

The Fed extended $1,322 billion of Federal Reserve Credit during 2008. That was 10 times the previous record of $133 billion set in 1999. The 2008 record held until the COVID-19 depression in 2020. Nonetheless, the Fed created extraordinarily large amounts of credit during four out of the six years following 2008. Federal Reserve Credit expanded by $192 billion in 2010, $493 billion in 2011, $1,105 billion in 2013, and $475 billion in 2014. Chart 12.20 illustrates these unprecedented developments.

Chart 12.21 shows total Federal Reserve Credit and the assets the Fed accumulated as a result of extending that credit. That chart shows that total Federal Reserve Credit expanded by $3,448 billion (437%) between 2007 and 2014, before contracting slightly, by $16 billion, over the next two years.

In that chart, Treasury securities and GSE-backed mortgage securities are grouped together as government securities, since

CHART 12.20 Federal Reserve Credit, Annual $ Change, 1940 to 2016

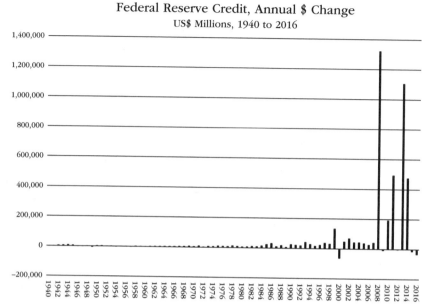

Federal Reserve Credit, Annual $ Change
US$ Millions, 1940 to 2016

Source: Data from the Federal Reserve's Annual Report for 2017, Tables 6.A and 6.B

GSE debt became government debt, at least effectively, if not officially, after Fannie and Freddie were nationalized in 2008.

The lines depicting total Federal Reserve Credit and government securities appear indistinguishable in this chart every year except for those years between 2007 and 2011, when the assets the Fed accumulated as collateral through its discounting operations are also visible. Otherwise, at least as far as can be distinguished in this chart, all the Federal Reserve Credit that the Fed created was used to acquire, and thereby to help finance, government debt. It should be noted, however, that up until the early 1930s, the assets the Fed accumulated as collateral by extending Federal Reserve Credit through discounting operations exceeded the government securities it acquired through extending Federal Reserve Credit through open market operations. That cannot be seen in this chart. It is shown and discussed in Chapters 2 to 4, however.

CHART 12.21 Federal Reserve Credit and Its Components,
1914 to 2016

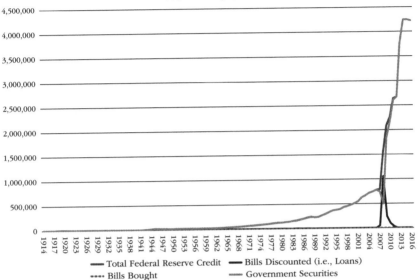

Federal Reserve Credit and Its Components
US$ Millions, 1914 to 2016

— Total Federal Reserve Credit   — Bills Discounted (i.e., Loans)
···· Bills Bought   — Government Securities

Source: Data from "*The Federal Reserve System's Weekly Balance Sheet Since 1914*" and accompanying spreadsheet. Johns Hopkins University, SAE/No.115/ July 2018. See Bibliography.[26]

Conclusion

In 2008, the United States was struck by the most severe financial and economic crisis since the Great Depression. The Fed's discounting operations prevented the collapse of the financial system. Its open market operations played a leading and indispensable part in restoring economic growth.

In the process, the Fed extended $3.4 trillion of Federal Reserve Credit between the end of 2007 and the end of 2014. Consequently, the monetary base of the United States leapt by 370% in only seven years.[27] Conventional wisdom suggests that such an extraordinary surge in the money supply over such a short period of time should have resulted in very high rates of inflation. It did not.

Chapter 15 analyzes inflation in the United States over the past century to explain why it didn't. First, however, Chapter 13 will discuss how Creditism fared between 2008 and 2019; and Chapter 14 will describe the extraordinary economic policy response to the COVID-19 pandemic during 2020 and the first half of 2021.

Notes

1. Ben Bernanke, quoted in the Financial Crisis Inquiry Commission Report, p. 354. https://www.govinfo.gov/content/pkg/GPO-FCIC/pdf/GPO-FCIC.pdf
2. Office of Management and Budget, The White House.
3. "The Rescue of Fannie Mae and Freddie Mac," Federal Reserve Bank of New York Staff Reports, p. 2. https://www.newyorkfed.org/medialibrary/media/research/staff_reports/sr719.pdf
4. The figures for total assets used in this chapter are taken from the Annual Reports and/or 10-K Reports filed by each company, p. xxv. https://www.govinfo.gov/content/pkg/GPO-FCIC/pdf/GPO-FCIC.pdf
5. Phil Angelides (2011), Financial Crisis Inquiry Report.
6. The source for the seven lending facilities is the 2008 Annual Report of the Federal Reserve System, pp. 51–55.
7. Monetary Authority includes the assets and liabilities of Federal Reserve Banks and Treasury monetary accounts that supply or absorb Bank Reserves.
8. Monetary Authority includes the assets and liabilities of Federal Reserve Banks and Treasury monetary accounts that supply or absorb Bank Reserves.
9. Marc Labonte, "Federal Reserve: Emergency Lending," Congressional Research Service, updated March 27, 2020. https://fas.org/sgp/crs/misc/R44185.pdf
10. Total credit did not actually contract quarter on quarter until the second quarter of 2009. It then contracted for five consecutive quarters. Of course, it would have contracted earlier had the government not borrowed more than $1 trillion during the second half of 2008.
11. The fourth round of QE began in October 2019 following a disruption in the repo market. Then it was expanded enormously

beginning in March 2020 as part of the policy response to the economic crisis caused by the COVID-19 pandemic.

12. Board of Governors of the Federal Reserve System 2008 Annual Report, p. 38

13. Board of Governors of the Federal Reserve System 2009 Annual Report, p. 88

14. Board of Governors of the Federal Reserve System 2010 Annual Report, p. 21

15. Board of Governors of the Federal Reserve System 2010 Annual Report, p. 21

16. Board of Governors of the Federal Reserve System 2012 Annual Report, p. 25

17. Monetary Authority includes the assets and liabilities of Federal Reserve Banks and Treasury Monetary accounts that supply or absorb Bank Reserves.

18. Monetary Authority includes the assets and liabilities of Federal Reserve Banks and Treasury Monetary accounts that supply or absorb Bank Reserves.

19. Monetary Authority includes the assets and liabilities of Federal Reserve Banks and Treasury Monetary accounts that supply or absorb Bank Reserves.

20. Monetary Authority includes the assets and liabilities of Federal Reserve Banks and Treasury Monetary accounts that supply or absorb Bank Reserves.

21. Monetary Authority includes the assets and liabilities of Federal Reserve Banks and Treasury Monetary accounts that supply or absorb Bank Reserves.

22. Monetary Authority includes the assets and liabilities of Federal Reserve Banks and Treasury Monetary accounts that supply or absorb Bank Reserves.

23. As discussed in Chapter 10.

24. Monetary Authority includes the assets and liabilities of Federal Reserve Banks and Treasury Monetary accounts that supply or absorb Bank Reserves.

25. Monetary Authority includes the assets and liabilities of Federal Reserve Banks and Treasury Monetary accounts that supply or absorb Bank Reserves.

26. Federal Reserve Credit is here comprised of total loans and securities held by the Fed.

27. US Monetary Base St. Louis Fed. https://fred.stlouisfed.org/series/BOGMBASE

CHAPTER 13

Creditism Between the Crises

So we don't react to, you know, to most things that happen in the financial markets. But when we see a sustained change in financial conditions, then that's something that has to play into our thinking. In fact, our policy works through changing financial conditions, so it's sort of the essence of what we do.

Fed Chair Jerome Powell[1]

Creditism nearly collapsed in 2008. A surge in government borrowing held it together, but, even with a string of trillion-dollar budget deficits, credit growth remained too weak to restore solid economic growth. The Fed did whatever it took to drive asset prices higher in order to create a wealth effect that would supplement credit growth. The combination of massive fiscal and monetary stimulus only managed to produce a lackluster economic recovery. This chapter describes the weakened state of Creditism between the crisis of 2008 and the end of 2019, just a few months before the start of the economic depression brought on by the COVID-19 pandemic.

Creditism in Crisis

Total credit began to contract in 2009. If it had contracted significantly or for very long, the US economy would have collapsed into a severe depression. It didn't, however. Total credit (not adjusted for inflation) declined by only 0.1% in 2009 and then began to grow again in 2010. By the end of 2019, total credit had expanded by $23 trillion, or 43%, above its pre-crisis 2007 peak, to $75 trillion, as shown in Chart 13.1.

Between 1981, when Reaganomics began, and the crisis of 2008, total credit had grown faster than the economy and, consequently, had been the leading driver of economic growth. That was reflected in the sharp rise in the ratio of total credit to GDP from 169% in 1981 to 378% in 2009 (see Chart 13.2). After the crisis, however, credit grew less than the economy. Credit

CHART 13.1 Total Credit = Total Debt, 1945 to 2019

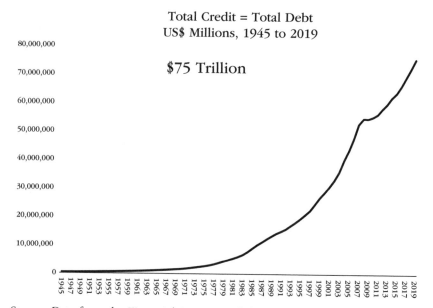

Source: Data from the Financial Accounts of the United States, the Federal Reserve

CHART 13.2 Total Credit to GDP, 1945 to 2019

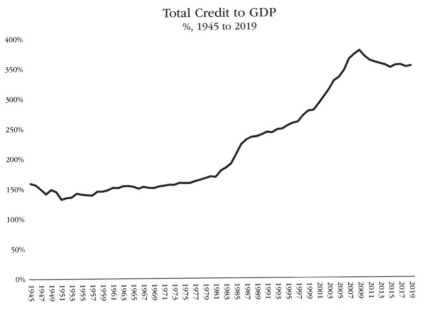

Total Credit to GDP
%, 1945 to 2019

Source: Data from the Financial Accounts of the United States, the Federal Reserve

growth adjusted for inflation averaged only 1.3% a year between 2008 and 2019, whereas real GDP growth averaged 1.7% a year. By 2019, the ratio of total credit to GDP had declined from its 2009 peak of 378% to 352%. The slump in that ratio indicates that credit growth had ceased to be the most important source of economic growth.

A glance at the change in the debt levels of the three main classifications of debtors reveals that it was a sharp contraction in the debt of the financial sector that weighed most heavily on the economy. Between 2008 and 2019, financial sector debt contracted by more than a third, falling from 122% of GDP to just 78%. Non-financial sector debt flattened out at around 250% of GDP. The debt of the rest of the world expanded from 11% of GDP to 21%. Chart 13.3 shows these trends.

CHART 13.3 The Ratio of Debt to GDP by Major Sector, 1945 to 2019

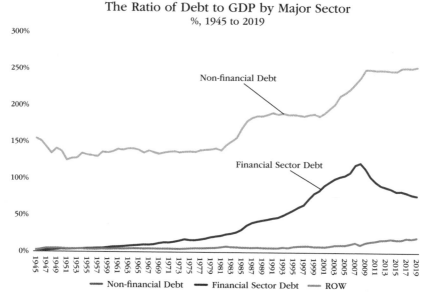

The Ratio of Debt to GDP by Major Sector
%, 1945 to 2019

Source: Data from the Financial Accounts of the United States, the
Federal Reserve

Financial Sector Debt

The collapse in the debt of the financial sector was due primarily to the unwinding of the debt obligations of the issuers
of asset backed securities. Their debt relative to GDP fell from
32% in 2007 to just 6% in 2019, as their business model (which
was designed primarily to hide the assets of banks in off-balance
sheet vehicles to enable the banks to avoid capital requirements)
became unacceptable, given the large role it had played in causing the financial crisis.

The debt of the rest of the financial sector also contracted
relative to the size of the economy. When the government
was forced to put the government-sponsored enterprises into
"conservatorship" to prevent their bankruptcy in 2008, their col-
lective debt obligations exceeded $8 trillion. That was more than
the US government's debt held by the public, which amounted
to $6.7 trillion at the end of that year and nearly 75% as much as

CHART 13.4 The Financial Sector Debt to GDP by Sub-Sector, 1945 to 2019

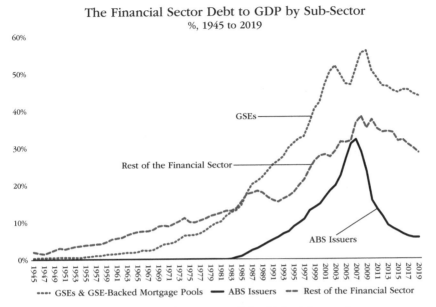

The Financial Sector Debt to GDP by Sub-Sector
%, 1945 to 2019

···· GSEs & GSE-Backed Mortgage Pools — ABS Issuers -- Rest of the Financial Sector

Source: Data from the Financial Accounts of the United States, the Federal Reserve

gross government debt.[2,3] Afterwards, the ratio of the GSEs' debt to GDP fell from a peak of 56% in 2009 to 44% in 2019. The combined debt of all the other sub-sectors of the financial sector also fell, from 38% of GDP in 2008 to 29% in 2019.

Chart 13.4 shows these trends for the financial sector.

Non-financial Sector Debt

As mentioned above, non-financial sector debt to GDP remained flat after 2008 at approximately 250%. However, the aggregate data for the non-financial sector masks extraordinarily important developments within that sector, as shown in Chart 13.5.

An explosion of government debt offset a large contraction in the debt of the household sector, as well as initial declines in corporate and non-corporate business debt and a subsequent decline in the debt of state and local governments.

CHART 13.5 Non-financial Sector Debt to GDP by Sub-sector, 1945 to 2019

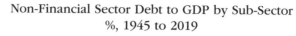

Non-Financial Sector Debt to GDP by Sub-Sector %, 1945 to 2019

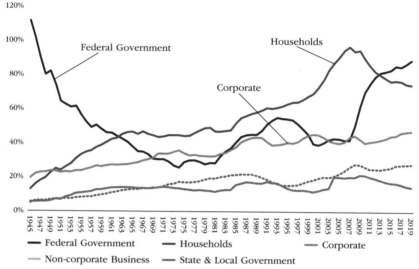

Source: Data from the Financial Accounts of the United States, the Federal Reserve

The growth in household sector debt had been an important driver of US economic growth from the mid-1980s and the principal driver of US economic growth from the turn of the century. It doubled relative to the size of the economy between 1984 and 2007, surging from 48% to 97% of GDP during those 23 years. By the end of that period, the household sector had taken on far more debt than it could bear. A tsunami of debt defaults by the sector ignited the global economic crisis the following year. Afterwards, the ratio of household sector debt to GDP collapsed back to 74% by the end of 2019 (see Chart 13.5).

Corporate debt and non-corporate business debt also declined relative to GDP during the years immediately after the crisis, although less dramatically than household debt.

CHART 13.6 US Government Budget Deficit (–) or Surplus, 2000 to 2019

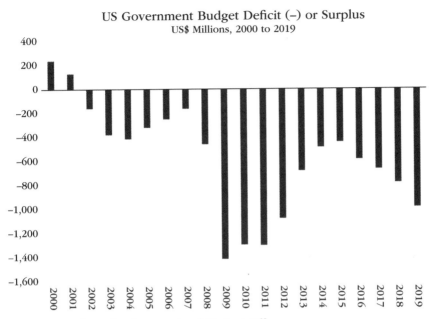

US Government Budget Deficit (–) or Surplus
US$ Millions, 2000 to 2019

Source: Data from the Congressional Budget Office

Only government debt expanded. Surging government debt was the crutch that kept the economy from falling over. As soon as the crisis began, the government began to borrow to finance extraordinarily large budget deficits. In 2007 the government's budget deficit was $161 billion. By 2009, it had leapt to $1.4 trillion. It remained above $1 trillion a year for the next three years (see Chart 13.6).

Those deficits provided the fiscal stimulus that kept the economy (and Creditism) from collapsing during the first postcrisis years when household spending and business investment plummeted. Chart 13.7 illustrates how rapidly government debt expanded in dollar amounts once the crisis began, just when household and corporate debt initially contracted.

Altogether, between 2007 and 2019, government debt more than tripled from $6.1 trillion to more than $19 trillion.[4] Without

CHART 13.7 Non-financial Sector Debt by Sub-sector, 1945 to 2019

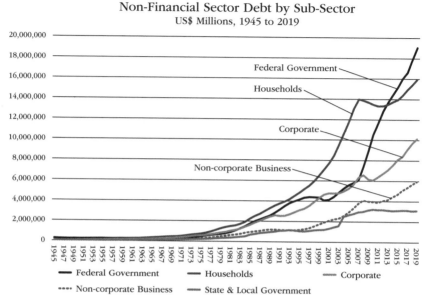

Non-Financial Sector Debt by Sub-Sector
US$ Millions, 1945 to 2019

Source: Data from the Financial Accounts of the United States, the
Federal Reserve

the increase in government spending that that debt financed, more households would have defaulted on their debts and more businesses would have failed. In that scenario, the debt levels of those sectors would have contracted far more than they actually did. The systemic banking sector crisis would have intensified, and the economy would have spiraled into a Great Depression, as it did during the 1930s.

When the worst of the crisis had passed, the government's budget deficit fell to a post-crisis low of $442 billion in 2015. By 2019, however, it had climbed back to nearly $1 trillion due to a new round of fiscal stimulus that combined both tax cuts and increased spending.

As a percentage of GDP, government debt soared from 42% in 2007 to 89% in 2019.[5]

Altogether, between 2007 and 2019, the total debt of all sectors of the economy combined increased by $22.9 trillion. Government borrowing of $13 trillion accounted for 57% of that total.

CHART 13.8 Total Credit, Annual Percentage Change, Adjusted for Inflation, 1990 to 2019

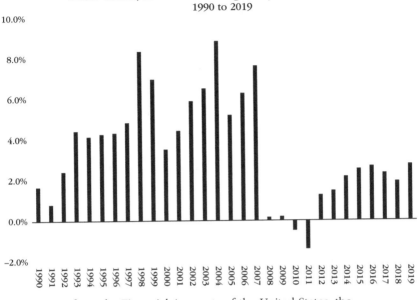

Total Credit, Annual % Change, adjusted for Inflation
1990 to 2019

Source: Data from the Financial Accounts of the United States, the Federal Reserve

Insufficient Credit Growth

Even with the extraordinary expansion of federal government debt, the annual growth rate for total credit adjusted for inflation remained very weak, as shown in Chart 13.8.

In 2008, total credit adjusted for inflation expanded by only 0.2%. In 2009, it grew again by 0.2%, even though the US government had to borrow to finance a $1.4 trillion budget deficit that year. Total credit adjusted for inflation contracted by 0.5% during 2010 and by 1.4% in 2011. It turned positive again in 2012, with 1.3% growth that year and 1.5% growth the next. Only in 2014 did total credit growth adjusted for inflation once again exceed the 2% "recession threshold" that had typically been required to keep the economy out of recession, but only just, with a growth rate of 2.2%. From there it rose to 2.7% in 2016. By 2018, it was back below 2%, however. In 2019, it

CHART 13.9 US Real GDP, Annual Percentage Change, 1981 to 2019

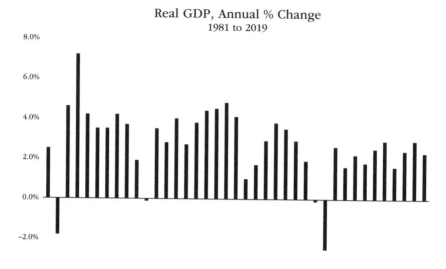

Real GDP, Annual % Change
1981 to 2019

Source: Data from the Financial Accounts of the United States, the Federal Reserve

reached a post-crisis peak of 2.9%, supported by an inflation rate that was 6/10 of 1% less than it had been in 2018 and a $1.2 trillion increase in government debt, which accounted for 36% of the increase in total debt that year.

Between 2008 and 2019, the average annual increase in total credit growth adjusted for inflation was only 1.3%. That compares with an average of 5.8% a year between 1981 and the eve of the financial crisis in 2007. Given the economy's reliance on credit growth, it is not surprising that economic growth was also much weaker when credit growth slowed down. Between 2008 and 2019, real GDP growth averaged just 1.7% a year, compared with average annual growth of 3.2% between 1981 and 2007 (see Chart 13.9).

If anything, given how weak credit growth was, it is surprising that the US economy managed to grow as much as it did

CHART 13.10 Credit Growth vs. GDP Growth, Adjusted for Inflation, 1952 to 2019

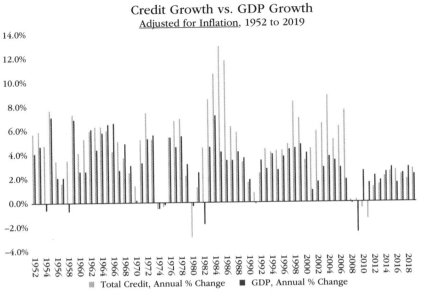

Credit Growth vs. GDP Growth
Adjusted for Inflation, 1952 to 2019

■ Total Credit, Annual % Change   ■ GDP, Annual % Change

Source: Data from the Financial Accounts of the United States, the Federal Reserve

after 2008. As explained in Chapter 11, between 1952 and 2009 the US economy went into recession all nine times that total credit adjusted for inflation grew by less 2%.

The economy did contract by 0.1% in 2008 and by 2.5% in 2009, years when total credit growth adjusted for inflation was only 0.2% a year. After that, however, the economy managed to grow, at least modestly, every year up through 2019 at a rate between 1.6% and 2.9% a year. With credit growth adjusted for inflation below the 2% recession threshold during five out of the ten years between 2010 and 2019, and never above 2.9%, economic growth was significantly stronger than would have been expected.

Chart 13.10, which compares credit growth and economic growth – both adjusted for inflation – back to 1952, demonstrates the marked weakness in both after 2007.

CHART 13.11 Household Net Worth, 1952 to 2019

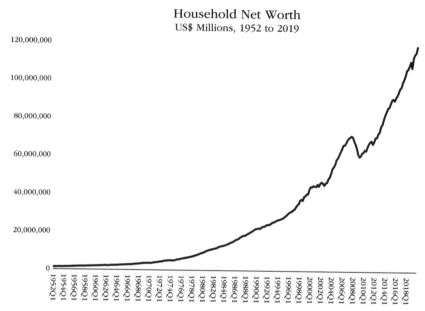

Household Net Worth
US$ Millions, 1952 to 2019

Source: Data from the Financial Accounts of the United States, the Federal Reserve

Asset Price Inflation

What was responsible for this break from the past pattern? Credit growth was too weak to drive the economy, so what did?

The answer is *asset price inflation*. The Fed, realizing that credit growth was insufficient to generate adequate economic growth, worked hard to push up the value of stocks and property through a combination of very low interest rates and the extension of Federal Reserve Credit on an unprecedented scale. Chart 13.11 shows the Fed's efforts were rewarded. Household net worth skyrocketed.

Household net worth is calculated by deducting all the liabilities of the American households from all their assets. It is essentially the wealth of the American public. It peaked at $71.3 trillion in the third quarter of 2007. It then fell $11 trillion (15%) to a trough of $60.3 trillion in the first quarter of 2009. From there, thanks to Quantitative Easing and extremely low interest rates, it began to rebound, as stock prices and property prices turned up. Between that post-crisis low and the end of 2019, household net worth nearly doubled to $118 trillion. More than $58 trillion of new wealth was created. Everyone who owned a home, a stock portfolio, or a pension benefited.

As wealth expanded, Americans spent more, and rising consumption made the economy expand through what is known as the wealth effect.

Asset price inflation was the supplement the economy required to grow despite weak credit expansion during the years after 2008. That growth supplement was engineered by the Fed.

Thus, massive fiscal stimulus combined with massive monetary stimulus saved Creditism from collapse after 2008 even though the private sector was too heavily indebted to take on enough new debt to make the economy grow.

Creditism was on government life support, but it survived.

Tightening

In late 2015, the Fed initiated a valiant, but, ultimately, foolhardy, experiment when it began to tighten monetary policy. It had two objectives for tightening.

First, the Fed had hoped to "normalize" monetary policy by pushing interest rates up from close to 0% to a more normal level, so that it would have the option to cut rates again during the next recession. It had also hoped to shrink the size of its balance sheet back to a more normal level, so that it could once again control the level of the federal funds rate by controlling the level of Bank Reserves through open market operations, rather than by paying interest on Bank Reserves as it had been forced to do since 2008.

Secondly, the Fed tightened monetary policy because it was concerned that a new asset price bubble was forming, particularly in the stock market. Chart 13.12 presents the ratio of household net worth as a percentage of disposable personal income. This can be thought of as a wealth-to-income ratio, since net worth reflects wealth and disposable personal income is income.

CHART 13.12 Households Net Worth as a Percentage of Disposable
Personal Income, 1952 to 2019

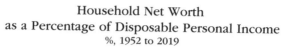

Household Net Worth
as a Percentage of Disposable Personal Income
%, 1952 to 2019

Source: Data from the Financial Accounts of the United States, the
Federal Reserve

This ratio averaged 548% between 1952 and 2019. It rose to
609% during the NASDAQ bubble and then crashed back to the
long-term average when that bubble popped. It rose to 666% at
the peak of the property bubble and then plunged back to the
long-term average again in 2009. By early 2015, it had climbed
back above 650%. The Fed felt compelled to tighten monetary
policy to try to prevent a new bubble from forming and popping.

The third round of Quantitative Easing ended in October
2014. The federal funds rate remained at a range between 0% and
0.25% from the end of 2008 until December 2015. That month, the
Fed hiked rates by 25 basis points. The Fed remained extremely
cautious in tightening monetary policy. The next increase in the
federal funds rate did not occur until one year later. There were
three rate hikes of 25 basis points each during 2017 and four

more during 2018. At the end of 2018, the federal funds rate was set at a range between 2.25% and 2.5%.

In October 2017, the Fed began to tighten even more aggressively when it started reversing Quantitative Easing. Instead of extending Federal Reserve Credit by acquiring US government securities and mortgage-backed securities guaranteed by Fannie Mae and Freddie Mac, as it had done during the three rounds of QE between early 2009 and October 2014, the Fed began contracting the Federal Reserve Credit that it had already extended by taking payment on some of those bonds when they matured. This process became known as *Quantitative Tightening*, or QT, for short.[6]

The Fed introduced QT gradually. Recall that at the peak of Quantitative Easing, during 2013, the Fed had expanded Federal Reserve Credit by $85 billion a month. During the final quarter of 2017, it contracted Federal Reserve Credit by just $10 billion per month. However, during the first quarter of 2018, the Fed increased QT to $20 billion per month and then to $30 billion per month in the second quarter, $40 billion per month in the third quarter and to $50 billion per month in the fourth quarter. By the end of 2018, Federal Reserve Credit outstanding had contracted by more than $400 billion from October 2017 when Quantitative Tightening began, as shown in Chart 13.13. Put differently, the Fed had contracted the country's monetary base by more than $400 billion during that time.

Capitulation

Eventually, the combination of rate hikes and Quantitative Tightening became too much for the stock market to withstand, but not until the wealth-to-income ratio had climbed to 698%, a record high, in the third quarter of 2018. Shortly thereafter, the US stock market took a dive. The S&P 500 Index fell from an all-time high of 2,930 on September 21, 2018, to 2,351 on December 24, 2018, a 20% drop in only three months. Chart 13.14 shows the impact that had on household sector wealth.

CHART 13.13 Federal Reserve Credit, 1990 to 2018

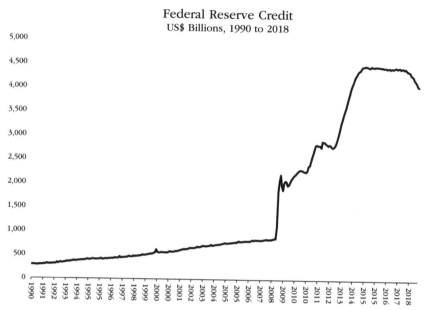

Federal Reserve Credit
US$ Billions, 1990 to 2018

Source: Data from the Federal Reserve Bank of St. Louis

During the fourth quarter of 2018, household net worth plunged $3.7 trillion, the largest drop ever up until then when measured in dollar terms, although not when measured in terms of percentage change. Suddenly, US economic data began to weaken significantly. Fed tightening was not the only reason for the weaker economy, but it was an important factor.

Recognizing that it had been too aggressive, the Fed announced a sudden change of plans. Following the January 2019 FOMC meeting, Chairman Powell stated the Fed had reconsidered its previously announced intention to continue hiking rates and to continue normalizing its balance sheet through further Quantitative Tightening. Instead, rate hikes were to be put on hold. Furthermore, the public was told that QT would be ended much earlier than had been previously indicated. That meant that there would continue to be a much larger amount

CHART 13.14 Household Net Worth, Quarter on Quarter Change, 1991 to 2019

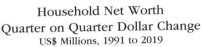

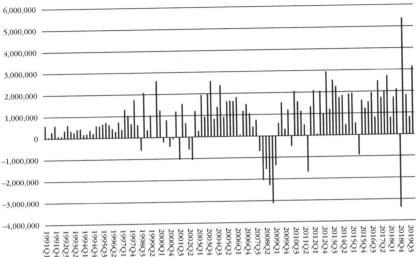

Source: Data from the Financial Accounts of the United States, the Federal Reserve

of Federal Reserve Credit outstanding than the Fed had signaled earlier. The abruptness of this monetary policy U-turn was jarring.

After the Fed's about-face, the stock market recovered, household net worth rose by a record amount in the first quarter of 2019, $5.4 trillion, and the economy began to strengthen.

In May, the S&P 500 Index fell again, however, this time by 6.6%. In response, the Fed let it be known in June that it would soon begin cutting the federal funds rate. This it did at its July 31st FOMC meeting, when it also announced that Quantitative Tightening would end in August, two months earlier than previously indicated. Altogether, the Fed contracted Federal Reserve Credit by $700 billion between October 2017 and August 2019, when Quantitative Tightening was finally brought to an end.

The very next month, a crisis erupted in the repo market. Interest rates there spiked to approximately four times the level where they should have traded. Why that occurred remains a mystery. At that time there was more than $1.5 trillion of reserves in the financial system. That should have provided far more than ample liquidity. Before 2008, Bank Reserves had been less than $40 billion for decades and had fallen as low as $4 billion in 2000, and yet the repo market had functioned smoothly.

Regardless of the reasons behind the repo market crisis, the Fed responded by flooding the financial markets with a new wave of liquidity, initially by entering into short-term repurchase agreements (repos) with a wide variety of counterparties. For good measure, it also cut the federal funds rate for the second time in two months. By October 9, the Fed's repo agreements had expanded the Fed's total assets by $190 billion, thereby reversing approximately 25% of its entire Quantitative Tightening program.

Then, on October 11, less than two months after Quantitative Tightening had ended, the Fed announced a new round of Quantitative Easing. The world was told that, starting that month, the Fed would begin buying $60 billion of Treasury bills a month until, at least, the second quarter of 2020. The Fed claimed that this program was not Quantitative Easing because its purpose was different from QE's purpose and because the Fed would be buying Treasury bills instead of Treasury notes. The Fed claimed the purpose of buying $60 billion a month of Treasury bills was to restore the smooth functioning of the repo market rather than to push down the yields on longer-term government bonds, which had been the purpose of the first three rounds of Quantitative Easing. The market disagreed and disparagingly began calling the new asset purchase program "The Not QE, QE," or simply QE4.

Before the year was over, the Fed cut the federal funds rate a third time, down to a range between 1.5% and 1.75%, 75 basis points below where it had been mid-year.

By year end, Federal Reserve Credit was back up to $4.1 trillion, an increase of $330 billion during the four months since QT ended in August (see Chart 13.15).

CHART 13.15 Federal Reserve Credit, 2000 to 2019

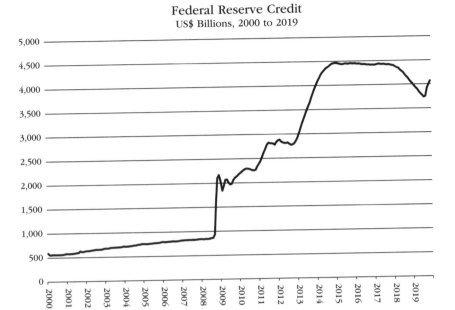

Federal Reserve Credit
US$ Billions, 2000 to 2019

Source: Data from the Federal Reserve Bank of St. Louis

The stock market revelled in the Fed's new liquidity injections. The S&P 500 index jumped 9.6% between the end of September and year end, and ultimately rallied by 14.5% to its pre-coronavirus high on February 9, 2020.

A trillion-dollar budget deficit, three interest rate cuts, and the launch of QE4 drove household sector net worth up by $11.1 trillion in 2019, the largest ever annual increase, as shown in Chart 13.16.

Moreover, by year end, the wealth-to-income ratio was also at an all-time high of 712%, far above its average of 548% since 1952 (see Chart 13.12).

Thus, it was in this state, heavily reliant on expanding government debt and underpinned by massive asset price inflation orchestrated by the Fed, that creditism encountered the coronavirus.

CHART 13.16 Household Net Worth, Annual Dollar Change, 1990 to 2019

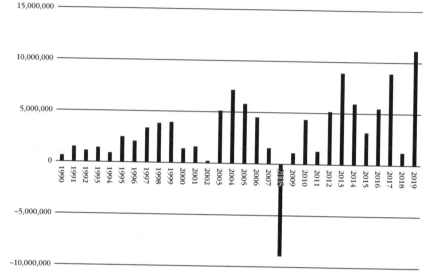

Household Net Worth, Annual Dollar Change
US$ Millions, 1990 to 2019

Source: Data from the Financial Accounts of the United States, the Federal Reserve

Notes

1. Fed Chair Jerome Powell at the FOMC Press Conference on January 30, 2019. See transcript, p. 12. https://www.federalreserve.gov/mediacenter/files/FOMCpresconf20190130.pdf
2. The difference between gross government debt and government debt held by the public is accounted for by intragovernmental debt.
3. The Debt to the Penny, TreasuryDirect. https://treasurydirect.gov/govt/reports/pd/debttothepenny.htm
4. Government debt here is defined as government debt securities and loans, as provided in the Fed's Financial Accounts of the United States.
5. See preceding footnote on government debt.
6. Up until October 2017, when the bonds the Fed owned matured, the central bank took the proceeds and reinvested the entire amount in bonds very similar to those that had matured.

CHAPTER 14

Pandemic

There's no monthly cap, no weekly cap (on the size of the Fed's asset purchases) . . . that language is open-ended, and it's meant to send a signal to the market that we're not going to be bound by, for example, $60 billion a month or anything like that. We're going to go in strong starting tomorrow.

Fed Chair Jerome Powell[1]

The COVID-19 pandemic struck the US economy with a severity and suddenness unprecedented in the country's history. The United States reported its first COVID-related death on February 29, 2020.[2] By the end of April, nearly 30 million Americans had lost their jobs[3] and the unemployment rate had soared to 14.7%, the highest since the Great Depression. The S&P 500 stock market index, which had recorded a new all-time high on February 19, lost 34% of its value by March 23. As a result, during the first quarter, household sector net worth plunged by a record $6.5 trillion. The economy contracted by 1.3% in the first quarter of 2020 compared with the fourth quarter of 2019 and then by a record-shattering 9.5% in the second quarter compared with the first.[4] It was an economic calamity exceeding any in living memory.

The Policy Response

The Initial Phase

Congress responded quickly and aggressively in supplying fiscal support during the initial phase of the crisis. The CARES Act was signed into law on March 27. It provided more than $2 trillion in emergency government funding for households, small and medium-sized businesses, and corporations. This government money enabled millions of Americans to pay their bills and put food on the table, even as stay-at-home orders were declared across many parts of the country. Government support for businesses, large and small, prevented many thousands of bankruptcies that would have crippled the economy for years to come. Moreover, the support the government provided to individuals and businesses also prevented a systemic collapse of the banking sector, as no bank could have survived the tidal wave of debt defaults that would have been inevitable without that government support.

Government borrowing ballooned as the surge in crisis-related spending was accompanied by exceptionally weak tax revenues. In April, the Treasury Department borrowed nearly $1.4 trillion. Government borrowing that month was greater than that of any full year, with the exception of the first three years following the crisis of 2008. In May, the government borrowed $760 billion more. In June, it borrowed an additional $716 billion (see Chart 14.1). That took government borrowing to $2.9 trillion for the second quarter of 2020 as a whole and to $3.4 trillion for the first half. During the 12 months ending June 30, 2020, the government borrowed $4.3 trillion, more than twice the previous record for any 12-month period preceding the pandemic. By mid-2020, total gross federal government debt reached $26.5 trillion.

The monetary policy response was even more extraordinary than the fiscal policy response. The S&P 500 set a new record high on Wednesday, February 19. By Friday of the following week, February 28, it had tumbled 13%. At an unscheduled

CHART 14.1 US Government Borrowing, Monthly, 2010 to June 2021

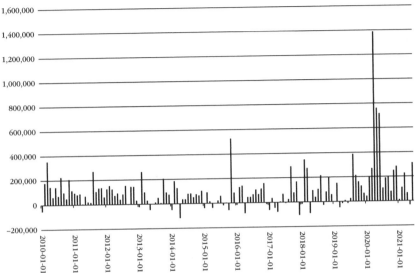

US Government Borrowing, Monthly
US$ Millions, 2010 to June 2021

Source: Data from the Federal Reserve Bank of St. Louis

FOMC meeting on March 3, the Fed cut the federal funds rate by 50 basis points to a range between 1.0% and 1.25%. Anxiety in the financial markets continued to mount.

On March 9, the Fed announced it would supply additional liquidity to the financial markets by increasing the amount it offered in daily overnight repo operations from at least $100 billion to at least $150 billion. On March 12, it was announced that the offer size would be increased to at least $175 billion beginning the following day.[5] These steps did nothing to calm the fears of the debt market. When the following day arrived, the growing sense of panic in the markets forced the Fed to attempt to provide liquidity on a very much larger scale. That day, March 12, the Fed announced it would immediately begin offering $500 billion in three-month repo operations plus $500 billion in one-month repo operations, in addition to the ongoing $175 billion in daily overnight repo operations.[6]

The Fed also announced on March 12 that it would begin buying Treasury securities across a range of maturities, rather than only Treasury bills as it had been doing at a rate of $60 billion per month since October 2019. Then, on March 13, the Fed let it be known that it would acquire $33 billion of government debt securities by the end of that day, an amount equivalent to more than 50% of its monthly purchases at that time.[7]

The next FOMC meeting was scheduled for the middle of the following week, March 17/18. With the stock market in free-fall and the bond market in a full-fledged panic, the Fed could not afford to wait until Wednesday to announce its next round of emergency measures. An unscheduled FOMC meeting was held on Sunday, March 15. At that meeting, the Fed cut the federal funds rate by 75 basis points to a range between 0% and 0.25%, taking it back down as close as possible to the zero percent lower bound. More importantly, the Fed announced that over the coming months it would purchase at least $500 billion more Treasury securities and at least $200 billion more agency mortgage-backed securities.[8]

The next day, Monday, March 16, the S&P 500 plunged a further 12%.

During the rest of that week, the Fed began rolling out a series of lending facilities, using its emergency authority under Section 13(3) of the revised Federal Reserve Act. These included the Commercial Paper Funding Facility (CPFF), the Primary Dealer Credit Facility (PDCF), and the Money Market Mutual Fund Liquidity Facility (MMLF), all designed "to support the flow of credit to households and businesses." The Fed also announced the establishment of temporary swap lines with nine other central banks, in addition to the standing swap lines that already existed with five central banks.[9] The stock market continued to fall.

By Friday March 20, the S&P was 32% below the record high it had set one month earlier. Trillions of dollars of wealth had evaporated in this stock market crash. The asset price inflation that the Fed had so carefully engineered to shore up economic growth in the face of weak credit growth gave way to extreme asset price deflation that, by itself, was certain to hurl the US economy into a severe recession if not reversed.

At last, on March 23, the Fed said the magic words, "The Federal Reserve will continue to purchase Treasury securities and agency mortgage-backed securities *in the amounts needed* to support smooth market functioning and effective transmission of monetary policy to broader financial conditions." Financial market participants understood correctly that the words "in the amounts needed" meant "whatever it takes."[10] The stock market bottomed that day. The S&P closed on March 23, 34% below the peak it had reached on February 19. Its subsequent recovery was spectacular. The S&P 500 set a new, all-time record high less than five months later on August 18, even as the unemployment rate remained above 10% and the economy remained in a severe crisis.

The Fed quickly made good on its commitment. In fact, the Fed had significantly increased its purchases of government debt even before its March 23 announcement. During the week ending Wednesday, March 18, the Fed had already purchased $118 billion of Treasury securities. During the week ending March 25, the Fed bought a further $338 billion worth of Treasury securities. That was followed by Treasury security purchases of $362 billion, $294 billion, $154 billion and $121 billion over the next four weeks, as shown in Chart 14.2. During those six weeks, the Fed acquired a total of $1.4 trillion of US government debt. The government sold an extraordinary amount of new debt during that period. The Fed's purchases made it possible for the government to borrow on that scale without pushing up interest rates.

The Fed also acquired a tremendous amount of agency mortgage-backed securities, as shown in Chart 14.3. During the six weeks between March 18 and April 22, the Fed bought just over $250 billion of such debt instruments. Its largest purchases of mortgage-backed securities occurred in mid-May, however. During the week of May 13, the Fed bought $178 billion worth. The following week, it bought $79 billion more, for a two-week total of $257 billion. These purchases allowed Fannie Mae and Freddie Mac to sell more debt at low interest rates during these months, money they used to pump more credit into the property market. Moreover, since money is fungible, regardless of

CHART 14.2 The Fed's Holdings of US Treasury Securities, Weekly Change, 2018 to June 30, 2021

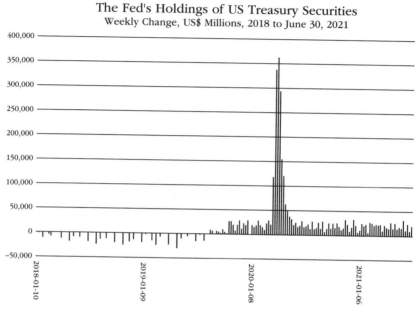

The Fed's Holdings of US Treasury Securities
Weekly Change, US$ Millions, 2018 to June 30, 2021

Source: Data from the Federal Reserve Bank of St. Louis

whether the Fed bought mortgage-backed securities or Treasury securities or simply extended loans, the money it created in this way quickly flowed into every corner of the financial markets, driving asset prices higher and yields lower.

As the reader will well understand by now, the Fed creates base money by extending Federal Reserve Credit, which it can do either by purchasing assets through open market operations or by making loans through a process that was known in the past as discounting operations. Chart 14.4 shows that, by extending Federal Reserve Credit, the Fed created $357 billion of base money during the week of March 18 and that during the following week, ending March 25, the Fed created a further $586 billion of base money.

To put the significance of that two-week total of $943 billion into perspective, consider that between the time the Fed began operations in 1914 and 2007, the eve of the crisis of 2008, the

CHART 14.3 The Fed's Holdings of Mortgage-Backed Securities, Weekly Change, 2018 to June 30, 2021

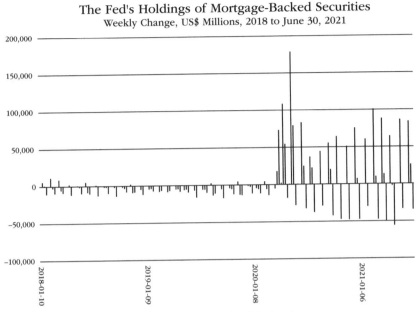

Source: Data from the Federal Reserve Bank of St. Louis

Fed had extended a total of only $902 billion of Federal Reserve Credit over 93 years. The Fed topped that by $41 billion during just these two weeks in March 2020.

The US central bank then went on to extend $557 billion more Federal Reserve Credit during the week of April 1 and a further $272 billion, $285 billion, and $205 billion over the next three weeks, respectively, bringing the six-week total to $2.3 trillion.

During the first half of 2020, the US government borrowed a total of $3.37 trillion. When the government spent the funds it borrowed by giving money to individuals and businesses, it provided desperately needed financial support that held the economy together through the first terrifying months of the pandemic.

CHART 14.4 Reserve Bank Credit, Weekly Change, 2018 to
June 30, 2021

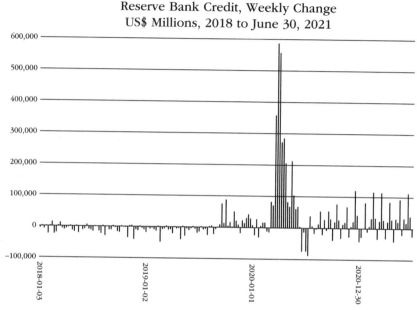

Source: Data from the Federal Reserve Bank of St. Louis

Over the same period, the Fed created $2.84 trillion of
base money by extending Federal Reserve Credit, an amount
sufficient to finance 84% of all the government's borrowing during that period. If the Fed had not created so much money, it
would not have been possible for the government to borrow
on that scale without driving interest rates sharply higher. Much
higher interest rates would have inflicted severe damage on the
economy that would have offset part, or even all, of the benefits resulting from the government's fiscal relief measures. Had
that occurred, the economic damage wrought by the pandemic
would have been far worse.

It must also be understood that the monetary stimulus the
Fed provided on such a great scale would have been far less
effective had it not been combined with the government's
aggressive fiscal stimulus. The money created by the Fed would
have driven asset prices much higher and interest rates to 0%

or lower, but that money would not have reached the broader economy had the government not sent out checks to individuals and made loans to the business sector.

Thus, it was fiscal and monetary policy working in coordination that held the United States economy together during the first crucial months of the pandemic.

The Second Phase

It is useful to think of the second quarter of 2020 as the initial phase of the pandemic-induced economic crisis. It was then that the economy came the closest to collapsing into a new great depression. It was also during the second quarter that the policy measures that prevented that outcome were put into place.

However, the fiscal and monetary support for the economy extended well beyond then. A second large fiscal stimulus bill amounting to $900 billion was passed in December 2020 and the $1.9 trillion American Rescue Plan Act followed in March 2021. Between mid-2020 and mid-2021, gross federal government debt increased by a further $2 trillion, from $26.5 trillion to $28.5 trillion.

Meanwhile, during those 12 months, the Fed extended an additional $1.44 trillion of Federal Reserve Credit through its $120 billion a month asset purchase program. By providing an amount of new credit equivalent to 72% of the increase in government debt during that period, the Fed made it possible for the government to borrow and spend on a large scale to support the economy without driving government bond yields up to levels that would damage the economy. The 10-year US government bond yield, which had fallen as low as 0.54% in March 2020, peaked at 1.74% in March 2021, but then fell back to just 1.45% at the end of June 2021.

Looking Ahead

At the time of writing, July 2021, the worst of the pandemic in the United States appears to be past. The 7-day average number of daily COVID-19 cases, which peaked near 260,000 in early

January 2021, has since fallen to 26,000, while the 7-day average number for deaths has declined from a peak of 3,352 to 284 over the same period.

No further pandemic-related fiscal stimulus bills are expected, although other large-scale spending bills appear likely. An infrastructure bill that could increase spending by $600 billion over eight years seems near enactment, while a social spending bill of up to $3.5 trillion to be disbursed over many years is being discussed. Although these proposed bills are large, given that they would be spread out over a number of years, they would not provide as much fiscal stimulus to the economy as the large COVID-related relief packages, which were largely disbursed over a period of only a few months.

Quantitative Easing continues at a pace of $120 billion per month. The Fed is expected to carry on its asset purchases at this level for most of the rest of 2021, before gradually bringing QE to an end through "tapering" by December 2022.

At this time, the fiscal support to the economy has already begun to fade, while it appears that monetary support will decline from the beginning of 2022. Therefore, unless a severe new wave of the pandemic occurs, it seems likely that this multitrillion-dollar experiment to support the economy through the pandemic will come to a close in late 2022. There is also every reason to believe that it will be judged to have been an extraordinary success. By the end of the second quarter of 2021, the size of the US economy exceeded its pre-pandemic peak and the unemployment rate had dropped back to 5.9% from a post-World War II record high of 14.8% in April 2020.

The Details: 2020 vs. 2008

The rest of this chapter will provide a more detailed look at how the Fed extended Federal Reserve Credit after the pandemic began. It will also show how the Fed's methods of providing that credit during the pandemic compared with the methods it employed during the crisis of 2008.

CHART 14.5 Federal Reserve Credit, Weekly Change, 2006 to
June 30, 2021

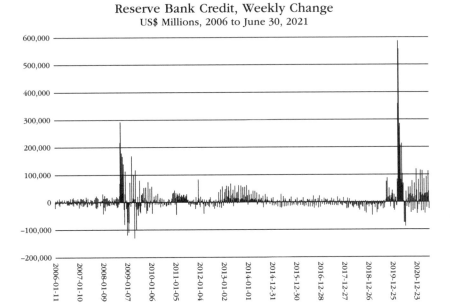

Reserve Bank Credit, Weekly Change
US$ Millions, 2006 to June 30, 2021

Source: Data from the Federal Reserve Bank of St. Louis

First, the Fed provided much more Federal Reserve Credit in
a short space of time during the initial phase of the 2020 economic crisis than during the crisis of 2008. Chart 14.5 shows that,
at the peak, the extension of Federal Reserve Credit was twice as
large during the COVID-19 crisis as it was at the peak of the previous crisis; $586 billion during the week of March 25, compared
with $292 billion during the week of October 1, 2008.

Next consider the breakdown of the extension of Federal
Reserve Credit between *securities bought outright* and *lending
operations*, as shown in Chart 14.6.

Two things are immediately discernable in this chart. First,
much more Federal Reserve Credit has been extended as the
result of the Fed acquiring securities outright than through
the Fed's lending operations. Second, Federal Reserve Credit
extended through lending operations tends to be extinguished
over time, whereas that supplied through *open market purchases*
only very rarely contracts.

CHART 14.6 The Breakdown of Federal Reserve Credit: Securities Bought Outright vs. Lending Operations, 2006 to June 30, 2021

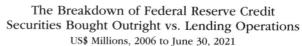

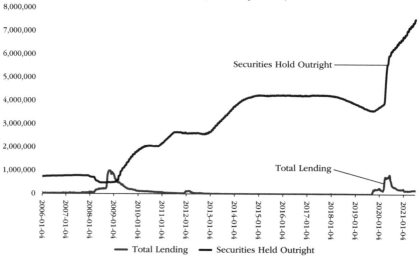

Source: Data from the Federal Reserve Bank of St. Louis

The *securities held outright* by the Fed increased by roughly $3.5 trillion over the seven years from the end of 2007 to the end of 2014 as the result of three rounds of Quantitative Easing. The Fed acted much faster in response to the pandemic. During just 16 months, between the end of February 2020 and the end of June 2021, the Fed added approximately $3.7 trillion to its security holdings, nearly doubling its securities held outright from $3.8 trillion to $7.5 trillion.

During those 16 months ending June 30, 2021, the Fed acquired $2.7 trillion of Treasury securities and $948 billion of agency mortgage-backed securities, increasing its total holdings of each to $5.2 trillion and $2.3 trillion, respectively, as shown in Chart 14.7.

The amount of Federal Reserve Credit created through the Fed's lending operations was on a much smaller scale. When the crisis of 2008 began, the Fed's initial response was to supply

CHART 14.7 Breakdown of Securities Held Outright, 2006 to June 30, 2021

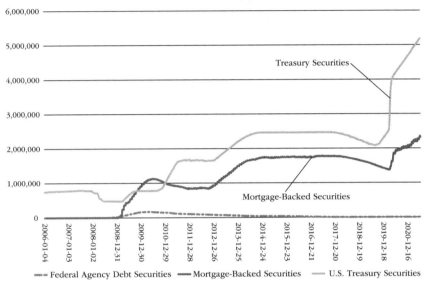

Breakdown of Securities Held Outright
US$ Millions, 2006 to June 30, 2021

- - Federal Agency Debt Securities   **——** Mortgage-Backed Securities   **----** U.S. Treasury Securities

Source: Data from the Federal Reserve Bank of St. Louis

liquidity very rapidly by lending to banks and a wide variety of other financial institutions, with the Fed obtaining some of the funds it lent by selling some of the Treasury securities it had bought in the past, as reflected in the 2008 dip in the securities the Fed held outright and in the dip in Fed's Treasury securities, which can be seen in Charts 14.6 and 14.7, respectively. Thus, in 2008, the assets it acquired as collateral in its lending operations briefly exceeded the securities it owned outright. Soon afterward, however, the first round of Quantitative Easing pumped very large amounts of Federal Reserve Credit into the economy, allowing the institutions that had borrowed from the Fed to repay their loans. Consequently, the loans extended by the Fed quickly contracted, while the securities the Fed acquired through open market purchases surged to more than $4.2 trillion by the time the third round of QE ended in October 2014.

The Fed's lending operations in response to the pandemic followed a similar pattern. Recall that Federal Reserve Credit was already expanding before the pandemic. Malfunctions in the repo market moved the Fed to inject large amounts of liquidity through repurchase agreements beginning in September 2019 and then to begin a new round of Quantitative Easing in October, at a pace of $60 billion of Treasury bill purchases a month.

When the pandemic struck, the Fed once again quickly injected large amounts of liquidity into the economy by extending loans to banks and numerous other institutions.

The assets the Fed accumulated as collateral through its lending operations increased from $143 billion at the end of February to a peak of $825 billion in early June, as shown in Chart 14.8.

By that time, however, enough liquidity had been injected into the financial markets through the Fed's asset purchases (QE) that the institutions that had borrowed from the Fed were able

CHART 14.8 Total Lending (formerly known as Discounting), 2006 to June 30, 2021

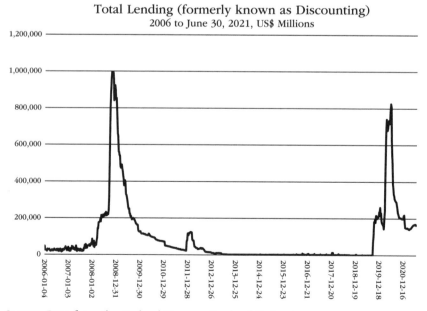

Source: Data from the Federal Reserve Bank of St. Louis

to begin repaying the Fed the money they had borrowed. By the end of the year, Fed lending had contracted back to $219 billion. By mid-2021, it had fallen further to $164 billion. At the peak, then, in early June 2020, the Fed's Lending Operations in response to the pandemic had expanded Federal Reserve Credit by $682 billion from the end of February, but, by the end of June 2021, that figure was reduced to only $20 billion.

Interestingly, the Fed's lending operations peaked at a higher amount, just under $1 trillion, during the crisis of 2008, than during the COVID-19 crisis at $825 billion. Perhaps the explanation is that the Fed provided an extraordinarily large amount of money quickly through QE this time, reducing the need for lending operations.

The Fed's total lending is comprised of four elements: central bank liquidity swaps, repurchase agreements, loans and credit facilities. Chart 14.9 presents the breakdown of total lending between 2006 and June 2021.

CHART 14.9 A Breakdown of Total Lending Between Repos, Central Bank Swaps, Loans & Credit Facilities, 2006 to June 30, 2021

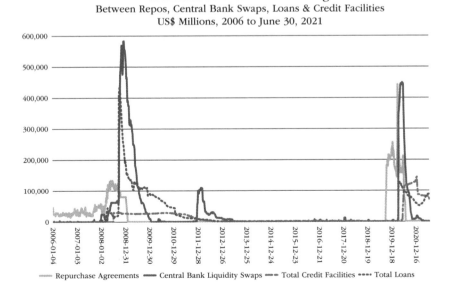

Source: Data from the Federal Reserve Bank of St. Louis

CHART 14.10 Central Bank Liquidity Swaps, 2006 to June 30, 2021

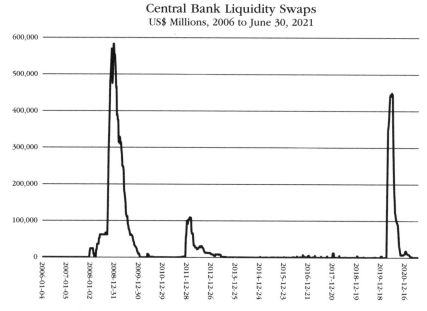

Source: Data from the Federal Reserve Bank of St. Louis

Central bank liquidity swaps have been the largest component of the Fed's total lending. These were larger during the crisis of 2008 than during 2020, having peaked at $583 billion in December 2008 versus a peak of $447 billion in early June 2020, as shown in Chart 14.10.

On the other hand, Federal Reserve Credit extended through repurchase agreements was much larger during 2020 than during the previous crisis. Repos peaked at $442 billion in March 2020 compared with $134 billion in May 2008. In both crises, repos outstanding fell back to $0 once large-scale asset purchases had re-liquified the financial markets (see Chart 14.11).

Federal Reserve Credit extended through more traditional kinds of loans played a larger role in the policy response to the crisis of 2008 than in 2020. Such loans peaked at $441 billon in October 2008. By April 2009, they were down to $100 billion and by the end of 2012 they had fallen below $1 billion. The peak in 2020 was significantly lower, at $130 billion in early

CHART 14.11 Repurchase Agreements, 2006 to June 30, 2021

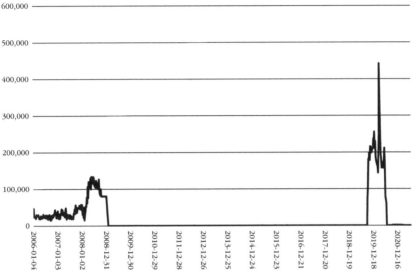

Repurchase Agreements
US$ Millions, 2006 to June 30, 2021

Source: Data from the Federal Reserve Bank of St. Louis

April. By mid-2021 they had been reduced to $91 billion (see Chart 14.12).

These loans were made up of:

1. Primary Credit, which peaked at $33 billion;[11]
2. The Money Market Mutual Fund Liquidity Facility, which peaked at $53 billion;[12]
3. The Primary Dealer Credit Facility, which peaked at $33 billion;[13] and
4. The Payroll Protection Liquidity Facility, which peaked at $91 billion.[14]

In the policy response to the COVID-19 pandemic, the first three of these hit their peak in April 2020, while the fourth peaked in June 2021.

The Fed also extended Federal Reserve Credit through other kinds of credit facilities, set up as LLCs using the Fed's

CHART 14.12 Loans, 2006 to June 30, 2021

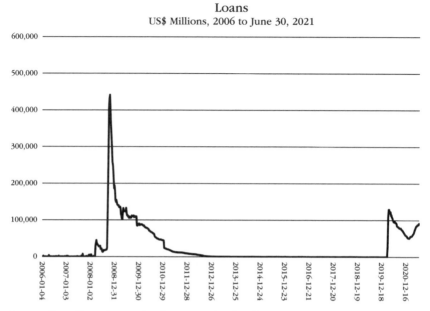

Loans
US$ Millions, 2006 to June 30, 2021

Source: Data from the Federal Reserve Bank of St. Louis

emergency lending authority under Section 13(3) of the revised Federal Reserve Act. Federal Reserve Credit extended through these credit facilities peaked at $29 billion in 2008, with Maiden Lane LLC, which had been established as part of the rescue of Bear Stearns, as the principal recipient (see Chart 14.13).

In the policy response to the COVID-19 pandemic, the amount of Federal Reserve Credit extended through this kind of credit facility peaked at $143 billion at the end of December 2020. The amount outstanding at mid-2021 was $72 billion.

These credit facilities included:

1. The Corporate Credit Facility LLC, which peaked at $46 billion;[15]
2. The Municipal Liquidity Facility LLC, which peaked at $21 billion;[16]
3. The MS Facilities LLC (Main Street Lending Program), which peaked at $54 billion;[17]

CHART 14.13 Total Credit Facilities, 2006 to June 30, 2021

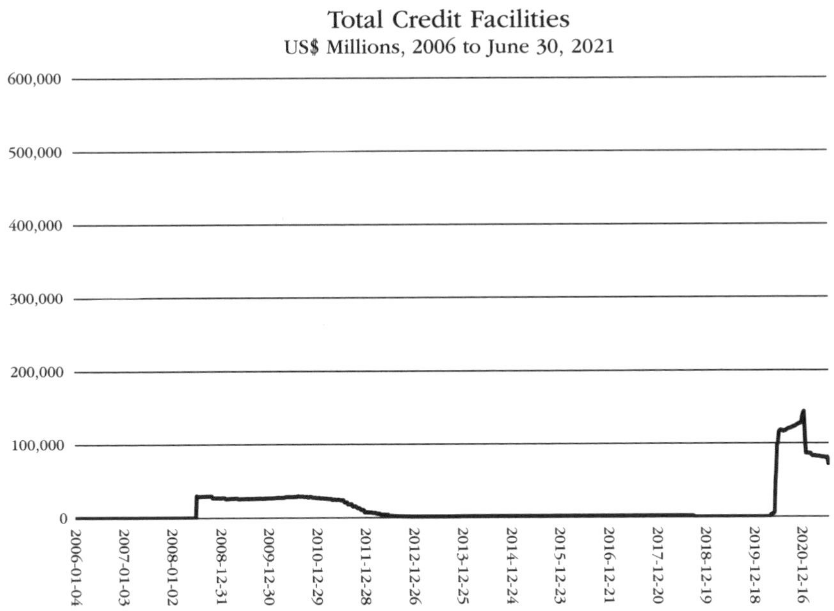

Total Credit Facilities
US$ Millions, 2006 to June 30, 2021

Source: Data from the Federal Reserve Bank of St. Louis

4. TALF II LLC, which peaked at $13 billion;[18] and
5. The Commercial Paper Funding Facility II LLC, which peaked at $13 billion.[19]

The first four hit their highest level at the end 2020. The fifth peaked in July 2020.

Federal Reserve Credit ended June 2021 at $8.0 trillion, an increase of $3.9 trillion or 95% from the end of February 2020, and a ninefold increase from the end of 2007 (see Chart 14.14).

Simultaneously, during those 16 months, the government borrowed $4.9 trillion. That means the Fed effectively monetized 80% of the government's borrowing during that period.

Economic textbooks teach that money creation on that scale should have caused very high rates of inflation or even hyperinflation. It did not. Chapter 15 will explain why it didn't.

CHART 14.14 Federal Reserve Credit, 2006 to June 30, 2021

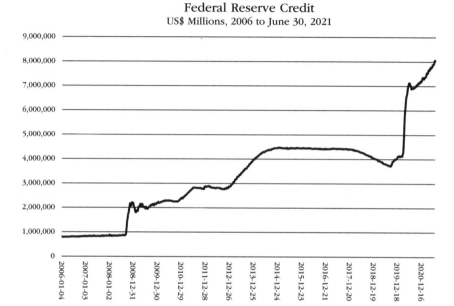

Federal Reserve Credit
US$ Millions, 2006 to June 30, 2021

Source: Data from the Federal Reserve Bank of St. Louis

Notes

1. Fed Chair Jerome Powell, March 15, 2020, Press Conference. See transcript: https://www.federalreserve.gov/mediacenter/files/FOMC presconf20200315.pdf
2. It was later confirmed that the first death actually occurred on February 6, but this did not become known until the second half of April.
3. Based on initial jobless claims.
4. Real Gross Domestic Product. Source: Federal Reserve Bank of St. Louis. https://fred.stlouisfed.org/series/GDPC1
5. Statement Regarding Repurchase Operations, New York Fed, March 11, 2020. https://www.newyorkfed.org/markets/opolicy/ operating_policy_200311
6. Statement Regarding Treasury Reserve Management Purchases and Repurchase Operations, New York Fed March 12, 2020. https:// www.newyorkfed.org/markets/opolicy/operating_policy_200312a

7. Statement Regarding Treasury Reserve Management and Reinvestment Purchases, New York Fed. March 13, 2020 https://www.newyorkfed.org/markets/opolicy/operating_policy_200313

8. Federal Reserve FOMC Statement, March 15, 2020. https://www.federalreserve.gov/newsevents/pressreleases/monetary20200315a.htm

9. Federal Reserve https://www.federalreserve.gov/newsevents/pressreleases.htm

10. Federal Reserve FOMC Statement, New York Fed, March 23, 2020. https://www.federalreserve.gov/newsevents/pressreleases/monetary20200323a.htm

11. Assets: Liquidity and Credit Facilities: Loans: Primary Dealer Credit Facility: Wednesday Level, St. Louis Fed, October 22, 2021. https://fred.stlouisfed.org/series/H41RESPPALDHNWW

12. Assets: Liquidity and Credit Facilities: Loans: Primary Dealer Credit Facility: Wednesday Level, St. Louis Fed, October 22, 2021. https://fred.stlouisfed.org/series/H41RESPPALDBNWW

13. Assets: Liquidity and Credit Facilities: Loans: Primary Dealer Credit Facility: Wednesday Level, St. Louis Fed, October 22, 2021. https://fred.stlouisfed.org/series/H41RESPPALDHNWW

14. Assets: Liquidity and Credit Facilities: Loans: Payroll Protection Program Liquidity Facility: Wednesday Level, St. Louis Fed, October 22, 2021. https://fred.stlouisfed.org/series/H41RESPPALDJNWW

15. Assets: Liquidity and Credit Facilities: Loans: Primary Dealer Credit Facility: Wednesday Level, St. Louis Fed, October 22, 2021. https://fred.stlouisfed.org/series/H41RESPPAABNWW

16. Assets: Liquidity and Credit Facilities: Loans: Primary Dealer Credit Facility: Wednesday Level, St. Louis Fed, October 22, 2021. https://fred.stlouisfed.org/series/H41RESPPAADHNWW

17. Assets: Liquidity and Credit Facilities: Net Portfolio Holdings of MS Facilities LLC (Main Street Lending Program): Wednesday Level, St. Louis Fed, October 22, 2021. https://fred.stlouisfed.org/series/H41RESPPAAENWW

18. Assets: Liquidity and Credit Facilities: Net Portfolio Holdings of TALF II LLC: Wednesday Level, St. Louis Fed, October 22, 2021. https://fred.stlouisfed.org/series/H41RESPPAATAL2HNWW

19. Assets: Liquidity and Credit Facilities: Net Portfolio Holdings of Commercial Paper Funding Facility II LLC: Wednesday Level, St. Louis Fed, October 22, 2021. https://fred.stlouisfed.org/series/H41RESPPAAC2HNWW

CHAPTER 15

Inflation

Inflation is always and everywhere a monetary phenomenon.
Milton Friedman, 1970[1]

Milton Friedman once famously said, "Inflation is always and everywhere a monetary phenomenon." But that is not true. The history of inflation in the United States over the past century demonstrates that inflation is not *always* a monetary phenomenon. Prices move higher and lower for non-monetary reasons, as well.

This chapter compares money supply growth and the inflation rate during each decade from the 1920s to the present. The evidence is clear: demand shocks and supply shocks have played at least as important a role as changes in the money supply in determining the rate of inflation. In fact, the link between money supply growth and inflation has become significantly weaker since the early 1980s; and, since 2008, money supply growth has had no impact on inflation whatsoever. Another factor – globalization – determines the inflation rate now. This has important implications for government policy.

A Century of Inflation

Over the past century, three factors have impacted the rate of inflation in the United States: the *money supply*, *demand shocks* and *supply shocks*. Increases in the money supply have led to inflation and decreases in the money supply have led to deflation. Similarly, there have been inflationary and deflationary demand shocks and inflationary and deflationary supply shocks.

The charts that follow – one for each decade – compare the annual rate of change for base money with the inflation rate. Base money is *currency in circulation* plus Bank Reserves, i.e., the deposits that banks hold in their reserve accounts at the Fed. This is the money that the Fed creates. The inflation rate used is Consumer Price Index: All Items (CPI). (Please note that all references to inflation, the inflation rate and money supply growth refer to the percentage change relative to one year earlier, unless otherwise stated.)

1919 to 1929

The first period covers the years 1919 to 1929.[2] That decade was remarkable in that it witnessed the highest rates of inflation and deflation during the century covered in this chapter. It also saw the century's sharpest contraction in the money supply. World War I was responsible for these wide swings in prices and the money supply.

Wars cause inflation. Government demand for war materials pushes prices higher; and central bank financing of government debt through money creation pushes prices higher. World War I ended in November 1918. Inflation peaked a year and a half later in June 1920 with prices 24% higher than one year earlier. See Chart 15.1.

By January 1921, prices had begun to fall. Exactly 12 months after the highest rate of inflation the United States was to experience during the twentieth century, the country suffered the worst deflation of the century. In June 1921, the annual rate of consumer price inflation was negative 16%.

CHART 15.1 Base Money *vs.* CPI: Percentage Change from Year Ago, 1919 to 1929

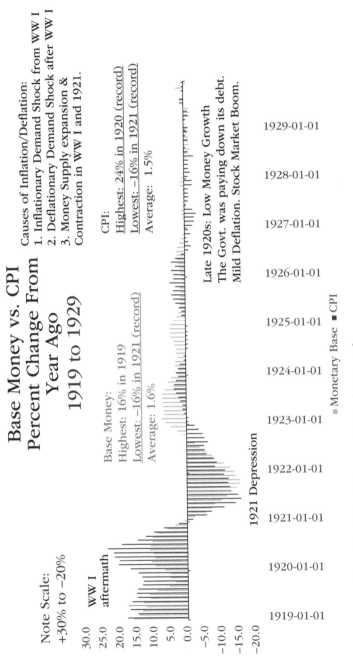

Base Money vs. CPI
Percent Change From
Year Ago
1919 to 1929

Note Scale:
+30% to −20%

Causes of Inflation/Deflation:
1. Inflationary Demand Shock from WW I
2. Deflationary Demand Shock after WW I
3. Money Supply expansion &
   Contraction in WW I and 1921.

CPI:
Highest: 24% in 1920 (record)
Lowest: −16% in 1921 (record)
Average: 1.5%

Base Money:
Highest: 16% in 1919
Lowest: −16% in 1921 (record)
Average: 1.6%

WW I
aftermath

1921 Depression

Late 1920s: Low Money Growth
The Govt. was paying down its debt.
Mild Deflation. Stock Market Boom.

30.0
25.0
20.0
15.0
10.0
5.0
0.0
−5.0
−10.0
−15.0
−20.0

1919-01-01
1920-01-01
1921-01-01
1922-01-01
1923-01-01
1924-01-01
1925-01-01
1926-01-01
1927-01-01
1928-01-01
1929-01-01

■ Monetary Base ■ CPI

Source: Data from the Federal Reserve Bank of St. Louis[3]

During the twentieth century, the Depression of 1921 was second only to the Great Depression of the 1930s in terms of severity. When the war ended, the government stopped buying war materials, so prices fell. Moreover, as described in Chapter 3, when the war ended, the Fed's balance sheet contracted sharply as the bills it had discounted to help finance the war were repaid. As the Fed's assets shrank, so did its liabilities. Currency in circulation, one of the two principal components of the money supply, contracted from $3.6 billion at the end of 1920 to $2.3 billion in March 1922. Consequently, base money contracted. At its trough in October 1921, it was down 16%. The contraction of the money supply compounded the blow to the economy that resulted from the end of government expenditure on the war.

A great deal can be learned about inflation from the economic boom and bust that accompanied and followed World War I. The very high rates of inflation during 1919 and 1920 had two causes. The first was an inflationary demand shock related to government spending during the war. The second cause was the expansion of the money supply as the Fed discounted bills in order to allow the government to finance its war expenditures at low interest rates.

The severe deflation of 1921 and 1922 also had two causes. The first was a deflationary demand shock when the government curtailed its spending at the end of the war. The second was the record setting contraction of the money supply when the Fed's assets and liabilities shrank. As will be seen shortly, even though the United States involvement in World War II was much longer and much more expensive than its involvement in World War I, the inflation rate was lower during World War II as the result of government-imposed price controls, while deflation was avoided after the war due to better central bank management of the money supply.

By 1923, the economy had recovered and the Roaring Twenties were soon underway. This period was remarkable in two important respects. Consumer financing became available for the first time on a very large scale. Households were able to buy automobiles and home appliances on monthly installment plans.

CHART 15.2 US Government Debt, 1900 to 1930

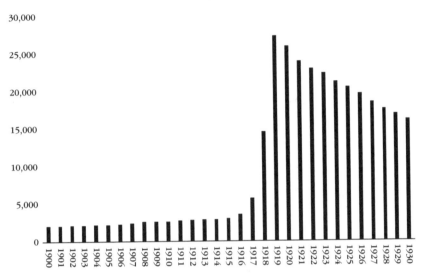

US Government Debt
1900 to 1930, US$ Millions

Source: United States Department of the Treasury

Home mortgages also became much more widely used. Rapidly increasing consumer debt is one reason the Depression of 1921 was so short-lived.

It is also noteworthy that the US government paid down its debt during this decade. Government debt peaked at $27 billion in 1919 and was reduced to $16 billion by 1930, as shown in Chart 15.2.

Just as large-scale government borrowing pushes up interest rates and "crowds out" the private sector by deterring private sector borrowing and investment, a large reduction in government debt tends to push interest rates down and therefore encourages private sector borrowing and investment. Moreover, the reduction in the amount of government bonds outstanding forced investors to invest elsewhere. This helps explain the extraordinary stock market boom of the late 1920s. With fewer government bonds to buy, investors were "crowded in" to the stock market. This pattern recurred 80 years later. The NASDAQ bubble formed when the government ran budget surpluses and paid down some of its debt between 1998 and 2000.

Base money growth rebounded following the 1921 Depression. But after 1923, the growth rate steadily declined during the rest of the decade. In 1928, base money began to contract. In April 1929, it fell as much as 2%. Prices began falling in July 1926 and fell consistently every month for the next three years. The deflation rate was -3.4% in April 1927 and -2.8% in June 1928. Weak money supply growth followed by a contraction in the money supply played a leading role in causing the deflation of the late 1920s.

For the decade, base money grew at an average annual rate of 1.6%. The inflation rate averaged 1.5% per year. These low averages mask very large swings in both the money supply and prices during the decade. The highest rate of money supply growth was 16% in 1919, while the lowest was -16% in 1921. Inflation peaked at 24% in 1920. Deflation was at its worst at -16% in 1921.

The 1930s

The Wall Street Crash of October 1929 brought the Roaring Twenties to an abrupt end. The Crash destroyed a tremendous deal of wealth and shattered business confidence. Prices began to fall. Then in late 1930 the first wave of bank failures began and turned what had been a recession up until then into the Great Depression.

In January 1930, the inflation rate had been 0%. By November prices were 5% lower than one year earlier. By mid-1931, they were 10% lower than in mid-1930 (see Chart 15.3). From then until March 1933, when Franklin Roosevelt became president, the annual deflation rate averaged 10%. Altogether, between the Crash and the presidential inauguration, the Consumer Price Index fell 27%.

Milton Friedman and Anna Jacobson Schwartz persuaded most of the economic profession that the Fed could have

CHART 15.3 Base Money vs. CPI: Percentage Change from Year Ago, The 1930s

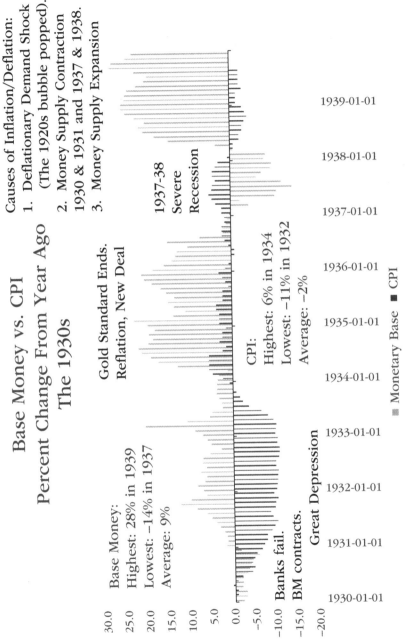

Base Money vs. CPI
Percent Change From Year Ago
The 1930s

Causes of Inflation/Deflation:
1. Deflationary Demand Shock (The 1920s bubble popped).
2. Money Supply Contraction 1930 & 1931 and 1937 & 1938.
3. Money Supply Expansion

Gold Standard Ends.
Reflation, New Deal

1937-38
Severe
Recession

Base Money:
Highest: 28% in 1939
Lowest: −14% in 1937
Average: 9%

CPI:
Highest: 6% in 1934
Lowest: −11% in 1932
Average: −2%

Banks fail.
BM contracts.
Great Depression

30.0
25.0
20.0
15.0
10.0
5.0
0.0
−5.0
−10.0
−15.0
−20.0

1930-01-01
1931-01-01
1932-01-01
1933-01-01
1934-01-01
1935-01-01
1936-01-01
1937-01-01
1938-01-01
1939-01-01

▦ Monetary Base ■ CPI

Source: Data from the Federal Reserve Bank of St. Louis[4]

prevented the Great Depression if it had expanded the monetary base aggressively in 1930. While that is very likely true, the contraction of the money supply during 1930 by itself was not large enough to account for the severe deflation that followed.

Base money contracted during 1930, but, at its lowest point, November, it was only down by 6% compared with one year earlier. The contraction in base money occurred because currency in circulation declined. When business slowed down, payrolls and prices fell. Consequently there was less need for cash.

Money supply growth resumed in January 1931 and continued through 1932 and into 1933 as the public's demand for cash increased as individuals became more fearful over the health of the country's banks and the security of their deposits. The Fed helped accommodate that demand through large-scale open market purchases in 1932 and 1933.

When the economic bubble of the 1920s popped, wealth was destroyed and credit contracted. Households and businesses no longer had the means to continue spending. They bought less and prices fell. Therefore, it was a *deflationary demand shock*, rather than a contraction of the money supply that was the main cause of the collapse in prices during the first years of the Depression.

President Roosevelt took the United States off the gold standard in April 1933 and then devalued the dollar in January 1934. Only then did deflation end. The devaluation of the dollar meant that foreign investors with gold could acquire US goods and assets at a much lower price than before. Consequently, gold flooded into the United States from abroad. That foreign capital inflow caused a new surge in US money supply growth. Between April 1934 and July 1936, base money grew at an annual average rate of 17%. The surge in the money supply, supported by expansionary New Deal fiscal policy, caused prices to begin to rise again from mid-1933.

Between May 1937 and June 1938, the country suffered another sharp economic slump, a recession within the depression. Fiscal austerity was to blame. The Roosevelt administration reduced the budget deficit from $4.3 billion in 1936 to only

$89 million in 1938. The unemployment rate rose from a low of 11% in mid-1937 back to 20% in mid-1938.[5]

The money supply also contracted during this period. The Treasury Department began sterilizing gold inflows into the United States by selling bonds. The gold inflows added to the money supply, but the bond sales by the Treasury withdrew money from the economy, reducing the money supply in much the same way the Fed removes money by selling bolds through open market operations. Sterilization continued until February 1938. Afterwards, the money supply began to expand again.

The Consumer Price Inflation Index peaked in October 1937 and then began to fall again. The annual change in the inflation rate peaked at 5% in May 1937, but fell back below zero in March 1938. Deflation persisted until the first months of 1940, even though continued capital flight out of Europe and Asia caused another strong surge in the money supply from March 1938. The Fed's gold assets increased by 68% during the last two years of the decade due to those capital inflows. That caused the US monetary base to increase by 54% during those 24 months.

Looking back over the decade, the deflationary demand shock that followed the collapse of the 1920s economic bubble was the most powerful factor affecting prices during this period.

The expansion of the money supply following the devaluation of the dollar in 1934 also had a powerful impact on prices. It was the main factor that brought the deflation of the early 1930s to an end. New Deal fiscal stimulus also played a role.

The contraction of the money supply in 1930 contributed to the deflation that followed, but was a less important factor than the deflationary demand shock mentioned above. It is also probable that the money supply contraction during 1937 played a role in bringing about the deflation of 1937 and 1938. On the other hand, moderate money supply expansion from 1931 to 1933 did not end deflation during those years. Nor did a very robust expansion of the money supply during 1938 and 1939 end the deflation that prevailed then.

For the decade as a whole, base money grew at an average rate of 9% a year. Prices, meanwhile, fell by an average of 2% a year. The highest rate of money supply growth was 28% in 1939. The lowest was a contraction of 14% in 1937. The inflation rate peaked at 6% in 1934. Deflation peaked at 11% in 1932.

The 1940s

European gold continued to pour into the US during 1940. The Fed's holdings of gold certificates increased by another 29% in that one year alone. That caused US base money to expand by 20% during 1940, with the peak rate of growth at 27% in February (see Chart 15.4).

Thereafter, capital controls were imposed in Europe. Moreover, Lend-Lease meant England no longer had to pay with gold for the war materials it bought from the United States. Instead, those purchases were financed with credit provided by the US government. Consequently, the gold inflows into the US ceased and US base money leveled off.

Altogether between the end of 1937 and the end of 1940, US base money had increased by 85%. The impact of this explosion of money on inflation was negligible. Prices fell during 1938 and 1939; and the annual inflation rate for the 12 months of 1940 averaged only 0.7%. These years do not lend strong support to the claim that money supply growth always results in inflation.

To be fair, it is usually argued that money supply growth always results in inflation with a lag. Milton Friedman wrote in *Money Mischief,* "over the past century and more in the United States, the United Kingdom, and some other Western countries, roughly six to nine months have elapsed on the average before increased monetary growth has worked its way through the economy and produced increased economic growth and employment. Another twelve to eighteen months have elapsed before the increased monetary growth has affected the price level appreciably and inflation has occurred or speeded up."[6] In this case, inflation did turn positive in February 1940, 26 months after the surge in the money supply began. But inflationary pressures remained very muted until the second quarter of 1941. By

CHART 15.4 Base Money vs. CPI: Percentage Change from Year Ago, The 1940s

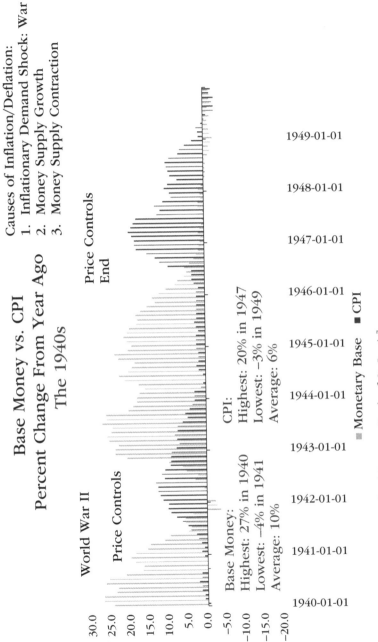

Source: Data from the Federal Reserve Bank of St. Louis[7]

then, Europe had been at war for a year and a half; and demand from Europe for US war materials and the United States' own military preparations that preceded its entry into the war had brought about a recovery in the US economy.

When inflation did begin to rise in the second quarter of 1941, the *inflationary demand shock* brought on by World War II was the principal reason. The extraordinary surge in the money supply that began in 1938 probably did contribute to the pickup in inflation; but, if so, its role was much less important than the inflationary demand shock resulting from the war.

The US inflation rate rose from 1.4% in March 1941 to a peak of 13.2% in May 1942. It certainly would have continued rising had the government not imposed price controls soon after the United States entered the war in December 1941. Of course, the price controls resulted in shortages of many consumer goods, which imposed a different kind of burden on the public. Nevertheless, the inflation rate moved back down to 0% by May 1944 and it remained below 3% through the first quarter of 1946.

Price controls kept inflation contained even though the money supply effectively doubled during the war. Between 1941 and 1945, the Fed's holdings of US government securities increased from $2.2 billion to $19.4 billion. The money supply doubled because the Fed created money to pay for the government bonds it acquired.

When the war ended, price controls were gradually removed. As controls were lifted, inflation took off. The inflation rate rose from 2.8% in March 1946 to a peak of 19.7% in March 1947. The annual growth rate of base money peaked at 27% in 1943 and then began to slow from the end of 1944. By July 1947, it was down to 0.2%. In March 1948, it turned negative and it remained negative (ranging between -0.1% and -2.4%) until the Korean War began in mid-1950.

This monetary restraint was an important factor in the rapid fall in the inflation rate after 1947. Prices stabilized during the second quarter of 1949 and then turned negative. Prices fell every month between May 1949 and June 1950, when the Korean War started.

The collapse in government expenditure after World War II also explains why the postwar inflation was so short-lived. Government outlays fell from $93 billion in 1945 to $30 billion in 1948. This was a deflationary demand shock that pushed prices lower.

Looking back over the decade, the inflationary demand shock brought on by the war was the principal cause of inflation during the decade. Money supply growth played a secondary role. When the war ended, the deflationary demand shock from the curtailment of government spending and monetary restraint both contributed to a rapid decline in inflation in late 1947 and during 1948. Of the two, the deflationary demand shock may have been more important than monetary restraint.

Base money grew at an average annual rate of 10% during the 1940s. Consumer price inflation increased on average by 6% a year. The highest rate of base money growth was 27% in 1940. The lowest was a contraction of 4% in 1941. Inflation peaked at 20% in 1947. Deflation peaked at 3% in 1949.

The 1950s

During the 1950s, money supply growth was tightly constrained and, other than during the Korean War, the inflation rate was low (see Chart 15.5).

The Korean War caused the inflation rate to jump from a low of -0.9% at the beginning of the decade to a peak of +9% in February 1951. Growth in the money supply was not to blame. President Truman insisted that the war be financed with tax increases rather than through money creation by the Fed in contrast to what had occurred during the two world wars. Consequently, money supply growth increased to only 5.3% in January 1952. That was its peak for the decade.

The inflationary demand shock of the war was responsible for the inflation that occurred during the 1950s. Government outlays increased from $43 billion in 1950 to $68 billion in 1952. After the war ended, however, this time there was no deflationary demand shock. Government spending didn't drop off after

CHART 15.5 Base Money *vs.* CPI: Percentage Change from Year Ago, The 1950s

Base Money *vs.* CPI
Percent Change From Year Ago
The 1950s

Causes of Inflation:
1. Positive Demand Shock:
   Korean War

Base Money:
Highest: 5% in 1952
Lowest: −1% in 1950
Average: 2%

CPI:
Highest: 9% in 1951
Lowest: −1% in 1954
Average: 2%

Korean War

Money Supply Growth and Inflation were both limited during the 1950s.

30.0
25.0
20.0
15.0
10.0
5.0
0.0
−5.0
−10.0
−15.0
−20.0

1950-01-01
1951-01-01
1952-01-01
1953-01-01
1954-01-01
1955-01-01
1956-01-01
1957-01-01
1958-01-01
1959-01-01

Monetary Base ■ CPI

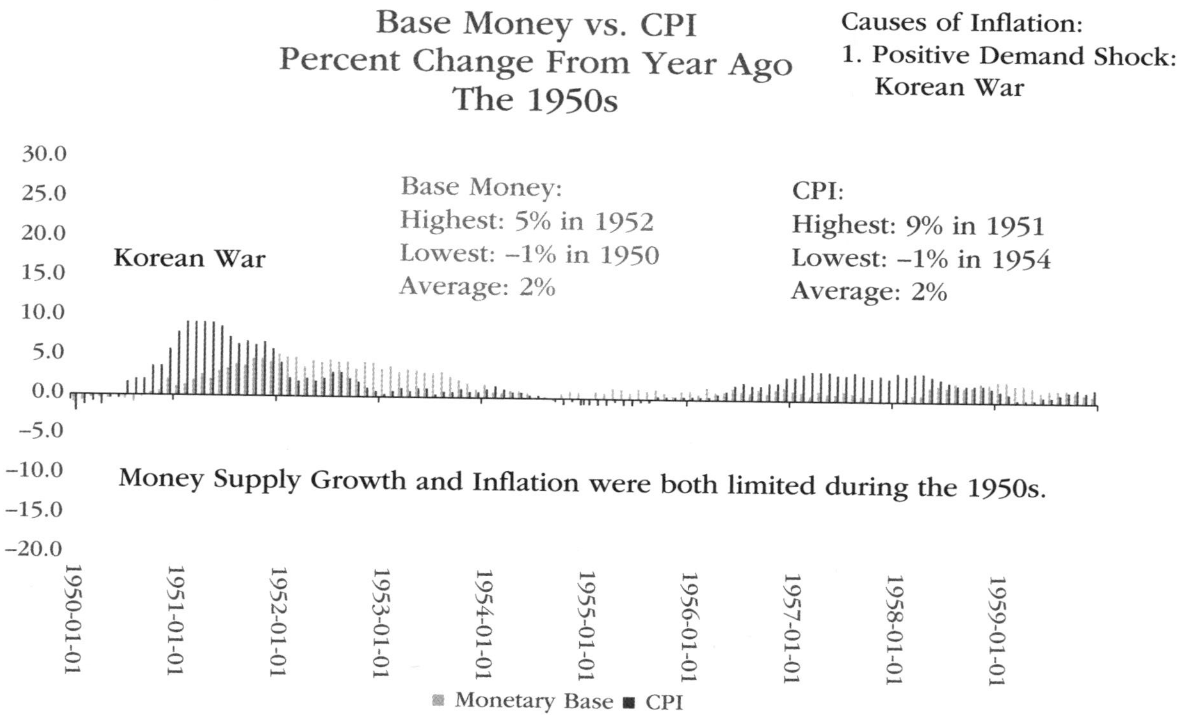

Source: Data from the Federal Reserve Bank of St. Louis[8]

the war. It continued to expand, reaching $92 billion in 1959. The military-industrial complex that President Eisenhower warned about when he left office in 1960 became entrenched during the 1950s.

Low money supply growth deserves the credit for the low inflation rates during the decade. Conservative fiscal policy helped. Although government spending increased steadily during the decade, so did tax receipts. Budget deficits were small up until 1959. Consequently, the Fed was not pressured to print money to help finance the budget deficits, as it came to be during the 1960s and beyond.

Base money and the inflation rate both grew at an annual average rate of 2% during the decade. The highest rate of base money growth was 5% in 1952. The lowest was -1% in 1950. CPI peaked at 9% 1951. Deflation peaked at -1% in 1954.

The 1960s

Money supply growth and inflation were both low at the beginning of the 1960s, but both accelerated as the decade progressed, as shown in Chart 15.6. Government spending on the Great Society social programs and the Vietnam War produced large budget deficits and the Fed was pressured to help finance them.

Between 1959 and 1969, the Fed's holdings of US government securities more than doubled from $27 billion to $57 billion. In 1959, the Fed owned 11% of all government bonds. In 1969, it owned 19% of a greatly expanded total.[9] The Fed created money to buy the bonds. Base money increased 58% during the decade as a result. Money supply growth would have been greater still, except that the United States lost $4.5 billion of gold, 21% of its holdings, during the 1960s.[10] The outflow of gold partially offset the money the Fed created to monetize the government's debt, making money supply growth less than it otherwise would have been.

The acceleration in money supply growth preceded the pickup in inflation and it was certainly an important factor in

CHART 15.6 Base Money vs. CPI: Percentage Change from Year Ago, The 1960s

Base Money vs. CPI
Percent Change From Year Ago
The 1960s

Causes of Inflation:
1. Inflationary Demand Shock: government spending on Vietnam & the Great Society
2. Money Supply Growth

Base Money:
Highest: 7% in 1969
Lowest: 0% in 1960
Average: 4.5%

CPI:
Highest: 6% in 1969
Lowest: 1% in 1961
Average: 2%

The Fed increased its purchases of US Government Bonds during the 1960s to help finance the Vietnam War and the Great Society programs; and to help support employment.

■ Monetary Base ■ CPI

30.0
25.0
20.0
15.0
10.0
5.0
0.0
-5.0
-10.0
-15.0
-20.0

1960-01-01
1961-01-01
1962-01-01
1963-01-01
1964-01-01
1965-01-01
1966-01-01
1967-01-01
1968-01-01
1969-01-01

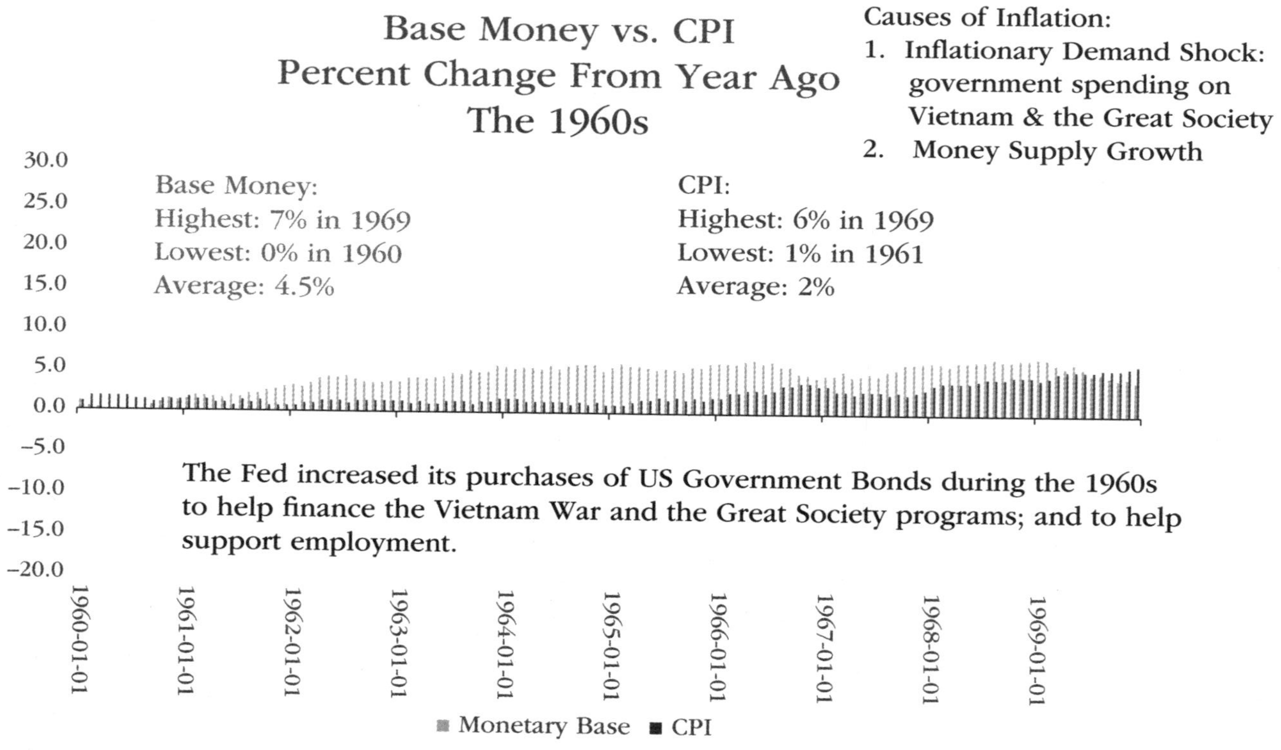

Source: Data from the Federal Reserve Bank of St. Louis[11]

driving prices higher. Government spending, which doubled during the decade, also pushed prices higher.

Base money grew at an annual average rate of 4.5%. Its growth rate increased from 0% in 1960 to 7% in 1969. The average inflation rate was 2%. CPI was lowest in 1961 at 1%. The highest rate of inflation was 6%, recorded in December 1969.

The large budget deficits and excessive money supply growth during the 1960s set the stage for the breakdown of the Bretton Woods international monetary system in August 1971 – and the inflationary firestorm that followed.

The 1970s

In 1970, the United States experienced a mild recession. The government responded with increased spending that produced a large budget deficit in 1971. Money supply growth accelerated as the Fed created more money to help finance the larger deficit. Base money growth increased from 4.1% in January 1970 to 8.6% in July 1971 (see Chart 15.7).

If the Nixon administration's priority had been preserving the Bretton Woods system, it would not have run large budget deficits or encouraged rapid money supply growth. That was not its priority, however. President Nixon's priority was being reelected in November 1972. The combination of fiscal and monetary stimulus in 1970 and 1971 was the final nail in the coffin for the Bretton Woods system.

The Bretton Woods system broke down because by the early 1970s (and, in fact, for a number of years before then) the United States no longer had enough gold to allow other countries to convert the dollars they had acquired into US gold, as the system required. The convertibility of dollars into gold was the foundation upon which the Bretton Woods system was built. The additional fiscal and monetary stimulus during 1971, which was certain to cause even more dollars to end up in foreign hands, made it clear to the rest of the world that the United States would not be able to live up to it obligation to

CHART 15.7 Base Money vs. CPI: Percentage Change from Year Ago, The 1970s

Base Money vs. CPI
Percent Change From Year Ago
The 1970s

Causes of Inflation:
1. Two Inflationary Supply Shocks: Oil
2. Money Supply Growth

Base Money:
Highest: 10% in 1973
Lowest: 4% in 1970
Average: 8%

CPI:
Highest: 13% in 1979
Lowest: 3% in 1972
Average: 7%

2nd Oil Shock
1978–1979

1st Oil Shock
1973–1974

Bretton Woods
breaks down

30.0
25.0
20.0
15.0
10.0
5.0
0.0
−5.0
−10.0
−15.0
−20.0

1970-01-01
1971-01-01
1972-01-01
1973-01-01
1974-01-01
1975-01-01
1976-01-01
1977-01-01
1978-01-01
1979-01-01

■ Monetary Base ■ CPI

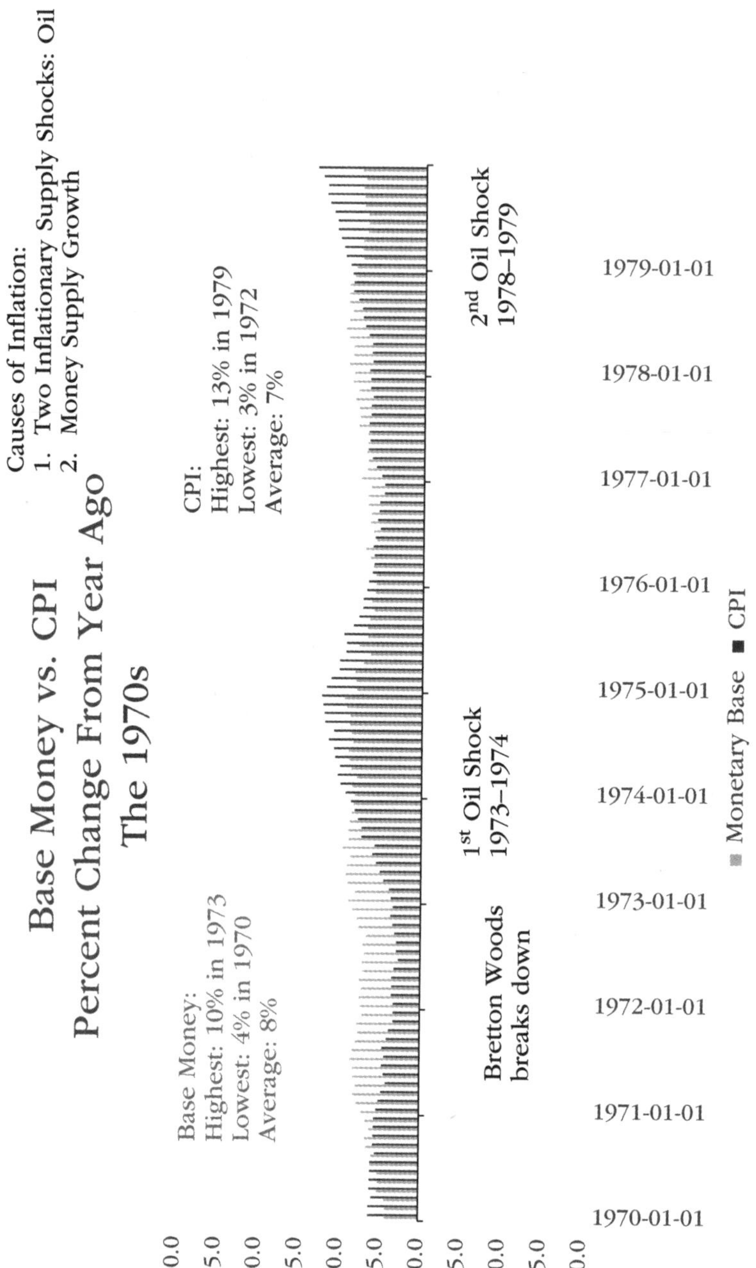

Source: Data from the Federal Reserve Bank of St. Louis[12]

convert dollars into gold for much longer. The redemption of dollars into gold accelerated. Nixon, therefore, had no choice but to end convertibility of dollars into gold in August 1971. Had he not done so, the United States would have been drained of all its gold and the Bretton Woods system would have collapsed anyway.

When Bretton Woods broke down, everything changed. Money was no longer backed by gold. Central banks were free to create as much money as they dared. Currencies were no longer pegged. They floated. Trade between nations no longer had to balance – so long as the trade deficits could be financed with money borrowed from abroad. In short, the orthodoxy that had governed economic policy making for more than a century was thrown out the window and a new paradigm began to take shape.

During the 1970s, these changes produced much higher rates of inflation, in the US and around the world. There were two inflationary oil supply shocks during the decade. The first in 1973–74 was the result of the Arab oil embargo. The second in 1978–79 was set off by the Iran–Iraq War. Oil prices spiked from $3.6 per barrel in July 1973 to $10 per barrel in March 1974. By the end of 1978, it had risen to $14.9 per barrel. It then spiked again to $39 per barrel by April 1980.[13]

First of all, it should be understood that the two oil shocks could not have occurred, or, at least, could not have persisted, if the world had remained on the Bretton Woods system. Many of the oil importing countries would not have had enough gold, dollars, or other gold-backed currencies to allow them to continue importing oil at the new elevated prices. As their gold reserves plummeted, they would have experienced severe economic crises and been forced to buy much less oil. The collapse in the demand for oil would have driven the price of oil back down.

In the post–Bretton Woods world, however, that scenario did not play out. The cash rich oil exporting countries deposited into US banks the money they earned from exporting oil and the US banks lent that money to the oil importing countries, enabling them to continue buying oil at the new high prices.

Therefore, oil prices remained elevated and the two inflationary oil supply shocks pushed inflation higher in the United States and around the world. The US inflation rate rose to above 12% in 1974, abated, and then climbed to more than 13% in 1979. It peaked at nearly 15% in March 1980.

Both oil shocks pushed the United States into painful recessions. Because the economy was weak, the government budget deficits were much larger during the 1970s (averaging 1.9% a year) than they had been during the 1950s (0.4% a year) and 1960s (0.7% a year). The Fed partially monetized those deficits by acquiring much more government debt with newly created money. The Fed's holdings of US government securities doubled during the decade, from $57 billion at the end of 1969 to $116 billion by the end of 1979. As a result of the Fed's purchases of government debt, money supply growth accelerated. Base money grew at an average annual rate of 8% during the 1970s. The inflation rate averaged 7% a year.

Both money supply growth and inflation would have been very much higher still had foreign central banks not stepped in and begun buying US government debt on a very large scale. At the beginning of the decade, the "rest of the world", i.e., foreign buyers, owned $10 billion worth of US government securities, 3% of the total outstanding. By the end of the decade, they owned $116 billion or 16% of the total.

Had foreign central banks not begun buying huge amounts of US government securities, in all likelihood, the Fed would have had to acquire much more government debt than it actually did in order to prevent the increased government borrowing from pushing up interest rates, which would have negatively impacted economic growth and employment. If the Fed had monetized even more government debt, the money supply growth would have been much larger and inflation much worse.

The breakdown of the Bretton Woods system made it possible for the "rest of the world" to buy more US government debt. Once money ceased to be backed by gold in 1971, central banks all around the world were free to create as much money as they wished. Some central banks began creating their own currencies very aggressively in order to buy US dollars in order to hold down the value of their currencies relative to the dollar, so as to support export-led growth for their economies. Once they accumulated the dollars, they had to invest them in US dollar-denominated assets. That explains why the "rest of the world" began buying so many US government bonds during the 1970s. The emergence of large-scale money creation by the central banks of the trade surplus countries was to have an extraordinary impact on the global economy during the decades that followed.

US base money doubled during the 1970s from $63 billion to $134 billion. It is important to understand that that surge in the US base money could not have occurred if the Fed had still been required to hold gold certificates to back the money it created. As noted in early chapters, up until 1968, the Fed had been required to hold 25% gold certificate backing for the dollars it created. In 1968, the Fed had only enough gold certificates to meet that requirement. That meant the Fed could not have created any more dollars unless the outflow of gold from the United States had been reversed or unless the gold certificate backing requirement was reduced. That requirement was removed altogether by an act of Congress in March 1968.[14] Consequently, the Fed was able to continue creating money and using it to buy government bonds in order to help finance the government's large budget deficits at interest rates that were lower than they otherwise would have been.

Looking back over the decade, the two inflationary oil supply shocks were the main reason for the high rates of inflation. The high rates of money supply growth were also a central reason the inflation rate rose as much as it did and remained as high as it did during this period.

The lowest annual rate of base money growth during the decade was 4% in 1970. The highest was 10% in 1973. It nearly reached 10% again in 1978. The lowest rate of inflation was 3% in 1972. The highest was 13% in 1979.

The 1980s

Globalization, in its modern form, got underway in the early 1980s when the United States began running very large trade deficits (see Chart 15.8). Under the gold standard or the Bretton Woods system, countries could not import more than they exported for very long because they were required to pay for their trade deficits with gold. Trade deficits drained money (i.e., gold) from their economies, caused severe economic slumps, unemployment, and deflation. Before long, spending fell, imports declined, and trade came back into balance.

All that ended when the Bretton Woods system collapsed. Afterwards, trade deficits did not have to be paid for out of a limited supply of gold reserves. They could be financed with money borrowed from abroad. Before long the United States began financing its extraordinarily large trade deficits by borrowing money from abroad, primarily money created by foreign central banks.

CHART 15.8 US Current Account Balance: 1947 to 2016

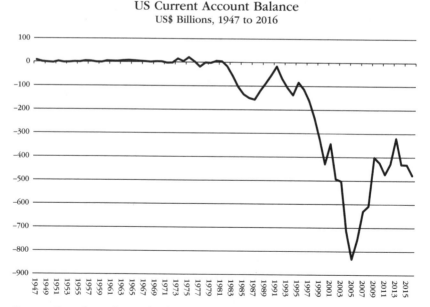

US Current Account Balance
US$ Billions, 1947 to 2016

Source: Data from the Federal Reserve Bank of St. Louis

This new arrangement of financing trade deficits by borrowing newly created money from the countries with large trade surpluses completely transformed the global economy. Its impact was far greater than any other economic development over the last 40 years. The economics profession has still not grasped the significance of this radical break from the past. That is why most economists failed to anticipate the crisis of 2008 and why contemporary economic theory remains unable to explain many of the most important economic developments that have occurred subsequently.

During the 1980s, money supply growth remained high, but inflation began to moderate. The deceleration in inflation is not what would have been anticipated, given the large budget deficits run by the Reagan administration. During the five years between 1982 and 1986, the government's budget deficit averaged 5% of GDP per year. These were by far the largest budget deficits during peacetime in the nation's history up until then. For the decade, the budget deficit averaged 3.8% a year, twice the level of the already high deficits experienced during the inflationary 1970s.

Considering that the budget deficits during the Johnson and Nixon years had played a leading role in the acceleration of inflation in the late 1960s and early 1970s, the Reagan administration's much larger budget deficits should have caused a new bout of inflation during the 1980s. But they didn't. The inflation rate peaked at 15% in 1980 and then fell to as low as 1% in 1986 (see Chart 15.9). Why didn't the Reagan deficits cause inflation to accelerate?

The Fed likes to take credit for bringing down inflation after 1980. And it is true that Fed Chairman Volcker did bring inflation down by provoking a harsh recession with very high federal funds rates from 1980 to 1982. However, after that, the Fed has had very little to do with bringing down the inflation rate. Base money grew at an average annual rate of more than 9% between 1983 and mid-1987. So, inflation didn't come down because the Fed reined in money supply growth. The Fed didn't rein in money supply growth.

CHART 15.9 Base Money vs. CPI: Percentage Change from Year Ago, The 1980s

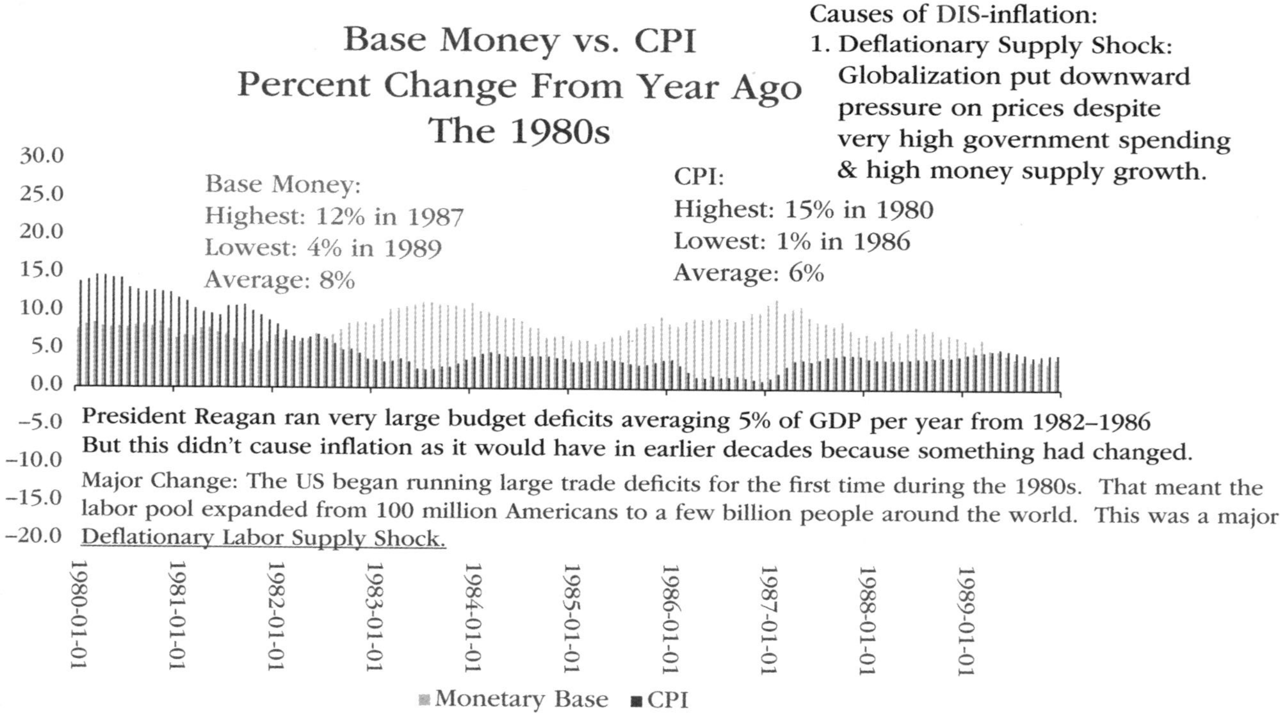
Base Money vs. CPI
Percent Change From Year Ago
The 1980s
Causes of DIS-inflation:
1. Deflationary Supply Shock:
Globalization put downward
pressure on prices despite
very high government spending
& high money supply growth.
Base Money:
Highest: 12% in 1987
Lowest: 4% in 1989
Average: 8%
CPI:
Highest: 15% in 1980
Lowest: 1% in 1986
Average: 6%
30.0
25.0
20.0
15.0
10.0
5.0
0.0
–5.0
–10.0
–15.0
–20.0
President Reagan ran very large budget deficits averaging 5% of GDP per year from 1982–1986
But this didn't cause inflation as it would have in earlier decades because something had changed.
Major Change: The US began running large trade deficits for the first time during the 1980s. That meant the labor pool expanded from 100 million Americans to a few billion people around the world. This was a major Deflationary Labor Supply Shock.
1980-01-01
1981-01-01
1982-01-01
1983-01-01
1984-01-01
1985-01-01
1986-01-01
1987-01-01
1988-01-01
1989-01-01
Monetary Base
CPI

Source: Data from the Federal Reserve Bank of St. Louis[15]

Inflation came down because the US began buying more and more goods from low wage countries and that drove down wages and prices in the United States. In other words, inflation came down because of a deflationary supply shock – a deflationary *labor* supply shock.

Supply and demand determine prices. Before the US started running very large trade deficits in the 1980s, if US money supply increased rapidly, that would boost demand and result in full utilization of US labor and industrial capacity, leading to inflation. After the US began running large trade deficits, US capacity constraints no longer mattered – only global capacity constraints mattered.

Globally, there are no labor constraints. Hundreds of millions of people will work for less than $10 per day. Consequently, after the early 1980s, rapid money supply growth in the United States no longer resulted in high rates of inflation. Once the United States began running large trade deficits, the deflationary supply shock that resulted from globalization and a near infinite pool of ultra-low-cost labor held US wages and prices down, regardless of how large the budget deficits or the money supply growth became.

This deflationary labor supply shock has continued to be the main factor determining the inflation rate during the decades that have followed.

Looking back over the decade of the 1980s, base money grew at an average annual rate of 8%. Inflation averaged 6% a year. Base money growth peaked at 12% in 1987. Its lowest rate of growth was 4% in 1989. Inflation peaked at 15% in 1980. It bottomed at 1% in 1986.

The 1990s

During the 1990s, the trends that developed during the 1980s continued. Money supply growth remained high. Base money doubled again during those 10 years. Nevertheless, the inflation rate continued to move down (see Chart 15.10). The deflationary

CHART 15.10 Base Money vs. CPI: Percentage Change from Year Ago, The 1990s

Base Money vs. CPI
Percent Change From Year Ago
The 1990s

Causes of DIS-inflation:

1. Deflationary Supply Shock:
   Globalization put downward
   pressure on prices despite
   high government spending
   & high money supply growth.

Base Money:
Highest: 16% in 1999
Lowest: 3% in 1996
Average: 8%

CPI:
Highest: 6% in 1990
Lowest: 1% in 1998
Average: 3%

Money supply growth was much higher than inflation.

This was the decade when China began running large trade surpluses with the US.

Y2K

1990-01-01
1991-01-01
1992-01-01
1993-01-01
1994-01-01
1995-01-01
1996-01-01
1997-01-01
1998-01-01
1999-01-01

30.0
25.0
20.0
15.0
10.0
5.0
0.0
-5.0
-10.0
-15.0
-20.0

Monetary Base   ■ CPI

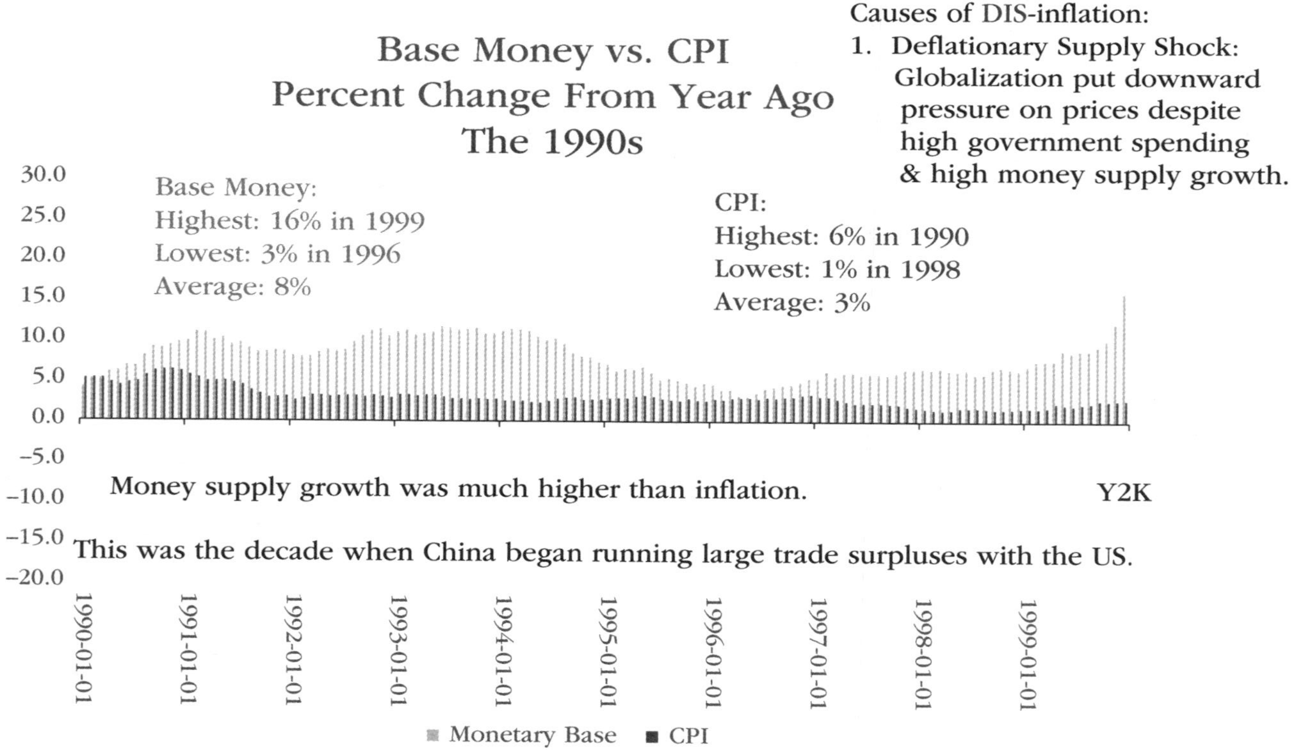

Source: Data from the Federal Reserve Bank of St. Louis[16]

labor supply shock explains the disinflation. This was the decade when China entered the global economy and began running large trade surpluses with the United States. By the end of the decade the US current account deficit had grown to nearly $300 billion, more than 3% of US GDP.

For the decade, base money growth averaged 8% a year. The average inflation rate fell to 3%. The highest rate of base money growth was 16% in 1999. That occurred because the Fed flooded the banks with money as a precautionary measure before Y2K. Other than that, the peak in base money growth occurred between late 1992 and mid-1994, at an annual average rate of 10% to 11%. The lowest rate of base money growth was 3% in 1996. CPI peaked at 6% in 1990. Its low was 1% in 1998.

2000 to Mid-2008

This section considers the years between 2000 and mid-2008 just before the economic crisis began. Base money growth slowed sharply after 2002. It fell from above 10% in 2002 to less than 1% during the first half of 2008. Inflation, on the other hand, rose during those years, from 1% in 2002 to 5% in mid-2008, as shown in Chart 15.11.

The acceleration in inflation over those years appears odd at first glance. Monetary policy was restrictive. The Fed hiked the federal funds rate by 425 basis points between mid-2004 and mid-2006, causing money supply growth to slow to lows not seen since 1960 (with the exception of two months in 2000 when the Fed unwound the Y2K money supply surge). Furthermore, the US current account deficit continued to widen, so the deflationary forces of globalization continued to exert downward pressure on US prices. What, then caused the pickup in the inflation rate?

The inflation rate accelerated because capital inflows from abroad resulted in such rapid credit growth in the United States that the country was blown into an economic bubble – despite the sharp reduction in the money supply growth engineered

CHART 15.11 Base Money vs. CPI: Percentage Change from Year Ago, 2000 to Mid-2008

Base Money vs. CPI
Percent Change From Year Ago
2000 to mid-2008

Base Money:
Highest: 13% in 2000
Lowest: −3% in 2000
Average: 5%

CPI:
Highest: 5% in 2008
Lowest: 1% in 2002
Average: 3%

Causes of DIS-inflation/Inflation:
1. Deflationary Supply Shock:
   Globalization
2. Inflationary Demand Shock:
   Global credit bubble

After 2002, Money supply growth slowed sharply.
But CPI picked up to 5% at the end of the period as the result of the global economic bubble.

■ Monetary Base ■ CPI

30.0
25.0
20.0
15.0
10.0
5.0
0.0
−5.0
−10.0
−15.0
−20.0

2000-01-01
2001-01-01
2002-01-01
2003-01-01
2004-01-01
2005-01-01
2006-01-01
2007-01-01
2008-01-01

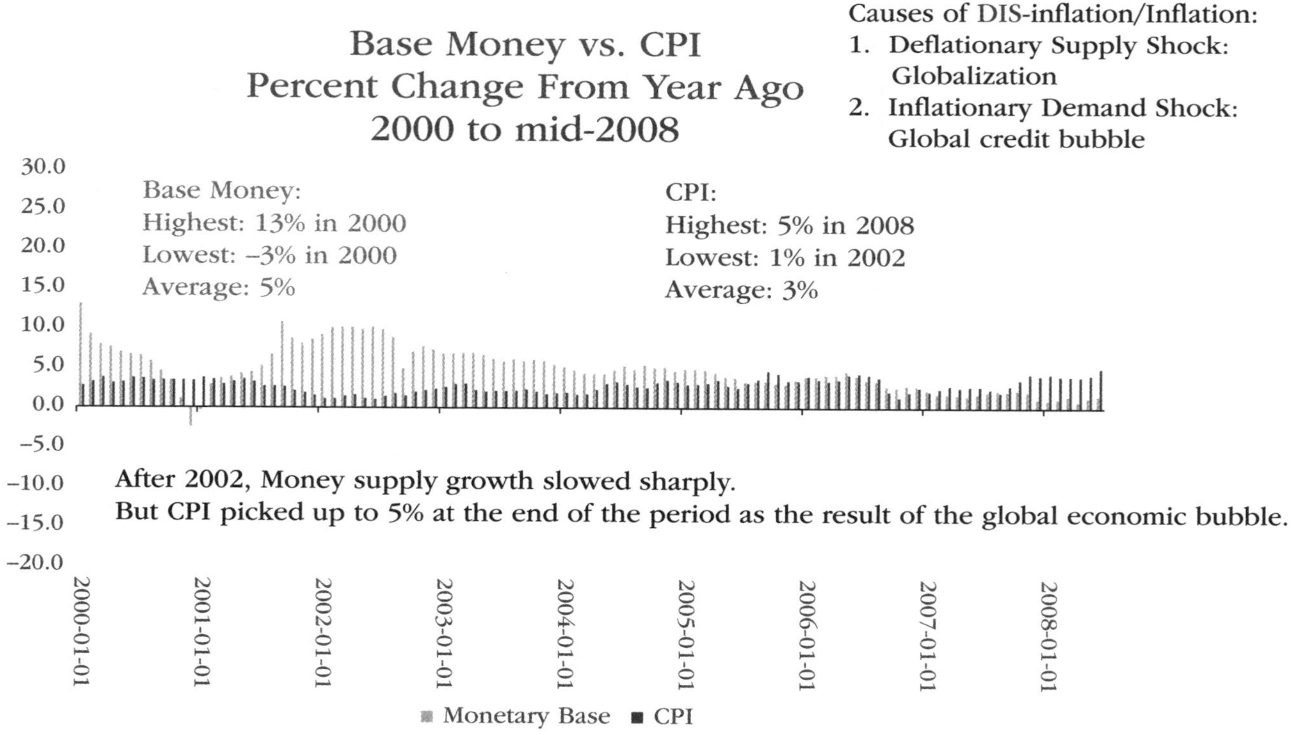

Source: Data from the Federal Reserve Bank of St. Louis[17]

by the Fed. Foreign capital inflows, the mirror image of the US current account deficit, peaked at $800 billion or 6% of GDP in 2006. As the capital inflows grew larger, credit expanded. Total US credit growth increased from 7% in 2000 to 10.5% in 2007. Rapid credit growth pushed up prices; both asset prices and consumer prices. The credit bubble of those years produced an inflationary demand shock that drove US inflation higher. When the bubble popped in the second half of 2008, the inflationary demand shock it had caused gave way to a deflationary demand shock once credit began to contract.

During these eight and a half years, base money growth averaged 5% a year, with much higher growth rates in the first half of the period than during the second half. Money supply growth peaked at 13% in January 2000. In December 2000, money supply contracted by 3%. The peak rate and the contraction were both related to the pre-Y2K money surge, which was partially unwound afterwards. The inflation rate averaged 3% a year. Inflation peaked at 5% in mid-2008, just before the crisis began. The lowest level of Inflation was 1% in 2002.

Mid-2008 to 2019

The period between mid-2008 and 2019 demonstrates in a dramatic fashion that changes in the money supply no longer have any discernable impact whatsoever on the rate of inflation. The following paragraphs will show that the largest annual increase in the monetary base ever recorded (109% in 2009) did not cause inflation to rise and that a very steep contraction in the monetary base in both 2016 and 2019 did not cause prices to fall. There could be no more conclusive proof than the evidence presented during this period that a fundamental economic change has occurred that has severed the causal link between changes in money supply growth and changes in the price level. The conclusion that must be drawn from these developments is that a paradigm shift has occurred in the way our monetary/economic system functions now that money is no longer backed by gold.

During the autumn of 2008, a systemic financial sector crisis came close to bankrupting every major financial sector institution in the United States. The Fed prevented that cataclysm by unleashing three tidal waves of money. See Chart 15.12.

Beginning with an extraordinary series of discounting operations that peaked at $1.5 trillion in late 2008, the Fed provided loans to all and sundry within the world of finance. Then followed three rounds of Quantitative Easing. QE1 began in December 2008 and lasted until March 2010. QE2 occurred between November 2010 and June 2011. QE3 extended for 24 months between October 2012 and October 2014.

In total, during the six years and four months between June 2008 and October 2014, when the third round of Quantitative Easing ended, the money supply increase by $3.2 trillion or by 365%. If inflation were always and everywhere a monetary phenomenon as Milton Friedman and other Monetarists believed, this flood of money should have quickly led to hyperinflation in the United States. It didn't. In fact, it was barely sufficient to prevent prices from falling. The inflation rate averaged 1.8% during that period.

During 2016, the monetary base contracted by 12% when the Fed entered into reverse repurchase agreements to absorb Bank Reserves. That was the largest contraction since 1937. During 2019, the monetary base shrank by 13% due to Quantitative Tightening, which began in October 2017 and ended in August 2019. Despite these exceptionally large declines in the monetary base, prices did not fall. The monthly inflation rate between January 2016 and July 2019 averaged 1.9%.

During this period, the highest annual rate of base money growth was 109% in 2009. The lowest was -13% in 2019. The largest rise in Inflation was 5.6% in mid-2008, before the crisis was fully underway. The highest rate of inflation after Quantitative Easing began at the end of 2008 was 3.9% in September 2011. The lowest rate of inflation was -2.1% in mid-2009.

CHART 15.12 Base Money vs. CPI: Percentage Change from Year Ago, Mid-2008 to December 2019

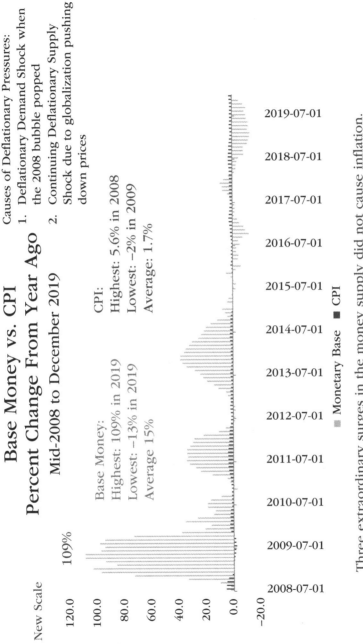

Base Money vs. CPI
Percent Change From Year Ago
Mid-2008 to December 2019

Base Money:
Highest: 109% in 2019
Lowest: −13% in 2019
Average 15%

CPI:
Highest: 5.6% in 2008
Lowest: −2% in 2009
Average: 1.7%

Causes of Deflationary Pressures:
1. Deflationary Demand Shock when the 2008 bubble popped
2. Continuing Deflationary Supply Shock due to globalization pushing down prices

New Scale

Three extraordinary surges in the money supply did not cause inflation. The money supply no longer determines prices.

■ Monetary Base ■ CPI

Source: Data from the Federal Reserve Bank of St. Louis[18]

2020 to Mid-2021

The Fed resumed creating money on a very large scale beginning in September 2019 in response to a disruption in the functioning of the market for overnight repurchase agreements. It then radically accelerated the amount of money it created beginning in March 2020 in response to the pandemic. Between September 2019 and June 2021, the monetary base surged by nearly $2.8 trillion, an 88% jump. The year-on-year peak rate of growth in the monetary base was 59% in May 2020. By June 2021, it had fallen back to 20%. Consumer price inflation moved up to 5.3% in June 2021.[19] See Chart 15.13.

The 5.3% jump in the CPI in June 2021 was the highest since a 5.6% increase in July 2008. However, it is important to understand that this figure was distorted by the deflation that

CHART 15.13 Base Money vs. CPI, Percentage Change from Year Ago, January 2020 to June 2021

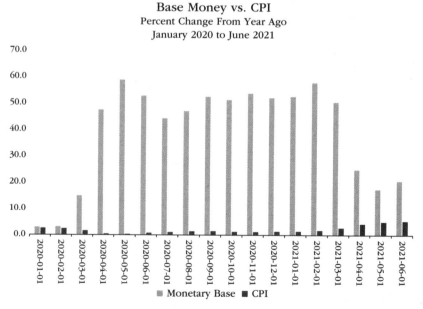

Source: Data from the Federal Reserve Bank of St. Louis[20]

occurred during the second quarter of 2020. While the June 2021 CPI index was 5.3% above its level in June 2020, it was only 6% above its level in June 2019, meaning that the average annual inflation rate during the two years between mid-2019 and mid-2021 was a much less alarming 3.0%.

The pickup in inflation during the first half of 2021 resulted from an inflationary demand shock and an inflationary supply shock. The government's extraordinarily aggressive fiscal policy response to the economic crisis caused by the pandemic produced the inflationary demand shock. Three very large rounds of fiscal stimulus, which included checks sent from the government directly to individuals, provided Americans with augmented purchasing power that fueled consumption and created higher than normal demand.

At the same time, the COVID-19 pandemic disrupted supply chains around the world, leading to supply shortages and higher prices for some goods. One of the most significant instances of this was a shortage of semiconductors used by the automobile industry. When the pandemic began, the automobile industry, mistakenly expecting a collapse in consumer demand, sharply reduced its orders from semiconductor manufacturers. By the time it became clear that there would not be a collapse in demand, it was too late for the semiconductor companies to produce all the semiconductors the automobile companies required. Consequently, there was a shortage of new cars and trucks during the first half of 2021. As a result of that shortage, the price of used cars and trucks jumped by roughly 40% in the second quarter of 2021 compared with one year earlier. That alone accounted for approximately one-third of the increase in the Consumer Price Index during the second quarter.

The elevated inflation of mid-2021 is unlikely to persist for long. The supplemental demand provided by the government's large fiscal stimulus packages has already begun to fade, and no other large government spending programs on the scale of the first three are expected. Therefore, the growth in consumer demand will slow during the quarters ahead. Demand will cool just as supply begins to expand as the supply bottlenecks stemming from the pandemic are overcome. The combination of weaker demand and increasing supply is likely to cause price pressures to abate.

By the end of 2022, the deflationary forces resulting from globalization are likely to once again become paramount, barring any new unexpected shocks. If so, the inflation rate may soon fall back below the Fed's 2% inflation target.

If large increases in the money supply inevitably produced high rates of inflation, as many believe, then the extraordinary surge in the US monetary base since March 2020 and the even larger increase in the monetary base following the crisis of 2008 should have set off hyperinflation in the United States. But that did not happen. The annual growth in the monetary base peaked at 59% in 2020. The average annual rate of inflation between mid-2019 and mid-2021 was 3%. The monetary base grew at a mind-boggling rate of 109% in 2009 and then by a further 34% in 2011 and by 39% more in 2013. And yet the peak rate of inflation following the financial crisis was 3.9%.

To put this into perspective, money supply growth peaked at what was then an unprecedented rate of 28% during World War II. Since 2008, growth in the money supply has exceeded the World War II peak four times (see Chart 15.14).

Why Prices Didn't Rise

From the end of 2008 to the middle of 2021, the US monetary base expanded at an average annual rate of 18%. Inflation, on the other hand, averaged just 1.7% a year. So why didn't the extraordinary surge in money supply growth cause very high rates of inflation?

The explanation is that, by 2008, money and the money supply had become largely irrelevant in terms of having a meaningful impact on prices. During the first half of the twentieth century, the money supply mattered because it determined how much credit could be created. The requirement that the Fed back the dollars it created by holding gold (or later gold certificates) and the requirement that the banking system hold a

CHART 15.14 Base Money *vs.* CPI: Percentage Change from Year Ago, 1919 to Mid-2021

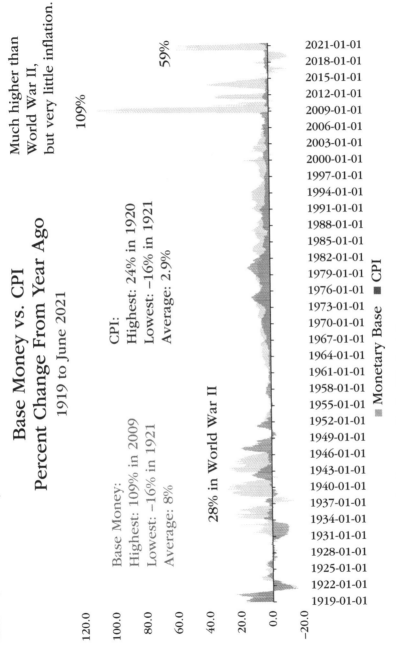

Base Money vs. CPI
Percent Change From Year Ago
1919 to June 2021

Base Money:
Highest: 109% in 2009
Lowest: –16% in 1921
Average: 8%

28% in World War II

CPI:
Highest: 24% in 1920
Lowest: –16% in 1921
Average: 2.9%

Much higher than
World War II,
but very little inflation.

109%

59%

■ Monetary Base ■ CPI

Source: Data from the Federal Reserve Bank of St. Louis[21]

substantial amount of reserves to back the money (i.e., bank credit) it created, meant that the supply of money and credit was tightly constrained. However, during the course of the second half of the century, the Fed was freed from the requirement to back dollars with gold certificates and the banking system was, for all intents and purposes, freed from the requirement to hold a meaningful amount of Bank Reserves. Moreover, non-bank financial institutions that were not subject to any reserve requirements began supplying a growing share of credit in the economy. Lastly, foreign central banks began pumping trillion of dollars of credit into the United States.

These changes meant that the money supply ceased to have any real influence over how much credit could be created in the United States. In the years leading up to the crisis of 2008, the financial system was free to create as much credit as it dared. The link between money and credit disappeared. More than that, money itself disappeared. When the Fed stopped backing dollars with gold certificates in 1968, dollars ceased to be money (as money had been defined in the past) and became simply another credit instrument issued by the government, a kind of non-interest bearing, small denomination government bond.

By 2008 – and long before – the money supply did not determine how much credit could be created. The only constraint on how much credit could be created was the financial ability of the borrowers to pay interest on the credit they borrowed. During the years leading up to 2008, the majority of the lenders in the US financial system misjudged – or simply ignored – that constraint and lent extravagantly. They then spiraled head-first toward bankruptcy when the borrowers defaulted. Afterwards, no amount of money supply growth could induce the financially crippled private sector to borrow and spend more. Consequently, a sevenfold increase in the money supply between mid-2008 and mid-2021 had almost no impact on inflation. Had the government not stepped in and begun borrowing on a multitrillion-dollar scale during the crisis of 2008, and again during 2020, then, in both instances, the economy would have collapsed, and severe deflation would have taken hold, just as occurred during the early 1930s after the economic bubble of the Roaring Twenties popped.

A new Great Depression was prevented by a policy response involving trillions of dollars of fiscal stimulus financed with trillions of dollars of money created by the Fed. Yet, despite this unprecedented fiscal and monetary stimulus, the average annual rate of inflation since mid-2008 has been 1.7%, below the Fed's 2% inflation target. These facts strongly support the idea that we are living in a new economic environment that opens up tremendous opportunities that did not exist in the past. Part Three describes those opportunities and the extraordinary benefits they offer if we make the most of them.

Notes

1. Friedman, Milton, Counter-Revolution in Monetary Theory. Wincott Memorial Lecture, Institute of Economic Affairs, Occasional paper 33, 1970, p. 11. https://miltonfriedman.hoover.org/friedman_images/Collections/2016c21/IEA_1970.pdf
2. This chapter begins with 1919 because the data series used for the monetary base, the St. Louis adjusted monetary base provided by the St. Louis Fed, begins that year.
3. 1919 to 2019: St. Louis Adjusted Monetary Base (AMBNS_PC1) January 2020 to June 2021: Monetary Base (BOGMBASE) CPI: Consumer Price Index for All Urban Consumers
4. 1919 to 2019: St. Louis Adjusted Monetary Base (AMBNS_PC1) January 2020 to June 2021: Monetary Base (BOGMBASE) CPI: Consumer Price Index for All Urban Consumers
5. St Louis Fed, FRED. https://fred.stlouisfed.org/series/M0892 AUSM156SNBR
6. Milton Friedman, *Money Mischief: Episodes in Monetary History*, p. 221. A Harvest Book, Harcourt Brace & Company, 1994.
7. 1919 to 2019: St. Louis Adjusted Monetary Base (AMBNS_PC1) January 2020 to June 2021: Monetary Base (BOGMBASE) CPI: Consumer Price Index for All Urban Consumers
8. 1919 to 2019: St. Louis Adjusted Monetary Base (AMBNS_PC1) January 2020 to June 2021: Monetary Base (BOGMBASE) CPI: Consumer Price Index for All Urban Consumers

9. Financial Accounts of the United States, Tables L.106 and L.109, the Federal Reserve.

10. Banking and Monetary Statistics 1941 to 1970, St. Louis Fed. https://fraser.stlouisfed.org/title/banking-monetary-statistics-1941-1970-41

11. 1919 to 2019: St. Louis Adjusted Monetary Base (AMBNS_PC1) January 2020 to June 2021: Monetary Base (BOGMBASE) CPI: Consumer Price Index for All Urban Consumers

12. 1919 to 2019: St. Louis Adjusted Monetary Base (AMBNS_PC1) January 2020 to June 2021: Monetary Base (BOGMBASE) CPI: Consumer Price Index for All Urban Consumers

13. West Texas Intermediate, St. Louis Fed, FRED. https://fred.stlouisfed.org/series/WTISPLC

14. Public Law 90-269, 82 Stat. 50 – An Act to eliminate the reserve requirements for Federal Reserve notes and for U.S. notes and Treasury notes of 1890. Source: Govinfo. https://www.govinfo.gov/app/details/STATUTE-82/STATUTE-82-Pg50

15. 1919 to 2019: St. Louis Adjusted Monetary Base (AMBNS_PC1) January 2020 to June 2021: Monetary Base (BOGMBASE) CPI: Consumer Price Index for All Urban Consumers

16. 1919 to 2019: St. Louis Adjusted Monetary Base (AMBNS_PC1) January 2020 to June 2021: Monetary Base (BOGMBASE) CPI: Consumer Price Index for All Urban Consumers

17. 1919 to 2019: St. Louis Adjusted Monetary Base (AMBNS_PC1) January 2020 to June 2021: Monetary Base (BOGMBASE) CPI: Consumer Price Index for All Urban Consumers

18. 1919 to 2019: St. Louis Adjusted Monetary Base (AMBNS_PC1) January 2020 to June 2021: Monetary Base (BOGMBASE) CPI: Consumer Price Index for All Urban Consumers

19. Consumer Price Index for All Urban Consumers: All Items in U.S. City Average, Percent Change, Seasonally Adjusted, St Louis Fed, FRED. https://fred.stlouisfed.org/series/CPIAUCSL#0

20. January 2020 to June 2021: Monetary Base (BOGMBASE) CPI: Consumer Price Index for All Urban Consumers

21. 1919 to 2019: St. Louis Adjusted Monetary Base (AMBNS_PC1) January 2020 to June 2021: Monetary Base (BOGMBASE) CPI: Consumer Price Index for All Urban Consumers

PART III

The Future

Introduction

We study history to better understand the present and to enable us to make better decisions for the future. The first two parts of this book presented a history of the extraordinary evolution of money and credit from the establishment of the Federal Reserve System in 1913 to the present. The final part presents important policy recommendations based on the lessons that can be derived from that history. Most crucially, Part Three shows that the Money Revolution opens up unprecedented opportunities for the United States to radically accelerate economic growth, enhance human well-being and strengthen US national security by investing aggressively in the Industries of the Future.

In recent years, the United States has experienced widespread economic discontent that has resulted in a bitter partisan divide in politics. At the same time, China has emerged as a geopolitical rival that threatens the United States' economic, technological, and military primacy and, therefore, US national security.

If the United States does not act quickly, the political divisions at home could tear the country apart, while Chinese hegemony becomes entrenched throughout the greater part of the world.

Fortunately, the United States has the means to stop and reverse its relative economic decline. The Money Revolution described in the first two parts of this book has created a set of circumstances that will allow the United States to carry out an Investment Revolution.

The objective of Part Three of *The Money Revolution* is to persuade the American public and US policymakers that the United States can and must make a multitrillion-dollar investment in new industries and technologies over the next 10 years in order to ignite a technological revolution that would turbocharge economic growth, consolidate the country's geopolitical preeminence, and vastly enhance human well-being, not only in the United States, but all around the world.

Part Three explains why the United States' current level of investment is dangerously inadequate. It shows how a multitrillion-dollar investment program could be structured and discusses the industries that should be targeted. It demonstrates how the investment program could be financed and it describes the extraordinary benefits that such a large-scale investment program could be counted on to deliver.

The Money Revolution of the twentieth century means that it is now possible to turn today's dreams for a better world into reality – not generations from now, but in our own lifetime. The financing is available. Only sufficient imagination is lacking. The goal of this book is to overcome that impediment, so that the first American Century need not be the last.

CHAPTER 16

America Must Invest

Basic research leads to new knowledge. It provides scientific capital. It creates the fund from which the practical applications of knowledge must be drawn. New products and new processes do not appear full-grown. They are founded on new principles and new conceptions, which in turn are painstakingly developed by research in the purest realms of science.

Vannevar Bush[1]

The purpose of the final part of this book is to advocate that the United States grasp the opportunity that the Money Revolution has made possible by undertaking a government-financed investment program in twenty-first century industries and technologies on such a large scale that it would be certain to succeed.

This chapter will summarize why such a large-scale investment program is possible and explain why it is urgently necessary. It will also discuss its ideal size, which industries it should target, and how it could be structured. Later chapters will describe how it could be financed and the transformational results it could be counted on to deliver.

Why a Large-Scale Investment Program Is Possible

Before the breakdown of Bretton Woods, there were hard constraints on how much the government could spend and on how much money the Fed could create.

If the government spent too much, as it did during the 1960s and 1970s, it overstimulated the relatively closed US economy and caused inflation. The large increase in government borrowing pushed up interest rates and "crowded out" the private sector. Moreover, increased government stimulus caused dollars to flow overseas as increased consumer demand pulled more imports into the US and as foreign investment by cash-rich US banks and corporations expanded. Large dollar outflows could not be tolerated because, up until August 1971, the governments of other countries had the right to exchange the dollars they accumulated for US gold; and any significant loss of gold would threaten the Fed's ability to continue backing dollars with gold.

At the same time, the Fed's freedom to create money was constrained by the legal requirement that it hold gold certificates to back the money it created and by the likelihood that increased money creation would lead to high rates of inflation.

All these constraints were eliminated after the US stopped backing dollars with gold following the breakdown of the Bretton Woods system and once the US started running large trade deficits with the rest of the world from the early 1980s.

Afterwards, the government found that allowing the trade deficit to widen meant that it could spend much more freely without causing inflation because importing goods from abroad, with no concern for the balance of trade, permitted the United States to circumvent the domestic bottlenecks in the labor market and in industrial capacity that had always led to inflation in the past. At the same time, the Fed was no longer required to back dollars with gold certificates and was therefore free to create as many dollars as it wished, so long as the increase in the money supply did not cause inflation, which it no longer did because the surge in imports from low-wage countries drove prices down.

As a result of these changes, the policy options available to the government and the Fed changed radically. During the 1960s and 1970s too much government spending and too much money creation led to double-digit inflation in the United States. After the United States began running large trade deficits in the early 1980s and as globalization gained momentum, inflation rates fell and then remained low regardless of how large the government's budget deficits became or how much money the Fed created. This was spelled out in considerable detail in Chapter 15.

These developments mean that we are living in a completely new policy environment. In the old world of gold-backed money and balanced trade, large budget deficits and excessive money creation did more harm than good. That is no longer the case. In the world in which we live, large-scale government investment in new industries and technologies financed by large-scale money creation has the potential to deliver a technological revolution that would not only generate much higher rates of economic growth, but also solve many of the world's most intractable problems and radically improve the well-being of everyone alive – all without creating high rates of inflation.

Why a Large-Scale Investment Program Is Necessary

There are three main reasons the US government must invest on a very much larger scale than it does at present.

The first and most compelling reason is that it must because it can. A multitrillion-dollar investment program is certain to produce technological breakthroughs that will improve the lives of every American – and everyone else as well. It is now possible for the US government to invest trillions of dollars in new industries and technologies at little to no cost, as Chapters 19 and 20 will demonstrate. Consequently, the cost-reward trade-off is overwhelmingly favorable. The cost is very close to zero. The rewards include a vast improvement in health and well-being, as well as greatly enhanced national security. It would be extraordinarily foolish for the US government not to fully exploit the opportunities open to it at this unique moment in history.

Second, our economic system is driven by credit growth. Capitalism has evolved into Creditism, as explained in Chapter 11. The crisis of 2008 occurred because the private sector was unable to take on any more debt. A surge in US government borrowing and spending prevented a collapse into a new Great Depression. The government is going to have to continue to borrow and spend to make total credit grow and to make the economy expand. It would be far wiser for the government to borrow to fund a large-scale investment program, rather than to borrow to finance unnecessary wars or excessive consumption.

Finally, as Chapters 17 and 18 will show, China is on the brink of overtaking the United States as the world's leading economic and technological superpower because it invests much more than the United States does, not only as a percentage of GDP, but in absolute amounts. If China surpasses the United States technologically, it won't be long before it becomes the world's dominate military power as well. "When China Rules the World"[2] it may be a benign ruler, overseeing a long era of peace and prosperity. On the other hand, it may not be. World history teaches that countries with great technological superiority rarely treat inferior powers kindly.

An artificial intelligence arms race has begun. Within 20 years AI is likely to reach parity with human intelligence. After that it will accelerate at an exponential rate. The country that gets there first will have the rest of the world at its mercy. The US government must ensure that the United States is that country. Pax Americana[3] has not been flawless. However, it has overseen a 75-year period of general peace and facilitated an extraordinary expansion of prosperity around the world.

The rationale for the US government to undertake a multi-trillion-dollar investment program would be irresistibly compelling even if no strategic rival to the United States were visible on the horizon. The fact that China is certain to overwhelm the United States technologically, economically, and militarily before the middle of this century if current trends continue makes such an investment program urgently necessary for reasons of national security as well.

How Much to Invest?

The US government should invest as much as possible, as quickly as possible. Chapters 19 and 20 show that the United States could easily finance a $10 trillion investment program over 10 years. But would that much investment over a decade cause the economy to overheat and lead to unacceptably high rates of inflation? If so, then the investment program could be slowed down until the capacity bottlenecks that caused the inflation were overcome. All capacity constraints are temporary. With sufficient investment they can be quickly resolved.

We might discover that the US economy could absorb that level of investment over 10 years without any significant stress. In that case, then more than $10 trillion should be invested.

The correct approach is for the government to set ambitious goals and to invest as much as possible and as quickly as possible to achieve them. There is no doubt that the government could invest multiples of what it is investing now. Chapter 21 describes the extraordinary benefits that could be expected if it does.

Which Industries to Target

The industries and technologies to target for increased investment should be decided after wide-ranging consultation with scientists in the public sector (including those from DARPA, the National Science Foundation, NASA, and the Departments of Health and Human Services, Energy, and Defense), as well as with business leaders and scientists in the private sector (including those from the leading US tech and pharmaceutical giants).

Artificial intelligence, quantum computing, genetic engineering, biotech, nanotech, renewable energy, neural sciences, and robotics stand out as likely candidates.

How to Structure the Investments

There are two ways the federal government could organize such a large-scale investment program.

First, some projects could be carried out entirely by the federal government, just as NASA was during the 1960s. That method succeeded then. NASA sent a man to the moon in less than a decade. Today, there is much talk of the private sector tech giants investing in "moon shot" projects that they expect to produce extraordinary returns in the future. The original "moon shot" was accomplished by the federal government – 50 YEARS AGO. There is no reason that fully government directed projects could not be successful again now.

Alternatively, the federal government could use a venture capital model to drive this program. The government could set up joint venture companies with thousands of the most promising scientists and entrepreneurs in the United States. The government could then fund those companies lavishly in exchange for a 60% equity stake. The scientists and entrepreneurs would own 40% of the equity and they would manage the companies.

Over time, many of those companies would make extraordinary technological breakthroughs and produce life-changing products that would make their shares incredibly valuable. As they do, they could be listed on NASDAQ, with the government (i.e., the American taxpayer) receiving 60% of the payout. Not only would the government eventually fully recover the investment it made in those companies, the profits and the capital gains might very well be high enough to pay off the entire national debt, or to abolish the income tax or both. This is no pipe dream. If one of these extraordinarily well-funded companies were to discover a cure for cancer or Alzheimer's Disease, which, with enough funding it almost certainly eventually would, it could well become the most valuable company in the world when listed on NASDAQ.

The government should adopt both these approaches: fully government-controlled investment projects and government funded joint ventures with the private sector. A government agency beat the private sector to the moon. Let the government sector and the private sector compete to see which will be the first to cure all the diseases, perfect quantum computing, and master artificial intelligence.

Government Sharing in the Profits

In recent decades, government investment in research and development has produced extraordinary breakthroughs that the private sector adopted and derived enormous profits from. For instance, as Mariana Mazzucato documents so brilliantly in her book, *The Entrepreneurial State,*[4] most of the technologies that make smartphones smart resulted from federally funded research programs – technologies such as semiconductors, GPS, touch screen technology, the voice recognition utilized by Siri and Alexa and, of course, the internet itself.

Similarly, federal government-funded research contributed to the creation of the algorithm that Google used to make its search engine the world's best. Google Search now has 93% global market share and Google's parent company, Alphabet, is one of the most valuable companies in the world.

Up until now, however, the federal government has not received a fair share of the profits that have been derived from the research it funds. The share of taxes paid by corporations has continued to shrink thanks to the success of the corporate lobbyists they pay in Washington. In 2018, corporate taxes amounted to only 1% of GDP, whereas the average from 1934 has been 2.6%.

Going forward, a structure will have to be put in place that ensures the federal government will earn income from licensing fees when the privates sector adopts and profits from the technologies that government investment brings forth. That would greatly reduce the cost of this investment program and finance additional investment in the decades that follow.

Conclusion

The next two chapters describe how and how much the United States invests currently. They also show why the current level of investment is sorely inadequate. Subsequent chapters show how the dangerous deficiencies in US investment can be remedied and detail the extraordinary benefits that will result once they are.

Notes

1. Vannevar Bush in *Science, the Endless Frontier*, A Report to the President, Director of the Office of Scientific Research and Development, July 1945.
2. See the book by Martin Jacques (2012), *When China Rules the World: The Rise of the Middle Kingdom and the End of the Western World*. Penguin, UK.
3. Pax Americana is the term given to the period of relative international peace resulting from the preponderance of US military and economic power, c.1945 to the present day.
4. Mariana Mazzucato, *The Entrepreneurial State: Debunking Public vs. Private Sector Myths*, revised edition. Public Affairs (October 27, 2015).

CHAPTER 17

Inadequate Investment

*We will see more technological change in the next 10 years –
than we saw in the last 50 years. And we're falling behind in
that competition. Decades ago we used to invest 2% of our GDP
on research and development. Today, we spend less than 1%.
China and other countries are closing in fast.*

President Biden[1]

Capital Grows

One of the most important things to understand about economics is that capital grows. Capital not only grows, it evolves and becomes more complex. As it does, it transforms the way people live and the environment in which they live.

Capital grows and evolves as a result of investment. The amount invested and the type of investments made determine the speed at which capital grows and the direction in which it evolves.

This chapter describes investment in America: its rate of growth, where the money is invested, and who is making the investments. The long-term future of the United States will be determined by how the country invests during the years immediately ahead.

This chapter also makes clear that the United States is quickly losing its position as the world's most powerful economy because it invests too little.

Investment

While there are several kinds of capital, in this chapter, the term "capital" refers to fixed assets. A fixed asset is any long-term tangible piece of property used in the production of income, and not expected to be consumed or converted into cash any sooner than at least one year's time. Fixed assets, when combined with labor and natural resources, generate income. When that income is saved and invested, it adds to the stock of fixed assets and generates still more income.

The capital stock of the United States increased 65-fold between 1952 and 2019, from $1 trillion to $65 trillion, as shown in Chart 17.1. The one time when capital did not grow during this period, 2009, there was an economic crisis.

CHART 17.1 The Capital Stock of the United States, 1925 to 2019

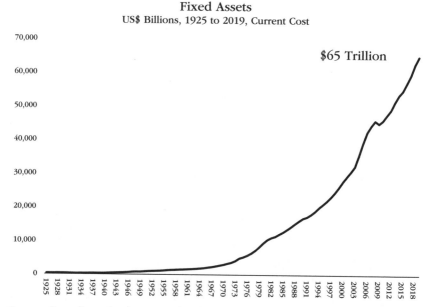

Fixed Assets
US$ Billions, 1925 to 2019, Current Cost

$65 Trillion

Source: Data from the Bureau of Economic Analysis

CHART 17.2 Annual Percentage Change in Fixed Assets, 1926 to 2019

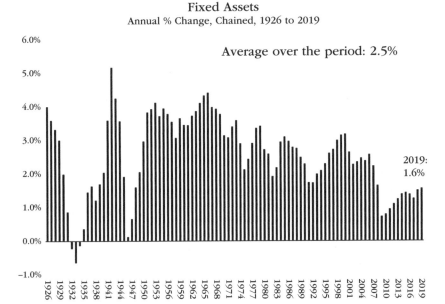

Fixed Assets
Annual % Change, Chained, 1926 to 2019

Source: Data from the Bureau of Economic Analysis

The rate of growth of the US capital stock has been slowing since World War II and has been particularly weak since 2008. The average annual growth rate since 1926 has been 2.5% a year. In 2019, it was 1.6%, and that was the highest growth rate in a decade (see Chart 17.2).

The growth in the capital stock has slowed because investment has been weak.

Chart 17.3 shows the annual percentage change in real gross domestic fixed investment from 1940.

Following the United States entry in World War II, investment in fixed assets surged at an extraordinary pace. In 1941, it leapt by 44%. In 1942, it grew by 44% more. And, in 1943, investment in fixed assets rose a further 21%. By 1944, the capital stock of the United States was 60% larger than it had been in 1940.

After the war ended, investment in fixed assets grew more rapidly during the 1950s and 1960s than during the following decades. The average annual rate of growth was 5.6% during the 1950s and 4.9% during the 1960s. During the first decade of this

CHART 17.3 Annual Percentage Change in Real Gross Domestic Fixed
Investment, 1940 to 2019

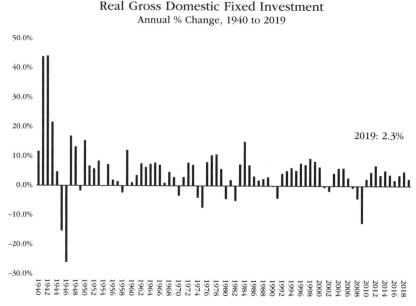

Source: Data from the Bureau of Economic Analysis

century, investment in fixed assets increased by an annual average of only 0.6%, the average being dragged down by a contraction of 4.2% in 2008 and an especially sharp contraction of
12.5% in 2009. Moreover, the rebound following the economic
crisis has also been weak. Between 2010 and 2019, the average
increase in fixed investment has been just 3.8% a year.

The slowdown in the growth rate of the capital stock and
the slowdown in investment have been responsible for the notable deceleration in economic growth in the United States during recent decades. Since 1950, the economy has grown at an
average rate of 3.2% a year, but during the 2010s only by 2.3%,
despite unprecedented monetary policy stimulus in the form of
trillions of dollars of Quantitative Easing (see Chart 17.4).

CHART 17.4 Annual Percentage Change in Real Gross Domestic
Product, 1940 to 2019

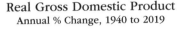

Real Gross Domestic Product
Annual % Change, 1940 to 2019

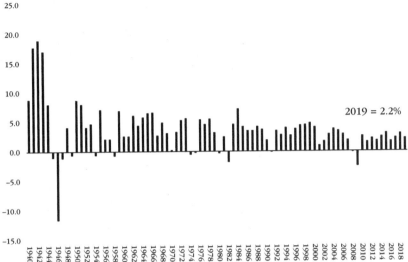

Source: Data from the Bureau of Economic Analysis

Inadequate government investment is the reason overall
investment growth slackened. Government investment as a percentage of GDP plunged from 7.1% in 1961 to just 3.5% in 2019,
as shown in Chart 17.5.

In 1961, government investment accounted for 32% of total
investment in the United States. By 2019, that ratio had fallen
to just 17%. The share of private sector investment rose from
68% to 83% over that period. Chart 17.6 shows the breakdown
of total investment between private investment and government
investment back to 1950.

The weakness in government investment has been particularly pronounced since the crisis of 2008, as illustrated in
Chart 17.7, which shows total investment, private investment,
and government investment from 1950 to 2019.

CHART 17.5 Government Investment as a Percentage of GDP, 1950 to 2019

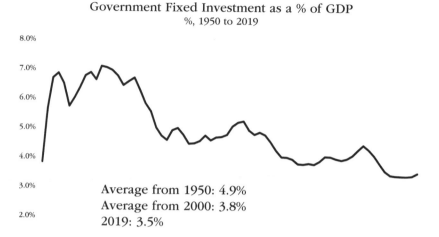

Government Fixed Investment as a % of GDP
%, 1950 to 2019

Average from 1950: 4.9%
Average from 2000: 3.8%
2019: 3.5%

Source: Data from the Bureau of Economic Analysis

In 2019, total investment was $4.5 trillion. Of that, $3.7 trillion was private investment and $753 billion was government investment. Notice that total investment has increased by 38% from the pre-crisis peak in 2007 and is up 64% from the post-crisis low in 2009. Private investment is up 40% from 2007 and is up 78% from 2009. But government investment is up only 27% from 2007 and up only 17% from 2009, a nominal increase of just 1.7% a year and a real, inflation-adjusted increase of only 0.1% a year. The failure of the government to invest much more over the last decade has depressed the growth in the country's capital stock. It has been a grave mistake that will weigh heavily on the economy for years to come.

Private Fixed Investment

This section describes how the private sector invests. The next section then discusses government investment.

CHART 17.6 The Breakdown of Total Investment Between Private Investment and Government Investment, 1950 to 2019

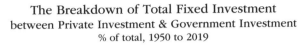

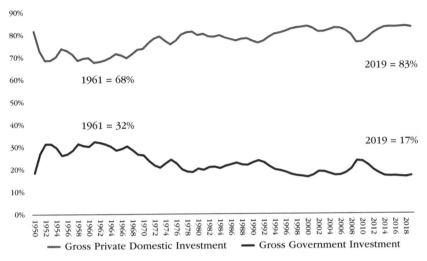

Source: Data from the Bureau of Economic Analysis

During 2019, the private sector invested $3.7 trillion in fixed assets. Of that amount, $2.9 trillion was for non-residential investment and $807 billion was for residential investment.

Non-residential investment was comprised of structures, $650 billion; equipment, $1.2 trillion; and intellectual property products, $1 trillion (see Table 17.1). We will look at each of these in closer detail, beginning with non-residential structures.

PRIVATE FIXED INVESTMENT IN STRUCTURES

Table 17.2 provides a breakdown of the $650 billion invested by the private sector in non-residential structures.

The main subcategories here are commercial and health care structures, $196 billion; manufacturing structures, $77 billion; power and communication structures, $129 billion; mining, exploration, shafts and wells, $121 billion; and other structures, $128 billion.

CHART 17.7 Total Investment, including Private and Government Fixed Investment, 1950 to 2019

Total Fixed Investment
Including Private & Government Fixed Investment
US$ Billions, 1950 to 2019

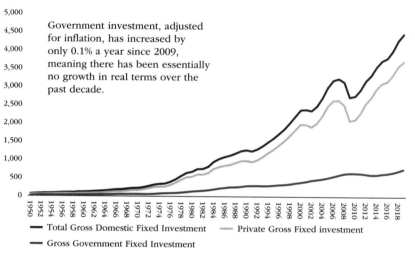

Government investment, adjusted for inflation, has increased by only 0.1% a year since 2009, meaning there has been essentially no growth in real terms over the past decade.

— Total Gross Domestic Fixed Investment   — Private Gross Fixed investment

— Gross Government Fixed Investment

Source: Data from the Bureau of Economic Analysis

TABLE 17.1 Private Fixed Investment, 2019

	2019 US$ Billions
Private Fixed Investment	3,702
Non-residential	2,895
Structures	650
Equipment	1,241
Intellectual property products	1,004
Residential	807
Structures	794
Equipment	13

Source: Data from the Bureau of Economic Analysis

TABLE 17.2 Private Fixed Investment in Structures, 2019

	2019 US$ Billions
Private Fixed Investment in Structures	1,444
Non-residential	650
Commercial and health care	196
Office	85
Health care	41
Multimerchandise shopping	14
Food and beverage establishments	9
Warehouses	33
Other commercial	14
Manufacturing	77
Power and communication	129
Power	107
Communication	22
Mining exploration, shafts, and wells	121
Petroleum and natural gas	114
Mining	7
Other structures	128
Religious	4
Educational and vocational	20
Lodging	40
Amusement and recreation	18
Transportation	17
Farm	7
Other	23
Residential	794

Source: Data from the Bureau of Economic Analysis

Notice that the largest individual item here is investment in petroleum and natural gas structures, $114 billion. The second largest is investment in power structures, $107 billion.

Private fixed investment in residential structures amounted to $794 billion in 2019.

CHART 17.8 Private Residential Investment, 1950 to 2019

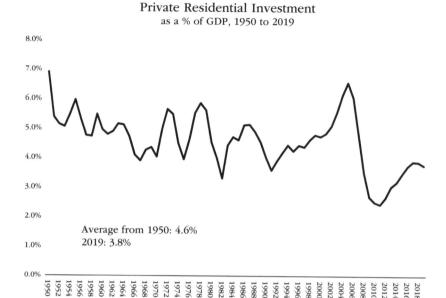

Source: Data from the Bureau of Economic Analysis

Chart 17.8 shows private residential investment as a per-centage of GDP from 1950. During that period, it has averaged 4.6% of GDP. The chart clearly highlights the residential invest-ment boom leading up to the crisis of 2008 and the bust that followed it.

PRIVATE FIXED INVESTMENT EQUIPMENT IN EQUIPMENT

The private sector invested $1.2 trillion in equipment during 2019. That was comprised almost entirely of non-residential equipment. The subcategories under non-residential equipment are information processing equipment, $397 billion; industrial equipment, $261 billion; transportation equipment, $310 billion; and other equipment, $282 billion. Table 17.3 provides a break-down of private sector investment in non-residential equipment in greater detail.

TABLE 17.3 Private Fixed Investment in Equipment, 2019

	2019 US$ Billions
Private Fixed Investment in Equipment	1,254
Non-residential equipment	1,241
Information processing equipment	397
Computers and peripheral equipment	122
Communication equipment	119
Medical equipment and instruments	105
Nonmedical instruments	40
Photocopy and related equipment	8
Office and accounting equipment	3
Industrial equipment	261
Fabricated metal products	23
Engines and turbines	16
Metalworking machinery	38
Special industry machinery, n.e.c.	47
General industrial, including materials handling, equipment	93
Electrical transmission, distribution, and industrial apparatus	44
Transportation equipment	310
Trucks, buses, and truck trailers	223
Autos	23
Aircraft	45
Ships and boats	8
Railroad equipment	12
Other equipment	282
Furniture and fixtures	52
Agricultural machinery	46
Construction machinery	50
Mining and oilfield machinery	24
Service industry machinery	38
Electrical equipment, n.e.c.	8
Other	65
Residential equipment	13

Source: Data from the Bureau of Economic Analysis

It is worth looking at those categories more closely. Under information processing equipment, we find computers and peripheral equipment, communication equipment, medical equipment, nonmedical instruments, photocopiers, and related equipment and office equipment.

Listed under industrial equipment are fabricated metal products, engines and turbines, metalworking machinery, special industry machinery, general industrial machinery, and electrical transmission, distribution, and industrial apparatus.

Under transportation equipment, are trucks, buses and truck trailers, autos, aircraft, ships, and railroads.

Other equipment includes furniture, agricultural machinery, construction machinery, mining and oilfield machinery, service industry machinery, electrical equipment, and others.

The largest individual items of investment in equipment were trucks, buses, and truck trailers, with $223 billion of investment in 2019. Next came computers and peripheral equipment, at $122 billion, and then communication equipment, at $119 billion.

PRIVATE FIXED INVESTMENT IN INTELLECTUAL PROPERTY PRODUCTS

The private sector invested $1 trillion in intellectual property products in 2019.

Investment in intellectual property as a percentage of GDP has increased sharply since 1950. It is now at a record high of 4.7% of GDP, as shown in Chart 17.9.

Table 17.4 presents a detailed breakdown of investment in intellectual property products. The major subcategories are software, at $411 billion; research and development, at $502 billion; and entertainment, literary, and artistic originals, at $91 billion.

Research and development (R&D) includes pharmaceutical and medicine manufacturing, chemical manufacturing, semiconductor, other computer, motor vehicles, aerospace, and others.

Classified under entertainment are movies, television, books, music, and others.

CHART 17.9 Private Investment in Intellectual Property Products, 1950 to 2019

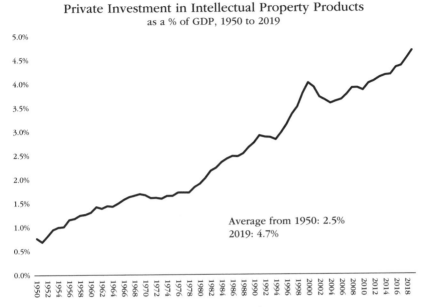

Private Investment in Intellectual Property Products
as a % of GDP, 1950 to 2019

Average from 1950: 2.5%
2019: 4.7%

Source: Data from the Bureau of Economic Analysis

Notice that the largest single item under intellectual property products is $90 billion invested in pharmaceutical and medicine R&D. Here it is worth pausing to note that the Fed is currently creating $120 billion each month through the latest round of Quantitative Easing. That means that it would require only 23 days of funding from QE to finance the private sector's entire annual budget for R&D in an industry that our lives literally depend upon.

Government Fixed Investment

Now, let's turn to government investment in fixed assets.

Total government investment in fixed assets amounted to $753 billion in 2019. That was divided between federal government investment of $322 billion and state and local government

TABLE 17.4 Private Fixed Investment in Intellectual Property Products, 2019

	2019 US$ Billions
Private Fixed Investment in Intellectual Property Products	1,004
Software	411
Research and development	502
Business	475
Manufacturing R&D	294
Pharmaceutical and medicine manufacturing	90
Chemical manufacturing, excluding pharmaceutical and medicine	10
Semiconductor and other electronic component manufacturing	37
Other computer and electronic product manufacturing	53
Motor vehicles, bodies and trailers, and parts manufacturing	27
Aerospace products and parts manufacturing	12
Other manufacturing	65
Non-manufacturing R&D	182
Scientific research and development services	10
All other non-manufacturing	172
Nonprofit institutions serving households	27
Entertainment, literary, and artistic originals	91
Theatrical movies	19
Long-lived television programs	51
Books	9
Music	9
Other	4

Source: Data from the Bureau of Economic Analysis

investment of $431 billion. The federal government investment was split between national defense, $176 billion, and nondefense, $146 billion, as shown in Table 17.5.

TABLE 17.5 Gross Government Fixed Investment, 2019

	2019 US$ Billions
Gross government fixed investment	753
Federal	322
National defense	176
Nondefense	146
State and local	431

Source: Data from the Bureau of Economic Analysis

Table 17.6 lays out a more detailed breakdown of how the government invests. Out of the $753 billion the government invested in fixed assets in 2019, $361 billion was invested in structures, $164 billion in equipment, and $228 billion in intellectual property products.

The federal government invested $93 billion in equipment for national defense. This included investments in aircraft, missiles, ships, vehicles, electronics, and others. It invested a further $75 billion in intellectual property products for national defense purposes and $111 billion more in intellectual property products unrelated to national defense.

State and local government invested $50 billion in equipment and $42 billion in intellectual property products.

Government investment in fixed assets has been declining as a percentage of GDP since the early 1960s. Chart 17.10 shows total government investment, as well as how that was divided between the federal government, and state and local government, as a percentage of GDP going back to 1929.

The level of total government investment was very high during World War II, nearly 20% of GDP. Nearly all of that wartime investment was carried out by the federal government, rather than by state and local government.

Since 1950, government investment in fixed assets has averaged 4.9% of GDP a year. During 2019, however, it was only 3.5%. Federal government investment in fixed assets has

TABLE 17.6 Gross Government Fixed Investment Breakdown, 2019

	2019 US$ Billions
Gross Government Fixed Investment	753
Structures	361
Equipment	164
Federal	114
National defense	93
Aircraft	23
Missiles	5
Ships	17
Vehicles	4
Electronics	8
Other equipment	36
Nondefense	20
State and local	50
Intellectual property products	228
Federal	186
National defense	75
Software	13
Research and development	63
Nondefense	111
Software	28
Research and development	83
State and local	42
Software	20
Research and development	22

Source: Data from the Bureau of Economic Analysis

averaged 2.6% of GDP a year since 1950. In 2019, that was down to only 1.5%. State and local government investment in fixed assets averaged 2.3% of GDP since 1950, but only 2.0% in 2019.

The surge in government investment during World War II ended the Great Depression and generated the prosperity that the United States enjoyed during the 1950s and the 1960s. The

CHART 17.10 Government Investment as a Percentage of GDP: Total, Federal, and State and Local, 1929 to 2019

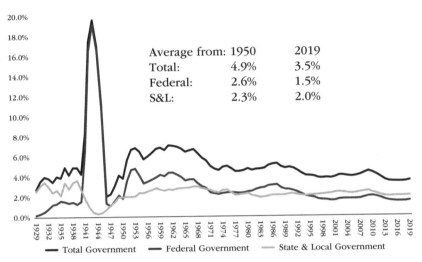

Government Investment as a % of GDP
Total, Federal and State & Local
%, 1929 to 2019

Average from:	1950	2019
Total:	4.9%	3.5%
Federal:	2.6%	1.5%
S&L:	2.3%	2.0%

— Total Government — Federal Government ⸺ State & Local Government

Source: Data from the Bureau of Economic Analysis

current weakness in government investment will retard future US economic growth long into the future.

The rate of growth of the federal government's capital stock has slowed sharply in recent decades and, during the last few years, has actually begun to contract.

Chart 17.11 shows the annual percentage change in the federal government's fixed assets, inflation adjusted, back to 1926. Of course, there was a big surge during World War II. The stock of federal government fixed assets increased by almost 100% during 1942 alone, and there were also very large increases in 1941, 1943, and 1944. It was this debt-funded government investment during World War II that ended the Great Depression.

Over this entire period, the average growth rate was 4.0% a year but, of course, that average is distorted by World War II.

CHART 17.11 Federal Government Fixed Assets, Annual Percentage Change, 1926 to 2019

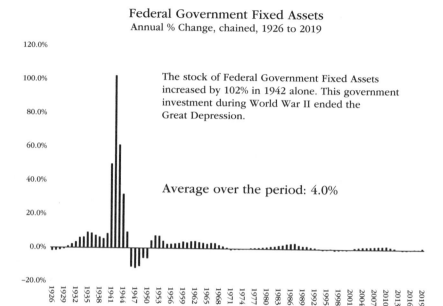

Federal Government Fixed Assets
Annual % Change, chained, 1926 to 2019

The stock of Federal Government Fixed Assets increased by 102% in 1942 alone. This government investment during World War II ended the Great Depression.

Average over the period: 4.0%

Source: Data from the Bureau of Economic Analysis

Stripping out the war years and, instead, beginning in 1951, the federal government's fixed assets have increased on average by 1.6% a year. The trend in growth has been very notably downward, as can be seen in Chart 17.12.

There was relatively strong growth in federal government fixed assets under President Eisenhower, President Kennedy, and President Johnson, and again under President Reagan. Otherwise, the increase has been anemic, at best.

There was no growth in 2013 and a contraction in 2014, 2015, and 2016. The average during the last three years was 0.4% annual growth.

This depletion of the federal government's capital stock is the result of inadequate government investment. It goes a long way in explaining the slowdown in the growth in US productivity, as well as the country's relative economic decline,

CHART 17.12 Federal Government Fixed Assets, Annual Percentage Change, 1951 to 2019

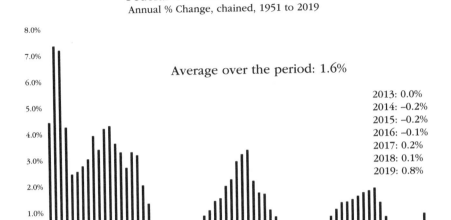

Federal Government Fixed Assets
Annual % Change, chained, 1951 to 2019

Average over the period: 1.6%

2013: 0.0%
2014: –0.2%
2015: –0.2%
2016: –0.1%
2017: 0.2%
2018: 0.1%
2019: 0.8%

Source: Data from the Bureau of Economic Analysis

particularly relative to China, which has grown its capital stock at breathtaking speed since the turn of the century.

The Competition

The United States can no longer afford to be complacent. In 2019, China invested twice as much as the United States relative to the size of its economy.

Investment in China accounted for 42% of Chinese GDP, whereas US investment made up only 20% of US GDP. Its much higher rate of investment explains why China's economy is growing much more rapidly than the US economy. Investment creates capital and capital generates income.

Chart 17.13 shows that China has been investing more relative to the size of its economy since 1970.

CHART 17.13 Annual Fixed Investment US vs. China, 1952 to 2019

Annual Fixed Investment as a % of GDP
The US vs. China
1952 to 2019

As a percent of GDP, China invest twice as much as the US.

━━ China: Gross Fixed Capital Formation as a % of GDP   ━━ US Gross Domestic Investment as a % of GDP

Source: Data for the US, the Bureau of Economic Analysis. Data for China, CEIC

But even in absolute dollar amounts, China is now investing much more than the United States. China has invested more in fixed assets than the United States has every year since 2011. In 2019, it invested 36% more – $1.6 trillion more – than the United States did (see Chart 17.14).

If these trends continue, China will soon overtake the United States to become the preeminent global superpower.

What's to Be Done?

The United States is rapidly losing its leading position in the global economy because it invests too little. Insufficient government investment is to blame. Government investment in fixed assets declined from 7.1% of GDP in 1961 to only 3.5% of GDP in 2019. If it had been 7.1% of GDP during 2019, that would

CHART 17.14 Annual Fixed Investment: US vs. China, 1957 to 2019

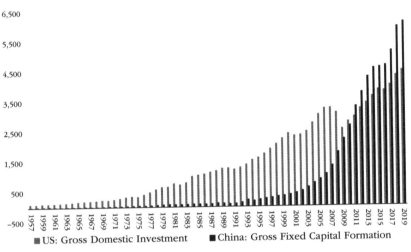

Annual Fixed Investment
The US vs China
US$ Billions, 1957 to 2019

■ US: Gross Domestic Investment   ■ China: Gross Fixed Capital Formation

Source: Data for the US, the Bureau of Economic Analysis. Data for
China, CEIC

have resulted in twice as much government investment in fixed
assets, $1.5 trillion instead of only $747 billion.

The US government must immediately begin to invest far
more than it has in recent years or else the United States will
soon become a vulnerable second-rate power.

The next chapter drills down to examine how and how
much the United States invests in Research and Development. It
reveals that the country's inadequate investment in R&D has put
US national security at risk.

Note

1. President Biden, Address to a Joint Session of Congress, The White
   House, April 29, 2021.

CHAPTER 18

R&D: The Future Depends on It

China may already have surpassed the U.S. in total (R&D) expenditures at some point in 2019.

Julia Phillips, chair of the National Science
Board's science policy committee[1]

Investment in Research and Development (R&D) is the decisive factor in determining which country leads the world economically, technologically, and militarily. From World War I to 2019, the United States invested more in R&D than any other country. In 2019, however, China overtook the US to become the world leader in R&D investment.

Unless the United States quickly retakes its lead by investing much more in R&D, China will displace the US as the undisputed global superpower within one to two decades. The United States must not allow that to happen. Fortunately, the country has the financial resources to ensure that it does not.

This chapter provides an overview of R&D in the United States at present. It describes the kind of R&D currently being conducted, who is carrying it out, and who is paying for it. It also provides international comparisons of overall R&D spending in the United States vs. the rest of the world. The chapter reveals that, while a great deal of extraordinary work in research and development is being done in the United States, current levels of investment are not enough, because China is investing more.

The final three chapters of this book will describe how the United States can undertake R&D investment on a vastly larger scale, thereby maintaining its global preeminence indefinitely.

Current Investment in R&D

The United States invested $580 billion in research and development during 2018. Chart 18.1 shows the level of R&D investment every year from 1953 to 2018. The data is presented in constant 2012 dollars in order to remove the influence of inflation.

The growth rate in R&D investment has been slowing since the 1950s. The average annual rate of growth between 1954 and 2018 was 4.3%. It has been below average during the last three

CHART 18.1 United States: Total R&D Expenditure, 1953 to 2018

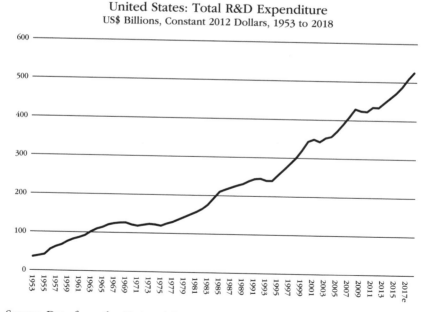

United States: Total R&D Expenditure
US$ Billions, Constant 2012 Dollars, 1953 to 2018

Source: Data from the National Science Foundation

CHART 18.2 Total R&D Expenditure, Annual Percentage Change, 1954 to 2018

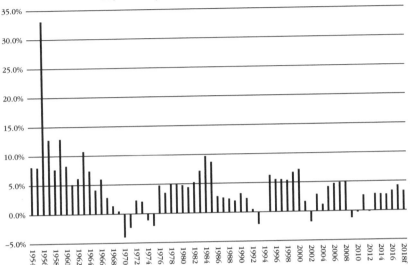

Total R&D Expenditure, Annual % Change
US$ Billions, Constant 2012 Dollars, 1954 to 2018

Source: Data from the National Science Foundation

decades. Average annual growth in R&D investment was 3.3% during the 1990s, 2.9% during the 2000s, and 2.4% between 2010 and 2018. Chart 18.2 shows the clear downward trend since the 1950s.

Out of the $580 billion total R&D investment in 2018, the business sector carried out $422 billion of the R&D, or 73% of the total. The Federal Government carried out $58 billion (10%), Higher Education $75 billion (13%), and other Non-Profit Organizations $24 billion (4%). See Table 18.1.

There is some considerable difference between who carries out the R&D and who funds it. In particular, the Federal Government funds a significantly higher share of the R&D than it carries out. It funds 22% of all R&D, but carries out (or performs) only 10%. On the other hand, Higher Education funds significantly less R&D than it performs. Higher Education funds only 4% of all R&D while it performs 13%. These discrepancies result

TABLE 18.1 Who Carries Out the R&D?

US R&D Expenditure by Performing Sector: 2018		
(Current Dollars)	US$ Billions	% of Total
Total	580	100%
Business	422	73%
Federal Government	58	10%
Non-Federal Government	1	0%
Higher Education	75	13%
Non-Profit Organizations	24	4%

Source: Data from the National Science Foundation

principally from the federal government funding the majority of the research carried out by US universities. The government also funds part of the research carried out by the business sector, although relatively little in comparison with what it provides to universities or in comparison with the business sector's total investment in R&D. Table 18.2 provides the breakdown of the sources of R&D funding in the US.

The business sector invested more than three times as much in R&D as the federal government did in 2018. Before 1980, however, the federal government led the country in investing in R&D. In fact, during the decade that followed the Sputnik shock in 1957, the federal government invested twice as much in R&D as the business sector did.

Business investment in R&D only overtook that of the federal government in 1980, but its lead over the government did not begin to become significant until the late 1980s. Afterwards, government investment in R&D began to stagnate, as shown in Chart 18.3.

Through the 1990s, government investment declined in real (inflation-adjusted) terms practically every year. Modest growth resumed during the 2000s, but did not last. Growth gave way to contraction again during most of the 2010s. In 2018, federal government investment in R&D was only 5% larger in real terms

TABLE 18.2 Who Funds the R&D?

US R&D Expenditure by Performing Sector: 2018		
(Current Dollars)	US$ Billions	% of Total
Total	580	100%
Business	404	70%
Federal Government	127	22%
Non-federal Government	5	0%
Higher Education	21	4%
Non-profit Organizations	23	4%

Source: Data from the National Science Foundation

CHART 18.3 R&D Expenditure by Source of Funds, 1953 to 2018

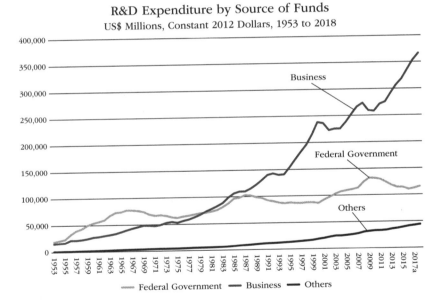

R&D Expenditure by Source of Funds
US$ Millions, Constant 2012 Dollars, 1953 to 2018

Source: Data from the National Science Foundation

than it had been in 1987. The failure of the US government to expand its investment in R&D during the past three decades has been an enormous error. It deterred US productivity growth and, consequently, economic growth. Moreover, it enabled China,

which has a very different attitude toward government investment in R&D, not only to catch up with the United States in
R&D spending, but to surpass it.

Allocation

The following paragraphs show how the business sector, the universities and the federal government allocate their R&D funding.

The Business Sector

In 2017, the business sector invested $400 billion in R&D. Man-
ufacturing Industries accounted for $257 billion or 64% of that
amount. Non-Manufacturing Industries made up the remaining
$143 billion, 36%.

Table 18.3 presents the breakdown of R&D spending by the
business sector across the Manufacturing Industries.

The Computer and Electronic Products industry invested
the most in R&D, $79 billion. That was followed by $66 billion
invested in Pharmaceuticals and Medicines, $26 billion in Aero-
space Products and Parts and $24 billion in Automobiles, Trail-
ers, and Parts.

Within the Non-Manufacturing Industries, $80 billion was
invested in the Information Industry (including $34 billion into
Software Publishers) and $37 billion in Professional, Scientific,
and Technical Services. Table 18.4 presents the breakdown
of the $143 billion invested by the business sector in Non-
Manufacturing Industries.

Universities

Universities in the United States spent $79 billion on research
and development during 2018. As mentioned above, most of
that money was provided by the federal government. Of the
$79 billion total, $62 billion was allocated to Science, $12 billion
to Engineering and $5 billion to Non-Science and Engineering.
Table 18.5 provides a more detailed breakdown of university

TABLE 18.3 Business Sector Investment in R&D: Manufacturing Industries, 2017

Manufacturing Industries	
Funds Spent for Business R&D Performed in the US, Selected Industries: 2017	
	All R&D $millions
All industries	400,100
Manufacturing industries	257,227
Chemicals	74,977
Pharmaceuticals and medicines	66,202
Other	8,775
Machinery	13,197
Computer and electronic products	78,575
Electrical equipment, appliances, and components	4,291
Transportation equipment	53,292
Automobiles, trailers, and parts	23,881
Aerospace products and parts	26,383
Other	3,028
Manufacturing n.e.c.	32,895

Note: n.e.c. – not elsewhere classified
Source: Based on data from the National Science Board, Science and Engineering Indicators: 2020

expenditure by field. Most notably, it shows that universities invested $46 billion in Life Sciences, 58% of all their R&D expenditure.

The Federal Government

The federal government invests in R&D primarily through various federal departments and agencies. During FY2018, the government allocated $136 billion in funding for R&D. Table 18.6 lists the departments and agencies ranked by the amount of their R&D funding.

The Department of Defense received $52 billion or 39% of the total that year. The Department of Health and Human

TABLE 18.4 Business Sector Investment in R&D: Non-manufacturing Industries, 2017

Non-Manufacturing Industries	
Funds Spent for Business R&D Performed in the US, Selected Industries: 2017	
	$ Millions
Non-Manufacturing industries	142,874
Information	80,252
Software publishers	34,264
Other	45,988
Finance and insurance	7,616
Professional, scientific, and technical services	36,922
Computer systems design and related services	13,327
Scientific R&D services	17,321
Other	6,274
Non-manufacturing n.e.c.	18,084

Note: n.e.c. – not elsewhere classified
Source: Based on data from the National Science Board, Science and Engineering Indicators: 2020

TABLE 18.5 Higher Education R&D Expenditures, by Field: FY 2018

(Dollars in thousands)	
R&D Field	All institutions
All R&D expenditures	79,436,487
Science	62,407,007
Computer and information sciences	2,407,676
Geosciences, atmospheric sciences, & ocean sciences	3,171,781
Life sciences	45,899,964
Mathematics and statistics	757,719
Physical sciences	5,256,018
Psychology	1,267,419
Social sciences	2,755,708
Sciences, n.e.c.	890,722
Engineering	12,386,784
Non-Science and engineering	4,642,696

Source: Data from the National Science Foundation

TABLE 18.6 Federal Research and Development Funding, By Agency, FY 2018

Federal Agencies ranked by their R&D funding for 2018		
Federal Research and Development Funding By Agency: FY2018	$ Billions	% of Total
All agencies	136	100.0%
Department of Defense	52	38.6%
Department of Health and Human Services	37	27.2%
Department of Energy	17	12.9%
National Aeronautics and Space Administration	12	8.7%
National Science Foundation	6	4.7%
Department of Agriculture	3	1.9%
Department of Commerce	2	1.5%
Department of Veterans Affairs	1	0.9%
Department of Transportation	1	0.8%
Department of the Interior	0.9	0.7%
Department of Homeland Security	0.7	0.5%
Environmental Protection Agency	0.5	0.4%
Smithsonian Institution	0.4	0.3%
Department of Education	0.3	0.2%
All other agencies	1	0.9%

Source: Data from the Congressional Research Service

Services came next with an allocation of $37 billion, which was 27% of the total. They were followed by the Department of Energy, which received $17 billion, 13% of the total; NASA with $12 billion, 9%; and the National Science Foundation, with $6 billion, 5%. These five received 92% of total agency R&D funding. They will be described in greater detail in Chapter 21.

Federal government investment in R&D through all government agencies peaked in 2010. The amount invested in 2018 was 10% below the peak. Chart 18.4 shows the federal government's

CHART 18.4 Federal Government Obligations for R&D and R&D Plant
by Selected Agencies: FYs 2008–2018

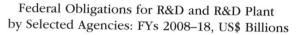

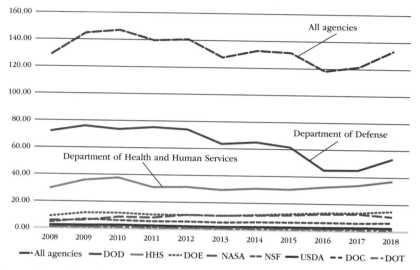

Source: Data from the National Science Foundation

R&D obligations for all agencies in total and for various individual agencies from FY2008 to FY2018. The United States would
be richer and more secure today if the government had substantially increased its R&D funding across that decade instead of
allowing it to stagnate.

Types of R&D

Research and development is divided into three classifications:
basic research, applied research, and experimental development.
During 2017, 17% of all R&D expenditure in the United States
was for basic research, 20% was for applied research, and 63%
for experimental development, as shown in Table 18.7.

   Basic research is experimental or theoretical work undertaken primarily to acquire new knowledge of the underlying

TABLE 18.7 Types of R&D

Types of R&D		
US R&D Expenditures by Type of Work: 2017		
	US$ Billions	% of Total
Total R&D	548	100%
Basic research	91	17%
Applied research	109	20%
Experimental development	348	63%

Source: Data from the National Science Foundation

foundations of phenomena and observable facts, without any particular application or use in view.

Applied research is original investigation undertaken in order to acquire new knowledge; directed primarily, however, toward a specific, practical aim or objective.

Experimental development is systematic work, drawing on knowledge gained from research and practical experience and producing additional knowledge, which is directed to producing new products or processes and to improving existing products or processes.[2]

Basic research is particularly important because applied research and experimental development are generally built on knowledge first derived from basic research. Vannevar Bush, who oversaw the Manhattan Project, described the importance of basic research as follows:

> *Basic research leads to new knowledge. It provides scientific capital. It creates the fund from which the practical applications of knowledge must be drawn. New products and new processes do not appear full-grown. They are founded on new principles and new conceptions, which in turn are painstakingly developed by research in the purest realms of science.[3]*

The business sector spends less on basic research than the government does because it can take a very long time before basic research can be turned into products that can be sold. Businesses, therefore, focus on experimental development, which is more likely to generate profits sooner. However, their experimental development programs often utilize knowledge that was generated through basic research paid for by the government.

Intel, Apple, Google, and SpaceX are prime examples of companies that prospered by incorporating the products, techniques, and capabilities generated by government funded basic research.

Table 18.8 shows R&D expenditure in the US by type of work and by source of funds. The top half of the table shows the dollar amounts and the bottom half shows the breakdown in percentage terms.

In 2018, the federal government funded 22% of all the R&D that was done in the United States. But it funded 42% of the basic research, 34% of the applied research, and just 13% of the experimental development, whereas, the business sector only funded 29% of the basic research, but 85% of the experimental development. As shown in the top half of Table 18.8, the federal government invested $40 billion in basic research, while the business sector invested only $28 billion in basic research.

In total, the United States invested $96 billion in basic research in 2018 (measured in current dollars). Here, it is worth pointing out that the Federal Reserve is now creating $120 billion per month through its current round of Quantitative Easing. That statistic helps put into perspective how little the United States is actually investing in basic research and also how easy it would be for the country to invest much more by using additional Quantitative Easing to finance the investment. With just 24 days of money creation through QE at its current pace, the United States could double its annual investment in basic research.

Chart 18.5 shows total expenditure on basic research in constant 2012 dollars from 1953 to 2018.

The growth rate for investment in basic research has been weak for decades, but during the past decade it has been

TABLE 18.8 R&D Expenditure: Types of Work and Source of Funds: 2018

Type of R&D	Total	Business	Source of Funding, US$ Millions, Current Dollars			
			Federal Government	Non-federal Government	Higher Education	Others
Total R&D	579,985	404,231	127,246	4,726	21,120	22,662
Basic research	96,490	27,973	40,365	2,497	13,140	12,516
Applied research	114,958	62,369	39,465	1,632	5,671	5,821
Experimental development	368,537	313,890	47,416	597	2,310	4,325

Type of R&D	Total	Business	Source of Funding, % of Total			
			Federal Government	Non-federal Government	Higher Education	Others
Total R&D	100%	70%	22%	1%	4%	4%
Basic research	17%	29%	42%	3%	14%	13%
Applied research	20%	54%	34%	1%	5%	5%
Experimental development	64%	85%	13%	0%	1%	1%

Source: Data from the National Science Foundation

CHART 18.5 US: Total Expenditure on Basic Research, 1953 to 2018

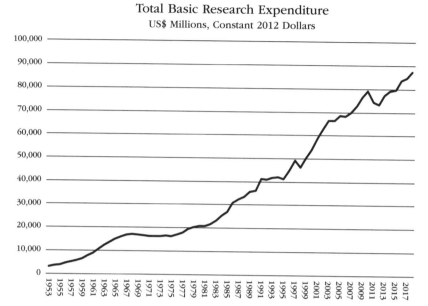

Total Basic Research Expenditure
US$ Millions, Constant 2012 Dollars

Source: Data from the National Science Foundation

particularly depressed. During the 10 years following the Sputnik shock in 1957, total investment in basic research grew at an average annual rate of 12.7%. During the 1990s, it increased only 3.6% a year on average, followed by 4.4% a year during the 2000s, and by only 1.5% during the 2010s. This weakening trend is clear in Chart 18.6, which presents the annual percentage change in expenditure in basic research going back to 1954.

Once again, insufficient government investment is primarily to blame for the tepid growth in the United States' total investment in basic research.

Chart 18.7 shows the breakdown of expenditure on basic research between the federal government, business, and higher education from 1953 to 2018, measured in constant 2012 dollars. Between 2013 and 2018, the federal government invested less in basic research each year than it did in 2002.

CHART 18.6 Annual % Change in Total Expenditure on Basic
Research, 1954 to 2018

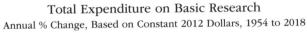

Total Expenditure on Basic Research
Annual % Change, Based on Constant 2012 Dollars, 1954 to 2018

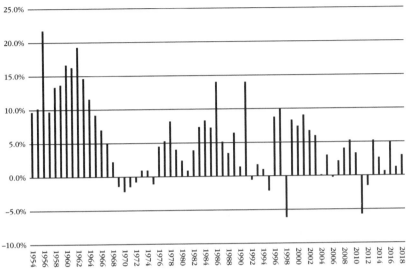

Source: Data from the National Science Foundation

During the 10 years following the launch of Sputnik, federal government investment in basic research expanded by an average of nearly 16% a year. Since 1970, the average annual growth rate has been just 2.4%. During the 2010s, it weakened still further to just 0.8%. Federal government investment in basic research actually contracted in real terms during 7 out of the last 13 years (see Chart 18.8).

This weak and declining government investment in basic research has been a terrible mistake. The United States economy today would have been a great deal stronger and the country's longer-term prospects very much brighter if the federal government had continued to aggressively expand its investment in basic research even after the United States had won the Space Race. Regrettably, it did not. As a consequence, the United States is once again confronting a new Sputnik moment now that

CHART 18.7 Expenditure on Basic Research: Federal Government, Business, and Higher Education, 1953 to 2018

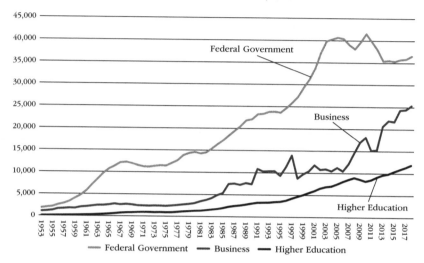

Expenditure on Basic Research:
Federal Government, Business, Higher Education
US$ Millions, Constant 2012 Dollars, 1953 to 2018

Source: Data from the National Science Foundation

China has overtaken the United States in total R&D investment and, concurrently, won the race to develop 5G.

International Comparisons

On January 15, 2020, the National Science Foundation published its biannual *Science and Engineering Indicators* for 2020. The report provides data on R&D trends in the United States and comparisons with other countries up to 2017. The report shows that the United States still invested more in R&D than any other country in 2017. However, the trends in the rate of annual R&D investment growth strongly suggest that China surpassed the United States in 2019.

Table 18.9 lists the eight countries that invested the most in R&D during 2017. The United States was in first place that year,

CHART 18.8 Federal Government Expenditure on Basic Research, Annual Percentage Change, 1954 to 2018

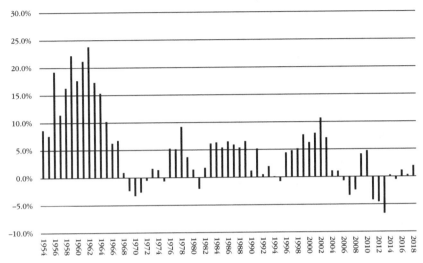

Federal Government Expenditure on Basic Research
Annual Percent Change
Based on Constant 2012 Dollars, 1954 to 2018

Source: Data from the National Science Foundation

TABLE 18.9 Gross Domestic Expenditure on R&D: 2017

Gross Domestic Expenditure On R&D: 2017	
Selected Countries	
US$ Billions (Current Dollars, based on purchasing power parity)	
United States	549
China	496
Japan	171
Germany	132
South Korea	91
France	65
India	50
United Kingdom	49

Source: Data from the National Science Foundation

CHART 18.9 Gross Domestic Expenditure on R&D by the United States, the EU, and Selected Other Countries, 1990–2017

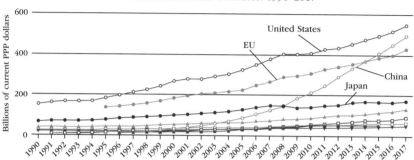

Gross domestic expenditures on R&D, by the United States, the EU, and selected other countries: 1990–2017

Source: National Science Board, Science and Engineering Indicators: 2020

followed closely by China, and then by Japan, Germany, and South Korea (see Chart 18.9).

The United States invested eight times more in R&D than China in 2000. By 2017, it only invested 10% more, $549 billion compared with $496 billion invested by China. Chart 18.10 illustrates the extraordinary surge in Chinese R&D investment relative to that of the United States.

Renewable energy provides one example of an important technology where China is investing much more in R&D than the United States. Between 2010 and the first half of 2019, China invested more than twice as much as the United States in renewable energy. China invested $758 billion, whereas the United States invested only $356 billion.[4]

At the time of the publication of the National Science Board's *Science and Engineering Indicators* for 2020, Julia Phillips, chair of the National Science Board's science policy committee, told *The Washington Post* that "China may already have surpassed the U.S. in total (R&D) expenditures at some point in 2019."[5]

Given recent trends in R&D spending by each country, it is likely that China did overtake the United States. Measured in dollars, on a purchasing power parity basis, China has increased its

CHART 18.10 Gross Domestic Expenditure on R&D: The US vs. China, 2000 to 2017

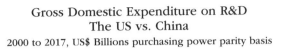

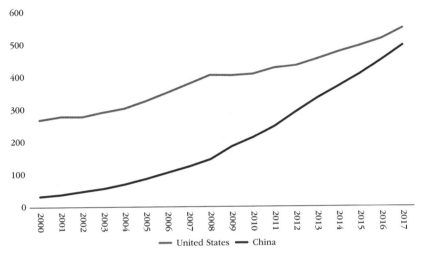

Source: National Science Board, Science and Engineering Indicators: 2020

investment in R&D by substantially more than the Uniteds States every year from 2009, as shown in Chart 18.11.

Moreover, Chinese investment in R&D has grown at an average of 17.4% a year since 2000, compared with only 4.3% average annual growth for the United States (see Chart 18.12).

During 2017, the most recent year comparable data is available, the growth rate of Chinese investment had slowed to 9.9%, whereas that of the United States was above average, at 6.3%. Nevertheless, the rate of growth in Chinese investment in R&D remained 57% larger. Assuming each country retained its 2017 rate of R&D investment growth every year this decade, China would invest nearly 40% more than the United States in R&D by 2030, as shown in Chart 18.13. Should the United States allow that scenario to play out, it will become a vulnerable, second rate power long before mid-century.

Next, Table 18.10 shows gross expenditure on R&D by type of work in the United States vs. China.

CHART 18.11 R&D Investment, Annual Dollar Change: The US vs. China, 2001 to 2017

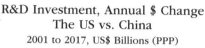

**R&D Investment, Annual $ Change
The US vs. China**
2001 to 2017, US$ Billions (PPP)

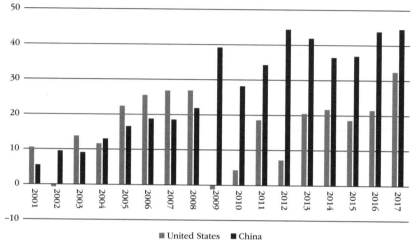

■ United States ■ China

Source: National Science Board, Science and Engineering Indicators: 2020

In the United States, 17% of all R&D expenditure is for basic research. In China, only 6% is spent on basic research. In China, 84% is spent on experimental development; whereas, the US only spends 64% on experimental development.

This suggests China is utilizing the knowledge derived from other countries' basic research to conduct its experimental development, which it then turns into products that it sells to the countries that funded the basic research in the first place. In 2017, China actually spent more on experimental development, $416 billion, than the United States, $348 billion.

The Second Great Divergence

5G, fifth generation wireless technology, is 100 times faster than 4G. China launched 5G in 50 Chinese cities in November 2019.

CHART 18.12 R&D Investment, Annual Percentage Change: The US vs. China, 2001 to 2017

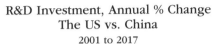

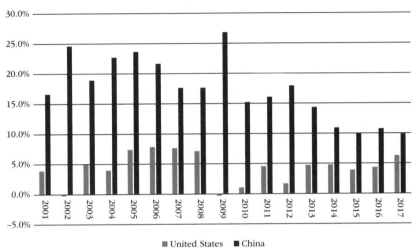

Source: National Science Board, Science and Engineering Indicators: 2020

By the end of 2019, there were more than 130,000 5G base stations in China. There will soon be millions.[6]

China has an enormous lead over the United States in 5G. Not only has China won the 5G race, the United States is not even in the race. Huawei is the world leader. Ericsson of Sweden is in second place. No American companies are even in the running.

5G supremacy will give China a great advantage in developing autonomous vehicles, drones, and augmented and virtual reality, as well as in developing the Internet of Things (IoT). Moreover, the nature of the 5G network makes it a national security risk for other countries because the 5G equipment can be used for espionage. If a country adopts China's 5G equipment, then the Chinese government would be able to access all the data transmitted across that equipment.

CHART 18.13 Gross Domestic Expenditure on R&D: The US vs. China, 2000 to 2030 estimate

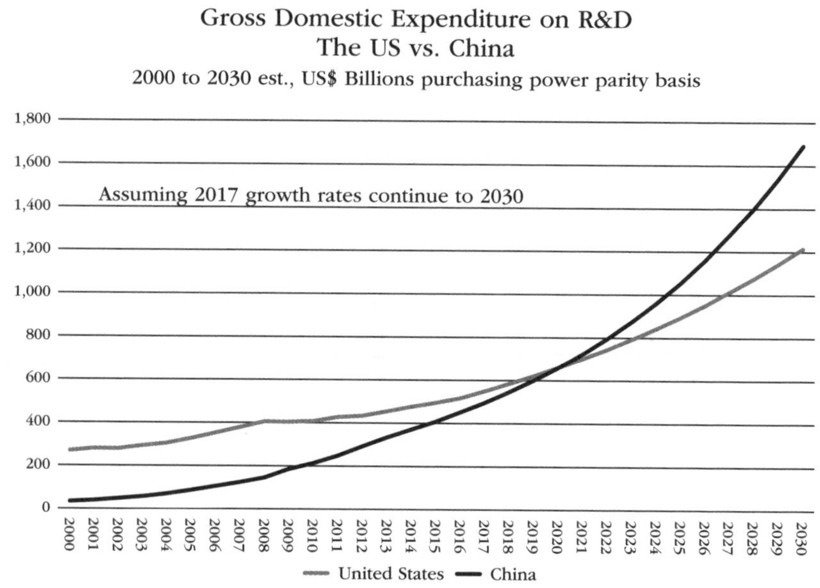

Gross Domestic Expenditure on R&D
The US vs. China
2000 to 2030 est., US$ Billions purchasing power parity basis

Source: National Science Board, Science and Engineering Indicators: 2020. Author's projections

TABLE 18.10 Gross Expenditure on R&D by Type of Work: The US vs. China, 2017

Gross expenditures on R&D, by type of work: The US vs. China 2017

(PPP billions of dollars and percent share)

	Total R&D PPP US$ Billions	Basic	Applied	Experimental Dev.
United States	549	92	109	348
China	496	28	52	416
Share of total (%)				
United States	100%	17%	20%	63%
China	100%	6%	11%	84%

Source: Based on data from the National Science Foundation

If China wins the AI Race, as it has won the 5G Race, then China will rule the world. The first country to achieve artificial general intelligence, the point where machines can perform any task that a human can, is likely to have the rest of the world at its mercy, because, after that, AI will quickly accelerate exponentially beyond human intelligence.

The Carnegie Endowment for International Peace published a report in October 2019 stating:

> . . . *some international relations analysts and historians point out that AI technology could bring about a "Second Great Divergence" of productivity – allowing countries and firms that are the earliest and most successful adopters to leap ahead of other peers – following the First Great Divergence brought about by the Industrial Revolution.*[7]

The Industrial Revolution enabled Western Europe to conquer most of the rest of the world. The AI Race is a winner take all contest. The winner will have the twenty-first century equivalent of a nuclear weapons monopoly.

China has a plan to win that race. They have given that plan a name. It is called Made in China 2025. It was announced by China's State Council in May 2015.

Made in China 2025 is stage one of an ambitious three-stage, state-led program with the ultimate aim of making China the world's leading manufacturing power by 2049. It established "Nine Priority Tasks." These are

1. improving manufacturing innovation,
2. integrating technology and industry,
3. strengthening the industrial base,
4. fostering Chinese brands,
5. enforcing green manufacturing,
6. promoting breakthroughs in 10 key sectors,
7. advancing restructuring of the manufacturing sector,
8. promoting service-oriented manufacturing and manufacturing-related service industries, and
9. internationalizing manufacturing.

The 10 key sectors to be promoted are

1. next-generation information technology,
2. high-end numerical control machinery and robotics,
3. aerospace and aviation equipment,
4. maritime engineering equipment and high-tech maritime vessel manufacturing,
5. advanced rail equipment,
6. energy-saving and new energy vehicles,
7. electrical equipment,
8. agricultural machinery and equipment,
9. new materials, and
10. biopharmaceuticals and high-performance medical devices.[8]

The United States doesn't have a plan. But it desperately needs one.

When the Soviet Union beat the United States into space by launching the world's first satellite in 1957, the US government responded by creating NASA in 1958. During the next three decades, the US government invested so aggressively in missile technology that the USSR could not keep up. It went bankrupt trying and ultimately collapsed because its government was unable to invest as much as the US government did. This policy response enabled the United States to retain its global preeminence for another 60 years.

China's lead in 5G technology is, at least, as great a threat to the United States as the Soviet Union's lead in the Space Race was. If China continues to invest more in R&D than the United States does, it will quickly surpass the United States and become the world's leading technological, economic, and military superpower.

The rest of this book will describe how the United States can prevent that from happening by investing much more in R&D than China can afford to do.

Notes

1. Quoted in "Science and engineering report shows continued loss of U.S. dominance," *Washington Post*, January 15, 2020.
2. *Science and Engineering Indicators* 2018, National Science Foundation, p. 44.
3. Vannevar Bush, "Science, the Endless Frontier," National Science Foundation, July 1945. https://basicresearch.defense.gov
4. Global Trends in Renewable Energy Investment: 2019, p. 56.
5. "Science and engineering report shows continued loss of U.S. dominance," *Washington Post*, January 15, 2020.
6. "What is the difference between 4G and 5G?" Just Ask Thales. https://www.justaskthales.com/en/difference-4g-5g/
7. "Competing With China on Technology and Innovation," The Carnegie Endowment for International Peace. October 2019.
8. "Made in China 2025" Industrial Policies: Issues for Congress, Congressional Research Service, August 11, 2020. https://fas.org/sgp/crs/row/IF10964.pdf

CHAPTER 19

America Can Afford to Invest

Reagan proved deficits don't matter.
Former Vice President Dick Cheney[1]

This chapter and the next will show that the US government can easily afford to finance a multitrillion-dollar investment program targeting the Industries of the Future over the next 10 years, even though it has already spent nearly $5 trillion supporting the economy through the COVID-19 pandemic. The ease with which the government was able to increase its debt by $2.8 trillion[2] during the second quarter of 2020 alone strongly supports this argument.

Estimates for Government Debt and GDP

The Congressional Budget Office (CBO) publishes a lengthy paper at least twice a year containing its projections for the US government's annual budget deficits, debt, and debt relative to GDP during the following 10 years, along with the assumptions underlying those forecasts.

Accurately projecting anything as complex as government debt or the size of the economy 10 years into the future is an impossible task. The CBO is required to make the attempt, nevertheless, in order to assist Congress to better understand how its decisions on spending and taxes will impact the country's debt during the years ahead.

In March 2020, just before the COVID-19 pandemic crashed the US economy, the CBO expected government debt to increase from $22.7 trillion in 2019 to $36.2 in 2030, a $13.5 trillion increase over 11 years. It also projected that the ratio of government debt to GDP would rise gradually from 107% of GDP in 2019 to 113% of GDP in 2030.[3]

The CBO's most recent 10-year projections,[4] published 16 months later in July 2021, show that, due to the pandemic, government debt is likely to climb to $39.4 trillion in 2030, $3.2 trillion more than the CBO had expected in March 2020. The latest projections also show that the ratio of government debt to GDP would be 121% in 2030 rather than 113%, as previously expected.

Despite this pandemic-related jump in government debt, this chapter makes the case that the US government could still easily afford to finance a multitrillion-dollar investment program targeting the Industries of the Future over the next 10 years.

The chapter begins by comparing the CBO's pre- and postpandemic projections for government debt and gross domestic product out to 2030.

It then goes on to show how the nation's finances would be affected if the government borrowed $10 trillion over the next decade to pay for a transformative investment program targeting the industries and technologies of the future. Several scenarios are presented, beginning with the most pessimistic, in which every last penny of the $10 trillion investment program is wasted so that nothing good whatsoever results from it. These paragraphs shows that even in that absurdly pessimistic scenario, the ratio of government debt to GDP in 2031 would be 151% of GDP. Japan exceeded that level of government debt to GDP 19 years ago in 2002.

At 151% of GDP, the ratio of government debt to GDP would be 41% higher than it had been 12 years earlier in 2019.

While large, an increase of that magnitude, in this worst-case scenario, would be far from unprecedented. It would be substantially below the 64% increase in that ratio during the seven years from 2007 to 2014; less than half the 91% increase experienced during the 12 years of the Reagan-Bush presidencies, encompassing 1981 to 1992; and less than a third of the 140% increase in the ratio of government debt to GDP that occurred during the five years between 1941 and 1946.[5]

The chapter concludes by explaining that, in reality, a 10-year, $10 trillion investment program targeting the Industries of the Future would bring about such an extraordinary surge in economic growth that by 2031, the ratio of government debt to GDP would most probably be lower than it was in 2019 and perhaps very much lower. The final chapter of this book describes the paradigm-shifting transformation of the US economy and of human well-being that such a large investment would bring about.

The CBO's Pre- and Post-Pandemic Projections

In its March 2020 10-year projections, the CBO expected government debt to increase by $1.1 trillion in both 2020 and 2021, and by $1.2 trillion in 2022. That cumulative increase of $3.4 trillion over three years was expected to take total government debt up from $22.7 trillion in 2019 to $26.1 trillion in 2022.

By the time the CBO had published its most recent 10-year projections in July 2021, government debt had already increased by $4.2 trillion during 2020 alone. That 2020 increase was nearly four times as much as the CBO had expected in March 2020. In its July 2021 projections, the CBO's estimate for the rise in government debt during 2021 had doubled relative to its March 2020 estimate to $2.2 trillion, while its estimate for the rise in government debt during 2022 had been revised up by $264 billion. In these latest projections, the CBO now expects that total government debt will climb to $30.5 trillion by the end of 2022, nearly $4.5 trillion higher than the CBO had expected in March 2020.

In its earlier projections, the CBO had estimated that the ratio of government debt to GDP would increase from 107% in 2019 to 108% in both 2020 and 2021 and then to 109% in 2022. The current projections, which include the actual data for 2020, show that, in fact, that ratio had jumped from 107% in 2019 to 128% in 2020; and that the ratio was expected to rise further to 130% of GDP in 2021, before declining back to 126% in 2022.

Looking further out, the CBO's March 2020 projections showed government debt climbing by $13.5 trillion over 11 years from $22.7 trillion in 2019 to $36.2 trillion in 2030, while the ratio of government debt to GDP was expected in increase gradually from 107% in 2019 to 113% in 2030. By contrast, the CBO's July 2021 projections now have government debt climbing to $39.4 trillion in 2030, $3.2 trillion more than the CBO had expected 16 months earlier.[6] The latest projections also show the ratio of government debt to GDP rising to 121% in 2030 instead of 113% as the CBO had projected in March 2020.

Chart 19.1 presents the CBO's March 2020 and July 2021 projections for the ratio of US Government debt to GDP from 2019 to 2030.

The sharp jump in the ratio of government debt to GDP in 2020 occurred not only because government debt surged but also because GDP shrank. In March 2020, the CBO had expected nominal GDP to grow by 4.2% during 2020, whereas, due to the pandemic, it contracted by 1%.[7] See Chart 19.2.

It is also interesting to note in Chart 19.2 that while GDP contracted, rather than expanding as expected in 2020, the CBO now looks for the rate of economic growth during 2021 and 2022 to be much more rapid than it had expected before the pandemic.

In fact, the CBO now projects that the US economy will actually be larger every year from 2022 to 2030 than it had expected in March 2020, as shown in Chart 19.3.

The CBO expects the economy to be larger over the next decade than it had earlier due to the extraordinarily aggressive fiscal and monetary policy the government employed to combat the economic fallout from the pandemic.

CHART 19.1 The CBO's Projections for Government Debt to GDP, Pre- and Post-Pandemic, 2019 to 2030 est.

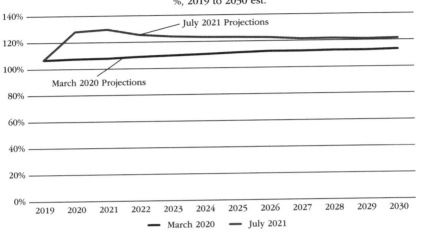

The CBO's Projections for Government Debt to GDP
Pre- and Post-Pandemic
%, 2019 to 2030 est.

Source: Data from the Congressional Budget Office

CHART 19.2 The CBO's Projections for GDP Growth, Pre- and Post-Pandemic, 2020 to 2030 est.

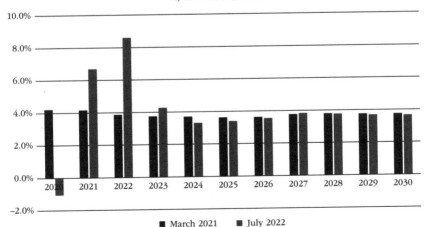

The CBO's Projections for GDP Growth
Pre- and Post-Pandemic
%, 2020 to 2030 est.

Source: Data from the Congressional Budget Office

CHART 19.3 The CBO's Projections for US GDP, Pre- and Post-Pandemic, 2019 to 2030

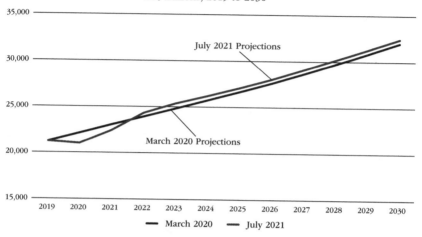

The CBO's Projections for US GDP
Pre- and Post-Pandemic
US$ Billions, 2019 to 2030

Source: Data from the Congressional Budget Office

The higher than previously expected economic output between 2022 and 2030 also explains why the CBO now expects the ratio of government debt to GDP to begin to decline in 2022 after peaking at 130% of GDP in 2021. The CBO's July 2021 projections show government debt to GDP declining every year from 2022, with the ratio at 121% at the end of 2030.

Chart 19.4 shows the CBO's most recent projections for both government debt and GDP out to 2030.

Investing in the Future

During the second quarter of 2020 alone, US Government debt increased by $2.8 trillion. That record-shattering government borrowing did not push US interest rates higher because the Fed created $2.9 trillion during February, March, and April that year to help finance that debt at low interest rates.

CHART 19.4 The CBO's Current Projections for Government Debt and Nominal GDP, 2019 to 2030 est.

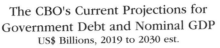

The CBO's Current Projections for
Government Debt and Nominal GDP
US$ Billions, 2019 to 2030 est.

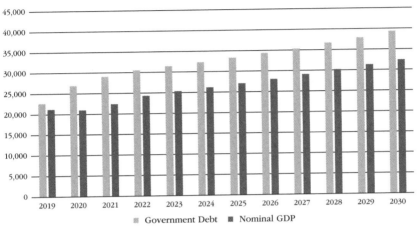

Source: Data from the Congressional Budget Office

Orthodox economic theory, as taught at universities, holds that large government budget deficits financed with money creation by a central bank inevitably cause high rates of inflation. In June 2021, the most recent data available, the inflation rate in the United States was 5.4%. A fall in prices one year earlier, when the economic impact of the pandemic was at its peak, explains much of the large increase in the Consumer Price Index (CPI) in mid-2021. For instance, although the price level was 5.4% higher in June 2021 than in June 2020, it was only 6.0% higher in June 2021 than in June 2019, meaning that the average increase in consumer prices over two years has been a much less concerning 3.0%.

Moreover, supply bottlenecks and other temporary factors have played an important role in pushing consumer prices higher during 2021. For example, a shortage of semiconductors has disrupted the production of new cars, which, in turn, has driven up the price of used cars by more than 40% year-on-year.

The increase in the price of used cars alone accounted for one-third of the increase in the CPI during the second quarter of 2021. Soon, the spike in used car prices will not only end but be reversed, resulting in disinflationary pressures during the quarters ahead.

The forces that have pushed prices higher during 2021 are largely transitory. They will not persist. If inflationary pressures begin to abate, as seems probable, despite an expected $6.4 trillion increase in government debt between the end of 2019 and the end of 2021, financed largely by what is likely to be $4.7 trillion of money creation by the Fed over the same period, what lesson must we learn from this extraordinary experiment?

If the inflation rate comes back down and returns to near its pre-pandemic anemic rates, despite the dire warnings from numerous pundits that hyperinflation would be the inevitable outcome of the government's aggressive policy response to the pandemic, the lesson should be unmistakably clear: we are living in a new economic environment in which the US government can deficit-spend trillions of dollars, financed by trillions of dollars of money creation by the Fed, without generating high rates of inflation or other destabilizing consequences.

At that point, logic and national self-interest would demand that US policymakers reassess the policy options now available to the United States and carefully examine the opportunities made possible by the new economic environment in which we find ourselves. Specifically, the question must be asked: What could be accomplished if the government took full advantage of these new circumstances to borrow and invest aggressively in the Industries of the Future?

Since the chances are high that the sky will not fall due to the multitrillion-dollar fiscal and monetary policy response to the COVID-19 pandemic, the rest of this chapter will show that America can *still* afford to invest on a multitrillion-dollar scale even after the pandemic-induced spike in government debt. It will illustrate how a $10 trillion government investment in new industries and technologies over the 10 years between 2022 and 2031 would impact the level of government debt under various scenarios and argue that such a large-scale investment program would be affordable even in an unrealistic worst-case scenario, where nothing good whatsoever comes from that huge investment. The chapter then discusses a much more realistic scenario in which a $10 trillion investment in the Industries of the Future ignites an extraordinary economic boom that would make the economy much larger and government debt much smaller over the next decade than it would be in the absence of that investment.

The amount of $10 trillion has been chosen simply because it is a very large round number. As mentioned in Chapter 16, the nation will not know how much it can invest over 10 years without causing unacceptably high rates of inflation until it tries. It may not be possible to invest so much so quickly. If not, then, the government could invest less until the bottlenecks causing the inflation are overcome; and then, when they are overcome, the amount invested could reaccelerate. On the other hand, it may prove possible to invest even more than $10 trillion. If it is possible, then the government should invest more. The correct approach is for the US government to begin investing on a much larger scale as soon as possible and to invest as much as it can as quickly as it can.

It would take some time to ramp up the investment program. The government could not simply turn on the taps and invest $1 trillion in the first year, for instance. Plans would have to be made, people would have to be hired and many other arrangements set in motion. The debt projections that will be presented below take that into consideration by assuming a relatively slow start, with $65 billion being invested in 2022, followed by $250 billion in 2023, $530 billion in 2024, $900 billion in 2025, and then a slower rate of increase from 2026 to 2031, as shown in Chart 19.5.

CHART 19.5 The $10 Trillion Investment Program, Investment per Year, 2020 to 2031

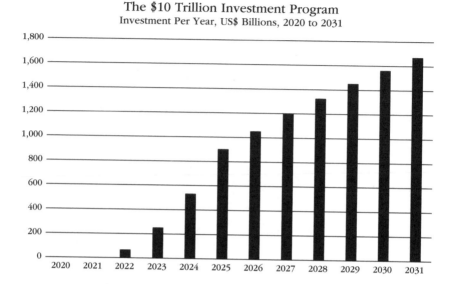

The $10 Trillion Investment Program
Investment Per Year, US$ Billions, 2020 to 2031

Extremely Conservative Assumptions

To assess the impact that level of investment would have on US government debt during those years requires making a number of assumptions. The following paragraphs will present a number of scenarios, beginning with the bleakest.

The first scenario adopts two unrealistically pessimistic assumptions. First, that the $10 trillion increase in government investment would have no impact on the size of the economy. Second, that it would have no impact on the amount of tax revenues that would be collected by the government. Later, we will relax those assumptions to present a more realistic picture.

Using the CBO's July 2021 projections as the base case and assuming that government debt increases above that in line with the $10 trillion government investment program as shown in Chart 19.5, then gross government debt would climb from $23 trillion in 2019 to $51 trillion in 2031, or by $10 trillion more than the CBO's July 2021 projections for 2031.

CHART 19.6 Government Debt After the $10 Trillion Investment Program, 2019 to 2031 est.

Government Debt
After the $10 trillion Investment Program
US$ Billions, 2019 to 2031 est.

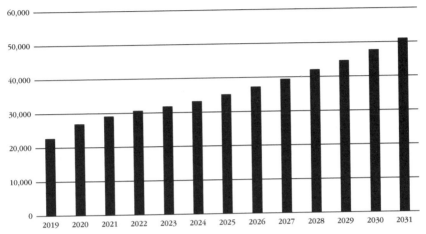

Source: Data from the Congressional Budget Office, incorporating the author's projections for the Investment Program

Chart 19.6 presents the growth in gross government debt from 2019 to 2031 under these assumptions.

Next, Chart 19.7 compares this worst-case scenario for government debt with GDP from 2019 to 2031, using the CBO's July 2021 projections for GDP.

Under these assumptions, the ratio of government debt to GDP would rise to 151% in 2031, in contrast to 121% in the CBO's July 2021 projections and to 113% in the CBO's pre-pandemic March 2020 projections for 2030. (Note that the 10-year projections made by the CBO in March 2020 only extended to 2030.)

Chart 19.8 shows the increase in this ratio over the next decade under each of these scenarios.

Chart 19.9 puts these scenarios into historical perspective by adding the actual data from 1940 to 2020 to the estimates extending out to 2031.

CHART 19.7 Government Debt and GDP After the $10 Trillion Investment Program, 2019 to 2031 est.

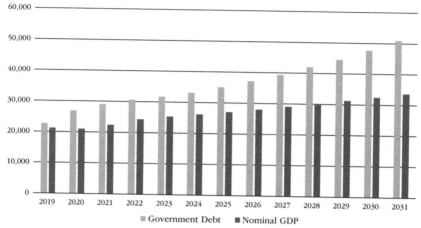

Source: Data from the Congressional Budget Office, incorporating the author's projections for the Investment Program

In this worst-case scenario, in 2031, gross government debt, at 151% of GDP, would be far higher than the previous peak of 119% in 1946. Below, it will be shown that the worst-case scenario is far too pessimistic. However, even if the ratio of US government debt to GDP did climb to 151% over the next 10 years that would not harm the US economy. Here, it is useful to look to Japan. The Japanese economic crisis began in 1990, 18 years before the crisis of 2008 hit the United States and 30 years before the COVID-19 pandemic. In response to Japan's economic crisis, the ratio of Japanese government debt to GDP rose from 64% in 1990 to 237% of GDP in 2019, as shown in Chart 19.10. In 2020, that ratio increased to 256% of GDP.

At the end of 2019, the year before the pandemic began, the ratio of Japanese gross government debt to GDP was 120% larger than that of the US government.

CHART 19.8 Government Debt as a Percentage of GDP, Three Scenarios, 2019 to 2031 est.

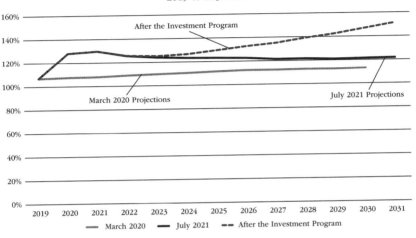

Government Debt as a % of GDP
Three Scenarios
2019 to 2031 est.

Source: Data from the Congressional Budget Office, incorporating the author's projections for the Investment Program

Over the next decade, if the US government goes $10 trillion deeper into debt by borrowing to finance a $10 trillion investment program targeting new industries and technologies, US government debt would reach 151% in 2031 (under the most pessimistic assumptions). Japanese gross government debt to GDP breached that level in 2002. In other words, 10 years from now, in 2031, after the fiscal fallout from the pandemic and after investing $10 trillion in new industries and technologies, in a scenario in which the investment proved entirely fruitless, the US government's debt relative to GDP would be at the level Japanese government debt to GDP hit 19 years ago.

Let it further be noted that Japan has neither suffered inflation or increased government borrowing costs as a result of the sharp rise in Japanese government debt over the last 30 years. Deflation is a greater threat than inflation in Japan and the Japanese government can borrow money for 10 years at interest

CHART 19.9 Government Debt as a Percentage of GDP, Three Scenarios, 1940 to 2031 est.

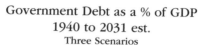

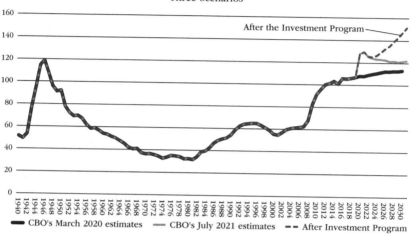

Source: Data from the Congressional Budget Office and the White House, Office of Management and Budget; incorporating the author's projections for the Investment Program

rates very close to and sometimes below 0% a year. At the time of writing, the yield on the 10-year Japanese government bond is 0.01%.

The Japanese experience strongly suggests that the US government could easily invest an additional $10 trillion over the next decade without driving inflation or interest rates significantly higher. If the government did invest on that scale, even in the worst-case scenario, in which the additional government investment failed to boost economic growth or tax revenues at all and contributed nothing whatsoever to the economy, then 10 years from now the ratio of US government debt to GDP would still be only 59% as large as Japanese government debt to GDP was at the end of 2020.[8]

That was the worst-case scenario. The following paragraphs will explain why the worst case must be dismissed and why a very much more positive outcome must be expected.

CHART 19.10 Japan: Gross Government Debt to GDP, Percentage of GDP, 1980 to 2019

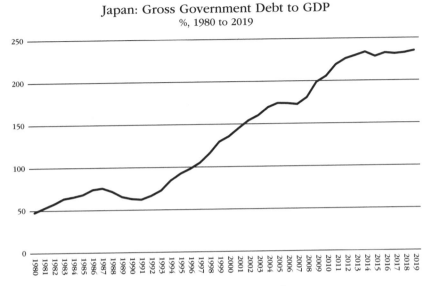

Japan: Gross Government Debt to GDP
%, 1980 to 2019

Source: Data from the International Monetary Fund

Toward a More Realistic Scenario

Accelerated Government Spending Would Boost Economic Growth

The worst-case scenario, outlined above, assumes that a 10-year, $10 trillion government-financed investment program targeting the Industries of the Future would have no impact on the size of the US economy. That assumption is unrealistic. Every country's economy (GDP) is made up of four parts: (1) personal consumption expenditure, plus (2) private investment, plus (3) net trade (i.e., exports minus imports), plus (4) government spending. For example, in 2022, if, in line with the investment schedule presented above, government spending were to increase by $65 billion relative to what the government had planned to spend that year, then the economy would be $65 billion larger that year than it would have been if government investment had not increased by $65 billion (all other factors remaining unchanged).

If we assume that the government invests $65 billion more in 2022 than currently anticipated in the CBO's July 2021 projections, then the US GDP would be $65 billion larger that year than the CBO's projections currently anticipate. And, if it invests $1.7 trillion more in 2031, (again, in line with the investment schedule presented above) then US GDP would be $1.7 trillion larger in 2031 than the CBO currently expects. In 2031, GDP would be at least $35.3 trillion instead of $33.7 trillion. That would knock seven percentage points off the ratio of government debt to GDP in 2031, bringing it down from 151% in the worst-case scenario outlined above to 144%.

Keep in mind, however, that these projections are still based on extremely conservative assumptions. They do not take into consideration the additional tax revenues the government would receive as the economy expanded. Furthermore, they only assume a $1 increase in economic growth for each $1 increase in government spending. The following paragraphs will explain why those assumptions are far too pessimistic.

Additional Economic Growth Would Boost Tax Revenues

Given that an additional $10 trillion would be invested between 2022 and 2031, the cumulative increase in the US GDP during all those years combined would be $10 trillion (at the very least). The larger the economy is, the more tax revenues the government collects. Since 1969, federal tax revenues have averaged 17.4% of GDP a year.[9] If we assume that tax revenues will amount to 17% of GDP over the next 10 years, then, given that the cumulative increase in US GDP between 2022 and 2031 would be at least $10 trillion, US tax revenues would be at least $1.7 trillion higher than they otherwise would have been.

That means the US government could invest $10 trillion in new industries and technologies, but recoup at least $1.7 trillion as the result of additional tax revenues. So, after tax, the $10 trillion investment program would generate at least an additional $1.7 trillion in tax revenues. That would reduce the estimated government debt level by at least $1.7 trillion in 2031, from $51.0

trillion to $49.3 trillion, thereby knocking another five percentage points off the ratio of government debt to GDP that year, lowering it from 144% to 139%.

That also means that the actual cost of the government-financed $10 trillion investment program would be $8.3 trillion after the government recouped $1.7 trillion in additional tax revenues. In other words, the government can finance investment at a discount. For every $100 the government invests, it receives a refund of $17. It obtains $100 worth of goods and services at a net cost of $83.

The Multiplier

Thus far, we have assumed that every one dollar of additional investment by the government would only generate an additional one dollar of economic growth. In other words, we have assumed that the "multiplier" on the government spending would be 1. This, too, is an overly pessimistic assumption. Economists have argued for generations about what the size of the multiplier on government spending actually is. Does a $1 increase in government spending make the economy grow an extra $2 (a multiplier of 2) or only by an extra $1.5 or by just $1.2? Some have even argued that the multiplier is less than one for one, that a $1 increase in government spending results in the economy growing by less than $1.

The case for a multiplier of less than 1 rests on the assumption that the government has to increase taxes to finance the increased government spending; and that the reduction in private sector spending and investment resulting from higher taxes more than offsets the boost to the economy from higher government spending. That would not be the case here, since we are assuming that the increase in government investment would be financed by increased government debt, not by higher taxes; and that the debt is entirely financed by the Fed so that the additional government borrowing would not push interest rates higher. This subject is the topic of the next chapter.

In truth, the multiplier on government spending varies depending on many factors, the most important of which is how the government spends the money. In the case we are considering, where all the additional government spending is invested in cutting edge technologies and industries, it is very probable that the multiplier would be exceptionally large. Large-scale investment of this kind would add to the United States' most productive type of capital stock, that generated from research and development (R&D). And capital generates income (i.e., economic growth), as discussed in Chapter 17.

An investment of an additional $10 trillion over 10 years in research and development, through a combination of government-directed programs and public-private sector joint ventures, would enormously enhance US productivity and ignite a new technological revolution that would result in an extraordinary acceleration of US economic growth.

Of course, the benefits would be cumulative. The investments made in R&D during the first five years would generate higher returns during the second five years when the innovations and breakthroughs they financed began to come to fruition. Within 10 years, it is likely that an investment program on this scale would have generated medical breakthroughs that would allow most Americans to live significantly longer, healthier, and more productive lives.

Therefore, the multiplier on government investment could easily reach two times by 2031, and quite possibly three or four times, if not more. If the multiplier were two times in 2031, GDP that year would be $37.0 trillion, $1.7 trillion larger than estimated above. If so, that would reduce the ratio of gross debt to GDP further to 133% that year (without considering the reduction in the debt that would result from higher tax revenues related to the higher multiplier).

The Fiscal Benefits of Improved Health

Furthermore, a $10 trillion investment in new industries and technologies would create medicines and medical procedures that would make the American workforce healthier and keep it healthy well past current life expectancy averages. If these breakthroughs extended the working life of the average American by only two or three years, the size of the active US workforce would be much larger in 2031 – and every subsequent year – than currently expected. That would bring in much higher US tax revenues, including much higher contributions to Social Security and Medicare through payroll taxes. Significantly higher payroll tax revenues would eliminate all concerns over the longer-term solvency of those programs. Moreover, a healthier population would reduce the amount of money the government would spend on Medicare, Medicaid, and Disability Insurance. In sum, just by making Americans healthier, this $10 trillion investment program would radically improve the long-term outlook for the US government's budget deficit and debt.

Income and Capital Gains

Finally, the discussion above has entirely ignored the extraordinary windfall profits that a $10 trillion investment program would begin to rain down on the government and society more generally. Unlike in the past, the government would earn licensing fees from the private sector companies that adopt and profit from the breakthroughs in technology that this government-financed investment program would produce. Even more importantly, many of the joint venture companies the government would set up with the private sector would earn extraordinarily large profits, 60% of which would accrue to the government (i.e., the US taxpayers), since the government would hold a 60% equity stake in those companies as discussed in Chapter 16.

This $10 trillion investment program would be structured to ensure that the government and, therefore, US taxpayers, directly share in the profits that would be derived from the innovations and breakthroughs that this investment program would be certain to produce. An investment program on this scale has the potential to generate technological miracles and medical breakthroughs with stratospheric market values. When these products hit the market and when these public–private joint venture companies are listed on the stock exchange, the government will share in the profits. It is not at all inconceivable that those profits could pay off the entire national debt; and, afterwards, allow a reduction in, or even the complete elimination of, the income tax.

What If Government Debt Is Higher?

The estimates in all the scenarios discussed above are built on the CBO's July 2021 projections for government debt and GDP out to 2031.

The CBO bases its projections on current laws rather than attempting to make assumptions about how the law could be changed and how those changes could impact the government's fiscal position in the future. The CBO's July 2021 projections for government debt only incorporate the CBO's assessment of the impact of the laws that Congress had passed up until May 18, 2021.[10] It is possible that Congress will enact new laws that cause US government debt to be higher over the next decade than the CBO's July 2021 projections foresee.

Therefore, let us quickly consider a scenario in which government debt exceeds the CBO's current projections by $2.5 trillion in 2031, implying that the government budget deficit would, on average, be $250 billion a year larger than the CBO now projects. That would take government debt up to $53.5 trillion 10 years from now after factoring in the $10 trillion the government would borrow to finance the investment program. If we also assume that the GDP in 2031 would remain at $33.7 trillion, meaning that the economy did not grow at all despite a $10 trillion investment in new technologies or due to the additional $2.5 trillion of additional government debt assumed in this scenario, then 10 years from now the ratio of government debt to GDP would be 159% instead of 151% as described in the most pessimist scenario discussed above.

Next, if we assume government debt exceeds the CBO's current projections by $5.0 trillion in 2031, implying that the government budget deficit would, on average, be $500 billion a year larger than the CBO now projects, that would take government debt up to $56.0 trillion 10 years from now. Retaining all the assumptions in the preceding paragraph, that would put the ratio of government debt to GDP at 166% in 2031.

Even using these very pessimistic assumptions concerning the outlook for government debt and economic growth, the ratio of government debt to GDP in 2031 would not be so high that it would undermine fiscal stability or damage the US economy in any other way. The ratio of government debt to GDP in Japan exceeded 159% in 2003 and it exceeded 166% in 2004. It ended 2020 at 256%. Japan remains one of the most prosperous nations in the world.

Therefore, there should be no doubt on this subject. America can afford to invest.

Notes

1. Dick Cheney quote. https://www.goodreads.com/quotes/9445209-reagan-proved-that-deficits-don-t-matter
2. The Debt to the Penny, TreasuryDirect. https://treasurydirect.gov/govt/reports/pd/debttothepenny.htm
3. Baseline Budget Projections as of March 6, 2020, Congressional Budget Office. https://www.cbo.gov/system/files/2020-03/56268-CBO-baseline-budget-projections.pdf
4. Additional Information About the Updated Budget and Economic Outlook: 2020 to 2031 Congressional Budget Office. https://www.cbo.gov/system/files/2021-07/57263-outlook.pdf
5. Source for Historical US Government Debt to GDP Ratios: Office of Management and Budget, Historical Tables. Table 7.1 – Federal Debt at the End of Year: 1940 to 2026, The White House. https://www.whitehouse.gov/omb/historical-tables/
6. Note: Although the CBO's July 2021 projections for government debt at the end of 2022 are nearly $4.5 trillion higher than its March 2020 projections had been, its July 2021 projections for government debt at the end of 2030 are only $3.2 trillion higher. This

appears odd. The explanation is that by July 2021, the CBO had significantly lowered its forecasts for US interest rates. As a result, its projections for the government's interest expense between 2021 and 2030 were reduced. The lower than anticipated interest expense during the course of the decade relative to what had been expected in March 2020, resulted in the increase in the CBO's projections for government debt in 2030 being lower than the increase in its projections for government debt in 2022 (both relative to its March 2020 projections).

7. Note: The CBO's GDP projections are for the Fiscal Year ending September 30.

8. IMF World Economic Outlook Database. https://www .imf.org/en/Publications/WEO/weo-database/2021/April/weo-report?c=158,&s=GGXWDG_NGDP,&sy=2019&ey=2026&ssm=0&scs m=1&scc=0&ssd=1&ssc=0&sic=0&sort=country&ds=.&br=1

9. Office of Management and Budget, Historical Tables. Table 2.3 – Receipts by Source as Percentages of GDP: 1934 to 2026, The White House. https://www.whitehouse.gov/omb/historical-tables/

10. Additional Information About the Updated Budget and Economic Outlook: 2021 to 2031, p. 1, Congressional Budget Office. https:// www.cbo.gov/system/files/2021-07/57263-outlook.pdf

CHAPTER 20

Monetize the Debt

Financing isn't a constraint; real resources are.

Stephanie Kelton[1]

The Fed has the power to create money, as this book has shown again and again.

It has exercised that power in a dramatic fashion during four great national emergencies: World War I, World War II, the financial crisis of 2008 and the COVID-19 pandemic of 2020. It should use that power now to finance a multitrillion-dollar investment program targeting the Industries of the Future over the next 10 years. If it does, the entire investment program could be carried out at no cost whatsoever to the American taxpayer. This chapter discusses the mechanics of how that could be done.

Financing the Investment Program at No Cost

As stated in Chapter 16, the correct approach is for the US government to invest as much as possible as quickly as possible, with the exact amount and speed to be determined through trial and error. The previous chapter used an example of a $10 trillion investment program carried out over 10 years to illustrate how the government's fiscal position would be impacted by such an investment under various scenarios. This chapter will use the same amount and time frame, $10 trillion over 10 years, to portray how the Fed's balance sheet would be affected by a large-scale investment program of this type.

This chapter will argue that the Fed should monetize the entire cost of the investment program. In this approach, when the investment program is announced, it would include a commitment from the Fed to finance the entire program by creating $10 trillion over 10 years and buying all the bonds the government would issue to fund the investments. Technically, the government would pay the Fed interest on all those bonds every year, but since the Fed is required to return all its profits to the government, the net cost to the government would be zero, or, at least, very close to zero.

The Fed would also specify that it would never sell those bonds and that it would always roll them over when they mature. Or, to make matters simpler still, the government could sell the Fed perpetual bonds that never mature. That would make it clear that the $10 trillion of government debt issued to finance the investment program would be cost-free debt, with the principal never to be repaid and the annual interest expense returned to the Treasury Department each year, forever.

For all intents and purposes, such an approach would cancel all $10 trillion of the debt the government would issue to finance the investment program. Debt never to be repaid and paying no net interest would be debt in name only. It could be forgotten as it would never cost the Treasury Department or American taxpayers anything.

However, to finance the investment program at no cost to the taxpayer, the Fed would have to stop paying interest on the Bank Reserves that commercial banks hold at the Fed. This would require the Fed to raise the required reserve ratio high enough to absorb all the Bank Reserves that would be created as a result of the Fed creating money to buy the government's $10 trillion of investment-related debt.

Here some background information is required.

Seigniorage and Bank Reserves

It is amazing how much money you can make when you make the money. The Federal Reserve is one of the world's most profitable institutions. Luckily for US taxpayers, the Fed is required to hand over all of its profits to the US Treasury Department every year. Between 1914 and 2020 the Fed gave the Treasury Department $1.6 trillion, as shown in Chart 20.1.

The US government debt is more than $1.6 trillion lower now than it would have been thanks to the transfer of the Fed's profits to the Treasury. It is *more* than $1.6 trillion lower because interest expense would have accumulated on the additional $1.6 trillion of debt and added to the government's total debt. Ninety-nine percent of the Fed's remittances to the Treasury occurred after 1971, when dollars ceased to be linked to gold. 60% occurred after 2008, as the Fed created trillions of dollars in

CHART 20.1 The Fed's Remittances to the US Treasury Department, 1914 to 2020

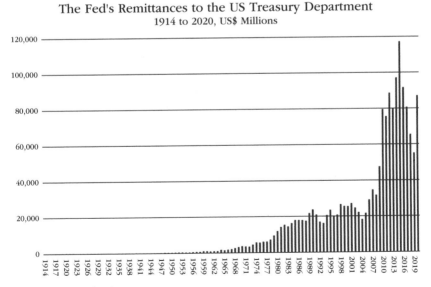

Source: The Federal Reserve

response to the economic crisis and, more recently, in response to the COVID-19 pandemic.

If the Fed were a corporation, in 2020, based on its remittances to the Treasury of $86.9 billion, it would have been the most profitable corporation in the world. Apple, which was the world's most profitable corporation in 2020, would have come in second place with $57.4 billion of earnings.[2]

Before the crisis of 2008, most of the Fed's earnings came from issuing Federal Reserve Notes. The Fed supplies currency to commercial banks upon demand, but it does not give the dollars away for free. The Fed is required to hold Treasury securities for the dollars it issues. So, in essence, the Fed provides the banks with dollars in exchange for government bonds. The Fed makes a profit in the process because it earns interest income on the government bonds it acquires but pays no interest on the currency it issues. This process is known as seigniorage.[3]

Chart 20.2 illustrates this in a simplified balance sheet of the Fed from 1945 to 2006. By 2006, the Fed had issued $783 billion

CHART 20.2 The Fed's Balance Sheet, Major Items Only, 1945 to 2006

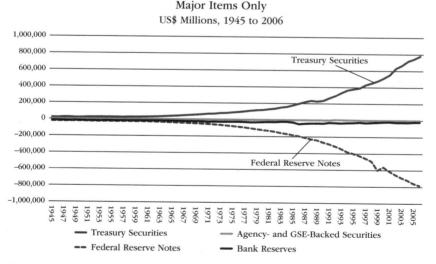

Source: Data from the Federal Reserve's Annual Reports

of Federal Reserve Notes and acquired $779 billion of government securities.

During the years following the economic crisis, the Fed's profits became very substantially larger as the result of Quantitative Easing. Between the end of 2007 and end of 2014, the Fed's total assets grew by $3.6 trillion as it bought government securities and mortgage-backed securities issued or guaranteed by the government-sponsored enterprises (GSEs). It acquired those bonds by making deposits into the reserve accounts at the Fed of the banks from which it purchased the bonds. The Fed earned a higher rate of interest on the bonds it acquired than it paid on the reserves held by the banks. Consequently, the Fed's profits soared, peaking at $117 billion in 2015 versus a pre-2008 crisis peak of $35 billion in 2007.

By 2014, the Fed's holdings of Treasury securities had increased to nearly $2.6 trillion and its holdings of GSE-related debt had jumped from zero in 2006 to almost $1.8 trillion. Meanwhile, on the liabilities side of the Fed's balance sheet, Bank Reserves has surged to nearly $2.4 trillion, while currency had grown to $1.3 trillion. Chart 20.3 illustrates these changes.

Notice that Bank Reserves did not increase in line with the Fed's holdings of Treasury securities and GSE-related debt. Between the end of 2007 and the end of 2014, the former increased by only $2.4 trillion, while the latter grew by $3.6 trillion. The $500 billion increase in currency accounts for part of the $1.2 trillion difference. That is because when the banks obtain currency from the Fed, the Fed debits their reserve accounts in exchange. In other words, as currency expands, it absorbs Bank Reserves. An increase in reverse repurchase agreements of $469 billion and a $219 billion increase in the deposits in the Treasury's General Account at the Fed made up most of the rest of the difference between the growth in the Fed's total assets and the growth in Bank Reserves. When reverse repurchase agreements and the deposits in the Treasury's General Account increase, they also absorb Bank Reserves. However, they don't increase on a permanent basis the way that currency steadily has in recent decades.[4]

CHART 20.3 The Fed's Balance Sheet, Major Items Only, 1945 to 2014

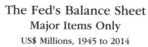

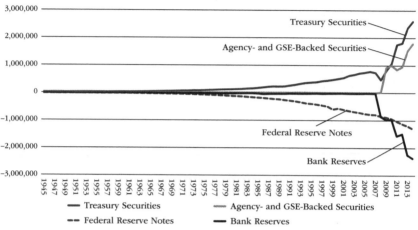

Source: Data from the Federal Reserve's Annual Reports

The Fed's interest income surged as it accumulated trillions of dollars' worth of interest earning assets. Meanwhile, its expenses remained limited. As mentioned above, the Fed does not pay interest on the currency it issues. It only began paying interest on Bank Reserves in 2008. The law prohibited the Fed from paying interest on Bank Reserves until Congress removed that prohibition that year. Even then, the interest rate the Fed paid on Bank Reserves was less than 0.25% per annum until December 2015.

Before 2008, there was no need for the Fed to pay interest on Bank Reserves. However, the Fed's policy response to the crisis disrupted the Fed's traditional operating procedures, making it difficult for the Fed to control the federal funds rate in the way that it had done in the past.

Traditionally, the Fed had controlled the federal funds rate by keeping Bank Reserves scarce. If it wanted the federal funds rate to rise, it could conduct an open market operation that would remove reserves from the banking system. More specifically, the

Fed would sell to a bank a government bond that it had bought in the past. In such a transaction, the Fed would collect payment for the bond by debiting the reserve account the acquiring bank held at the Fed, thereby reducing that bank's reserves and, therefore, the reserves of the entire banking system. With fewer reserves in the system, the federal funds rate would rise.

Conversely, if the Fed wanted the federal funds rate to fall, it would acquire a government bond from a bank by crediting that bank's reserve account at the Fed. The injection of new reserves would make reserves more plentiful throughout the banking system, causing the federal funds rate to fall.

After 2008, however, Bank Reserves were no longer scarce. In response to the crisis of 2008, the Fed injected trillions of dollars into the banking sector, first through discounting operations and then through open market operations (QE). Afterwards, so long as Bank Reserves remained superabundant, the Fed could no longer control the federal funds rate as it had in the past. Small-scale open market sales would have no impact on the federal funds rate. Only the complete reversal of Quantitative Easing would have served to make the reserves of the banking system scarce enough to enable the Fed to adjust the federal funds rate using the methods it had employed before 2008.

The federal funds rate was set at a range between 0% and 0.25% from December 2008 and December 2015. In December 2015, the Fed decided to begin tightening monetary policy with a 25-basis point rate hike which took the federal funds rate to a range of 0.25% to 0.5%. In order to make this decision effective, the Fed began paying just above 0.25% interest on the reserves banks held in their reserve accounts at the Fed. That ensured that the banks would not lend to anyone at less than 0.25%, since they could earn a little more than 0.25% by holding reserves at the Fed.

Between December 2015 and December 2018, the Fed gradually increased the federal funds rate to a range of 2.25% to 2.5%. It accomplished this by increasing the interest rate it paid on Bank Reserves to just above 2.25% (see Chart 20.4).

CHART 20.4 The Effective Federal Funds Rate, 2008 to mid-2021

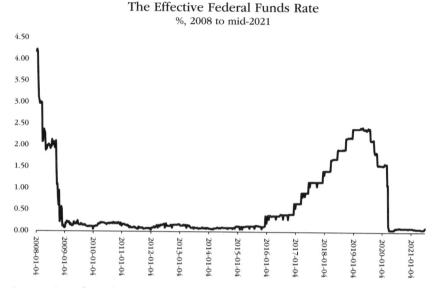

The Effective Federal Funds Rate
%, 2008 to mid-2021

Source: Data from the Federal Reserve Bank of St. Louis

When the Fed began moving the federal funds rate up by paying more interest on Bank Reserves starting in December 2015, its profits began to fall. Until then, nearly all of the interest income it earned on the bonds it had acquired through its Quantitative Easing program had gone straight to the Fed's bottom line as profits. Once it began hiking the interest it paid on Bank Reserves, however, the interest it paid to banks had to be deducted from its interest income. That reduced the Fed's profits and, therefore, the amount of money the Fed handed over the Treasury Department each year thereafter. When the Fed began reducing the size of its assets through Quantitative Tightening in October 2017, that further reduced the Fed's profitability. By 2019, the Fed's profits had fallen by more than half from the peak, to $55 billion. In 2020, they rebounded sharply back to $86.9 billion, first because the Fed acquired an additional $3.2 trillion of interest-earning assets during the year and, second, because it also slashed the rate of interest it paid on Bank Reserves back very close to 0% in March, as part of its policy response to the pandemic.

The Fed's Balance Sheet Projected to 2031

This section describes how the Fed's balance sheet would evolve between 2019 and 2031, assuming the US government finances a $10 trillion investment program between 2022 and 2031 and assuming that the Fed creates $10 trillion in order to monetize the cost of the entire investment program. It is also assumed that the Fed continues its ongoing asset purchase program at the current pace of $120 billion a month through the end of 2021 and then tapers its asset purchases by $10 billion each month starting in January 2022, thereby bringing this round of Quantitative Easing to an end in December 2022. Under these assumptions, the Fed's total assets would increase by a total of $2.1 trillion during 2021 and 2022 as the result of Quantitative Easing, and by a further $10 trillion between 2022 and 2031 as a result of financing the investment program.

Altogether, therefore, the Fed's assets would increase from $7.4 trillion at the end of 2020 to $19.5 trillion at the end of 2031, or by $12.1 trillion over 11 years. This would come on top of the $3.2 trillion (76%) jump in the Fed's total assets during 2020. The total increase between the end of 2019, the eve of the pandemic, and 2031 would be $15.3 trillion or 366% over 12 years.

While that would be a very large increase in over just a dozen years, it would still be less than the 417% increase in the Fed's total assets during the seven years between 2007 and 2014 in the aftermath of the crisis of 2008. Chart 20.5 shows the increase in the Fed's total assets out to 2031, given the assumptions described above.

In that scenario, and also adopting the unrealistically pessimistic assumption that the $10 trillion investment program would have no impact on the size of the US economy whatsoever, then the Fed's total assets relative to the size of the US economy would increase from 35% of GDP in 2020 to 58% of GDP in 2031, as depicted in Chart 20.6.

That would mean that 10 years from now, after the Fed had financed much of the government's policy response to the

CHART 20.5 The Fed's Total Assets Projected to 2031 est.

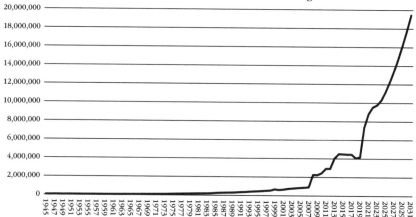

The Fed's Total Assets Projected to 2031
US$ Billions, 1945 to 2031 est.
Assuming the Fed Ends QE in December 2022
and Monetizes the $10 Trillion Investment Program

Source: Data from the Federal Reserve's Annual Reports, incorporating the author's projections for the Investment Program

COVID-19 pandemic, as well as a $10 trillion investment program that had failed to generate a single cent of economic growth, then the ratio of the Fed's total assets to GDP, at 58%, would be at the same ratio that the Bank of Japan's (BOJ) total assets to Japanese GDP reached in 2014 and only 56% as large as that Japanese ratio was on the eve of the pandemic in 2019, when it reached 104%. By the end of 2020, the ratio of the BOJ's total assets to Japanese GDP had spiked to 127% due to Japan's policy response to the pandemic. Given that Japan has not experienced any harmful consequences as the result of the BOJ accumulating assets in excess of the size of Japan's GDP, the growth in the ratio of the Fed's total assets to GDP to 58% by 2031 should be easily manageable even in an unrealistic worst-case scenario as the one presented here. The ratio of the BOJ's total assets to GDP from 2000 to 2020 is shown in Chart 20.7.

It should also be noted that the ratio of the European Central Bank's[5] total assets had reached 62% of the Euro Area's GDP

CHART 20.6 Fed's Total Assets as a Percentage of GDP, 1945 to 2031 est.

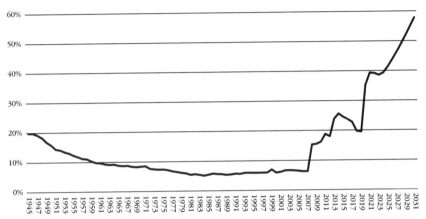

Fed's Total Assets as a % of GDP
1945 to 2031 est.
Assuming the Fed Ends QE in December 2022
and Monetizes the $10 Trillion Investment Program

Source: Data from the Federal Reserve's Annual Reports, and the Bureau of Economic Analysis, incorporating the author's projections for the Investment Program

at the end of 2020.[6] That is already larger than the Fed's total assets relative to US GDP would be in 2031 in the scenario discussed above.

How, then, would a $12.1 trillion expansion of the Fed's total assets between 2020 and 2031 impact the major items on the Fed's balance sheet, and, in particular, how large would interest-bearing Bank Reserves grow in this scenario?

How the Fed's balance sheet evolves on the asset side would depend on the split between the Fed's purchases of Treasury securities and its purchases of agency and GSE-backed securities. The evolution of the liabilities side of the balance sheet would be determined primarily by the growth in currency in circulation. Chart 20.8 presents one scenario of what the evolution of the four major items on the Fed's balance sheet could look like between 2019 and 2031.

CHART 20.7 BOJ Total Assets as Percentage of GDP, 2000 to 2020

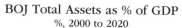

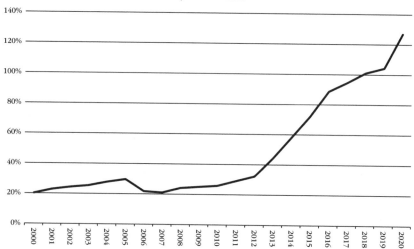

Source: Data from the Federal Reserve Bank of St. Louis

CHART 20.8 The Fed's Balance Sheet Projected to 2031, Major Items Only, 1945 to 2031 est.

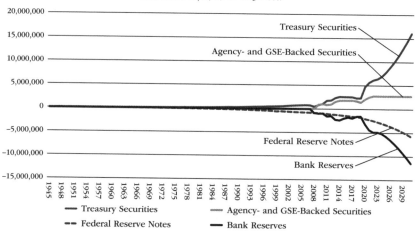

Source: Data from the Federal Reserve, incorporating the author's projections

In this scenario, on the asset side of the Fed's balance sheet, the Fed's holdings of Treasury securities would increase to $16.1 trillion in 2031, while its holdings of agency and GSE-backed securities would rise to $2.8 trillion that year. On the liabilities side of the balance sheet, currency in circulation (Federal Reserve Notes) would grow to $5.8 trillion in 2031, while Bank Reserves would expand to $11.5 trillion. The appendix to this chapter explains the assumptions behind these estimates.

The increase in Bank Reserves is what interests us most here. That is because, since 2008, the Fed has paid interest on Bank Reserves. That interest expense reduces the Fed's profits and, therefore, its remittances to the Treasury Department. In the scenario discussed here, in 2031, Bank Reserves would be $8.3 trillion larger than they were in 2020 as the result of the money created by the Fed during the 11 intervening years.

Given the Fed's current operating procedures for controlling the federal funds rate, if the federal funds rate were above 0%, the Fed would have to pay interest to the commercial banks on the additional $8.3 trillion of Bank Reserves.

Therefore, even though the Fed would still return all the profits it earned on the interest income from its portfolio of government bonds and mortgage-backed securities to the Treasury Department, those profits would be reduced by the amount of interest the Fed would have to pay on the banks' reserves. Consequently, Fed financing of the $10 trillion investment program would not be cost-free. There would be a cost. That cost would be determined by the federal funds rate. For instance, if the federal funds rate were 1.0%, the Fed would have to pay the banks 1% on the additional $8.3 trillion of Bank Reserves that would exist in 2031 as the result of the Fed financing the investment program. That would amount to $83 billion per year. Of course, if the federal funds rate were 0%, then there would be no cost. On the other hand, if the federal funds rate moved up to 5%, then the cost would be $415 billion per year.

However, the Fed can and should avoid paying any interest on Bank Reserves by reverting to its traditional operating procedure. Instead of paying interest on Bank Reserves to control

CHART 20.9 Bank Reserves as a percentage of Bank Deposits, 1945 to 2031 est.

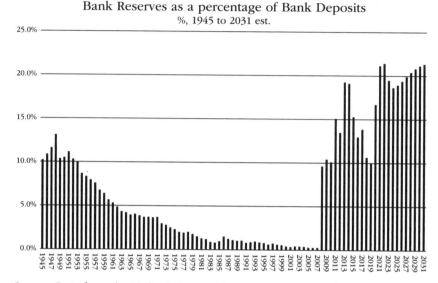

Source: Data from the Federal Reserve, incorporating the author's projections

the federal funds rate, the Fed could raise the required reserve ratio as high as necessary to make reserves in the banking system scarce again, despite the additional $8.3 trillion of new Bank Reserves that would be created as the Fed acquires $12.1 trillion of new government bonds, and agency and GSE-backed securities, between the end of 2020 and the end of 2031.

Chart 20.9 presents an estimate of the level of Bank Reserves relative to the size of the banking sector's customer deposits out to the end of 2031.[7] It puts that increase in Bank Reserves into perspective by showing the ratio of reserves to total deposits for private depository institutions in the United States beginning in 1945.

The ratio of Bank Reserves to total liabilities was 13.1% in 1948. The Fed did not pay interest on Bank Reserves then. In 2013, that ratio hit 19.2%. The Fed paid less than 0.25% interest on Bank Reserves that year.

The ratio of Bank Reserves to total deposits will increase as the Fed monetizes the debt the government issues to finance the

$10 trillion investment program. That ratio will rise from 16.7% in 2020 to 21.3% in 2031.

At its most recent Federal Open Market Committee meeting (June 15-16, 2021), the Fed indicated that it was unlikely to begin increasing the federal funds rate from its current near 0% lower bound to 0.25% until 2023. Therefore, the Fed is likely to pay only a very small amount of interest on Bank Reserves until, at least, 2023. However, before the Fed does begin to hike interest rates, it should revert to its traditional method of pushing rates higher by making excess Bank Reserves scarce. It could accomplish this by raising the required reserve ratio as high as necessary to absorb all excess Bank Reserves.

For instance, in 2023, the ratio of Bank Reserves to bank customer deposits is expected to be 19.5%, as shown in Chart 20.9. If the Fed decides to increase the federal funds rate that year, it should set the required reserve ratio of Bank Reserves to bank customer deposits at precisely 19.5%. Then banks would be legally required to hold that level of reserves. Therefore, there would be no excess reserves in the banking sector.

Over time, as the ratio of Bank Reserves to bank customer deposits changed, as in the projections shown in Chart 20.9, the Fed could adjust the required reserve ratio so that it would also be exactly the same level as the actual ratio of Bank Reserves to bank deposits. For instance, in 2024, the required reserve ratio could be reduced to 18.6% and then raised again to 19.3% in 2026, and so on. The large increase in the required reserve ratio is not without precedent. Between July 1936 and May 1937, the Fed doubled the required reserve ratio on demand deposits of central reserve city banks from 13% to 26%, as shown in Table 4.1 in Chapter 4.[8]

The much higher required reserve ratio would be, in effect, a windfall profits tax on the commercial banks. It would prevent them from profiting from the Fed financing the government's investment program, to which they had contributed nothing. There is no justification for the Fed paying interest to commercial banks on the Bank Reserves that the Fed had created, when the Fed could simply increase the required reserve ratio instead. The banks themselves would have done nothing to earn those reserves. They would not have obtained them as the result of making a successful loan to a small business in Kansas City, Missouri, for instance, nor from financing a multibillion-dollar merger in the tech industry, nor, even, from making a large successful bet on the direction of the price of pork bellies. Banks do not obtain reserves as the result of earning profits. Banks do not "earn" reserves. Bank Reserves are created by the Fed, entirely independently from any action taken or decision made by the banking sector.

Bank Reserves expand in only one way. They expand when the Fed makes a deposit into the reserve accounts that the commercial banks hold at the Fed. Therefore, there is absolutely no reason the Fed should pay interest on those reserves, thereby lowering its own profits and, consequently, reducing the remittances it hands over to the Treasury Department (i.e., US taxpayers) each year, while, in the process, boosting the earnings of the commercial banks directly in line with the amount of interest paid. Raising the required reserve ratio high enough to absorb all excess reserves in the banking sector would simply eliminate these unearned bank profits and place this money with the US taxpayers where it belongs.

Even if the Fed did increase the required reserve ratio as described above, it is very likely that the profitability of commercial banks would improve considerably, nevertheless, as the $10 trillion investment program supercharged economic growth. An additional benefit of this approach would be that a much higher level of Bank Reserves would also ensure that the banks would have more than enough reserves to withstand any future economic crisis. Then, rather than the banks being too big to fail, they would be too well reserved to fail.

With this approach, the Fed would not have to pay interest on the currency it issues or on the Bank Reserves it creates, as was the case before 2008. That would mean that the government would earn seigniorage not only on the currency it issues, but also on the Bank Reserves the Fed creates when it purchases government bonds, and agency and mortgage-backed securities.

Raising the required reserve ratio as high as necessary to absorb all the Bank Reserves created by the Fed would make all the debt issued by the government to fund the $10 trillion investment program cost-free debt. It would also make most of the debt issued by the government to fight the economic fallout from COVID-19 cost-free debt, while, at the same time, making all the debt the Fed acquired through its numerous rounds of Quantitative Easing between the crisis of 2008 and the beginning of the pandemic cost-free debt. Reverting to the Fed's traditional method of controlling the federal funds rate by keeping Bank Reserves scarce would boost the Fed's profits by hundreds of billions of dollars during the decades ahead and make it possible for the US government to finance a transformative $10 trillion investment program over the next 10 years at no cost whatsoever to US taxpayers.

Before us is a once-in-history opportunity for the US government to invest in new industries and technologies on an enormous scale at essentially no cost. The deflationary forces of globalization, in combination with the ability of central banks to create money without gold backing, makes this possible. It is an opportunity that we must not let slip past us.

What Could the Negative Consequences Be?

In the worst-case scenario outlined above, by 2031, the ratio of government debt to GDP would rise to 151% and the Fed would create $12.1 trillion between 2020 and 2031 to help finance the increase in government debt at low interest rates.

What are the negative consequences that could result from such a large increase in government debt and Federal Reserve Credit? Three possibilities immediately jump to mind:

1. A sharp increase in consumer price inflation (CPI).
2. A new round of steep asset price inflation that would significantly worsen income inequality.
3. The loss of confidence in the US dollar, imperiling its status as the world's preeminent reserve currency.

The following paragraphs will discuss – and dismiss – each of those concerns in turn.

Consumer Price Inflation

The surge in government debt during World War II caused high rates of consumer price inflation, which the government attempted to restrain through price controls. At the beginning of the war, the phenomenal increase in government spending to manufacture war materials and to carry out the war pulled the United States out of the Great Depression and quickly led to full employment and full industrial capacity utilization. Consequently, the economy overheated and wages and prices rose. In other words, the war generated an inflationary demand shock. That wartime experience is discussed in Chapter 15.

The early months of the COVID-19 pandemic produced a set of circumstances nearly opposite to those of World War II. The countrywide lockdown prevented consumers from spending and businesses from investing. Unemployment surged to Depression Era levels. Demand collapsed. As it did, prices fell. In March 2020, consumer price inflation fell 0.3% compared with one month earlier. In April and May, CPI fell a further 0.7% and 0.1% month-on-month, respectively. During those months the United States experienced a deflationary demand shock (see Chart 20.10).

During June 2020, the relaxation of lockdowns, combined with enhanced purchasing power resulting from the $2 trillion CARES Act, which had been signed into law on March 27, brought about a rebound in spending that pushed prices 0.5% higher compared with May. From July to October 2020, price pressures moderated, as the purchasing power from the CARES Act dissipated.

A new $900 billion stimulus bill was enacted in December, followed by the American Rescue Plan Act in March, which pumped $1.9 trillion more into the economy. Enhanced purchasing power stemming from the December and March stimulus bills fueled demand during the first half of 2021, just as

CHART 20.10 Consumer Price Inflation, Monthly Percentage Change, January 2018 to June 2021

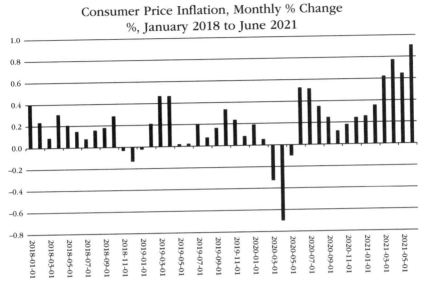

Consumer Price Inflation, Monthly % Change
%, January 2018 to June 2021

Source: Data from the Federal Reserve Bank of St. Louis

COVID-induced supply bottlenecks began to disrupt supply chains around the world, leading to shortages of many goods.

The combination of increased demand with curtailed supply pushed prices higher. Between March and June 2021 the month-on-month increase in consumer prices ranged from 0.6% and 0.9%.

By June, the year-on-year increase in CPI had risen to 5.4%, the highest since 2008. This was above the Fed's inflation target of an average of 2% over the long run. However, the high year-on-year increase in inflation was due in large part to a base effect, since prices had fallen between March and May 2020. For instance, the price level in June 2021 was only 6.0% higher than it was in June 2019, meaning that prices had risen by a significantly less worrying rate of 3.0% a year on average over those two years.

At the time of writing, it appears likely that inflationary pressures will abate during the second half of 2021 and into

2022. No further stimulus bills are expected. That suggests that demand will weaken once consumers have exhausted the relief money they received from the government during the first months of 2021.

Moreover, the supply bottlenecks that helped push prices higher during the first half of 2021 are likely to be overcome during the quarters ahead. As they are, price pressures are likely to lessen. For example, during the first half of 2021, a shortage of semiconductors disrupted the production of new cars and trucks. That led to a 40% year-on-year jump in the price of used cars and trucks during that period. That surge in used car prices accounted for nearly a third of the month-on-month rise in CPI during the second quarter of 2021.

When semiconductor supply bottlenecks are overcome and the production of new cars returns to normal, the price of used cars and trucks is very likely to fall sharply. That deflation in used car prices will offset a significant part of any remaining inflationary pressure that persists into 2022.

Therefore, with demand likely to weaken just as supply recovers, inflation should be substantially lower in 2022 than in 2021. In other words, the inflation of mid-2021 is likely to prove to be transitory, just as the Fed has said that it would be.

But what impact would a 10-year, Fed-financed, multitrillion-dollar investment program have on prices?

Assuming that a $10 trillion investment program is adopted and phased in gradually as discussed in Chapter 19, its impact on inflation would likely be modest. Even in 2031, when the investment program is at its peak, at $1.7 trillion, that would still produce only a 6.8% increase in government debt that year (under unrealistically pessimistic assumptions that ignore the positive impact that increased investment would have on tax revenues). That increase in government debt would be only 36% as large as the 18.7% jump in government debt during 2020 relative to 2019.

Assuming that the Fed created enough money to finance all of the investment program, the Fed's total assets would increase by 9.4% in 2031 compared with 2030. The consequences of that should be modest given that the Fed's total assets soared by 76% in 2020 vs. 2019.

These comparisons suggest a 10-year, $10 trillion investment program could be carried out without causing high rates of inflation.

Altogether, during the 11 years between 2020 and 2031, government debt would increase by 89% and the Fed's total assets would expand by 164%. Compare that with developments following the crisis of 2008. During the seven years between 2007 and 2014, government debt increased by 98% from $9.0 trillion to $17.8 trillion[9]; and the Fed's total assets expanded nearly five-fold, from $915 billion to $4.5 trillion. And, yet, there was no significant spike in inflation then. The Consumer Price Index peaked at just 3.9% in 2011 and then fell back below 0% in early 2015. The Core Consumer Price Index, which excludes food and energy, never rose as high as 2.4%. In fact, between the crisis of 2008 and the start of the pandemic, the Fed struggled to prevent deflation. Policymakers would have welcomed higher inflation, since the economic damage caused by deflation is far greater than the damage caused by inflation.

There was very little inflation following the crisis of 2008 because the deflationary pressures stemming from globalization outweighed the inflationary pressures that would have been expected to arise from such a large increase in government debt and such a large increase in the monetary base. This subject was discussed in greater detail in Chapter 15.

Therefore, so long as globalization survives, a jump in government debt and in the Fed's total assets resulting from a large investment program would be unlikely to cause a worrying rise in US consumer price inflation. However, as mentioned in Chapter 16, if the large-scale investment program did begin to push inflation to undesirably high levels at any time, the investment program could be slowed down until the supply bottlenecks responsible for the inflation had been overcome. Then the investment program could reaccelerate.

Asset Price Inflation and Rising Income Inequality

Asset price inflation leading to greater income inequality is probably a greater risk than the return of persistently high rates of consumer price inflation. Following the crisis of 2008, the five-fold expansion of Federal Reserve Credit, combined with very low interest rates, drove up stock prices and property prices to such an extent that household sector net worth practically doubled between 2009 and 2019. Those who owned stocks and property became much richer, while those who did not were left far behind.

The policy response to the pandemic has produced a similar outcome. The S&P 500 Index bottomed on March 23 when the Fed announced "QE Infinity." By the end of August, it had recovered all of its losses and began to set new highs. The new money that the Fed would create to finance the investment program between 2022 and 2031 is likely to continue driving asset prices higher. Should that occur, income inequality could become more extreme.

Great income inequality is undesirable because it undermines democracy. Therefore, if the investment program threatens to exacerbate it, legislative action should be brought to bear to reverse it. Significantly higher tax rates could be imposed on the highest income brackets; and capital gains exceeding $1 million, for instance, could be taxed at significantly higher rates. Inheritance taxes on estates above $50 million dollars could also be raised enough to prevent income inequality from worsening. The wealthiest Americans would have no grounds to object to paying higher taxes on the additional wealth they accumulated as the direct result of government policy, additional wealth that was entirely unconnected to any effort made on their part.

Therefore, while the surge in government debt and money creation necessitated by the urgent need to invest in the Industries of the Future may continue to push asset prices higher, the new wealth created by that investment need not be allowed to threaten democracy in America. It can be taxed, with the tax revenues being used to invest in new industries and technologies; investments that would improve the well-being of every American.

A Threat to the Dollar Standard?

There simply is no alternative to the dollar standard, nor will there be any time within the foreseeable future.

First of all, all the other major central banks in the world are creating enormous amounts of their currencies in response to the pandemic, just as the Federal Reserve is. In fact, some were doing so even before the pandemic began. The Bank of Japan was the pioneer of Quantitative Easing and it has been conducting QE for decades. As of March 31, 2021, the BOJ's assets amounted to 131% of Japan's GDP. The European Central Bank total assets amounted to 62% of the Euro Area's GDP at the end of 2020, while the People's Bank of China's total assets equaled 38% of China's GDP.

The ratio of the Fed's total assets to US GDP was 35.6% at the end of June 2021. This is likely to increase during the second half of the year due to the ongoing policy response to COVID-19. But the same is likely to be true for all the other major central banks in the world. The ratio of their total assets to GDP will rise for the same reason. So, on a relative basis, the policy response to this pandemic will leave the US dollar no less attractive than it was at the end of 2019.

Once the investment program is underway, it is more likely to strengthen the position of the dollar rather than to weaken it, given the extraordinary enhancement to the US economy that it would bring about.

The US dollar emerged as the principal international reserve currency in the aftermath of World War II because the United States had won the war and held most of the world's gold. However, the dollar has remained the principal international reserve currency during the half century since money ceased to be backed by gold because the United States' enormous annual trade deficits have flooded the world with dollars.

For example, between 2014 and 2018, China's trade surplus with the United States averaged approximately $1 billion per day.[10] Chinese companies sold their goods in the United States. They were paid in US dollars. Once China had the dollars, it had to invest them in US dollar-denominated assets, like US government securities. Consequently, China's stockpile of dollars grew by more than $1 billion a day.

China could have exchanged some of those dollars into some other currency, euros, for instance. However, whomever China bought the euros from would then have owned the dollars and they would have had to invest them in US dollar-denominated securities. Dollars are like farmland. When a farmer sells the farmland, it does not disappear. Someone else owns it. The same is true for dollars.

Therefore, the gigantic pool of dollars that currently exists in the world is going to continue to circulate around the globe for generations to come. Moreover, as long as the United States continues to have a large trade deficit every year, that stockpile will become larger and larger. And, all those dollars will have to be invested in US dollar-denominated assets if they are going to generate any investment income.

The Chinese yuan is not going to replace the dollar as the preeminent international reserve currency. There are relatively few Chinese yuan circulating in the world because China always has a very large trade surplus. It never has a trade deficit that throws yuan out into the global economy in the way that the US trade deficit throws dollars into the global economy every hour of every day. That is not going to change. Nor does the currency of any other country pose a threat to US dollar hegemony for the same reasons.

There will never be a return to a gold standard unless civilization collapses and we return to a Mad Max world in which trade can only be conducted through barter. Our civilization is built on credit. There is $84.6 trillion of US dollar-denominated credit in the United States alone as of mid-2021. That credit structure would completely collapse if anything remotely resembling a return to the gold standard were attempted. All around the world, that reality is understood by every single policymaker holding any position of influence. There is no going back to a gold standard.

As for Bitcoin, its value lies primarily in its usefulness in allowing wealthy individuals to move large sums of money around the world illegally, in the (mistaken) belief that their Bitcoin transactions are going undetected by national and international authorities. The authorities are watching; and those individuals who use Bitcoin for this purpose who lack sufficient political influence are likely to eventually be brought to account. If the Bitcoin mania were to become too widespread among the general public, it would be outlawed. No one should doubt the power of the US government to put an end to the possession and trading of Bitcoin by any American (and for that matter, by most other nationalities) anywhere in the world. The government arrests people who counterfeit money, just as it arrests Americans who don't pay their taxes, regardless of where in the world they live. Bitcoin is certainly no threat to the dollar, nor will it ever be.

Therefore, the very large expansion of US government debt and of Federal Reserve Credit that would be required to fund a multitrillion-dollar investment program would not undermine the dollar or the dollar standard.

Appendix

The Assumptions Underlying the Projections

The projections discussed in this chapter and depicted in its charts are not intended to be precise forecasts, but merely very rough estimates of possible outcomes under a specific set of assumptions. They involve far too many variables, as the future always does, to forecast with any great degree of certainty. Nevertheless, it is hoped that they are useful in enabling the reader to imagine how the Fed's total assets, the composition of the Fed's balance sheet and the ratio of Bank Reserves to customer deposits could evolve in the scenario outlined in this chapter, in order to demonstrate how the proposed investment program could be financed by the Fed at no cost to US taxpayers.

The following paragraphs discuss the most important assumptions that have been incorporated into these projections.

First, it is assumed that the Fed's total assets would increase by $12.1 trillion between 2020 and 2031 for the reasons described above.

Next, Chart 20.8, which projects the evolution of the four major items on the Fed's balance sheet out to 2031, requires assumptions concerning the kind of assets the Fed would acquire and, most importantly, how much currency would expand each year out to 2031.

Regarding the assets the Fed would acquire, during the second half of 2021 and until Quantitative Easing ends in late 2022, it is assumed that the Fed would continue to acquire twice as many Treasury securities as mortgage-backed securities, as it has been doing since the second quarter of 2020. From 2023 to 2031, it is assumed the Fed would acquire only Treasury bonds. That would take the Fed's holdings for Treasury securities up from $4.7 trillion in 2020 to $16.1 trillion in 2031, an increase of $11.4 trillion. Meanwhile, the Fed's holdings of agency and GSE-backed securities would increase from $2.0 trillion in 2020 to $2.8 trillion in 2022 (an increase of $720 billion over two years), from which point they would remain stable out to 2031. Adding the Fed's holdings of Treasury securities together with its holdings of agency and GSE-backed securities, the Fed's total assets would increase by $12.1 trillion, from $7.4 trillion in 2020 to $19.5 trillion in 2031. Since money is fungible, it does not matter that part ($720 billion) of the $12.1 trillion the Fed would create would be used to buy agency and GSE-backed securities instead of all $12.1 trillion being used to buy Treasury securities, because the $720 billion that would be spent to acquire the agency and GSE-backed securities would still find its way into Treasury securities.

The more consequential question is: How much would currency in circulation expand between 2020 and 2031? That question is more important for this inquiry because, as currency expands, it absorbs Bank Reserves. We are interested in how large Bank Reserves will become because, under the Fed's current process for controlling the federal funds rate, the Fed must pay interest on Bank Reserves. Therefore, the growth in currency affects the quantity of Bank Reserves and the quantity of Bank Reserves affects the size of the Fed's profits and, therefore, the Fed's remittances to the Treasury.

Between 1971 and 2019, US currency in circulation expanded by 7.5% a year on average. However, during the extraordinary circumstances surrounding the COVID-19 pandemic, currency expanded by 16% during 2020. The large increase in currency outstanding during this period seems to have been caused both by the large increase in the amount of dollars created by the Fed and by the public's desire to hold more cash during this period of crisis and uncertainty. It is very difficult to estimate with any degree of certainty what the demand for cash will be going forward. Here, in light of the extraordinary amount of money the Fed is expected to create by 2031 in this scenario, it is assumed that currency in circulation will expand by 10% every year between 2021 and 2031.

In that case, currency in circulation would reach $5.8 trillion in 2031, an increase of $3.8 from 2020. The increase in currency would absorb Bank Reserves as it expands. Therefore, Bank Reserves would not grow exactly in line with the $12.1 trillion increase in the Fed's total assets (even though the Fed would deposit money into the banks' reserve accounts at the Fed when it acquires the additional Treasury securities and agency and GSE-backed securities). Instead, Bank Reserves would expand by $8.3 trillion (i.e., $12.1 trillion less the $3.8 trillion expansion of currency in circulation).

Finally, Chart 20.9, which projects the ratio of Bank Reserves to bank customers' deposits, requires one additional assumption concerning the annual growth rate of customer deposits at banks.

Between 1971 and 2019, deposits by the banks' customers increased by an average of 6.7% a year. However, during 2020, they jumped by 21.4% compared with the end of 2019. This 2020 surge in deposits resulted from the stimulus associated

with a $4.5 trillion increase in government debt that year,[11] com-
bined with money creation of $3.2 trillion by the Fed. Again, it is
very difficult to project with any degree of certainty the annual
growth rate of deposits out to 2031. However, given the large
increase in government borrowing and the large increase in the
amount of money that the Fed would create in this scenario,
here it has been assumed that deposits will increase by an average annual rate of 10% a year between 2021 and 2031.

One of the main purposes of making all the projections discussed above is to estimate how high the required reserve ratio
would have to be raised in order to make Bank Reserves scarce
enough so that the Fed would no longer have to pay interest
on Bank Reserves to control the federal funds rate – even after
the Fed created an extraordinary amount of Bank Reserves as it
acquired government bonds to finance the proposed $10 trillion
investment program.

A large number of variables and an even larger number of
assumptions concerning those variables are involved in reaching the projections shown in Chart 20.9. For instance, if the Fed
creates less than $12.1 trillion, all the variables discussed here
would change. If currency grows by less than 10% a year, then
the level of Bank Reserves and the ratio of Bank Reserves to
deposits would both be higher than projected. Similarly, if customer deposits grow by less than 10% a year, then the ratio of
Bank Reserves to deposits would be higher than projected.

However, none of these uncertainties undermines the main
argument being presented here. No matter how high the ratio of
Bank Reserves to customer deposits climbs, the required reserve
ratio could be increased to **WHATEVER LEVEL IS REQUIRED**
to absorb **ALL** excess Bank Reserves until Bank Reserves are
once again made scarce, thereby allowing the Fed to control the
federal funds rate without paying interest on Bank Reserves, just
as it did up until 2008.

Raising the required reserve ratio to that requisite level
would enable the Fed to avoid paying interest on Bank Reserves,
making it possible for the Fed to create money and finance the
entire cost of the proposed investment program in a way that
would cost US taxpayers nothing whatsoever.

Notes

1. Stephanie Kelton, *The Deficit Myth*, p. 207. PublicAffairs, New York, 2021

2. Apple's 2020 Form 10-Filing, p. 19 United States Securities and Exchange Commission. https://s2.q4cdn.com/470004039/files/doc_financials/2020/ar/_10-K-2020-(As-Filed).pdf

3. The Treasury Department ultimately reaps the benefits of seigniorage because the Fed pays the Treasury all the profits it earns through this process.

4. Reverse repos and deposits in the Treasury's General Account at the Fed are not shown in these charts.

5. Technically, the Eurosystem's total assets to Euro Area GDP.

6. Weekly Financial Statements of the Eurosystem, European Central Bank, reproduced by St. Louis Fed. https://fred.stlouisfed.org/series/ECBASSETSW#0

7. The key assumption here involves the growth rate of the banks' customer deposits. The assumptions behind these projections are also discussed in the appendix to this chapter.

8. 1936 Annual Report of the Board of Governors of the Federal Reserve System, p. 11.

9. Office of Management and Budget, Historical Tables. Table 7.1 – Federal Debt at the End of Year: 1940–2026, The White House. https://www.whitehouse.gov/omb/historical-tables/

10. US Trade in Goods by Country US Census Bureau, Foreign Trade. https://www.census.gov/foreign-trade/balance/c5700.html

11. Debt to the Penny, TreasuryDirect. https://treasurydirect.gov/govt/reports/pd/debttothepenny.htm

CHAPTER 21

An Investment Revolution

I believe this nation should commit itself to achieving the goal, before the decade is out, of landing a man on the moon and returning him safely to Earth.

President John F. Kennedy[1]

Introduction

A century and a half ago, Jules Verne published *Twenty Thousand Leagues Under the Sea, From the Earth to the Moon,* and *Around the World in 80 Days*. At the time, submarines and space travel were considered to be wild fancies of the imagination, while a trip around the world in only 80 days was seen as an extremely unlikely bet. Fifty years later submarines were commonplace. One hundred years later men walked on the moon. Today, a trip around the world in 80 *hours* can be easily arranged by any travel agent.

Science fiction has become reality. The lesson to be drawn from this – and, more generally, from the extraordinarily rapid technological advances during the past 250 years – is that what the human imagination can envision, human ingenuity can accomplish.

The Money Revolution described throughout this book makes possible a multitrillion-dollar, government-financed Investment Revolution that would make today's science fiction real. Before us lies the opportunity to cure all the diseases, radically expand life expectancy, develop cheap and limitless clean energy, rehabilitate the environment, and solve many of the other most intractable challenges confronting humanity.

Insufficient imagination, rather than insufficient funding, is the greatest impediment to carrying out an investment program large enough to achieve these objectives.

This chapter sets out to overcome that impediment by comparing the amounts the US government invests in research and development (R&D) now with the amounts that it could afford to invest; and by emphasizing what could be accomplished if the government invested as much in R&D as it could afford to do. It begins by taking a closer look at how – and how much – the US government currently invests in R&D. It then presents estimates of how much more lavishly those initiatives could be funded if the government took full advantage of the Money Revolution to invest on a much more aggressive scale.

There is no need to wait generations for our dreams of a healthier and more prosperous future to become reality. We have the means to make those dreams come true in our lifetime. Money is no object. We must recognize that fact and invest accordingly.

Government Investment in R&D

During 2018, the US government invested $136 billion in R&D through various departments and agencies, as mentioned in Chapter 18. Here, it is worth pausing to consider that the Federal Reserve is currently creating nearly that much money every month. It creates $120 billion a month through its asset purchase program. This shows how easy it would be for the government to finance R&D investment on a very much larger scale, simply by having the Fed create more money to finance the investment.

TABLE 21.1 Federal R&D Funding by Agency: FY2019, Top Five

Federal R&D Funding by Agency: FY2019	
	US$ Millions
Department of Defense	55,832
Department of Health and Human Services	38,647
Department of Energy	17,793
NASA	15,287
National Science Foundation	6,520

Source: Data from the Congressional Research Service

The FY2019 R&D budgets for all the federal agencies are not yet available at the time of writing. However, those for the five most well-funded agencies, which accounted for 92% of the total in FY2018, have been made public. They are show in Table 21.1.

They are the Department of Defense ($55.8 billion), the Department of Health and Human Services ($38.6 billion), the Department of Energy ($17.8 billion), NASA ($15.3 billion), and the National Science Foundation ($6.5 billion).[2]

The following paragraphs will describe the types of R&D investments each of those agencies undertakes.

Department of Defense

The Department of Defense (DOD) receives the largest allocation of government R&D funding among all government agencies, 38% of the total in FY2018. The DOD's mission is to provide the military forces needed to deter war and ensure our nation's security. Its R&D funding supports the development of the nation's future military hardware and software and the science and technology base upon which those products rely.

Within the DOD, the Defense Advanced Research Projects Agency, or DARPA, is of particular interest. It was established as part of the United States' response to the Soviet Union's launch of Sputnik in 1957. Its mission is to make pivotal investments in breakthrough technologies for national security.

Since then, DARPA has produced remarkable results. Its website states:

For sixty years, DARPA has held to a singular and enduring mission: to make pivotal investments in breakthrough technologies for national security. DARPA has repeatedly delivered on that mission, transforming revolutionary concepts and even seeming impossibilities into practical capabilities. The ultimate results have included not only game-changing military capabilities such as precision weapons and stealth technology, but also such icons of modern civilian society such as the Internet, automated voice recognition and language translation, and Global Positioning System receivers small enough to embed in myriad consumer devices. DARPA explicitly reaches for transformational change instead of incremental advances.[3]

DARPA received $3.4 billion in funding for FY2019.[4]

The National Institutes of Health

The Department of Health and Human Services (HHS) receives the second largest allocation of government R&D funding after the Department of Defense. It received 27% of the total in FY2018.

The National Institutes of Health (NIH) is part of HHS and receives 97% of the total HHS R&D funding.

The National Institutes of Health is the primary agency of the federal government charged with performing and supporting biomedical and behavioral research. It also has major roles in training biomedical researchers and disseminating health information. The NIH mission is "to seek fundamental knowledge about the nature and behavior of living systems and the application of that knowledge to enhance health, lengthen life, and reduce illness and disability."[5]

Table 21.2 shows the NIH received $36 billion in R&D funding in FY2019. The table also shows how that funding was distributed between NIH institutions and centers.[6]

TABLE 21.2 National Institutes of Health Funding: FY2019

National Institutes of Health Funding FY2019	
	US\$ Millions
National Cancer Institute	6,144
Allergy/Infectious Diseases	5,523
Heart, Lung, and Blood Institute	3,488
National Institute on Aging	3,083
Neurological Disorders/Stroke	2,274
Diabetes/Digestive/Kidney	2,030
National Institute of Mental Health	1,870
General Medical Sciences	1,726
Child Health/Human Development	1,506
National Institute on Drug Abuse	1,420
Human Genome Research Institute	576
Biomedical Imaging/Bioengineering	389
The Other 18 Institutes/Centers	5,985
Total	36,014

Source: Data from the Congressional Research Service

Since NIH is the primary federal agency charged with enhancing health and lengthening life, it is useful to compare the funding it receives for particular purposes against the leading causes of death in the United States, which are shown in Table 21.3.[7]

■ Heart Disease killed 667,457 Americans in 2017, accounting for 23.5% of all deaths in the United States that year. The Heart, Lung, and Blood Institute received \$3.5 billion in R&D funding in FY2019.

■ Cancer killed 599,108 Americans in 2017 (21.3% of all US deaths). The National Cancer Institute received \$6.1 billion in R&D funding in 2019. Note that the Fed is currently creating \$120 billion a month. Therefore, with just two weeks of funding from Quantitative Easing (QE), the National Cancer Institute's annual R&D budget could be increased by a factor of 10.

TABLE 21.3 The Leading Causes of Death in the United States in 2017

The Leading Causes of Death in the United States in 2017

	Deaths in 2017	% of Total Deaths
Heart Disease	667,457	23.5%
Cancer	599,108	21.3%
Unintentional Injuries	169,936	6.0%
Chronic Lower Respiratory Disease	160,201	5.7%
Stroke & Cerebrovascular Disease	146,383	5.2%
Alzheimer's Disease	121,404	4.3%
Diabetes	83,564	3.0%
Influenza & Pneumonia	55,672	2.0%
Kidney Disease	50,633	1.8%
Suicide	47,173	1.7%

Source: Data from the Medical News Today

- Alzheimer's Disease killed 121,404 Americans (4.3% of all US deaths) and debilitated hundreds of thousands more. The National Institute on Aging received $3.1 billion in R&D funding.
- Diabetes killed 83,564 Americans and Kidney Disease killed 50,633 more, together accounting for 4.8% of all US deaths. The National Institute of Diabetes and Digestive and Kidney Diseases received $2 billion of R&D funding.

In light of the opportunities opened up by the Money Revolution described in the first two parts of this book, the questions we need to ask in relation to the NIH's budget are

1. How many lives could be saved every year if the government invested much more in R&D funding for NIH; and
2. How much money would it take *to permanently eradicate* all these diseases?

The Department of Energy

The Department of Energy (DOE) received the third largest share, 13%, of the government's R&D funding in FY2018.

The "DOE conducts basic scientific research in fields ranging from nuclear physics to the biological and environmental sciences; basic and applied R&D relating to energy production and use; and R&D on nuclear weapons, nuclear nonproliferation, and defense nuclear reactors."[8]

The DOE's mission is to "ensure America's security and prosperity by addressing its energy, environmental and nuclear challenges through transformative science and technology solutions."[9] Its activities are classified under three broad categories, Science, National Security and Energy, each with a number of subcategories. Table 21.4 provides a breakdown of how the DOE's funding is allocated.

Among the subcategories, basic energy sciences receives the most R&D funding, at $2.2 billion; followed by energy efficiency and renewable energy ($2.1 billion); and weapons activities: research, development, test and evaluation ($2.0 billion). Other areas of particular interest include nuclear energy ($1.3 billion); high energy physics ($980 million); advanced scientific computing research ($936 million); nuclear physics ($690 million); and fusion energy sciences ($564 million).

NASA

The National Aeronautics and Space Administration (NASA) was created in 1958, after the Soviet Union successfully sent Sputnik, the first man-made satellite, into orbit in 1957. By 1969, NASA had landed a man on the moon.

Today:

> *NASA has research programs in planetary science, Earth science, heliophysics, astrophysics, and aeronautics, as well as development programs for future human spacecraft and for multipurpose space technology such as advanced propulsion systems. In addition, NASA operates the International Space Station as a facility for R&D and other purposes.*[10]

NASA was the recipient of the fourth largest share of government R&D funding in FY2018. It received 9% of the total.

TABLE 21.4 Department of Energy R&D, FY2019

Department Of Energy R&D US$ Millions	
	US$ Millions
Science	6,585
Basic Energy Sciences	2,166
High Energy Physics	980
Biological & Environmental Research	705
Nuclear Physics	690
Advanced Scientific Computing Research	936
Fusion Energy Sciences	564
Other	545
National Security	4,406
Weapons Activities	2,014
Naval Reactors	1,789
Defense Nuclear Nonproliferation R&D	576
Defense Environmental Cleanup Technol. Devel.	28
Energy	4,721
Energy Efficiency & Renewable Energy	2,067
Fossil Energy R&D	740
Nuclear Energy	1,326
Electricity Delivery R&D	132
Cyber Energy Security	9
Advanced Research Projects	366
Total	15,712

Source: Data from the Congressional Research Service

Table 21.5 shows how its $15.3 billion FY2019 budget was distributed between R&D work for Science, Aeronautics, Space Technology, Deep Space Exploration Systems, and Spaceflight Operations, including funding for the International Space Station.

National Science Foundation

The National Science Foundation received the fifth largest share of government R&D funding in FY2018, with 5% of the total.

TABLE 21.5 National Aeronautics and Space Administration R&D, FY2019

National Aeronautics and Space Administration R&D, US$ Millions	
NASA	
	US$ Millions
Science	6,906
Earth Science	1,931
Planetary Science	2,759
Astrophysics	1,192
The James Webb Space Telescope	305
Heliophysics	720
Aeronautics	725
Space Technology	927
Deep Space Exploration Systems	5,051
Spaceflight Operations	1,678
R&D Total	15,287

Source: Data from the Congressional Research Service

The National Science Foundation (NSF) supports basic research and education in the nonmedical sciences and engineering. Congress established the foundation as an independent federal agency in 1950 and directed it to "promote the progress of science; to advance the national health, prosperity, and welfare; to secure the national defense; and for other purposes." The NSF is a primary source of federal support for U.S. university research, especially in mathematics and computer science. It is also responsible for significant shares of the federal science, technology, engineering, and mathematics (STEM) education program portfolio and federal STEM student aid and support.[11]

Table 21.6 shows how the NSF's $8.1 billion of R&D funding was deployed.

TABLE 21.6 National Science Foundation Funding, FY2019

National Science Foundation Funding, US$ Millions	
	US$ Millions
Research & Related Activities	6,520
Education & Human Resources	910
Major Research Equipment & Facilities Construction	296
Agency Operations & Award Management	330
National Science Board	4
Office of the Inspector General	15
Total	8,075

Source: Data from the Congressional Research Service

Working Miracles

A great deal of important research and development work is being done in the United States, as Chapter 18 and the preceding paragraphs have shown. But we must ask ourselves, a great deal relative to what? As we have seen, the United States is not investing "a great deal" relative to China. China overtook the United States in R&D investment in 2019 and, if current trends continue, will vastly outspend the United States on R&D within a matter of only a few years.

Nor is the United States investing a great deal in R&D relative to what it has invested in the past. Federal government investment in R&D peaked a decade ago. The level of its investment was 10% less in 2018 than it was in 2010.

Most importantly, the United States is certainly not investing as much in research and development as it could afford to do. The preceding two chapters have demonstrated that the US government could easily finance an additional $10 trillion investment in R&D over the next decade.

Therefore, here, let's consider what an additional $10 trillion investment would look like between now and 2031 in comparison with the level of R&D investment that would result if federal government R&D investment remains flat for another decade.

In FY2018, the federal government invested $136 billion in R&D through its various departments and agencies. If we assume that level of investment will remain flat for the next 10 years, then government investment in R&D would total $1.36 trillion between 2022 and 2031.

An additional $10 trillion investment would mean the US government would invest $11.36 trillion over the next 10 years rather than $1.36 trillion. That would represent an increase of 735%. That amount of investment would ensure that the United States retained its position as the world's most powerful nation.

In 2017, the growth rate of Chinese R&D investment was more than 50% larger than that of the United States. If that trend continues, then China will invest 44% more in R&D than the United States by 2031. Should that occur, the United States' technological lead would be lost to China – probably forever – in which case the United States would no longer be the master of its own destiny.

However, were the US government to invest an additional $10 trillion in R&D over the next decade, in line with the investment schedule presented in Chapter 19, then the United States would greatly outspend China on R&D, just as it outspent the Soviet Union following Sputnik. In that scenario, the United States would invest two-thirds more than China in R&D in 2031, rather than nearly one-third less. Chart 21.1 illustrates the large lead the United States would have over China in R&D investment if the US implements that investment program. An investment gap of that magnitude would guarantee US national security for generations.

Applying a 735% increase in investment to the R&D budget of each of the federal agencies would mean the Department of Defense would invest $4.7 trillion in R&D over the next decade rather than $558 billion as it would if its level of investment remained flat at the FY2019 level each year. The R&D budget for the Department of Health and Human Services, 97% of which would be allocated to NIH, would be $3.2 trillion rather than $386 billion. The Department of Energy would have $1.5 trillion of R&D funding rather than $178 billion. NASA would invest $1.3

CHART 21.1 Gross Domestic Expenditure on R&D: the US vs. China, 2000 to 2031 est.

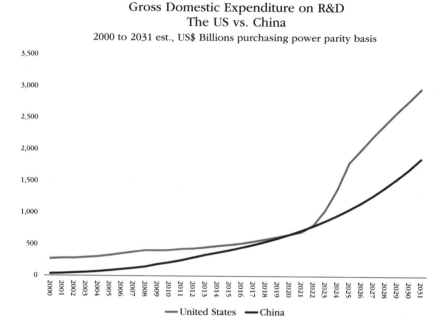

Gross Domestic Expenditure on R&D
The US vs. China
2000 to 2031 est., US$ Billions purchasing power parity basis

━━United States ━━China

Source: Based on data from the National Science Foundation, incorporating the author's projections to 2031.

trillion instead of $153 billion. And the National Science Foundation would have $545 billion to invest, rather than $65 billion. See Table 21.7.[12]

Likewise, a 735% increase in the R&D funding available to the National Institutes of Health would provide the NIH with $3 trillion over the decade instead of $360 billion if funding were to remain flat. The National Cancer Institute would have more than half a trillion dollars to invest to cure cancer rather than only $61 billion. The Heart, Lung, and Blood Institute's R&D funding would jump to nearly $300 billion, rather than just $35 billion. The National Institute on Aging would be allocated $257 billion with which to attempt to cure Alzheimer's Disease instead of $31 billion. And the Diabetes, Digestive, and Kidney Institutes would have $170 billion in R&D funding rather than $20 billion. See Table 21.8.

TABLE 21.7 Federal R&D Funding by Agency: With and Without a $10 Trillion Investment Program

Federal R&D Funding by Agency:			
With and Without a $10 Trillion Investment Program, US$ Millions			
			10 Year Budget
	FY2019	Flat	Plus $10 trillion
Total*	136,000	1,360,000	11,360,000
Department of Defense	55,832	558,320	4,663,614
Department of Health and Human Services	38,647	386,470	3,228,161
Department of Energy	17,793	177,930	1,486,239
NASA	15,287	152,870	1,276,914
National Science Foundation	6,520	65,200	544,612

*The Total for FY2019 assumes no change from FY2018
Source: Data from the Congressional Research Service, incorporating the author's assumptions.

TABLE 21.8 National Institutes of Health Funding, Selected Institutes, With and Without a $10 Trillion Investment Program

National Institutes of Health Funding, Selected Institutes			
With and Without a $10 Trillion Investment Program, US$ Millions			
			10 Year Budget
	FY2019	Flat	Plus $10 Trillion
Total NIH	36,014	360,140	3,008,228
National Cancer Institute	6,144	61,440	513,205
Heart, Lung, and Blood Institute	3,488	34,880	291,351
National Institute on Aging	3,083	30,830	257,521
Diabetes/Digestive/Kidney	2,030	20,300	169,565

Source: Data from the Congressional Research Service, incorporating the author's assumptions.

The preceding paragraphs have assumed that the $10 trillion in additional funding would be allocated so that each department or agency would receive a 735% increase in R&D funding, in line with the increase in total funding. Of course, that need not be the case. For instance, perhaps it would be appropriate to increase the R&D budget of the National Institutes of Health by 15 times rather than by 8.4 times, taking the additional NIH funding from part of the new R&D funding that would have been allocated to the Department of Defense, which, in that case, would still see its R&D funding quadruple in comparison with what it would receive if its funding remained flat at the FY2019 level.

In that scenario, NIH would have $5.4 trillion to invest in R&D over the decade. The National Cancer Institute's 10-year R&D budget would be $922 billion; that of the Heart, Lung, and Blood Institute, $523 billion; and that of the National Institute on Aging, $462 billion. Would that amount of R&D investment suffice to cure cancer, heart disease, Alzheimer's and all the other diseases? It just might. If not, then double it. As we approach the second quarter of the twenty-first century, the United States has the financial resources to work miracles.

America's New Manifest Destiny

Just as Jules Verne's works of science fiction foretold the future, the dreams of the visionaries of our time are very likely to become reality during the decades ahead.

Elon Musk, CEO of SpaceX and Tesla, intends to make us "a multi-planet species" and is building rockets that he believes will enable humans to begin colonizing Mars during this decade.

Aubrey de Grey, chief science officer of the SENS Research Foundation and the editor-in-chief of the journal *Rejuvenation Research*, is working to slow aging to the point where people will live youthful, healthy lives for hundreds of years.

Ray Kurzweil, renowned futurist, author, and inventor, whom Forbes Inc. called the "the rightful heir to Thomas Edison," has written that, by 2040, people will have the option to "live forever."

Google has hinted at plans to "cure death."

Yuval Noah Harari, bestselling author of *Sapiens*[13] and *Homo Deus*,[14] believes that it is humanity's inevitable destiny to strive for immortality, and, even, happiness.

This book has argued that it is imperative for the United States to invest in research and development on a much larger scale for reasons of national security. However, beyond and above the national security rationale, there is a moral imperative for investing much more, as well.

The Money Revolution of the last century gives the United States the power to induce a technological revolution that would vastly enhance human well-being.

We must make the most of this opportunity. We can explore the universe and embed life, including human life, on other planets. At the same time, we can eliminate all the pollution from our own planet to ensure that it continues to be capable of sustaining life here.

We can use quantum computing and artificial intelligence to find out what is really going on around us at the subatomic level, in the stellar realm and within our own minds; and to illuminate dark matter and discover new dimensions.

We can cure all the diseases and stop aging, at which point we will have a great deal more time to work on reversing aging and even "curing" death.

All these things are within our grasp.

The United States must make the most of the Money Revolution by carrying out an investment and technological revolution that will turn these twenty-first century dreams into twenty-first century realities.

Here is America's new Manifest Destiny.

Notes

1. John F. Kennedy in special State of the Union message on May 25, 1961.
2. Federal Research and Development (R&D) Funding: FY 2020, Congressional Research Service https://fas.org/sgp/crs/misc/R45715.pdf
3. About DARPA, DARPA's website: https://www.darpa.mil/about-us/about-darpa
4. Budget, DARPA's website: https://www.darpa.mil/about-us/budget
5. "About NIH, What We Do, Mission and Goals," National Institutes of Health. http://www.nih.gov/about-nih/what-we-do/mission-goals
6. Federal Research and Development (R&D) Funding: FY 2020, Congressional Research Service https://fas.org/sgp/crs/misc/R45715.pdf
7. "What are the leading causes of death in the US?" Medical News Today. https://www.medicalnewstoday.com/articles/282929.php
8. Federal Research and Development (R&D) Funding: FY 2020, Congressional Research Service. https://fas.org/sgp/crs/misc/R45715.pdf
9. Mission, Department of Energy. https://www.energy.gov/mission
10. Federal Research and Development (R&D) Funding: FY 2020, Congressional Research Service https://fas.org/sgp/crs/misc/R45715.pdf
11. Federal Research and Development (R&D) Funding: FY 2020, Congressional Research Service. https://fas.org/sgp/crs/misc/R45715.pdf
12. These paragraphs which discuss "applying a 735% increase in investment to the R&D budget of each of the federal agencies" are simply intended to illustrate how dramatically a $10 trillion investment program would increase the United States' R&D efforts. They are not intended to suggest that these government agencies should be put in charge of making all the new investments. As discussed in Chapter 16, the best approach would probably involve a combination of entirely government-directed investment programs and public-private joint ventures.
13. Yuval Noah Harari (2015), *Sapiens: A Brief History of Humankind*. Harper.
14. Yuval Noah Harari (2017), *Homo Deus: A Brief History of Tomorrow*. Harper.

Conclusion

The brilliant economist, Joseph Schumpeter, taught that economic growth is driven by waves of innovation, such as the railroad boom of the mid-nineteenth century, and later the development of the chemicals industry, electricity, and automobiles.

The breakdown of the Bretton Woods international monetary system in 1971 set off another similarly transformative innovation; this time an innovation in the way our economic system functions, one that has removed all limits on the amount of credit that can be created, while simultaneously eliminating the labor and industrial capacity bottlenecks that, in the past, had resulted in high rates of inflation when credit expanded rapidly.

With the collapse of Bretton Woods, an international monetary system that had constrained how much credit could be created was suddenly replaced by a system that permits limitless credit creation. At the same time, an international trading system that had comprised dozens of relatively closed national economies, each compelled to prevent persistent trade imbalances, was replaced by a new system, globalization, that encompasses the entire world and in which labor and industrial capacity are excessive, rather than scarce.

This new monetary system, operating within a new international trading order, has been the most powerful Schumpeterian innovation of our age. It vastly expands the resources at humanity's disposal. With money no longer backed by gold, there are no longer any limits on how much credit central banks and commercial banks can create. At the same time, the labor and industrial constraints that had caused inflation and held economic growth in check simply no longer exist.

The financial and economic fetters that had long restrained us are no longer binding. We are living in a new, much larger economic environment, which presents us with the possibility to accomplish much more than had ever been possible before.

The only impediment left to overcome is insufficient imagination. Policymakers are captive to outdated economic theories that most of them never really understood in the first place. The best of those theories were appropriate for the age when they were developed, but not for our age. This is not the early twentieth-century world of Ludwig von Mises, when gold reserves limited how much credit could be created. Nor is it Milton Friedman's 1960s, when the size of the US workforce and the depth of industrial capacity within the United States dictated how much the US government could spend without setting off an inflationary firestorm.

This is the twenty-first century. It presents opportunities that did not exist in the past. We must recognize those opportunities, grasp them, and extract every last benefit from them as quickly as we can and for as long as we can. If we do, we will greatly improve our lives and our children's lives. Then, our children's children will recall hearing of diseases like cancer and Alzheimer's the way we only remember hearing of diseases like smallpox and cholera; and they will live in a clean and sustainable environment, never knowing the stench of gasoline.

A multitrillion-dollar investment program targeting new industries and technologies is certain to yield miracles. There is nothing to stop the United States from making that investment. We are like fish in a fishbowl that has been dropped into the ocean. All we have to do is realize that the walls that had long confined us no longer do – and swim out the top. There, a new world of superabundance awaits.

About the Author

Since beginning his career as an equities analyst in Hong Kong in 1986, Richard Duncan has served as global head of investment strategy at ABN AMRO Asset Management in London, worked as a financial sector specialist for the World Bank in Washington D.C., and headed equity research departments for James Capel Securities and Salomon Brothers in Bangkok. He also worked as a consultant for the IMF in Thailand during the Asia Crisis.

Richard is now the publisher of Macro Watch, a biweekly video-newsletter he launched in 2013. To learn more about Macro Watch, visit his website:

http://www.richardduncaneconomics.com/

Also by Richard Duncan:

The Dollar Crisis: Causes, Consequences, Cures

The Corruption of Capitalism: A Strategy To Rebalance The Global Economy And Restore Sustainable Growth

The New Depression: The Breakdown Of The Paper Money Economy

Bibliography

Books

Walter Bagehot. *Lombard Street: A Description of The Money Market.* Henry S. King & Co. London; 1873

Barry Eichengreen. *Golden Fetters: The Gold Standard and the Great Depression.* Oxford University Press; 1992

Milton Friedman and Anna Jacobson Schwartz, *A Monetary History of the United States, 1867–1960.* First Edition. Princeton University Press; November 21, 1963

Milton Friedman, *Money Mischief: Episodes in Monetary History.* Mariner Books; March 31, 1994

Irving Fisher. *100% Money.* 1935. http://fisher-100money.blogspot.com

The Financial Crisis Inquiry Report. Submitted by THE FINANCIAL CRISIS INQUIRY COMMISSION, Pursuant to Public Law 111-21 January 2011. https://www.govinfo.gov/content/pkg/GPO-FCIC/pdf/GPO-FCIC.pdf

Yuval Noah Harari. *Sapiens: A Brief History of Humankind.* Hardcover – Illustrated, Harper; February 10, 2015

Yuval Noah Harari. *Homo Deus: A Brief History of Tomorrow.* Hardcover – Illustrated, Harper; February 21, 2017

Ray Kurzweil. *The Singularity Is Near: When Humans Transcend Biology.* The Viking Press; September 22, 2005

Allan H. Meltzer. *A History of the Federal Reserve.* University of Chicago Press.
Volume 1: 1913–1951. (2004)
Volume 2, Book 1: 1951–1969. (2014)
Volume 2, Book 2: 1970–1986. (2014)

Mariana Mazzucato. *The Entrepreneurial State: Debunking Public vs. Private Sector Myths.* Revised edition. PublicAffairs; October 27, 2015

Stephanie Kelton. *The Deficit Myth: Modern Monetary Theory and the Birth of the People's Economy*. Illustrated edition. PublicAffairs; June 9, 2020

Joseph Schumpeter. *Business Cycles: A Theoretical, Historical, and Statistical Analysis of the Capitalist Process [Volumes One and Two]*. First Edition 1939. Reprinted Martino Fine Books; January 25, 2017

Federal Reserve System: Purposes and Functions series, 1939–2016. Board of Governors of the Federal Reserve System. Ten editions: 1939, 1947, 1954, 1961, 1963, 1974, 1984, 1994, 2005, 2016. See the Fiftieth Anniversary Edition, 1963. https://fraser.stlouisfed.org/series/federal-reserve-system-4526

Acts of Congress

The Federal Reserve Act of 1913. FRASER. Federal Reserve Archival System for Economic Research. Federal Reserve Bank of St. Louis. https://fraser.stlouisfed.org/title/federal-reserve-act-975

The Gold Reserve Act of 1934. FRASER. https://fraser.stlouisfed.org/scribd/?title_id=777&filepath=/files/docs/meltzer/sengol34.pdf

The Employment Act Of 1946. FRASER. https://fraser.stlouisfed.org/files/docs/historical/trumanlibrary/srf_014_002_0002.pdf

Papers

"The Federal Reserve System's Weekly Balance Sheet Since 1914". Cecilia Bao, Justin Chen, Nicholas Fries, Andrew Gibson, Emma Paine, and Kurt Schuler. 2018. Johns Hopkins University, Institute for Applied Economics, Global Health, and the Study of Business Enterprise, Studies in Applied Economics & Center for Financial Stability (working paper series), No. 115, July. https://sites.krieger.jhu.edu/iae/files/2018/07/Federal-Reserve-Systems-Weekly-Balance-Sheet-Since-1914.pdf ; and accompanying spreadsheet via: https://sites.krieger.jhu.edu/iae/working-papers/studies-in-applied-economics/

"How Currency Gets into Circulation". The Federal Reserve Bank of New York, https://www.newyorkfed.org/aboutthefed/fedpoint/fed01.html

"Reserve Requirements: History, Current Practice, and Potential Reform". Federal Reserve Bulletin, June 1993. Board of Governors of the Federal Reserve System. https://www.federalreserve.gov/monetarypolicy/0693lead.pdf

"Why Are Banks Holding So Many Excess Reserves?" Todd Keister and James J. McAndrews. Federal Reserve Bank Of New York. Current Issues in Economics and Finance. Volume 15, Number 8. December 2009. https://www.newyorkfed.org/medialibrary/media/research/current_issues/ci15-8.pdf

"Monetary Policy 101: A Primer on the Fed's Changing Approach to Policy Implementation". Jane E. Ihrig, Ellen E. Meade, and Gretchen C. Weinbach (2015). Finance and Economics Discussion Series 2015–047. Washington: Board of Governors of the Federal Reserve System, http://dx.doi.org/10.17016/FEDS.2015.047

"How Does the Fed Adjust Its Securities Holdings and Who Is Affected?" Ihrig, Jane E. and Mize, Lawrence and Weinbach, Gretchen Cope. Board of Governors of the Federal Reserve System Finance and Economics Discussion Series. (September 2017). FEDS Working Paper No. 2017-99, Available at SSRN: https://ssrn.com/abstract=3042513 or http://dx.doi.org/10.17016/FEDS.2017.099

"The International Gold Standard and U.S. Monetary Policy from World War I to the New Deal". Leland Crabbe. The Federal Reserve Bulletin, June 1989. https://fraser.stlouisfed.org/files/docs/meltzer/craint89.pdf

"Reserve Requirements". Board of Governors of the Federal Reserve System https://www.federalreserve.gov/monetarypolicy/reservereq.htm

"Science, The Endless Frontier: A Report to the President" by Vannevar Bush, Director of the Office of Scientific Research and Development, July 1945. https://www.nsf.gov/about/history/nsf50/vbush1945.jsp

National Institutes of Health. "What We Do". https://www.nih.gov/about-nih/what-we-do

US Monetary Policy and Financial Markets, Ann-Marie Meulendyke, Federal Reserve Bank of New York, 1998, p. 38 https://files.stlouisfed.org/files/htdocs/aggreg/meulendyke.pdf

The Carnegie Endowment For International Peace. "Competing With China on Technology and Innovation", October 2019. https://carnegieendowment.org/2019/10/10/competing-with-china-on-technology-and-innovation-pub-80010

Other Sources

Federal Reserve Bulletin. The Board of Governors of the Federal Reserve System. https://www.federalreserve.gov/publications/bulletin.htm

The Board of Governors of the Federal Reserve System, Annual Reports, 1914 to 2020. (Note: The Federal Reserve Board, Annual Reports, 1914 to 1934.) FRASER https://fraser.stlouisfed.org/title/annual-report-board-governors-federal-reserve-system-117?browse=1910s

Financial Accounting Manual for Federal Reserve Banks. Federal Reserve Notes. The Board of Governors of the Federal Reserve System. https://www.federalreserve.gov/aboutthefed/chapter-5-federal-reserve-notes.htm

Historical Statistics of the United States: From Colonial Times to 1957, Chapter 10, Banking and Finance. https://www2.census.gov/library/publications/1960/compendia/hist_stats_colonial-1957/hist_stats_colonial-1957-chX.pdf

FRASER. Federal Reserve Archival System for Economic Research. Federal Reserve Bank of St. Louis. https://fred.stlouisfed.org

Factors Affecting Reserve Balances – H.4.1. Board of Governors of the Federal Reserve System. https://www.federalreserve.gov/releases/h41/

Financial Accounts of the United States – Z.1. Board of Governors of the Federal Reserve System. https://www.federalreserve.gov/releases/z1/default.htm

Banking And Monetary Statistics: 1914–1941. Board of Governors of the Federal Reserve System. https://fraser.stlouisfed.org/title/banking-monetary-statistics-1914-1941-38?browse=1940s#6408

Banking And Monetary Statistics: 1941–1970. Board of Governors of the Federal Reserve System. https://fraser.stlouisfed.org/title/banking-monetary-statistics-1941-1970-41

White House, Office of Management and Budget. Historical Tables https://www.whitehouse.gov/omb/historical-tables/

Bureau of Economic Analysis, U.S. Department of Commerce. https://www.bea.gov

International Monetary Fund. World Economic Outlook Database. https://www.imf.org/en/Publications/SPROLLs/world-economic-outlook-databases#sort=%40imfdate%20descending

The Debt to the Penny and Who Holds It. TreasuryDirect. https://treasurydirect.gov/govt/reports/pd/debttothepenny.htm

National Science Foundation. National Patterns of R&D Resources. https://www.nsf.gov/statistics/natlpatterns/

National Patterns of R&D Resources: 2017–2018 Data Update https://ncses.nsf.gov/pubs/nsf20307/

National Science Board. The State of U.S. Science and Engineering 2020 https://ncses.nsf.gov/indicators

R&D Data. https://ncses.nsf.gov/indicators/data

National Science Foundation. National Center for Science and Engineering Statistics. Higher Education Research and Development Survey. https://www.nsf.gov/statistics/srvyherd/

Federal Research and Development Funding: FY2020, Congressional Research Service. https://fas.org/sgp/crs/misc/R45715.pdf

Congressional Budget Office. Budget and Economic Data. https://www .cbo.gov/about/products/budget-economic-data#3

Monthly Treasury Statement. Bureau of the Financial Service. https:// fiscal.treasury.gov/reports-statements/mts/

Index